The Author

Ruth Bennett White has taught college, high
school, and junior high school courses in foods, nutrition, and general home economics for many years,
both in this country and in Turkey and Nigeria. Her
other contributions in the field of nutrition include
lectures, articles in both scientific and popular pub-
lications, and extension work with 4-H Clubs. She has
done research in nutrition and the chemistry of food
at the University of Iowa, Cornell University, and
Columbia University. Mrs. White is a member of local
and national home economics associations; member of
the Official Publication Committee, California Home
Economics Association; member of the American
Home Economics Association and the International
Federation Home Economics Liaison Committee; and
was a delegate to the Eleventh International Congress
of Home Economics in Bristol, England, in 1968. She
is at present associated with her husband, Carl M.
White, in the Ford Foundation.

Ruth Bennett White

YOU AND YOUR FOOD

Third Edition

PRENTICE-HALL, INC., Englewood Cliffs, N. J.

Related Prentice-Hall Books

BUILDING YOUR LIFE
by Judson T. Landis and Mary G. Landis

EXPLORING HOME AND FAMILY LIVING
by Henrietta Fleck and Louise Fernandez

FOOD AND YOUR FUTURE
by Ruth Bennett White

LIVING WITH YOUR FAMILY
by Henrietta Fleck, Louise Fernandez, and Elizabeth Munves

PERSONAL ADJUSTMENT, MARRIAGE, AND FAMILY LIVING
by Judson T. Landis and Mary G. Landis

UNDERSTANDING AND GUIDING YOUNG CHILDREN
by Katherine Read Baker and Xenia F. Fane

YOU AND YOUR FOOD, THIRD EDITION
by RUTH BENNETT WHITE

© 1961, 1966, 1971 by Prentice-Hall, Inc.,
Englewood Cliffs, N. J.

Printed in the United States of America.

ISBN 0-13-972950-X

PRENTICE-HALL INTERNATIONAL, INC., *London*
PRENTICE-HALL OF AUSTRALIA, PTY. LTD., *Sydney*
PRENTICE-HALL OF CANADA, LTD., *Toronto*
PRENTICE-HALL OF INDIA PRIVATE LTD., *New Delhi*
PRENTICE-HALL OF JAPAN, INC., *Tokyo*

10 9 8 7 6 5 4

Acknowledgments

The author extends thanks to the many individuals and organizations who have made contributions to the preparation of this book.

For supplying pictures and other materials: the United States Department of Agriculture; the Institute of Home Economics; the United States Department of Commerce; the United States Department of Health, Education, and Welfare; Cornell University; Columbia University; numerous land grant colleges; a great number of commercial organizations; and many home economists in business.

For reading all or parts of the manuscript and for supplying many important suggestions: Dr. Charles Glen King, Columbia University; Dr. John L. Buchanan, Columbia-Presbyterian Hospital, New York; Miss Helen Mohns, Birmingham, Alabama; Miss Kate B. Anderson, Cleveland, Ohio; Mrs. Josie M. Pittman, Durham, North Carolina; Sister M. Cuthbert, Alverno College, Milwaukee, Wisconsin; Mrs. Evelyn Moss, Palisades Park, New Jersey; Miss Jerline Kennedy, Dallas, Texas; and Miss Margaret A. Learson, Boston, Massachusetts.

For encouragement and guidance in writing this book: Dr. Amy L. Daniel, University of Iowa; Miss Frances Zuill, formerly of the University of Iowa; the late Martha Van Rensselaer, Cornell University; the late Flora Rose, Cornell University; Dr. Helen Judy Bond, New Hope, Pennsylvania; Dr. Anna Dooley, New York, New York; and Mrs. Grace Coleman, New York, New York.

For teaching units from the manuscript and evaluating the material from the standpoint of teacher and student: Miss Helen O'Brien, Livingston, New Jersey; Mrs. Grace Coleman, New York, New York; Mrs. Lila Jeanne Eichelberger, Champaign, Illinois; and Miss Elsie Friebel, Columbus, Ohio.

For counseling concerning content and approach: Mrs. Sallie Hilley, Abilene, Texas; Miss Margaret Booher, Tucson, Arizona; Mrs. Margaret Pritchard Larsen, Berkeley, California.

Finally, I wish to pay tribute to my parents, Sarah and A. L. Bennett, who encouraged me as a teen-ager in cooking and helping in the management of the meals of our big family; to my husband, Carl, for his devoted faith and loyalty as I have written this book; and to our two daughters, Sherril and Caroline, who, with their father, were enthusiastic about new dishes in family meals along the way.

R.B.W.

Contents

Illustration Credits

Abbott Laboratories, 98, 212. Adolph's Ltd., 219, 226, 227. American Can Company, 178. American Dry Milk Institute, Inc., 50. American Institute of Baking, 52, 92, 122, 195, 203 (top), 301, 321. American Molasses Company, 76, 326. American Spice Trade Association, 25, 45, 60, 69, 97 (center right), 128, 158, 161, 179, 244, 250, 328, 336. Christa Armstrong/Rapho Guillumette, 207, 298. *Better Homes and Gardens*, 94, 134, 231. Betty Crocker of General Mills, 97 (top left). The Borden Company, 51, 62, 74, 203 (middle), 300. Calavo Growers of California, 204. Calumet Baking Powder, 46, 47, 110, 176, 177. Campbell Soup Company, 120, 314, 338. Cereal Institute, Inc., 172. Cornell University, 186, 187. Dallas (Texas) Independent School District, 174. Dow Chemical Company, 333. Dudley-Anderson-Yutzy, 243, 322 (top). Evaporated Milk Association, 35, 154. Fort Lee (New Jersey) High School, 116. Florida Citrus Commission, 82, 87, 203 (bottom), 249, 347. Frigidaire Division, General Motors Corporation, 54. The Kellogg Company, 108. Lever Brothers, 262, 263, 264. Bernard L. Lewis, 49, 156, 332. Melamine Council, 283. Millard M. Halter High School, Wellston, Missouri, 206 (top). National Dairy Council, 9, 37, 38, 43, 66, 149 (top), 201, 282. National Livestock and Meat Board, 106, 216, 223, 224, 225, 228, 229, 230, 232, 233, 235, 236, 237, 251, 252, 288, 289. National Presto Industries, Inc., 38, 139 (middle and bottom), 146, 147, 298 (top right). The Nestlé Company, 107. Poultry and Egg National Board, 61, 63 (top and bottom), 75, 78, 202 (bottom), 208, 240, 241 (top), 242, 244, 245. *Progressive Grocer*, 54, 101. Procter & Gamble, 307. Richmond (California) Union High School District, 111, 127, 175. Safeway Stores, Inc., 221 (top left). Sealtest Kitchens, 40, 97 (bottom right), 99, 204. San Diego (California) Public Schools, 297. Hanna W. Schreiber/Rapho Guillumette, 25. Stokely-Van Camp, Inc., 96, 144, 145. Swans Down Cake Flour, 192, 193, 268, 269, 272, 273, 274, 275, 276. Tabasco, 180 (bottom), 234, 246. United Fresh Fruit and Vegetable Association, 23, 36, 67, 77, 83, 84, 91, 92, 93, 97 (middle left, bottom left, top right), 101, 111, 131, 132, 133, 136, 139 (top), 143, 148, 149 (bottom), 152, 155, 157, 165, 200, 202 (top), 206 (bottom), 238, 256, 278, 284, 296, 306, 322 (bottom), 340. United Fruit Company, 71, 204. United States Department of Agriculture, 31, 70, 72, 73, 221 (bottom left and all right), 241, 297, 302, 303, 334. Universal C. I. T. Credit Corporation, 327. Vanilla Growers of Madagascar, 53, 266, 344. Wong & Wong, 140. Cover, National Dairy Council

Foreword

You and Your Food was a pioneer venture in fusing the latest scientific knowledge of a balanced diet with its practical application. This third edition brings the subject up to the minute.

TO YOUNG PEOPLE: All the subjects you study have their place in your preparation for mature life, but nothing has a closer daily relation to the "you" you are creating than *the food you choose to eat daily*. YOU and YOUR FOOD are inseparable. Americans often choose food unwisely and sometimes miss meals entirely, not for lack of food or money, but because of lack of interest and knowledge. It takes effort to acquire this knowledge, and it takes further effort to apply what you learn if it is to help you toward attractiveness, stamina and mental alertness, resistance to ills, and a vitality that gives sparkle to your life now and as you grow older.

This book provides accurate information—obtained from scientific labor—about the many and relative values in your daily foods so that you can make wise choices in your meals and snacks. You will learn not only WHAT you need to eat daily, but also WHY you need the balance from different foods, and HOW to cook and serve these foods in a variety of balanced meals. And in the process you will also learn how to shop wisely for food, how to care for it, and how to save time, energy, and money.

It is hoped that young people of both sexes will study this book, for the roles of men and women are not so separate today as formerly. Both need to know how to manage their own diet as well as that of their families when they are married.

TO PARENTS: Our study of food is a new science. Research shows that some mothers, who may not have had the opporunity to learn this science, do not know how to give their family a balanced diet. Many fathers also do not know how to select meals when they eat away from home—or when they help with shopping and preparing meals at home. Encourage your young people to bring this text home and share with you what they learn. Encourage them to practice what they learn by allowing them to help plan and prepare family meals and to share the responsibility for food shopping. The whole family can benefit from this experience now, and your young people will be better prepared for later mature responsibilities.

TO TEACHERS: *You and Your Food* is written to help you teach and to help your students learn what you teach. Effective instruction is fortified by personalizing the study so that your students will want to learn and to practice what they learn as they progress. The book is organized in such a manner that all phases are integrated; that is, the study of food is related not only to nutrition, but also to the management of time, energy, and money in planning, preparing, and serving balanced meals and good snacks to meet individual needs.

The *focus* of the book is on the practical use of newer knowledge for better family meals and snacks: units 2–5 center in breakfast; the next three in lunch; units 9–11 in dinner. Together with a strong introductory unit giving the overall view of the text material and basic guides and charts referred to throughout the book, these ten units provide the foundation your students need to distinguish between the factual and the fraudulent in making wise choices in the use of food.

To facilitate teaching and learning, *each chapter forms a complete lesson plan.* Headings within the chapter amplify the main points in presenting basic information under the topic to be studied, along with teaching and learning aids at the end of each chapter.

The sequence was designed so that each unit builds on the preceding one and, at the same time, is a complete entity. This will enable you to adapt the sequence to fit the needs of your particular students or community. Wherever you begin, however, teach unit 1 first to establish a solid base for the course and to help motivate the student. The last unit is meant for students who have completed the basic study in the first eleven units. However, you can teach any of these six chapters in combination with any other unit.

The study aids at the end of each chapter utilize many different teaching methods and help the student to bring the knowledge gained to the home. The Cookbook, planned to supplement each unit, provides a wide variety of cooking experiences for each food, showing how to use it in many different ways as a part of balanced meals. *Basic recipes* are given that are easy to follow step by step, many supported within the text by "how-to" photographs. Variations are given to fit individual family tastes and to encourage students to use imagination in cooking.

Scientific knowledge is constantly growing. The author has tried to encourage the student to use nutritional information that is trustworthy today and to seek additional knowledge continuously throughout life. If those who study this book are motivated to improve their food habits, and thus to live fuller lives individually and when they are managing their own families, then *You and Your Food* will have fulfilled its purpose.

Ruth Bennett White

Food, Nutrition, and You

Looking Ahead
with "You and Your Food"

What Is in This Book for You?

Why do you eat? Part of the answer is that you like to eat and you don't like to go hungry. But you can't stop there. The truth is that we all share personal hopes and desires which food helps us to achieve. You want to be vigorously alive in mind and body. You want to grow to full manhood or womanhood with a healthy, good-looking body, bright eyes, clear skin, glossy hair, and sound teeth.

Many things help you achieve these goals, but one of the essentials is good food. Of course wisely chosen food does its job even if someone else does the choosing for you. As you get further along in life, however, it becomes increasingly important to be independent of others in this as in other matters. If you want to learn how to choose food wisely for your-

self, this book is written for you. By the time you have finished reading it, you will be able to use food to help improve your life and help you reach important goals in health and appearance.

Your Teen-age Growth and Your Food

Adults may outdo teen-agers in some things, but not in rate of growth or personal development. You enter your teens as a girl or boy, and you leave them as a young adult. This miracle of growth involves changes in your body, and often greatly alters your appearance. This is your last spurt of growth to reach the pattern set down for you by heredity. These changes can be seen in your height, and in the size of your hands and feet and legs. A new body form develops, and the fresh "bloom" of maturity begins to appear.

Inside your body, changes are also taking place. Glands are working faster, and more red blood cells are being made. Your body is achieving a new chemical balance. Where does the strength come from for all of these rapid changes? It comes from the food you eat daily in your meals and snacks.

You Can See How Food Affects Life by Studying Animals

When scientists first discovered what a big difference the wise choice of food can make in health and personal appearance, this knowledge was used in animal feeding. The results were startling. Animals fed "balanced" diets were much finer looking in every respect. They were larger, with sleeker coats of hair, brighter eyes, and more perfectly formed bodies. They were also healthier.

Of all the animals, the one that has food needs nearest those of human beings is the white rat. He lives some 30 times as fast as we do. In one year a scientist can feed the white rat a certain type of diet, and find out what it would take 30 years to learn by feeding a person that diet. Thus in three years we can see the effect of good or poor eating habits in the whole life of a human being. Scientists have learned how food can affect several generations of these small animals who eat man's diet. From experiments with animal feeding and studies of human beings, we have learned that a good-looking, healthy body is the result not only of good breeding, but also of good feeding.

Modern Science Reveals How Food Does Its Job for You

Modern science is providing us with dependable knowledge which can improve family living. But are these discoveries within our reach? Can we who are not scientists understand and apply them in our daily lives? Yes. The only barrier is the specialized language of science. One of the main objects of this book is to translate the newer knowledge of food into language which has meaning for you. When you acquire this newer knowledge and practice it in your daily life, it will help you attain your personal goals.

A Wise Use of Food Is a Part of Good Family Management

Women report that the management of food is the household task which takes the largest share of their time, energy, and money. Depending on the family income, the food budget may take from 20 to 50 percent or more of the income. Naturally, on a very high income it would not take as much as 20 percent, but on a very low one it may take more than 50 percent. That is a big slice of money! Studies now show that with adequate knowledge of food you can save 20 percent or more on the food budget and still be well fed. This adds up to several hundred dollars in a year, and thousands in a normal life.

Today a homemaker goes into a modern supermarket and sees thousands of items from which to choose. Much of this food is packaged, and some of it she cannot see. There is no one to answer her questions. She must make her decisions on what to buy on the basis of what she knows about food, in relation to the amount of money she has to spend. Whether she uses the family money wisely or not depends on the thoroughness of her knowledge, for what she selects will affect the health and welfare of her whole family. If you wish to make wise choices of food when you go marketing, then this book will help you by showing you what the good home manager needs to know about food.

Need for You to Understand Food Values

In 1968 the U.S. Department of Agriculture released shocking figures on the national dietary survey made in 1965. Despite an abundance of good, nutritious food, despite the highest per capita income in the world, only 50 percent of our population chose "good" diets in 1965. (If we eat a good diet, we get our full quota of daily recommended nutrients, or more.) In 1955, 10 percent more people ate a good diet than in 1965, and 20 percent chose a poor diet, or 2 persons in every 10 compared with 1 in every 10 in 1955. (A "poor" diet supplies less than two-thirds of the allowances recommended on pages 450–451.)

We ate less milk and milk products, less vegetables and fruits, less cereal and foods made from flour at home. The only food group that showed a gain was meat, and the price for that, especially red meat, went up considerably. This means that our diets are less nourishing. Why— because of ignorance, indifference, or both?

High income alone does not assure a good diet. The study showed that 9 percent of those with an income of $10,000 or more a year chose a poor diet, and only 63 percent in this category chose a good diet. By comparison, 37 percent in the lowest income groups (under $3,000 a year) had diets rated good, with 36 percent rated poor.

One person involved in making the study said that many consumers seemed confused by the multiplicity of choices available in food stores. Thousands of convenience foods in various forms are pouring into markets, thus increasing the consumer's opportunities to make poor choices, unless she knows foods. For example, in 1967 Americans spent more than $2 billion on snack foods!

You should understand the meaning of a good diet and acquire the facts you need to provide it. You who have your full life before you must avoid a low-quality diet and strive to achieve a good diet.

This chart shows the difference between the percent and kinds of foods families purchased in 1965 as compared with 1955. There is a nutritional downtrend! (This is shown in U.S.D.A. statistics.)

PERCENT DOWNWARD	
Milk group	10%
Vegetables and fruits	9%
Flour and cereal	20%

PERCENT UPWARD	
Meat	10%
Bakery goods	14%
Soups and nonessential convenience foods	27%

What Makes a Food Valuable?

A food is made of different parts called "nutrients" (nū'trĭ ĕnt). In order to make wise decisions about what foods to buy and to use in meals, we must first know what the body needs, and what foods provide the nutrients that meet these needs.

Scientists find that about 50 individual nutrients are required to build the body. Many others are useful, even though they may not be necessary. But in common practice we need to be concerned with only five groups or classes. They are: carbohydrates (kär′bō hī′drāt), fat, protein (prō′tēn), minerals (mĭn′ēr ăl), and vitamins (vī′tȧ mĭn).

Your task is easier if you know that wise selection of foods containing these five classes of nutrients usually provides all the 50 nutrients you need for life and growth. This makes it all the more advisable that you have adequate information about different foods if you are to plan meals intelligently. But before we define what is meant by these different food groups, a word should be said about calories (kăl′ȯ rē).

Calorie is a word that everyone uses. What does it mean? A calorie is a unit to measure the amount of energy or heat given off when a carbohydrate, fat, or protein is burned inside the body. Food is like coal or oil in this respect. All three give off energy-heat when burned. You can measure a pint of sand and a pint of whipping cream in the same cup. These two are alike in one respect (volume), but different in other respects. Thus when a carbohydrate or a protein food is burned in the body, each gives off the same number of calories (4 calories per gram of food). But when fat is burned it gives off 2¼ times more heat or energy than either of these (9 calories per gram of food). This accounts for the fact that a little fat goes a long way. The first need of your body is for calories to give you the energy for working, playing, and even breathing.

But when you eat more calorie-rich foods in a day than you need for your activities, the extra calories are changed to fat and stored as body fat. In this study you will learn how to plan meals and cook them to meet your need for calories, but not to supply so many that you gain excess weight.

The particular importance of each of the five groups of nutrients is as follows:

(1) *Carbohydrate* is the name given to the starches and sugars in food. It usually makes up the largest percentage of calories in the daily diet. Carbohydrates give energy or fuel, and an excess is stored as fat. Foods containing carbohydrates are widely grown, inexpensive, and have a mild flavor. We depend on cereal-bread, potatoes, and other vegetables and fruits as the best foods for carbohydrates. Cane sugar is 100 percent carbohydrate, but this does not mean it is the best carbohydrate food. The value of a carbohydrate food is judged by the amount of vitamins, minerals, and protein which it may also contain. Recent research shows starch is a far more valuable source of calories than sugar—for our appearance, for general health, and for its possible role in controlling some forms of heart disease. (This is discussed further in Units 4, 6, 7, and 10.)

(2) *Fat* is the most concentrated food for energy or fuel. It gives you 2¼ times more calories than either protein or carbohydrate.

Fats and carbohydrates are the two nutrients we depend on to supply calories. You will understand more fully the function of individual nutrients as you proceed in this study. Fat has other important jobs to do for you, as you will learn in Unit 10. Examples of fat foods are:

beef

veal

lamb

pork

nuts

lentils

Protein — animal

— vegetable

peas

fish

cheese

poultry

milk

dried beans

eggs

eggs

milk cheese meat

Minerals

green, leafy vegetables

whole grain cereal

dried fruits

raisins

Liquid fats and vegetable oils containing polyunsaturated fatty acids

saf-flower

pea nut

corn soy

cotton seed

oliv

Carbohydrates — Sugars

honey

jam preserve

white sugar

brown sugar

syrup

molasses

jelly

milk   cheese

fruit

vegetables

Vitamins

eggs

meat

whole grain cereal   enriched bread

Fats containing saturated fatty acids

vegetable shortening   butter

margarine

lard

cream

Fats in foods may contain all types of fatty acids

nuts

meat

— Starches

macaroni

spaghetti

bread

cereal

rice

parsnips

potatoes

corn

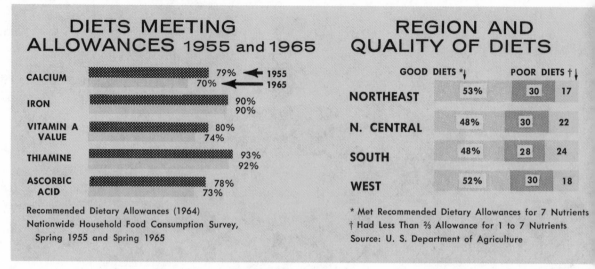

DIETS MEETING ALLOWANCES 1955 and 1965		
CALCIUM	79% ◄ 1955	
	70% ◄ 1965	
IRON	90%	
	90%	
VITAMIN A VALUE	80%	
	74%	
THIAMINE	93%	
	92%	
ASCORBIC ACID	78%	
	73%	

Recommended Dietary Allowances (1964)
Nationwide Household Food Consumption Survey,
Spring 1955 and Spring 1965

REGION AND QUALITY OF DIETS

	GOOD DIETS *↓	POOR DIETS †↓	
NORTHEAST	53%	30	17
N. CENTRAL	48%	30	22
SOUTH	48%	28	24
WEST	52%	30	18

* Met Recommended Dietary Allowances for 7 Nutrients
† Had Less Than ⅔ Allowance for 1 to 7 Nutrients
Source: U. S. Department of Agriculture

Diets in five households in ten surveyed in 1965 rated "good," as compared with six out of ten surveyed in 1955. About 20 percent of the diets in 1965 and 15 percent in 1955 rated "poor."

butter, margarine, lard, vegetable and fish oils, and the fat of meat.

(3) *Protein* is one of the most important nutrients in food, as you will learn in Unit II. It is essential for growth, health, and life itself. All foods do not contain equally valuable proteins for the body. You need adequate information about the protein in different foods to plan your meals and use your food money wisely. The foods which contain the most valuable proteins are: milk, cheese, meat (lean), fish, poultry, and eggs. Some plant foods such as dried beans, peas, lentils, nuts, and peanut butter are economical sources of protein when properly balanced with other foods. Many people all over the world do not get enough good protein food for good health. Protein is discussed more fully in Chapter 6.

(4) *Minerals* (and vitamins) do not give calories but are essential to build and repair cells, and to maintain the life pro-

cesses. They are unevenly distributed in foods. Some important foods are quite low in calcium, iron, and iodine. In this study you will learn which foods to select to incorporate these minerals into your meals and snacks.

(5) *Vitamins* form a part of an important team in building body tissue. With minerals and protein, they are often referred to as "protective" nutrients. This is because they are so critically important in maintaining health rather than in providing fuel. The vitamins most likely to be low in the diet are: vitamins A, C—also known as ascorbic (á skôr′bĭk) acid, D—also known as the sunshine vitamin, and three B vitamins—thiamine (thī′á mēn), riboflavin, (rī′bŏ flā′vĭn), and niacin (nī′á sĭn). In this study you will learn how these vitamins can help you, and what foods to eat to supply them.

Water is not a nutrient, but is essential for the use of nutrients. It provides the fluid for the blood and all body cells, and aids in the digestion, absorption, and use of food.

Some young people, and older ones, think that it does not matter what one eats, so long as one takes vitamin and mineral pills. Research has proved this false. *Pills are no substitute* for foods, since foods contain known and unknown nutrients not found in pills.

Recommended Daily Dietary Allowances

All through this book you will find references to the recommended daily dietary allowances. What does this mean? The Food and Nutrition Board of the National Research Council (a group of leaders in the sciences relating to food and nutrition) meets at intervals in the United States to review nutrition research and to set up dietary standards. In view of the research, the Board determines the "recommended allowances" for nutrients needed in the American diet for sound nutrition and optimum health of all our people. Amounts may change and other nutrients may be added as knowledge of nutrition increases.

When the Food and Nutrition Board met in 1963, it considered overweight as one of our major nutritional problems and recommended 200 to 300 less calories daily for adults and 100 fewer calories per day for children 4 to 6 years and for teen-agers. Calcium for children aged 1 to 9 was changed from 1 gram daily to 0.8 gram. Since the amounts of certain B vitamins are needed in relation to calories consumed, riboflavin, thiamine and niacin were slightly lowered and a few minor

changes were made in the vitamin C requirements. These changes in vitamin and calcium recommendations are so slight, however, as to make little difference in planning daily meals.

Some nutrients are so abundant in the foods we eat that we scarcely have to give thought to including them in the diet. Phosphorus is such an example. This mineral is necessary, along with calcium, for bone and tooth formation and for performing many other functions. But since it is abundant in our foods, it is not in the table on pages 450–451.

Your Daily Food Plan Can Help You Reach Your Goals

The experience of various nations with diverse food patterns shows us that people can survive by eating quite different combinations of food. In the past, people

In what ways can this snack help a teen-ager to maintain a good appearance?

A Guide To Good Eating

USE DAILY...

DAIRY FOODS

3 TO 4 GLASSES MILK – CHILDREN
4 OR MORE GLASSES – TEENAGERS
2 OR MORE GLASSES – ADULTS

CHEESE, ICE CREAM AND OTHER MILK-MADE
FOODS CAN SUPPLY PART OF THE MILK

2 OR MORE SERVINGS

MEATS, FISH, POULTRY, EGGS,
OR CHEESE – WITH DRY BEANS,
PEAS, NUTS AS ALTERNATES

MEAT GROUP

VEGETABLES AND FRUITS

4 OR MORE SERVINGS

INCLUDE DARK GREEN OR
YELLOW VEGETABLES;
CITRUS FRUIT OR TOMATOES

4 OR MORE SERVINGS

ENRICHED OR WHOLE-GRAIN
ADDED MILK IMPROVES
NUTRITIONAL VALUES

BREADS AND CEREALS

This is the foundation for a good diet. Use
more of these and other foods as needed for
growth, for activity, and for desirable weight.

The nutritional statements made on this chart have been reviewed by
the Council on Foods and Nutrition of the American Medical Association and found consistent with current authoritative medical opinion.

2ND EDITION–COPYRIGHT 1958. NATIONAL DAIRY COUNCIL, CHICAGO 6

who lived by the sea ate mostly sea food, and those who grew mostly rice ate it as the chief item of diet. Then a healthy diet was not always possible. Today the picture has changed—we are not content just to survive; we want to use food to help us feel and look as well as possible. Fortunately, a healthy diet is possible for many more millions of people all over the world. This is because of our modern knowledge of nutrition, the science of food as it relates to your health and life. Today we can better preserve food, and its health values, by improved methods of freezing, refrigerating, canning, and drying it. By improved transportation, foods can be moved in excellent condition to almost any part of the world. If you have adequate income to buy the food you need, your problem is not difficult. In some parts of the world people still do not have either the food or the money to buy what they need.

In our country we have an abundance of all the foods we need for good health. Our problem is to balance the health

NATIONAL FOOD SUPPLY

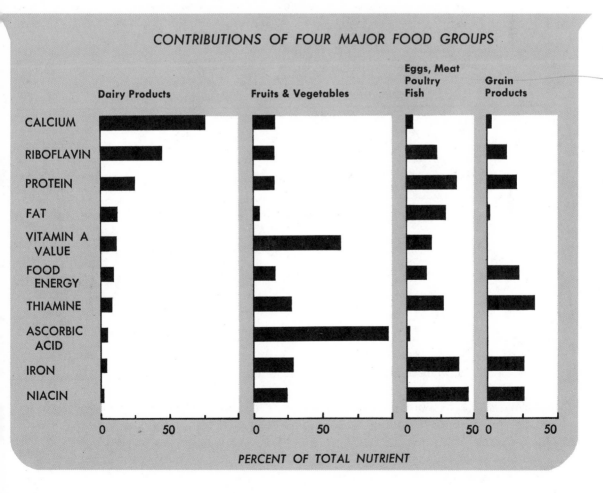

CONTRIBUTIONS OF FOUR MAJOR FOOD GROUPS

PERCENT OF TOTAL NUTRIENT

A GUIDE FOR A DAILY BALANCED DIET

MILK AND MILK PRODUCTS	Children 3-4 cups (8-oz. cups) Teenagers 4 cups or more Adults 2 cups or more Milk may be fluid whole, skim, buttermilk; evaporated; dry; cheese; ice cream
EGGS	1 daily or 4 per week (2 eggs may be used as an alternate for meat)
FRUITS	2 or more servings daily* 1 serving orange, grapefruit, or whole citrus juice, tomato juice, or other fruit rich in vitamin C (such as strawberries and cantaloupes in season; or guava, mango, or papaya) 1 serving other fruit—fresh, frozen, canned, or cooked
VEGETABLES	2-3 servings daily* 1 serving (½ to ¾ cup) dark-green or deep-yellow vegetable, at least every other day 1 serving potato or alternate 1 serving other vegetable of choice
MEAT	1 lean serving (about 3-4 oz. cooked) Beef, veal, lamb, pork; poultry, fish, and shellfish Include liver and sea food at least once each week
CEREAL - BREAD	4 or more servings** Whole grain, enriched, or restored
OPTIONAL FOODS	FAT: some vegetable oil or other fat to season food, if desired SUGAR: some preserves, syrups, and other foods to improve flavor of meals, if desired

* Count as 1 serving ½ to ¾ cup of cooked vegetable or fruit, or a portion as ordinarily served such as a whole orange, ½ grapefruit or cantaloupe, or a whole potato, banana, apple, pear.

** Count as 1 serving 1 slice of bread; 1 oz. ready-to-eat cereal; ½ to ¾ cup cooked cereal, rice, macaroni, spaghetti, noodles, cornmeal, or grits.

needs of the body with a variety of properly prepared foods in our daily meals. This can be done quite well on any income level if you have adequate information. What broad principles can guide you in meal planning to provide the balance of nutrients you need for good health and good looks?

(1) Eat a variety of foods daily to supply sufficient calories for your activity, but not so many as to cause you to gain excess weight.

(2) Eat enough good protein foods in each meal for growth and health, but still keep your food bill reasonable.

(3) Eat a variety of foods in each meal

A PATTERN OF FOOD FOR DAILY MEALS

	Food	Chief Nutrient it Gives
BREAKFAST	FRUIT: whole orange or half grapefruit, or ½-¾ cup whole juice; or 1-1½ cup tomato juice	Vitamin C
	EGG AND/OR CEREAL: cooked or ready to eat (whole grain, enriched, or restored)	High-grade protein, iron, other vitamins and minerals
	BREAD: whole grain or enriched	Calories, B vitamins
	BUTTER, FORTIFIED MARGARINE, OR OTHER FAT	Calories, vitamin A (butter and margarine)
	MILK: one 8-oz. glass or more	Calcium, riboflavin, high-grade protein, vitamin A (if whole)
LUNCH	LEAN MEAT, fish, poultry; or eggs; or cheese; or dried beans, peas, lentils, or peanut butter	High-grade protein, B vitamins, minerals
	VEGETABLE: cooked or raw	Vitamins C and A, minerals
	BREAD: whole grain or enriched	Calories, B vitamins
	BUTTER, FORTIFIED MARGARINE, OR OTHER FAT	Calories, vitamin A
	MILK: one 8-oz. glass or more	Calcium, riboflavin, protein, vitamin A
	DESSERT: choice of fresh, frozen, or cooked fruit; milk desserts; others	Fruit: vitamin C Milk desserts: same as milk Others: calories
DINNER	FRUIT OR VEGETABLE JUICE; or fresh fruit cup or melon (if desired, but not essential if salad is served or dessert is fresh fruit)	Vitamin C, other vitamins and minerals
	MEAT: lean beef, veal, pork, lamb, poultry, fish, shellfish; organ meats; or cheese, eggs, dried beans, peas, or lentils	High-grade protein, B vitamins, minerals
	VEGETABLES: dark-green or deep-yellow, cooked or in salad Potato or equal Other vegetable of choice if not served at lunch	Vitamins C and A, minerals Calories, vitamins, minerals Calories, vitamins, minerals
	SALAD: dark-green leafy instead of cooked, or alternate with appetizer or dessert if fresh fruit	Vitamins C and A, minerals
	BREAD: whole grain or enriched, if needed	Calories, B vitamins
	BUTTER, FORTIFIED MARGARINE, OR OTHER FAT	Calories, vitamin A
	MILK: one 8-oz. glass or more	Calcium, riboflavin, protein, vitamin A, thiamine
	DESSERT: Fruit—fresh, frozen, canned, cooked Milk—ice cream, custards, puddings, cheese Others—cakes, cookies, pies	Fruit: vitamin C Milk desserts: same as milk Others: calories

to provide essential vitamins and minerals needed for growth of body tissue and maintenance of vigorous health.

These are principles to guide you. How can you put them into practice in your daily meals and snacks? As indicated, a balanced diet may be achieved by many different food combinations. For instance, in our country during World War II a daily food guide called the "Basic Seven" was developed, which arranged the food we need in seven groups. You may be familiar with it. Families who followed this guide had a better diet than those who followed no guide in planning meals. More recently the research division of the U. S. Department of Agriculture, in the Institute of Home Economics, has proposed a daily food guide which divides the foods we need into four groups. These groups are listed and explained in the illustration on page 10. In addition, add other foods to complete meals and to provide food energy and other food values.

The idea of this arrangement is to use large groupings of foods, and let each family find variety within the broad group that fits its individual income and tastes. This is a logical arrangement, and gives more flexibility than the Basic Seven arrangement. But the fact that it is so general means that each family must subdivide these large groups in order to plan balanced meals.

A DAY'S BALANCED MENUS*

BREAKFAST	LUNCHEON	DINNER
Whole sliced orange	Baked Beans	Ham with scalloped
Egg, blindfolded	Brown bread	potatoes
Crisp bacon	Butter or margarine	Turnip greens
Whole wheat toast	Cabbage and pineapple	Salad—orange, carrot,
Butter or margarine	salad	celery
Milk	Deep-dish cherry pie	Corn sticks—butter or
	Milk	margarine
		Baked apple, milk
		Milk

SNACK: fruit milk shake; or milk and fruit; or milk and cookie; or fruit juice; or fruit

* These menus are suitable for any age group in the family. A small child and an inactive adult would eat smaller portions. A teenager would take second helpings of milk, vegetables, fruits, bread, and meat rather than sweet-fat desserts to meet the extra need during rapid growth. A teenage boy would need a "hearty" breakfast. See page 109 for an example of this type menu.

HOW TO KEEP A DAILY FOOD RECORD

These Foods I Ate and Drank on Sunday
(Give Name of Food and Amount as Indicated)

	Milk and Milk products	Fruits and Vegetables	Meat, poultry, fish, eggs, dried beans, nuts, or peanut butter	Cereal-bread
FOOD GROUPS				
BREAKFAST				
1 whole medium orange		1		
1 egg			1	
1 slice bacon*				
1 slice toast				1
1 glass milk (8 oz.)	1			
DINNER				
1 slice roast pork			1	
1 baked sweet potato		1		
½ cup cooked turnip greens		1		
¾ cup cabbage-pineapple salad		1		
½ cup canned apricots—2 oatmeal cookies		1		1
1 glass milk (8 oz.)	1			
SUPPER (OR LUNCH)				
1 peanut butter sandwich (4 teaspoons peanut butter, 2 slices whole wheat bread)			1	2
¾ cup seedless fresh grapes		1		
2 cups hot cocoa	1½			
½ cup ice cream	¼			
SNACK:				
1 glass milk, 1 cookie	1			½
TOTAL FOOD	4¾	6	3	4½

* Bacon is not counted as a meat, but as a fat.

WEIGHT—HEIGHT TABLES*

BOYS

Age Years	Average Weight Pounds	Range in Weight Pounds	Average Height Inches	Range in Height Inches
4	38.2	33.7– 42.7	40.9	39.0–42.8
5	43.2	37.7– 48.7	43.9	41.9–45.9
6	47.6	41.3– 53.9	46.1	44.0–48.2
7	52.5	45.4– 59.6	48.2	46.0–50.4
8	58.2	49.5– 66.9	50.4	48.1–52.7
9	64.4	54.6– 74.2	52.4	50.0–54.8
10	70.7	59.2– 82.2	54.3	51.8–56.8
11	77.6	64.5– 90.7	56.2	53.6–58.8
12	85.6	69.8–101.4	58.2	55.3–61.1
13	95.6	77.4–113.8	60.5	57.3–63.7
14	107.9	87.8–128.0	63.0	59.6–66.4
15	121.7	101.1–142.3	65.6	62.5–68.7
16	131.9	113.0–150.8	67.3	64.5–70.1
17	138.3	119.5–157.1	68.2	65.6–70.8

GIRLS

Age Years	Average Weight Pounds	Range in Weight Pounds	Average Height Inches	Range in Height Inches
4	37.3	32.5– 42.1	40.9	39.0–42.8
5	42.0	36.1– 47.9	43.6	41.6–45.6
6	46.4	39.6– 53.2	45.8	43.7–47.9
7	51.2	43.7– 58.7	47.9	45.7–50.1
8	56.9	47.5– 66.3	50.0	47.7–52.3
9	63.0	51.9– 74.1	52.0	49.6–54.4
10	70.3	57.1– 83.5	54.2	51.6–56.8
11	79.0	63.5– 94.5	56.5	53.7–59.3
12	89.7	71.9–107.5	59.0	56.1–61.9
13	100.3	82.3–118.3	60.6	58.0–63.2
14	108.5	91.3–125.7	62.3	59.9–64.7
15	115.0	98.8–131.2	63.2	60.9–65.5
16	117.6	101.7–133.5	63.5	61.3–65.7
17	119.0	103.5–134.5	63.6	61.4–65.8

* From "Basic Body Measurements of School Age Children," Office of Education, U. S. Department of Health, Education, and Welfare. The ranges given include the cases which fell within the middle two-thirds of those in the sample.

We shall start with the four-group arrangement of food for a daily meal guide in this study. But for purposes of simplicity and thoroughness, we shall subdivide the groups, and you will find this subdivision in the table on page 12. What foods do you think of when you start to plan breakfast, for instance? You probably think of bread or cereal in some form, milk, eggs, and fruit or fruit juice, and you may think of some kinds of meat. And so it is with lunch or dinner. It is milk and milk products, eggs, fruits, vegetables, cereal-breads, meats, fats, and sugars that make your meals. In order to plan or to select balanced meals, you need to understand what each of these foods contributes to your health, and in what respects. The tables on pages 10–15 will help you learn to plan balanced meals. The table on page 11 shows what percentage of various nutrients comes from each food group. The table on page 12 gives a variety of food from which to choose, and the table on page 13 gives a pattern to follow in planning daily menus. These last two tables have been used to produce the sample menu on page 14. Page 15 gives an example of how to keep a record of the kinds and amounts of food that you eat daily.

Foods Are Most Useful Working Together for You

Scientists have learned that nutrients in food work better together than alone. In fact, there is waste when you have enough calcium from your milk, for instance, but not enough vitamin C or vitamin D from other foods to help use the calcium for growth of bones, or to maintain teeth.

The following example will show you how the best use of the nutrients in one food depends on having, in the same meal, nutrients in other foods. Suppose you decide to build a concrete walk. You set up the frame and measure and mix the water and cement in proper amounts, but there is no sand. You look around for some sand, and when you can't find it, you think, "What does it matter? All that's missing is just one little thing that hardly counts." So you pour the mixture of water and cement into your frame, but it does not make concrete. Without sand in just the right amount, the water and cement cannot make concrete that will stand up to weather and wear.

It is the same with foods. You need a variety of food in the proper amounts in your meals if you are to enjoy the good health and fine appearance you desire.

Well-balanced diets are not planned by instinct, tradition, or simple little rules of balancing color, texture, and flavor alone. Well-balanced diets are planned by understanding the distinct nutritive values in different foods which we enjoy eating and need to eat. When you understand this, you can plan your meals intelligently whatever your income level. By acquiring this information while you are young, you can have a better diet over the years. The benefits from a good diet add up slowly, but you can be sure that a continuous good diet will give you an attractive appearance, more vitality, and a greater enjoyment in living.

Let us consider these foods that make your meals. Since milk is the most nearly perfect food, and is so important to your life, we will consider it first.

WORDS TO WORK WITH

Calorie (kăl'ŏ rĭ): a measure of heat. The *large calorie* is the unit used to express the heat-producing or energy-producing value of food.

Carbohydrate (kär'bŏ hī'drāt): a sugar or starch needed for energy.

Mineral (mĭn'ẽr ăl): an inorganic chemical nutrient such as calcium, iron, or iodine needed for growth and the maintenance of life.

Nutrient (nū'trĭ ĕnt): a substance in food that nourishes the body.

Nutrition (nū trĭsh'ŭn): the sum of the processes by which a body takes in and uses food; the study of such processes, in relation to their effect on growth and health.

Protein (prō'tēn): a nutrient found in milk, cheese, eggs, lean meat, and some other foods. It is essential for building and repairing cells and for maintaining life.

Vitamin (vī'tȧ mĭn): a nutrient essential for growth and body maintenance.

THINKING IT OVER

1. Why is selecting a well-balanced diet such an important responsibility for a teen-ager now? How do good eating habits affect your future life?

2. In what ways may ignorance and food prejudices contribute to a poor use of your food money? Give examples of how this may affect your health and appearance.

PROBLEMS TO SOLVE

1. Learn to look at your food habits critically.

   (1) Keep a record of the food you eat for one week—compare each day's diet with the recommendations in the table on page 12.

   (2) Evaluate what you eat daily and make a plan to improve if necessary.

3. What is meant by a balanced meal? A day's balanced diet? What guide would you use to achieve balanced meals?

4. Do you think most people use the most scientific knowledge of food in planning the meals and snacks they eat? How do you account for this?

5. Explain what is meant by the following terms: nutrition, nutrient, carbohydrate, protein, minerals, vitamins, calorie.

2. Check yourself for good nutrition. On what points can you improve?
   (1) What factors other than food may affect your nutrition?
   (2) Can you make a well-balanced plan to improve your nutrition?
   (3) Can you form a habit of following this plan?

3. Check your weight and find what it is in relation to your theoretical normal weight.

FURTHER READING

Foods and Nutrition

Bibliography of Books, Pamphlets, and Teaching Aids on Foods and Nutrition. American Home Economics Association, Washington, D.C., 1963.

Composition of Foods, Raw, Processed and Prepared. Handbook No. 8, U.S. Department of Agriculture, Washington, D. C., rev. 1964.

Conserving the Nutritional Values in Food. Home and Garden Bulletin 90. U.S. Department of Agriculture, Washington, D. C., 1963.

Dietary Evaluation of Foods Used in the United States. U.S. Department of Agriculture, Washington, D. C., 1961.

Food: The Yearbook of Agriculture. U. S. Department of Agriculture, Washington, D. C., 1959.

Handbook of Food Preparation. American Home Economics Association, Washington, D.C., 1964.

Improving Teenage Nutrition. Agricultural Department Program, January, 1964. U.S. Department of Agriculture, Washington, D.C.

"Nutritional Fitness for Teenagers," Mary M. Hill. *Nutrition Com. News,* July–August, 1963. U.S. Department of Agriculture, Washington, D.C.

Proceedings of Nutrition Education Conference, January, 1962. U.S. Department of Agriculture, Miscellaneous Publication No. 913. Washington, D.C.

Recommended Dietary Allowances (revised 1963). National Research Council Food and Nutrition Board, National Academy of Sciences, Washington, D.C.

Statements and Decisions of the Council on Foods and Nutrition of the American Medical Association. American Medical Association, Chicago, Ill., 1961.

Teaching Nutrition, 2nd ed., E. Eppright, M. Pattison, H. Barbour. Iowa State University Press, 1962.

You Aren't Alone in Nutrition Education. Folder. American Home Economics Association, Washington, D.C., 1962.

You Can Prevent Food-borne Illness. Public Health Service Publication 1105. U.S. Department of Health, Education, and Welfare. Washington, D.C., 1964.

Management of Family and Food Budget

"Consumer Education and the Home Economist," Bymers. *Journal of Home Economics,* May, 1963. American Home Economics Association, Washington, D.C.

Convenience Foods in the Grocery Basket. U.S. Department of Agriculture, Washington, D.C., 1962.

Family Fare: Food Management and Recipes. U.S. Department of Agriculture, Washington, D.C., 1960.

Family Food and Stockpile for Survival. Home and Garden Bulletin 79. U.S. Department of Agriculture, Washington, D.C., 1963.

Family Food Budgeting for Good Meals and Good Nutrition. Home and Garden Bulletin 94, January, 1964. U.S. Department of Agriculture, Washington, D.C.

Family Food Plans and Food Costs. Home Economics Research Report 20. Agricultural Research Service. U.S. Department of Agriculture, Washington, D.C., 1963.

"Food and Nutrition Relative to Family Life," *Journal of Home Economics,* April, 1964. AHEA, Washington, D.C.

Food for Families with School Children, Home and Garden Bulletin 13, U.S. Department of Agriculture, Washington, D.C.

Journal of Family Economics-Home Management. Edited by Beatrice Paolucci and Jean Schlater. American Home Economics Association, Washington, D.C., Volume II, 1963. Volume III, 1964.

Mind Your Manners, Betty Allen, Mitchell P. Briggs. J. B. Lippincott Co., Philadelphia, Pa., 1965.

Trading Stamps and Their Impact on Food Prices. U.S. Department of Agriculture, Washington, D.C., 1958.

Voices of the Consumer. American Home Economics Association, Washington, D.C., 1963.

What Consumers Should Know About Food Additives. Leaflet No. 10, Food and Drug Administration, Washington, D.C.

Equipment for Management of Family Food

Arrangement of Kitchen Centers, Steidl. Cornell Extension Bulletin E1028. Cornell University, Ithaca, New York.

Home Freezers . . . Their Selection and Use. U.S. Department of Agriculture, Washington, D.C., 1961.

Household Equipment Principles, Helen J. VanZante. Prentice-Hall, Inc., Englewood Cliffs, N.J., 1964.

Shopper's Guide to U.S. Grades for Food. Home and Garden Bulletin 58. U.S. Department of Agriculture, Washington, D.C., 1964.

Tools for Food Preparation and Dishwashing. Home and Garden Bulletin 3. U.S. Department of Agriculture, Washington, D.C.

Careers in Home Economics

Facts About a Very Important Profession. American Home Economics Association, Washington, D.C., 1962.

"Fifty Years of Achievement in American Home Economics," Zuill. *Journal of Home Economics*, Sept., 1959. American Home Economics Association, Washington, D.C.

It's Not Too Early to Start Thinking About Your Home Economics Future. American Home Economics Association, Washington, D.C., 1960.

Meet the Young Home Economist. American Home Economics Association, Washington, D.C., 1963.

National Leaders Look at Home Economics. American Home Economics Association Washington, D.C., 1963.

unit **2**

Milk and Milk Products for Your Meals and Snacks

Chocolate
Onions

Milk:
A Good Food
in Meals and Snacks

Milk is One of Nature's Best Foods

No one food, by itself, has all of the nutrients which the body needs for full growth and health. Milk is the most nearly perfect. It is the baby's first food, and we need the nutrients found in milk as we grow older. A survey in New Jersey of 9000 boys and girls in their junior and senior years of high school showed that only one girl out of ten had the recommended amount of milk in her daily diet.

In this unit you will learn how milk can help your health and appearance, including your figure. You will also learn how to use it in meals and snacks, of which it should be a part. There are many forms of milk on the market today, some with low fat and low calorie content but containing most of the nutrients you need from milk. Before we consider how it can help your looks and vitality, let us take a look at these different varieties of milk and how to buy and care for them.

Kinds of Milk and Milk Products

(1) *Fluid milk* is the kind that is left by the milkman at your home, or that you buy in containers at the store. There are several varieties:

(a) *Whole milk* averages about 86.9 percent water, 5 percent carbohydrate in the form of milk sugar, 3.9 percent butterfat, 3.5 percent protein, and 0.7 percent minerals, and it contains vitamins which are too tiny to measure in terms of percent. When the fat is broken into tiny particles and blended throughout the milk, the milk is called "homogenized" (hŏ mŏj'ĕ nīzed). Homogenized milk has a creamy color and a smooth taste, and usually has vitamin D added to help the body use the calcium in the milk for bones and teeth. (See page 65 for explanation of vitamin D.) It costs a few more cents per quart, but if you do not take vitamin D in other forms, it is worth the extra cost during growth. (The nutritive values in milk are discussed in Chapters 2–6.)

(b) *Skim milk* has the same nutritive values as whole milk except that the cream is removed. In removing the cream, the vitamin A and about one-half the calories are lost. Skim milk can be purchased with added vitamin A and D at about the same cost as whole milk.

(c) *Buttermilk* is skim milk with a lactic acid culture added to make it sour. It is easy to digest and has one-half the calories of whole milk.

(d) *Yogurt* (yō'gŏŏrt) is whole milk prepared with a special bacterial culture, making a firm curd. Some B vitamins can be made in the intestinal tract, when certain fragments of protein and certain bacteria are present. Yogurt seems to provide a good environment for this type of bacterial growth. Commercially made yogurt is too expensive to substitute for milk, but is a pleasant dessert occasionally with a dash of nutmeg or served over fresh fruit. You can make yogurt inexpensively at home by mixing thoroughly ¼ cup plain yogurt with 1½ cups nonfat dry milk and 1 quart of warm water. Pour this into dessert bowls, or leave it in one bowl, and set it in a warm place until the milk becomes a firm curd. Chill and serve with a spoon of jam on top as dessert, or beat and drink as milk.

(e) *Chocolate milk* costs more, in proportion to its nutritive content, than whole milk. Some people are willing to pay more for the flavor.

(2) *Evaporated milk* has about 60 percent of its water removed. This is done by heating milk in a vacuum at approxi-

It is highly important to have milk or milk products as a part of every meal. What foods in this dinner contain them?

mately 140°F and water is evaporated without harming the milk. The price of evaporated milk is about one-half the price of fresh milk. Evaporated milk can be stored on a shelf in a dry cool place until opened. When opened, it should be stored in the coldest part of the refrigerator, just as all fresh milk is stored.

(3) *Dried or powdered milk* is made by spraying milk under high pressure into a current of dry air; or by evaporating the water on hot rollers, or hot rollers in a vacuum. It is sold as whole dried milk, skim milk, and cream. The most popular form is dried skim milk. This is also called nonfat milk solids. Dried skim milk costs around one-third as much as fluid whole milk or fluid skim milk to which has been added vitamins A and D. It is used by many homemakers who wish to fortify at low cost the nourishment in such dishes as baked foods, creamed dishes, and desserts, without adding high calories. If you have sufficient storage space and use large amounts of non-fat dry milk regularly, you may save on some brands as much as two cents per quart in the 20 quart size compared with the three quart size. However, there may be exceptions to this rule, and it pays to read the label and take time to figure out the cost. Premeasured milk costs about two cents more per quart than the bulk packaged non-fat dry milk. Dried milk is 37 percent protein and 8 percent minerals. To make one quart of fluid skim milk from nonfat dry milk follow the directions on the package (quantities may vary but usually manufacturers recommend 1⅓ cups nonfat dry milk to one quart of water).

(4) *Sweetened condensed milk* is made by adding up to 40 percent sugar to milk

that has been evaporated. It is not a substitute for milk, but is excellent for desserts.

(5) *Ice cream* is a favorite milk product the world over. It is made from cream, milk solids, sugar, gelatin, and a flavoring ingredient. Air is whipped into this mixture and it is frozen to a smooth texture. One-third pint of ice cream gives around 200 calories, less than most pies or frosted cake. Sherbet is made like ice cream, but with milk, or milk and fruit juices. If eggs are added, it becomes a frozen milk dessert.

(6) *Cheese* is a good substitute for milk in many respects. It is made from pasteurized milk and keeps longer than milk. Food value, taste, and cost vary in different kinds of cheese. Labels tell whether milk solids are added to cheese. Cheddar cheese is a type many people like best. It is made from whole milk and may be mild, medium or sharp in flavor. It is often processed. Processed cheese is popular, constituting one-third of all cheese produced in the United States. Such cheese is ground and to this is added milk and an emulsifier. This mixture is heated to a temperature which pasteurizes the product and destroys the ripening enzymes and bacteria. It is molded and sealed, and will keep at room temperature until opened. Then it should be stored in the refrigerator. It is preferred by many homemakers because it blends smoothly in cooking. Cottage cheese is not as rich in fats, minerals, and vitamins as cheddar, but it is as good in protein. (See suggestions on page 41 for use of cheese in meals, and recipes on pages 361–364.)

Europeans drink less milk, but eat more cheese than we do. A choice dessert is cheese and crackers, or cheese and fresh fruit. Suitable dessert cheese includes such varieties as Camembert, Gruyère, Roquefort, blue cheese, Liederkranz, and other sharp cheeses. Cheese may be used in many different ways at lunch and dinner as a meat substitute, or at breakfast with eggs. It is also good food for snacks.

(7) *Butter* is made by churning sour or sweet cream until the solid separates as butter from the liquid. Commercial butter is 80 percent fat. It may be unsalted, or it may have 3 percent salt added, which tends to keep it from deteriorating as fast as sweet butter. It is sold in one pound prints, four sticks to a pound, or whipped and sold in half pound cartons, the latter being the more expensive. Good quality butter should be smooth in texture, pleasant in aroma, even in color, and delicate in flavor. Color and butter flavoring may be added to commercial butter without stating this on the package. Keep butter in the refrigerator in a tight container to prevent the absorption of odors. Freeze surplus butter to retain the fresh flavor, and use it as needed. (See Chapter 23 for discussion of fat in the diet.)

Pasteurization of Milk

Pasteurization (păs′tĕr ĭ zā′shŭn) is the process of heating milk to destroy harmful bacteria without seriously altering the nutritional value. People who own their own cows pasteurize their milk by bringing it to a boil for about three seconds.

In the days before we had laws requiring pasteurization of milk sold to the public, such diseases as typhoid fever, undulant fever, septic sore throat, and dysentery were spread through raw milk.

Milk—our first food.

Our governments, often local and state, set health standards that must be met by the farmers and all those who handle milk. The cows must be tested and be free from disease. Dairy barns, milking equipment, and the people who milk cows and handle milk must be clean and free from communicable disease. This is for your protection. But if you leave milk sitting outside the refrigerator, this care may be partially lost. Keep milk under refrigeration until the moment of use, and do not leave milk exposed in the kitchen or out in the sun while you cook a meal.

The values of milk which are discussed in this book are based on pasteurized milk.

How to Cook with Milk

Some of the health values in foods are lost by poor care and cooking. This is true of milk. Scientists find that:

(1) High temperatures in cooking milk or cheese affect both the taste and the health value. You may have noticed that a brown ring develops quickly on the sides of a pan when milk is heated quickly. Tiny particles of white also stick to the bottom and sides. Sometimes a "skin" forms on top. What is happening?

The brown is due to the burning of milk sugar. This spoils the flavor and color and destroys one of the best natural sugars in any food. The white particles are proteins. How can you save them? Cook milk at a low temperature and in a covered pan, either in a double boiler or directly over low heat. Even when milk is heated this way, a small amount of protein may cling to the bottom and sides of the pan, and a thin skin may rise to the top. In this case, scrape off all that clings to the pan. Covering the pan prevents the formation of the skin on top and saves most of the riboflavin. Cocoa cooked in this way makes a much more pleasant and nourishing drink. A high temperature causes cheese to be tough and "stringy." The processed cheeses are preferred by some for cooking because they blend smoothly.

(2) Light destroys riboflavin, a B vitamin richly found in milk. This is especially true when the sun shines directly on milk (as it may outside your door), or when milk is heated in the light. But when milk is heated in a covered pan that does not admit light, there is almost no loss of riboflavin.

Milk delivered at the door should be placed in a covered box. Some dairies supply these free. The paper containers or brown bottles in which some milk is sold protects the riboflavin content.

Use of Milk in Snacks

Few young people eat all of their daily food at meals. One study of school children showed that between 15 and 17 percent of the calories in the day's diet came from snacks. It also showed that these calories came mostly from rich carbohydrate foods. What does this mean to you?

It means that you need to think about what kind of food you are eating at your snacks, and how much. The snack should contribute to your total day's need of food, but never so much that you gain

AMOUNTS OF MILK PRODUCTS TO EQUAL MILK IN CALCIUM

1 inch cube Cheddar cheese	½ cup milk
½ cup cottage cheese	⅓ cup milk
½ cup ice cream	¼ cup milk
2 tablespoons cream cheese	1 tablespoon milk

ALTERNATES FOR MILK IN COOKING

1 cup fresh whole milk	½ cup evaporated whole milk, plus ½ cup water
1 cup skim milk	⅓ to ½ cup dry skim milk powder plus 1 cup water or follow directions on label
1 cup sour milk or buttermilk	1 cup fresh or reconstituted dry, or evaporated milk plus 1½ teaspoons lemon juice or ⅓ teaspoon vinegar

ALTERNATES FOR WHOLE FRESH MILK IN PLANNING MENUS FOR OVERWEIGHTS

1 glass whole milk (8 oz.)	1 glass skim milk plus 2 teaspoons butter or fortified margarine
1 glass whole milk	1 glass buttermilk plus 2 teaspoons butter or fortified margarine
⅓ pint ice cream	½ glass skim milk
1 glass whole milk	1¼ oz. Cheddar cheese
2 tablespoons table cream	2 teaspoons butter or fortified margarine

excess weight. Milk is a first-rate snack food. It gives an immediate "lift," few calories, and a variety of nutrients you need for your "sparkle" in life.

Milk may be used for a warm weather snack as: plain milk, ice cream, yogurt, or a milk shake made with fresh or frozen fruit or a flavoring of your choice; milk with bread, cookies, cake, or pie; milk with fruit or cereal; cheese and bread or cheese and fruit.

Cold weather snacks could include any of the above, but instead of cold milk, hot cocoa, hot eggnog, or different types of toasted cheese sandwiches might be substituted. Whatever you eat for a snack (unless it is a fruit juice), have a little milk with it.

 WORDS TO WORK WITH

Homogenized (hŏ mŏj′ ê nīzd): having fat particles broken up into smaller units, so that they are permanently and evenly distributed, as throughout milk.

Yogurt (yō′gŏŏrt): a firm curd, made from whole milk with a special bacterial culture and having the same nutritive content as whole milk. (Also spelled *yoghurt*.)

Pasteurization (păs′tĕr ĭ zā′shŭn): the process of heating milk long enough to destroy harmful bacteria.

THINKING IT OVER

1. Give an example of why milk is one of our best foods.
2. What is meant by the following: whole milk, skim milk, buttermilk, homogenized milk, yogurt, chocolate milk, evaporated milk, condensed milk, dried milk, cheese, milk solids?
3. What kind of milk do you buy for drinking at home? Which kind do you buy for cooking?
4. Observe the amount of water in milk, and note as you go forward in your study how important small percentages of protein and minerals may be to you.
5. How can you save money in buying milk and still meet your health needs?
6. Why are chocolate milk and condensed milk not exact substitutes for milk?
7. How does the pasteurizing of milk protect your health?
8. What effect do high temperature and light have on milk, and how would this influence the way you cook with milk?
9. Explain the best way to cook with milk.

PROBLEMS TO SOLVE

1. Checking the milk you use daily:
   (1) For three days keep a record of the milk you drink at meals and between meals (in any form).
   (2) Record the cheese you eat at meals or between meals.
   (3) Record the amount of ice cream you eat at meals and between.
2. How much milk and milk products are you getting daily?
   (1) How does the amount you get compare with the recommended amount?
   (2) Can you make a plan that will help you meet your particular needs?
   (3) Check yourself daily for a week to see if you can follow this plan.

3. Plan a menu for snacks for five days, in which you use milk in some form.
4. Make a plan showing how you would organize your work to serve a snack to your friends.
5. Arrange an exhibit of different kinds of milk.
6. Try using dry skim milk in beverages.

APPLYING WHAT YOU KNOW

1. Plan a menu for a snack and prepare to serve it at school, using dried milk and evaporated milk in one or more of the following forms:
   (1) Cold milk shake
   (2) Hot cocoa
   (3) Milk shake with fruit
2. Select appropriate dishes to serve your snack attractively.

EVALUATING

1. How could your snack taste better and be more attractive next time?
2. What made the atmosphere in which you ate pleasant or unpleasant?
3. Was your work done in an orderly and efficient way, with correct cooking practices?
4. Which kind of milk would you select on a low budget? A moderate budget? A high budget?
5. What other forms of milk could you use in snacks?
6. How did your snack contribute to your total food needs for the day?

HOME EXPERIENCE

1. Plan and prepare a snack for your family or friends at home.
2. Make a collection of good recipes for snacks using milk in some form.
3. Bring to school your family's favorite recipe which uses milk in a beverage.

3

Milk:
The Best Food
for Calcium

Milk Helps Build Good Posture and Good Teeth

You need many different nutrients to build good teeth and good bones for posture. Calcium (kăl′sĭ ŭm), a mineral, is one of these. Calcium is the most abundant mineral in the body, and most of it is found in the bones.

In a way, the construction of the body is like that of a skyscraper. The skyscraper has to be supported by an inner structure of steel. The muscles and skin of your body are supported by an inner structure of bone. The bones make up a large part of the total weight and bulk of the body, and 99 percent of the calcium found in the whole body is in the bones and teeth.

Perhaps you may think of the bones and teeth not as living, but as something more like stone or steel. In reality the bones and teeth are living structures and are constantly undergoing change. This means that the demands for calcium are of two kinds. The food we eat must supply calcium both for growth of bones and teeth, and for the maintenance of life processes. A growing girl or boy naturally needs more calcium than an adult. To meet this need, nutritionists recommend that a girl in her teens include in her daily diet 1.3 grams of calcium (a gram is one twenty-eighth of an ounce). A teen-age boy needs 1.4 grams daily. On the other hand, adults need 0.8 gram daily.

Milk is the Best Food for Calcium

Calcium is very low in most foods, but one quart of milk contains 1.15 grams of calcium. It is easy to drink a quart of milk a day and still be able to eat the other foods you need for good health. The comparisons in the table show how difficult it is to get needed calcium from other foods. You can see from this how important milk is in supplying calcium daily. You may not be surprised to learn that diet studies repeatedly show that many teen-agers are not getting the amount of calcium which they need. A calcium deficiency in your diet may affect your posture, the soundness of your teeth, and other aspects of your health.

The calcium is more easily used by the body when it comes from milk (and other animal foods) than when it comes from vegetables and fruits. However, including green vegetables in the daily diet helps add to your calcium intake.

AMOUNT OF FOOD REQUIRED TO GIVE ONE GRAM CALCIUM

3½	cups milk
55	slices of enriched white bread
77	cups cooked white rice
14	cups of cooked brown rice
62	average-size potatoes
28	pounds beef
26	cups cooked carrots
22	cups cooked snap beans
20	medium-size oranges
125	apples
125	bananas
5	ounces Cheddar cheese
37	ounces cottage cheese

Who Grows to His Full Height?

Full height for one person is not full height for another, because of differences in heredity. But whatever your possible height may be, in order to reach it you need proper food. Scientists have learned by experimenting with animals that not only does the choice of food influence the height of the individual animal, but a continually poor diet in calcium has an even greater influence on height in the next generation.

The pictures on page 31 show how much better the bone growth of one animal is than the other. What made this difference? Milk! The large animal had milk, meat, potato and bread, while the smaller one had only meat, potato, and bread. The findings in the laboratory show that proper food ranks with heredity in determining height, and many people probably fail to reach their full height because of poor choices of food in their daily diet.

How Did Primitive Man Get Along with Little Milk?

If calcium is so important for bone growth, and so low in common foods such as meat, cereal-breads, and the like, where did the Eskimo and the American Indian get their calcium?

These people ate the entire animal, fish or fowl, including the calcium-rich bones, tails, fins, and heads of fish and the blood, liver, bone-marrow, cartilage, and some bones of animals. Stefansson, the Arctic explorer, reports that Eskimos boiled bones until they were soft, and ate them as food. What appears on the surface to be a restricted diet turns out to be richer in some minerals and vitamins than the diets of many Americans.

Studies made of Eskimos in Greenland show that tooth decay among them rose from 4.5 percent to 44.5 percent after they had lived in or near the white man's village for 40 years, and had substituted white flour, white rice, and white sugar for a part of their native diet.

Why Is Calcium So Important in Maintaining Your Life?

Building teeth and bones is not the only important work of calcium. The body is made so that it maintains an almost constant level of calcium in the blood stream, day and night, to carry on these functions:

(1) Calcium is needed to help the heart muscle contract. We depend on a strong heart beat to send the blood through the body with its nutrients and oxygen to nourish every cell.

(2) Calcium is needed to give firmness to the liquid part of cells.

(3) Calcium contributes to blood clotting.

(4) When calcium in the blood is below normal, irritability of nerves is increased.

(5) Calcium is needed for the work of muscles and the response of nerves to stimulation.

What Happens When You Do Not Eat the Calcium-rich Foods Needed?

The body is no mere machine, though it has often been compared to one. If it were like a machine, the heart beat and other functions that need calcium would stop if you failed to include enough in the food you eat. What happens when you fail to include the calcium you need in your daily meals and snacks? The blood takes calcium from places where it is stored in your bones. This comes first from the end of the long bones as illustrated on the next page. X-rays of adult bones of people believed to be "normally" nourished have shown that they are often calcium-poor. The home diets of these people showed low calcium content. Thus you can see that if the diet is too low in calcium while you are growing, continuous "stealing" of calcium from bones will affect the soundness of these structures as you get older. It is like "robbing Peter to pay Paul."

Food makes the difference. The rat at top had a diet low in calcium and vitamins. His twin below, who ate well-balanced foods, weighs twice as much and has strong, well-formed bones.

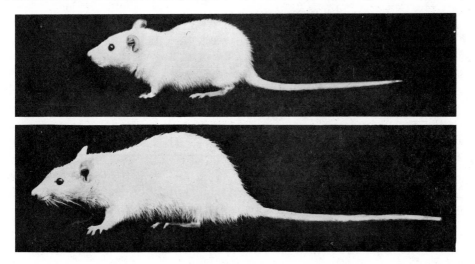

A calcium-poor diet over the years may cause bones to be more fragile, joints to enlarge, and legs to cramp. Lack of sufficient calcium may also affect posture and teeth.

The Relation of Atomic Fallout to Nutrition and Health

Since the testing of nuclear weapons began, you have read of fallout and radioactive strontium 90 (strŏn' chē ŭm) with possible ill-effects on food and health. Much harm can be done to health by anxieties, especially when they are based on misinformation or half-truths. What are the facts? Although more research is needed over a long span of time to get a clear picture, certain things are known right now. You may have heard that strontium 90 from milk and other foods is deposited in the bones like calcium. Some people have erroneously concluded that milk should be dropped from the diet for this reason.

In an experiment where one group of animals was fed a high calcium diet, compared with another group that was fed a low calcium diet, it was found that those eating the high calcium diet deposited *less* strontium 90 in the bones than those eating a low calcium diet. It would seem that a more liberal intake of calcium with a higher reserve in the body may actually reduce the deposit of radioactive strontium 90.

Calcium-rich Diets Bring Extra Benefits

Animal experiments at Columbia University show that there are extra benefits in having extra calcium in the daily diet. For instance, when more than adequate amounts of calcium in the form of milk were added, these benefits followed: more calcium was laid down in the bones, there was higher vitality, infant mortality was decreased, and the animals which had a more generous calcium intake lived longer by approximately 10 percent. Commenting on these results, Dr. H. C. Sherman says, "Here . . . are findings which clearly show that nutrition ranks with heredity as a factor in determining the length of life." *

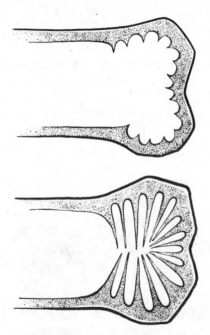

Diagram shows big end bones from which the blood can take calcium to do its work when calcium is lacking in the food. Poorly developed inner projections of bone in the picture at the top indicate low calcium reserve. The strong, deep projections toward the center of the bone at the bottom show good calcium deposits.

Chemistry of Food and Nutrition, 8th ed., The Macmillan Company, New York, N.Y. 1952.

FOODS RICH IN CALCIUM

RECOMMENDED DAILY ALLOWANCE:
GIRLS 13-19, 1.3 GRAMS; BOYS 13-19, 1.4 GRAMS; ADULTS, 0.8 GRAMS.

Name of Food and Measure*	Approximate Grams of Calcium**
Milk, 1 quart	1.15
Cheese, (Cheddar) 1 ounce	.21
Cheese, (Swiss) 1 ounce	.26
Collard greens, cooked, ½ cup	.23
Kale, cooked, ½ cup	.12
Mustard greens, cooked, ½ cup	.15
Turnip greens, cooked, ½ cup	.19
Broccoli, cooked, ½ cup	.10
Dry beans, cooked, ½ cup	.18
Salmon, with bones, 3 ounces	.16
Sardines, with bones, 1½ ounce	.16
Clams, raw meat, 4 ounces	.11

* Other common foods are lower in calcium, in portions we eat daily, than those listed. See page 451 for complete recommendations.
** Figures adapted from Handbook 8, *Composition of Foods*, U.S.D.A.

Phosphorus Teams Up with Calcium for Bones and Teeth

In 1968 the Foods and Nutrition Council of the National Academy of Sciences recommended, for the first time, that the diet should contain the same amount of phosphorus as calcium. These two minerals must work together if bone and tooth structures are to be properly built. Fortunately, milk contains phosphorus in just the right proportion. Phosphorus is also found in all meats and eggs, but these foods are low in calcium. If you get the daily recommended amount of milk, you will meet your need for phosphorus.

THINKING IT OVER

1. Why is calcium such an important mineral for good posture and sound teeth?

2. In what other ways is calcium important for your health and appearance?

3. How much calcium does a teen-age girl need? A teen-age boy? An adult?

4. Why is milk such an important food for calcium in the daily diet?

5. How does milk compare with other foods in calcium content?

6. Can you meet your daily need for calcium without including milk in your meals and snacks? Explain.

7. What happens to your body when you do not meet your calcium need through the food you eat?

8. Show practical ways to use milk in your meals and snacks.

9. What steps would you take to teach a younger brother or sister to like milk if he or she did not like it naturally?

10. What benefits carry over into later life if you continue to eat a calcium-rich diet?

PROBLEMS TO SOLVE

1. Learning to check on your growth: Check your weight and height once each month and record them. How near do you approach the estimated weight for your age and height (see page 16)? See how much you change in three months; six months; one year.

2. Learning to improve your diet in calcium: Show how you would use these foods in one day's menus: 1 quart milk, 1 egg, 1 dish cereal, 4 ounces lean meat, 1 ounce cheese, 1 orange, 1 tomato, 4–8 lettuce leaves, ½ cup Brussels sprouts, 1 sweet potato, 3 pats margarine, 4 slices whole wheat bread, 1 banana, 3 oatmeal cookies.

3. Examining a soup bone to see calcium splinters: As a class, have the butcher split a long soup bone lengthwise. If possible, compare the bones of a mature beef with a veal bone. The purpose is to examine the calcium splinters laid down in the ends of the long bone. Record what you see. What does this indicate? Compare with the drawing of end bones on page 32.

APPLYING WHAT YOU KNOW

1. Planning menus using milk in soups.
   (1) Plan three balanced luncheon menus using inexpensive forms of milk in a milk soup.
   (2) Plan a dinner menu using potato soup as the main dish in a balanced meal.

2. Using inexpensive forms of milk, prepare one or more of the following soups: potato soup; New England clam chowder; cream of tomato soup; cream of pea soup; cream of asparagus soup; cream of celery soup; corn chowder.

3. Serve the soup you have prepared as part of a balanced meal. Discuss service of a soup and table manners in eating it.

EVALUATING

1. In what ways would you use dried milk at breakfast to increase the health values in your diet? At lunch? At dinner?

2. In what dishes would you prefer to use evaporated milk? Why?

3. Why would you cover a milk soup when it is cooking, and why would you cook it over low heat?

4. Why is a milk soup a good main dish for lunch? What would you add to make it more nourishing?

HOME EXPERIENCE

Talk over with your mother what you have learned, and plan a balanced supper using a milk soup. Prepare and serve the soup. Report results to your teacher.

Milk:
The Best Food
for Riboflavin (Vitamin B₂)

A Quart of Milk Daily Is
Important for Riboflavin

If milk gave us nothing of importance but calcium, that alone would justify using at least one quart daily during growth, and a pint or more through life. But milk in its many forms is also our best food for riboflavin (rī′bŏ flā′vĭn) of which you as a teen-ager need 1.3 to 2 milligrams daily, depending on your sex and age. (See table page 39.) One quart provides 1.68 milligrams and meets a teen-age girl's recommended daily needs.

Evaporated or dry milk may be combined with fruit juice for a refrigerator ice cream that is quick to make and inexpensive.

How Riboflavin Helps Us

Riboflavin was first called the "growth-promoting" vitamin, but now we know it promotes more than growth. If there is too little of this vitamin in the diet, scientists have found, an animal cannot grow, and the state of health is so poor that life is scarcely more than just existing. It affects our own health, vigor, and appearance throughout life.

Riboflavin helps vision in many ways. In the lower animals and poultry (where life span is completed in a few short years), cataracts (kăt′á răkt) followed by blindness develop on the eyes when the diet is low in riboflavin. (A cataract is a cloudy growth that sometimes develops on the eyes of older people.) Riboflavin, along with other nutrients, helps prevent this condition and aids all ages in adjusting their eyes to bright light.

Riboflavin helps the body "burn" sugars and starches. We get our energy for work and living from the "burning" of the food we eat by its combination with oxygen. When the diet does not contain enough riboflavin, this job cannot be done. Red-streaked eyes of the alcoholic are one example of what can happen. Though alcohol contains calories that give energy and fuel, it does not contain riboflavin (or any other nutrient needed for the building of tissue). If one continues to get too many calories from foods or drinks that are too low in riboflavin, red-streaked eyes may follow. The body makes an effort to make up for this shortage. It builds a greater network of blood vessels,

When meat, poultry, fish or vegetables are added to cheese sauce, an excellent main dish for lunch or supper results. (Recipe on page 427.) If weight is a problem, what would you use instead of a patty shell?

Steps in Making White Sauce: (1) Measure fat accurately and melt in pan that does not admit light. (2) Add accurately measured flour and blend. (3) Add milk and blend. (4) Cook in top of double boiler or over low direct heat until sauce is thick and smooth. (See recipe and alternate method page 427.)

bringing more blood to the eyes to supply more riboflavin. It "burns" protein also.

Naturally, anything that interferes with good nutrition shows up more quickly under the added responsibility of pregnancy and nursing a baby. A startling observation has been made in experimenting with animals. When the diet of the pregnant animal was quite low in riboflavin, half the litter might be born with their toes grown together or a cleft palate or some other deformity. When the same mother was given adequate riboflavin, all the young in the next litter were normal.

One of the most common signs of a riboflavin deficiency is in the cracking of the lips, especially in the corners of the nouth. When food in the diet is too low in riboflavin content, the skin and hair may become either too oily or too dry. Girls or boys who have excessively dry or oily skin or hair might well look into the amount of riboflavin they are getting in their meals and snacks.

Nerve tissue also needs riboflavin for healthy functioning. When animals have a diet too low in riboflavin, they "go to pieces" under emotional strain. There seems to be a change in body tissue that shows up in weak and trembling legs and inability to grasp with the paws. This vitamin also helps maintain a healthy digestive tract.

A noodle ring filled with mixed vegetables and meat and topped with cheese sauce.

Use a cheese sauce on cooked cauliflower or any cabbage to enhance flavor and add nourishment.

Comparison of the Riboflavin Content of Milk with That of Other Foods

Yeast, liver, and kidney are richer in riboflavin than milk is. However, for practical reasons we cannot depend on eating these foods every day. Green leafy vegetables are also a good source of this vitamin, for it is in the leaf that riboflavin is made. It is from eating green leaves and grass that the cow gets her riboflavin to pass on to us in milk. Some remains in her tissue, but not much. It takes from one-half to three-quarters of a pound of beef to give the riboflavin in one cup of milk! The dark meat of chicken is richer in this vitamin than the white meat. The table on the next page shows the amounts of riboflavin in the common foods we eat. By studying this table you can see how difficult it is to meet your need of riboflavin daily unless you have milk with your meals.

How to Save Riboflavin in Cooking

Unfortunately, milk often loses much of its riboflavin content during cooking. This loss can be kept to a minimum, however,

FOODS RICH IN RIBOFLAVIN

RECOMMENDED DAILY ALLOWANCE:
GIRLS 12-16, 1.4 MILLIGRAMS; GIRLS 16-18, 1.5 MILLIGRAMS
BOYS 12-14, 1.4 MILLIGRAMS; BOYS 14-18, 1.5 MILLIGRAMS

Name of Food and Measure*	Milligrams of Riboflavin**
Milk, 1 quart	1.68
Cheese, (Cheddar) 1 ounce	.12
Liver, 4 ounces	4.50
Beef heart, 4 ounces	1.00
Egg, 1 whole	.14
Sirloin steak, 3 ounces	.16
Hamburger, 3 ounces	.16
Turnip greens, cooked, ½ cup	.30
Mustard greens, cooked, ½ cup	.13
Broccoli, cooked, ½ cup	.11
Asparagus, cooked, ½ cup	.15
Prunes, cooked, ½ cup	.10
Spinach, cooked, ½ cup	.18
Kale, cooked, ½ cup	.13
Oysters, ½ cup	.24
Ham, 3 ounces	.18
Squash, winter, baked, ½ cup	.15

* Other common foods are lower than those listed in the amounts we eat daily.
** Figures adapted from Handbook 8, *Composition of Foods*, U.S.D.A. (1950, revised 1958). (See the complete daily dietary recommendations in appendix, pages 450-451.)

if certain rules are followed. The loss of riboflavin is greater when milk is heated in the presence of light. Keep milk out of light and you will protect the riboflavin in it. You can save this vitamin by simply using a pan that does not admit light, and covering the pan when you cook.

Riboflavin, like sugar, goes into solution in liquid. When milk is evaporated to produce dry or evaporated milk, the riboflavin stays with the "milk solids." Any food that contains milk solids is rich in riboflavin, calcium, and protein from milk. When you use these less expensive forms

Have you tried to make a cheese soufflé? It is a dish that will delight the family or guests, and it is easy to prepare.

of milk in cooking, you are getting rich nourishment for the money spent.

Extra Benefits from Extra Riboflavin

As in the case of calcium, there is evidence to indicate that you get extra benefits from including more riboflavin in your diet than is considered adequate. This shows up in: (1) better growth in children; (2) greater freedom from disease in all ages; (3) higher adult vitality with a longer "prime of life" and a delay in the onset of old age. What this means is a longer, healthier life, with fewer years when we may be dependent on others.

Fortunately, all forms of milk are rich in riboflavin. If you know food values, you can meet this need on a low food budget, as well as on a more liberal one.

WORDS TO WORK WITH

Riboflavin (rī′bŏ flā′vĭn): vitamin B₂, essential for growth, health, and life itself.
Cataract (kăt′á răkt): a clouding of the eye which may result in blindness.

THINKING IT OVER

1. What is a second important reason why you need a quart of milk daily?
2. In what way does riboflavin help your vision? Your hair and skin? Your nervous system?
3. When you eat a rich starch or sugar food such as a candy bar or spaghetti, why do you need milk with it?
4. How may the overeating or overdrinking of foods or beverage with "empty" calories affect your appearance?
5. Which part of a plant is richest in riboflavin? How can you use this knowledge to improve your life?
6. What foods besides milk are rich in riboflavin?
7. How can you meet your need of riboflavin through milk if you have a low income?
8. Explain how light and heat affect this vitamin, and how you can retain it by proper care and proper cooking.
9. What are the benefits from including extra riboflavin in the diet? How can this help you as you get older?
10. How can thorough knowledge of the values of milk help you plan meals intelligently and cook them properly?

PROBLEMS TO SOLVE

1. How would you change the following meals to include enough riboflavin in each meal and give a completely balanced meal?
   Breakfast: 2 doughnuts, tomato juice, coffee
   Lunch: hamburger, pickle, cherry pie, coke
   Dinner: spaghetti and meat balls, bread and butter, celery, milk, cake

2. Look up in a reference book (such as Volume 9 of *Richards Topical Encyclopedia*) the story of how cheese is made. Share what you learn with the class.

3. Decide what kinds of cheese are most suitable to serve: as appetizers, in sandwiches, in sauces, with desserts.

APPLYING WHAT YOU KNOW

Prepare and serve as a part of a balanced meal one or more of the following *cheese dishes* for each meal (see Cookbook for recipes):

(1) Breakfast
   Cheese *omelet;* or egg fried on cheese; or eggs shirred with grated cheese.

(2) Lunch
   Welsh rarebit; welsh rarebit with added vegetables or meat or both; cheese *omelet;* cheese *soufflé;* cheese sandwich; variations of toasted cheese *sandwiches; salads.*

(3) Dinner
   (a) *Appetizers* with fruit juice or with salads as first course; grated over the top of soup; in dips for parties and first course.
   (b) As a *meat substitute,* in main course of dinner with macaroni; Spanish rice; potatoes au gratin; cheese soufflé.
   (c) As a *sauce,* over cauliflower, other vegetables, left-over meat.
   (d) As a *dessert,* with crackers or fresh fruit; with apple pie, pumpkin pie, apricot pie, other fruit pies; cheese cake.
   (e) Cooked in *breads,* as quick breads; yeast breads.
   (f) *Salads,* as cottage cheese with fruit; cheese in dressings; cubed in fruit or vegetable salads.
   (g) In *gelatin* base using *meat* or *fish;* as salmon mousse with cottage cheese.

2. Planning menus.
   (1) Plan one week of menus using cheese at breakfast two days; at lunch three days; at dinner as a meat substitute one day; and as a dessert one day.

EVALUATING

1. Did you cook with cheese? Was it smooth or stringy or lumpy? If not smooth, what was the cause? How can you correct this?

2. Why can you add cheese to different dishes? What does it contribute to the meal?

3. Which cheese is best suited for cooking? For dessert? How would you use cottage cheese? Is cheese a complete substitute for milk? Explain.

4. Did you keep the cheese out of the light as much as possible while cooking it? How? Why do you need to protect cheese from light?

5. Which do you prefer in cooking—a mild, medium, or sharp cheese? Why? Have you tried the others?

HOME EXPERIENCE

Talk over with your mother what you have learned. Plan with her a balanced menu for a family meal which includes cheese. Cook and serve the cheese dish as a part of this meal. Report results to your teacher.

chapter 5

Vitamin A in Milk
Helps Health and Looks

Vitamin A Discovered Through Butter

The discovery of vitamin A in 1913 was a dramatic event in the science of nutrition. Experiments were conducted at two separate universities independently of each other, and results of each experiment were similar.

Two groups of twin animals, A and B, were fed good diets. The diets were identical except for one thing. Group A had butter as a source of fat. Group B had lard. The animals in group A grew and thrived with sleek hair, bright eyes, good color, fine physique, and general vigor.

It was quite another story in Group B. These animals developed sore eyes, coarse hair, dry skin; they failed to grow normally and died.

This was amazing! Investigators immediately saw that there was "something special" in butter, not present in lard. They quickly set off on a trail of research to find this "something," and they found it—vitamin A in butter. Vitamin A had made all of the difference in the health and appearance of the two groups of animals. The discovery marked a great leap forward for the health and welfare of humanity.

Further study of fats followed. It was discovered that egg yolk and cod liver oil had this same vitamin, but that most of the commercial fats and vegetable oils lacked it. Today we know that for those who need a low fat or low calorie diet skim milk with added vitamin A is a real boon.

The Nature of Vitamin A

Pure vitamin A is colorless. It is called a "fat-soluble" vitamin, since it is soluble (dissolves) in fat and not in water. This means that we need a suitable fat in the same meal with vitamin A if it is to be well used by the body. Butter and whole milk provide a suitable fat.

Mineral oil, often taken as a laxative, is not a suitable fat. It prevents the absorption of vitamin A (and other fat-soluble vitamins—D, E, and K). Vitamin A is not easily destroyed by light or heat, but there is some loss when yellow peaches and apricots are dried.

This vitamin is stored in the liver when there is an excess in the diet. While it is possible to "overflow" the storage capacity, and get too much vitamin A, this is not likely to happen. Sherman found that it took eighty times the adequate amount

Why is cottage cheese low in vitamin A? What can sour cream or whole milk add to it?

of vitamin A to reach maximum storage in the white rat. For people, it is more probable that not enough of this vitamin is eaten. Studies of family diets repeatedly show that vitamin A is one of the nutrients not adequately represented. This is especially true for most teen-age diets. Your concern, then, is to eat daily enough of the foods that will give you this important nutrient. This is easy to do when you know the foods rich in it.

Milk and Its Products Help Meet Your Need for Vitamin A

One quart of milk daily supplies about one-third (1560 International Units) of the recommended daily allowance (5000 I. U.) for vitamin A. Two tablespoons of butter, and 9 ounces of ice cream each supply about a sixth, and 4 ounces of cheddar cheese about one third. Taken together, this quart of milk and milk products could just meet your daily need. But this is not practical in daily meal-planning. You need other foods to bring more vitamin A into your daily diet. Liver and some fish liver oils are the best sources; green leafy vegetables stand next in importance, followed by yellow vegetables and yellow fruits. The big sea fish feed on the tiny sea fish, and these eat plant life in the ocean to make vitamin A. Old fish and animals have more vitamin A in their livers than young ones. They have had a longer period to store it. Similarly, the cow eats green leaves, and changes the yellow-red carotene (kăr'ŏ tēn) from plants into vitamin A. The vitamin A content of milk is richer when the cow has a rich supply of carotene in her diet from fresh green pasture.

FOODS RICH IN VITAMIN A*

RECOMMENDED DAILY ALLOWANCE FOR 13-19 YEAR OLDS (GIRLS AND BOYS): 5,000 UNITS

Name of Food and Measure	Units of Vitamin A
VEGETABLES	
GREEN (cooked, ½ cup)	
Green leafy (kale, turnip greens, collards, mustard greens, spinach, other greens)	10,000
Broccoli	2,550
Green peas	575
Green beans	415
Brussels sprouts	260
YELLOW	
Sweet potatoes (5x2x2 inch)	11,410
Carrots, ½ cup	9,065
Winter squash, yellow, ½ cup	6,345
Yellow sweet corn, (one 5-inch ear)	390
FRUITS	
Cantaloupe, ½ with 5-inch diameter	6,190
Apricots, ½ cup, dried, cooked	3,450
6 halves, canned	2,475
Tomato, 1 medium, raw	1,640
½ cup, canned or juice	1,270
Orange juice, frozen (6-ounce can)	670
Prunes, 8-9 cooked	1,105
Peaches, raw, 1 medium	880
Banana, 1 medium, raw	430
OTHER FOODS	
Liver, 4 ounces	60,660
Milk, 1 quart	1,560
Cheese, Cheddar, 1-inch cube	400
Egg, 1 whole	550
Butter, 1 tablespoon	460
Cereal grains, dried beans, peas, lentils, nuts, sugars, and some fats contain no or almost no vitamin A	

* Figures in this table are adapted from Handbook 8, *Composition of Foods,* U.S.D.A., except that for green leafy vegetables, which is from H. C. Sherman, *Chemistry of Food and Nutrition,* 8th Edition, New York: The Macmillan Company, 1952.

In the table on page 44 are listed the foods that are highest in vitamin A. Notice that the green leafy and yellow vegetables and yellow fruits are superior to milk in vitamin A. As you shall soon see, you need them for this and other reasons. However, since many people do not eat these foods every day, the daily quart of milk is quite important.

When the body changes carotene from vegetables and fruits into vitamin A, there is a waste of up to 50 percent or more. But vitamin A from animal foods is ready to be used directly by the body.

How Vitamin A in the Diet Helps Your Looks and Health

Vitamin A helps general health by its influence on the mucous membrane (mū′-kŭs), which lines the mouth, nose, ears, eyes, lungs, digestive and urinary tracts, and glandular organs. Studies have shown that too little vitamin A in the diet results in: an increase in respiratory disease; skin, ear and sinus infections and inflammation; and infections of the alimentary tract. On the other hand, when vitamin A is adequate, there is greater resistance to respiratory disease and other types of infection. This vitamin is used in the treatment of tuberculosis.

Vitamin A is important for vision. Sore eyes are found where the diets of families and nations are poor.

In our country most of us get enough vitamin A to prevent serious eye disease. But do your eyes adjust quickly when you go from a lighted street into a dark theater? Enough vitamin A in the diet helps you adjust quickly from light to dark or the reverse. Our country used this

knowledge during World War II. You may have read in your social studies of how flyers were given large amounts of vitamin A so that their eyes could adjust quickly from darkness to light or light to darkness. Vitamin A is just one nutrient working for you with others to help prevent "night blindness." Night blindness often causes automobile accidents.

In addition, vitamin A has an important part to play in building strong, good-looking teeth. It helps harden the enamel, and gives the white pearl color which is so attractive.

One of the first things that happens in experimental animals and in persons under observation when vitamin A is too low is a change in the skin and hair. As you progress in this study, you will learn that other nutrients, or the absence of them, also affect the quality of the skin and hair. When vitamin A is deficient, the hair becomes drier and coarse. Little "goose pimples" may form around the elbow. Blackheads, whiteheads, and pimples appear, especially across the back of the shoulders and at places where hair grows

Add dried herbs and spices to biscuit dough for a delicious meat pie topping.

out of the skin. When vitamin A is increased in the diet sufficiently, these symptoms disappear. You can see then that the cream and butter which you eat may do more for your skin than the cream you rub on it.

Delayed Effect of Too Little Vitamin A in the Diet

If food could talk, it would tell us what it can do for us—and it does, through our health and appearance. But we have to understand the sign language that food "speaks." This requires time and study. For example, it was found that when twin animals had the same diet through two generations except that one had whole milk and the other had skim, it made a difference in their health, appearance, and length of life. At first the animals grew equally well, and looked equally at-

tractive. But the animal on the skim milk was getting much less vitamin A, and when the reserves stored in his body were used up, his hair began to look rough. This was even more noticeable in the second generation. The animals on a good diet except for vitamin A could not grow normally; their coat of hair was much rougher, and they were unable to produce and nurse healthy babies.

When the vitamin A was doubled in the normal basic diet, the animals looked better, and lived longer. Then four times as much vitamin A was added to the basic diet, and the health record and length of life were further improved.

This study tells us that we cannot always see the immediate value of a good diet, or the harm of a poor one. It takes time for food habits to show their good or ill effect on us.

 WORDS TO WORK WITH

International Units: the "measuring stick" for vitamin A and vitamin D, instead of weight.

Carotene (kăr′ȯ tēn): a substance in green and yellow plants from which the animal body can make vitamin A.

Mucous membrane (mū′kŭs): tissue lining body cavities such as the nose, ears, mouth, and digestive and urinary tracts.

Steps in Making Biscuits (see recipe, page 360): (1) Preheat oven to 450°F. Sift dry ingredients, including dry milk, together thoroughly. (2) Make a hole in center and add water (or milk) and vegetable oil. Mix lightly with a circular motion, keeping dough smooth. (3) Place dough on lightly floured board or wax paper and knead (turn under) 4 or 5 times. (4) Roll dough to a thickness of ¼ to ½ inch. (5) Dip biscuit cutter or small glass in flour and cut biscuits, placing them about 1 inch apart on a lightly greased cookie sheet. (6) Bake in very hot oven (450°F). In 10 to 12 minutes golden brown biscuits are ready to serve.

Bake your own bread and increase the calcium, riboflavin, protein, and other nutrients in it by adding milk.

THINKING IT OVER

1. How was vitamin A discovered, and why is it called "fat-soluble"? How does this influence meal-planning?

2. In what ways does vitamin A help your health? Your appearance?

3. What animal foods would you include in meals for vitamin A? Which plant foods?

4. How could you drink skim milk and meet your need for vitamin A during growth?

5. Why is vitamin A used more easily by the body when it comes from animal foods

rather than plant foods? In what form does this vitamin occur in plants?

6. Explain why a diet low in vitamin A may not show any harmful effects immediately.

7. How does vitamin A help build good-looking teeth?

8. About how much of your daily need for vitamin A can be met through milk? What other foods would you eat to boost this vitamin in your meals and snacks?

PROBLEMS TO SOLVE

1. Checking the vitamin A in your diet.
   (1) Write down the food you ate at meals and between meals yesterday.
   (2) Underscore the foods you ate containing vitamin A and rate yourself. Did you have milk in each meal or snack? Did you have a green vegetable? A yellow vegetable or fruit?

2. Plan balanced menus for three days, underlining foods rich in vitamin A in each meal and snack.

3. What foods for vitamin A would you include on a low-cost daily food budget?

APPLYING WHAT YOU KNOW

1. Learning to enrich baked foods with low-cost milk.
   (1) Plan balanced breakfast, luncheon, and dinner menus including quick bread such as biscuits.
      (a) Use a low-cost type of milk to make the biscuits (see recipe, page 360).
      (b) Discuss variations for biscuits: how to use at breakfast as the bread; how to use at lunch or supper with a creamed meat, Welsh rarebit, or a creamed vegetable; how to use for dessert as a part of a shortcake.

EVALUATING

1. Decide on the standard for a good drop biscuit; rolled biscuits.
   (1) Did your biscuits meet this standard? How can you improve?
   (2) What would you do to change a drop biscuit into a rolled one?
   (3) What are the advantages of the drop biscuit over the rolled?
   (4) Compare the cost of homemade biscuits with that of biscuit mix, ready-to-cook biscuits, and ready-to-eat biscuits.

2. Prepare a biscuit mix.
   (1) Study biscuit recipes and decide how you can prepare your own biscuit mix.
      (a) Decide how much you would mix at a time, what ingredients you would put in the mix, and what you would add (see recipe, page 360).
      (b) Compare the cost with ready-mix that you buy. Compare the time used.
      (c) Where would you store the mix until ready to use?

HOME EXPERIENCE

Discuss with your mother what you have learned about using dried milk in baking. Plan with her a balanced menu for a meal including drop biscuits. You prepare and serve the biscuits. Report results to your teacher.

Protein in Milk
Helps Growth and Vitality

What Is Protein?

The word *protein* (prō′tēn) comes from a Greek word meaning "of first importance." Indeed protein is of first importance, for it is a necessary part of every living cell. Plants can make it if there is nitrogen (nī′trō jĕn) in the soil, but man must get it from the food he eats. Protein does many things for you. You need it during growth to help make muscle cells, red blood cells, and cells of the skin, hair, teeth, bones, and nerve tissue. You need it throughout your life to repair and replace worn tissue.

Foods contain not only different amounts but different kinds of protein—

Milk shake with ice cream and cake—a party refreshment that tastes good, looks good, and is good.

Applesauce, dry skim milk, and sour cream make a quick, flavorful topping for desserts such as gingerbread.

and the kind of protein you eat is of great importance. For instance, in countries where the diet is mostly from plant foods (cereals, vegetables, and fruits), the people do not enjoy a high degree of health, their appearance is not good, and they do not live a long life. The report of a study made by the Food and Agricultural Organization of the United Nations points out the relation of good-grade protein in the diet to health and length of life. For example, in India in 1952, the average amount of animal protein eaten each day by each person was 6 grams, and the average length of life was 27 years. In Mexico this figure was 16 grams, with the average length of life at around 40 years. But in Australia, Canada, France, West Germany, Denmark, United Kingdom, and the United States, the average amount of protein eaten daily was from 30 to 65 grams. The average length of life in these countries was from 60 to 70 years. What, then, is the difference between the protein in animal and plant foods? Is it necessary that you under-

stand this distinction in order to plan your meals intelligently? Yes, it is. And if you do understand this difference you can also save money on your food budget in many ways.

Just as you are made of many parts, such as hands, arms, feet, legs, head, and internal organs, a protein is also made of many parts or fragments. There are about 22 known protein fragments, and these parts are called amino acids (ă mē′nō). Each one has a special name, and does a particular job in building certain tissues in the body. Not all of these amino acids have to be present in every food you eat. The body can make some of them, provided you have the right combination of other foods in your meal. But there are eight which the body cannot make, and which are essential for life and growth. You must therefore include in your daily meals and snacks some food which contains all of the "essential" amino acids. Such a food is called a "complete" protein food, for it can maintain your life in a high state of health, and can promote

Quick Ice Cream (see recipe, page 367): (1) Beating the chilled milk. (2) Pouring the ice cream into the tray to freeze. This ice cream can be made inexpensively at home.

normal growth. Milk, milk products, lean meat, fish, poultry, and eggs are the complete protein foods.

On the other hand, cereal-breads and vegetables (fruits contain practically no protein) lack one or more of the essential amino acids, and they are called "partially incomplete" protein foods. These foods could keep you alive, but your state of health would not be as good, nor would you grow as normally, as when the protein in your diet is complete. However, the protein in vegetables and cereal-breads is well used when you drink milk or at the same meal eat some cheese, lean meat, or eggs. The most important plant foods for protein are dried beans, peas, lentils, and nuts. Indeed these foods are so good in this respect that they may be used as an alternate for meat, if you eat in the same meal some cheese or eggs, or have milk to drink. Thus the protein in animal foods balances the weaker protein in plant foods when they are eaten together. This is one of the big reasons why you need to eat a variety of foods in a meal instead of eating only one or two that may suit your fancy.

You cannot always judge the value of a protein food by reading the amount it contains in a percentage table. For instance, gelatin is 100 percent protein. On the surface this would seem to indicate that gelatin is a marvelous protein food. The facts are just the opposite. When animals on an otherwise adequate diet were fed gelatin as the only source of protein, they failed to grow, their appearance became increasingly bad, and they died. But when only the protein from milk was added to this same diet, the animals not only lived, they grew normally. Milk protein is what made the difference. It is of great importance that you understand this difference in order to plan balanced meals, and in addition save money on your food budget.

In planning each meal, you should first select a *complete protein food*. But it is expensive and unnecessary to meet all of your protein need from milk, meat, and eggs, for animal foods cost more to produce and more to buy than cereals and vegetables. If you eat more animal protein foods than you need to grow and to repair worn tissue, the extra protein is

51

simply burned for energy. Today it is considered adequate if one-half to two-thirds of your protein comes from animal foods, and the remainder from vegetables and cereal-breads.

If you eat daily the foods recommended in the chart on page 12, they will supply an abundant balance of animal and plant foods to meet your protein needs as well as your other needs for growth, good health, and attractive appearance.

How Much Protein Do You Need Daily?

Your protein need is greater during the rapid-growth period of your teens than when you are grown. When a girl reaches 14, she needs 55 grams of protein daily. When she is grown, her estimated need is the same except in pregnancy, when she needs 10 to 20 grams more. Since boys grow larger, they need 60 grams daily from 14 to 22 and 65 after that. How does milk meet this need?

How Milk Helps Meet Your Protein Need

A quart of milk daily meets over half the protein need of everyone, except women during pregnancy or lactation. This is because a quart of milk contains 36 grams of protein. Cheese is also important for protein, for the protein is in the curd or solid part of milk, from which cheese is made. One and one-half ounces of cheese gives you 9 to 12 grams of protein. The protein in milk and milk products is easily and completely digested, and is thus economically used by the body.

How Adequate Protein Helps Your Appearance and Vitality

Having enough high-quality protein foods in your meals and snacks helps give you good posture, for physicians point out that good posture relates not only to good bone structure, but also to good muscle structure. In the past many people considered a fat baby superior to a lean one, and fatness at middle and old age was considered not only normal but desirable. Today we know that there is better health when the body does not have excess fat, and when the tissue is lean and firm. It takes protein of high quality to build the healthy lean tissue that we admire in a girl as she swings a tennis racket or glides through the water with ease, or in a couple as they move gracefully across a dance floor. These results of strong muscle tissue we can see. But we must have special knowledge if we are to see the many hidden ways in which protein of

How many ways can ice cream be served with cake for a family meal? for a party?

high quality improves vitality and appearance.

For example, many children are stunted in growth because they do not have enough protein food of high quality. This is very noticeable when babies are weaned from breast milk. Breast milk supplies the growing baby with plenty of good protein to meet its needs. It has been observed that babies, regardless of nationality, grow very similarly on breast milk. But what a change takes place when the baby is weaned! Then we see how important milk is. In some parts of the world, the baby eats mostly starchy food. He may look plump or even fat, but he does not grow normally, for his body cannot make muscle tissue out of starchy and sweet foods. If the child continues on an inadequate protein diet, he is stunted when he is an adult. On the other hand, a baby that has milk and the other protein foods he needs after he has been weaned continues to grow normally, and reaches the full growth which is normal for him. Today it is known that growth is not so much a matter of national differences as of an adequate diet.

Also, your resistance to respiratory and intestinal diseases is greatly increased when you eat enough high-quality protein daily. Furthermore, enough good-quality protein helps the healing of wounds, and it is therefore important after surgery. Physicians report that teen-agers with tuberculosis give evidence that they have not been getting enough high-quality protein food. Other studies show that when children eat too much bread, cereals, cookies, and other sweets and fats, with too little milk, eggs, lean meat, vegetables, and fruits, it affects them in many ways.

They are stunted in growth and irritable in disposition, and have a low resistance to disease and infections.

There are other "hidden" ways in which high-quality protein is valuable to us, such as in helping make enzymes (ĕn′zīm) to digest our food, hormones to keep our bodies in proper chemical balance, and antibodies to help us have resistance to certain diseases. These are a few of the reasons why protein has been called a nutrient "of first importance."

Summary of How One Quart of Milk Daily Helps Your Appearance and Health

We are born needing the nutrients in milk, and this need continues throughout life. In planning meals, milk is a basic food to include, because it gives so much that we need for what it costs. Milk gives the variety of minerals, vitamins, and

Ice cream and homemade chocolate pudding make a parfait with an ice cream parlor look.

Why should you clean the refrigerator before marketing? Use baking soda in warm water to wash the interior for a clean, healthful place for food.

(2) A quart of milk daily helps you easily meet your riboflavin requirement. As with calcium, it is quite difficult to satisfy your need for this important nutrient unless you use milk or its products generously in your meals and snacks. Riboflavin is essential for growth, for vision, for a good complexion, for healthy nerve tissue, and for the proper use of carbohydrates and proteins in your diet.

(3) A quart of milk also stands high in meeting the daily protein need during growth and after you are grown as well. It contains all of the known amino acids, it is therefore most valuable for an economical use of the vegetables and cereal-breads which you eat. Although milk contains only 3.5 percent protein by weight, compared with 9 to 16 percent protein in cereal-breads, the protein in milk is of greater worth to you. This is because the value of a protein food must be judged not by the amount it contains but by

Floating Island—easy to make, delicious to eat, and beautiful to see. Why is this a good dessert for those who have a weight problem? (See recipe, page 366.)

high-quality protein that make the many tissues of the human body.

(1) We need milk every day because it is the best common food in our diet for calcium, which forms a part in many life processes but is especially needed for bones and teeth. Soils where plants are grown vary in calcium content. A single field may vary from one end to the other. Hence the calcium content of vegetables and fruits also varies. But a cow eating a diet from poor soil steals calcium from her bones to keep her milk at a constant level. If you drink a quart of milk daily, you can depend on its containing one gram of calcium. In a world where heat, light, storage, and poor cooking methods cause loss of health values in foods, this is indeed a beneficial certainty.

whether it is a "complete" protein or not. Not only is the protein in milk completely used by the body, but milk protein costs less than either egg, beef, or lamb protein.

(4) In addition, you can get from that quart of milk about one-third of your recommended daily supply of vitamin A. And it is well used by the body, for vitamin A appears in the fat of milk, which is needed for its absorption. Cream and butter contain both saturated and unsaturated fatty acids (see Chapter 23).

(5) The sugar in milk is one of the best sugars in food. It requires only one step in digestion, and gives as quick energy as a snack food. In addition, the 165 calories in a glass of whole milk (eight ounces) have "staying power" because milk also contains protein, fat, vitamins, and minerals. By contrast, one ounce of chocolate candy gives you 145 calories that are "empty," that is, they give energy and little more.

(6) In addition to the major contributions of milk, it also contains a variety of other nutrients needed by the body. The thiamine in a quart of milk may meet about one-fourth of the recommended daily need. Though milk has a low iron content, the iron it does contain is excellently used by the body.

In the past, people falsely concluded that though milk is an important food for babies and growing children, it is not needed by adults. They looked at the percentage table and noted that milk is 87 percent water, and reasoned that a food so full of water could not amount to much. Indeed, in those days many people valued milk most for its fat content. You can see in the table on page 452 what milk contains. But now you understand what these figures mean—that milk is a very valuable food. Therefore you can see why your meals and snacks should include milk—not so much of it as to take the place of other important foods, but enough to meet your body's needs now and when you are grown.

We enjoy the vitality and vigor of young people who are healthy and look it, for such people are usually pleasant companions. Milk helps you achieve these goals.

 ## WORDS TO WORK WITH

Protein (prō′tēn): see page 17.

Amino acid (ă mē′nō): a part or fragment of a protein.

Nitrogen (nī′trŏ jĕn): a colorless, odorless, tasteless element that is a part of all living tissue.

Enzyme (ĕn′zīm): a substance able to produce chemical changes in food and aid in its digestion.

 ## THINKING IT OVER

1. In what ways is protein a nutrient of first importance to you?

2. What does "complete protein" mean?

3. In what ways can adequate information about "complete" and "partially complete" protein foods affect your health? Your

appearance? The amount of money you spend on food?

4. What percent of protein would you select daily from animal foods? Plant foods?

5. Can you judge the importance of a protein food by the percentage of protein it contains? Explain your answer, and give examples to prove your point.

6. In what ways does an inadequate amount of complete protein in the diet affect health? Appearance? Length of life?

7. Why is a quart of milk the most nearly perfect food in your daily diet, and why do you need it throughout life? How can it help you meet the recommended daily need for: calcium, riboflavin, vitamin A, protein, thiamine?

8. Under what circumstances would you include in your daily diet more protein than the recommended amount?

9. Explain why it is so important to care for milk properly, and how it should be used in cooking so as to save as much nourishment and flavor as possible.

PROBLEMS TO SOLVE

1. Checking the protein in your diet: Make a record of the food you ate at meals and between meals yesterday. Total all milk and milk products. Using the table on page 452, figure out how much protein you had in the day's diet. How much came from milk and milk products.

2. Learning how high heat affects the protein in milk: Dissolve six tablespoons of dry milk in a cup and a half of cold water. Heat half a cup over high heat uncovered; heat one-half cup uncovered in the top of a double boiler; and one-half cup in an uncovered pan over low direct heat. Repeat the same experiment, but *cover* each pan before heating. Compare the results. How do you account for the difference? What does this indicate to you about

cooking with milk? What is lost that you can't see when the pan is uncovered?

3. Plan balanced menus for one week, using one quart of milk in each day's menu.

4. Write a story on "How My Study of Milk Will Help My Life."

APPLYING WHAT YOU KNOW

1. Use of milk in desserts.
   (1) Discuss the different ways milk may be used in desserts.
   (2) Which milk desserts are most suited to each season?
   (3) Which form of milk would you use for cooking on a low, moderate, or high food budget? Why?
   (4) Compare the health value, the ease in storage and care, and the flavor and cost of different forms of milk.
   (5) Compare the ready-mix milk desserts with homemade ones in cost, food value, and time and energy used.

2. Prepare one of the following desserts using the less expensive forms of milk:
   (1) Vanilla, chocolate, or butterscotch pudding.
   (2) Tapioca, rice, or bread pudding.
   (3) Refrigerator ice cream.
   (4) Floating Island.

3. Discuss the standard for the dessert you make and see if you can reach that standard. If not, understand your mistake and try again.

4. Plan three menus each for lunch and dinner using milk as the dessert.

HOME EXPERIENCE

Discuss with your mother what you have learned, and choose a dessert you can prepare using milk. You prepare and serve this dessert as a part of the family meal. Report results to your teacher.

FURTHER READING

Annotated Bibliography of Strontium and Calcium Metabolism in Man and Animals. U.S.D.A., Washington, D.C., 1961.

Bicycle Rider of Beverly Hills, William Saroyan. Charles Scribner's Sons, Inc., New York, N.Y., 1952. Informal memoir of the author's childhood, describing his delight at the end of a bicycle ride in drinking all the cold buttermilk he could hold.

Cheese Buying Guide for Consumers. U.S.D.A., Washington, D.C., 1961.

Cheese in Family Meals. U.S.D.A., Washington, D.C., 1966.

Choice Cheese Cakes. Leaflet of recipes. The Borden Co., New York, N.Y.

Facts About Pasteurization of Milk. U.S.D.A., Washington, D.C., 1956.

Getting Enough Milk. Home and Garden Bulletin 57. U.S.D.A., Washington, D.C., 1965.

Know Your Butter Grades. U.S.D.A., Washington, D.C., 1960.

Milk and Cream, Definitions and Standards. Food and Drug Act. U.S. Dept. of Health, Education, and Welfare, Washington, D.C., 1953.

Milk Consumption in the Nation's Schools. U.S.D.A., Washington, D.C., 1958.

1,001 Dairy Dishes. Sealtest Kitchens, New York, N.Y., 1963.

White Magic. Leaflets on nonfat dry milk. Michigan State University Extension Service, East Lansing, Mich.

"You Don't Outgrow Your Need for Calcium," P. P. Swanson and E. Willis. *Iowa Farm Science* 9:12–24 (March, 1955).

VISUAL AIDS

For Form and Figure, Eat Well. Poster. National Dairy Council, Chicago, Ill.

Health Educational Materials, National Dairy Council, 111 N. Canal St., Chicago, Ill., 1965.

Food value of one quart of milk when you are 13 to 15 years old. Wall chart, 19″ x 25″, 14¢; leaflet size 8½″ x 11″, 4¢. No. EA27. No. EB36.

Posture Teaching Aids for Girls. 4 posters, 3 colors on white, 11″ x 17″. 30¢. No. EA91.

Comparison Cards for Teenagers. 42 cards, $1.75 per set. No. EB43T.

Creative Cooking with Cottage Cheese. 10 page booklet, 3¢ each. No. EB91.

unit 3

Eggs in Your Meals

How Eggs Help Your Health and Appearance

Why are eggs an important food in your diet? Just as milk supports the life of a newborn animal, the nutrients in an egg are so well balanced that they can make the complete body of a chicken. A food that can do this is worthy of our study.

Eggs Assist in the Formation of Red Blood Cells

The red blood cells transport the oxygen you breathe to all cell tissues, and they remove certain wastes. The fluid part of the blood carries the nutrients

Hot eggnog is a good way to use eggs in a beverage. Do you know why raw eggs are not desirable in beverages or in other dishes? (Recipe for hot or cold eggnog, page 369.)

Grade A eggs are a good choice for breakfast. What would you serve with this plate of ham and eggs for a balanced breakfast? What nutrients are lacking as this breakfast now stands?

from food to nourish each cell. Thus the blood is very important to your life, health, and appearance, for your body is dependent for its very life on what the blood brings. This is true of the nourishment from your little toe to the hair cells and skin on the top of your head.

In order to make red blood, the body needs several minerals, protein, and vitamins. Among the minerals, it is iron that gives us most concern. This is because iron must be present for the making of hemoglobin (hē′mŏ glō′bĭn), a protein pigment which gives the blood its red color. It also carries oxygen to the cells so that the food can be "burned," and removes some of the waste (carbon dioxide). You can see, then, that if iron is lacking in sufficient amounts in your food, this can interfere with the formation of red blood.

How many red blood cells do you need? An average healthy person has between 4½ and 5 million red blood cells per cubic millimeter (mĭl′ĭ mē′tēr) of blood. (A cubic millimeter is about one drop of

liquid.) These tiny blood cells are busy day and night doing their job for you. They can travel through the whole body in 30 seconds, and they live about four months. As the red cells are destroyed, nature re-uses part of the iron to make new cells. The blood makes up 7 percent of the body weight, and about half of the iron in the whole body is in the blood. If you collected all of the iron from your whole body on a small scale, it would weigh one-tenth of an ounce. That is enough to make one small nail. Though the amount is small, do not underestimate its great importance. When iron is too low, it naturally follows that you do not have as rich hemoglobin as you need, and you may have too few red blood cells. This condition is called anemia (à nē′mĭ à) and is sometimes referred to as "nutritional anemia" because the right amount

Grade AA eggs are best for poaching. Why should you cover the pan when you poach eggs?

Steps in Cooking an Omelet (see recipe, page 373): (1) Tip skillet and lift edge of omelet gently so that uncooked mixture runs under cooked portion to even the tender quality. (2) For cheese omelet, add grated cheese when eggs are moist but firm. (3) When cheese begins to melt and bottom of the omelet is golden brown, fold it over on itself and serve on hot plate. (4) What would you serve with this cheese omelet for breakfast? for lunch?

and variety of nutrients in the diet can prevent it, or cure it.

Anemia may be caused by many different things, such as loss of blood from bleeding of wounds, or loss of blood by menstruation in women and girls. It may also be caused by not eating enough of the foods containing iron, or by poor absorption of iron from the food you eat. The iron found in plant foods, for instance, is not as well used by the body as the iron in animal foods. We need to include in the daily diet enough foods rich in iron to give the body what it needs to build red cells. Some of the so-called "laziness" or undue fatigue of adolescence is often related to anemia. In addition to fatigue, anemia may also cause lower resistance to infection. It may or may not be accompanied by paleness.

It is not surprising to find that girls and women are more inclined to be anemic

Blindfolded eggs, fried chicken livers and onion rings make a quick main protein dish for lunch or supper. Can you think of a good dessert to balance it?

Poached eggs on toast. Can you tell which egg is Grade AA and which is Grade A?

than boys and men, for iron is lost every day during the menstruation period. Also, a woman needs more iron-rich foods when she is expecting a baby or nursing one. A reserve supply of iron is established in the baby during the last month of pregnancy. You learned that milk is low in iron. Nature has wonderfully made up for this weakness in milk, for the new-born baby has 40 percent more red blood cells per unit of blood than an adult. This gives the baby a vigorous start. But it is still necessary that the first foods which are added to its diet be selected for rich iron content as well as rich vitamins; this is the chief reason that babies are given egg yolk quite early. Two egg yolks contain as much iron, for instance, as a three-ounce hamburger. Eggs are not a substitute for milk, but the yolk is a good food to balance its weakness in iron.

FOODS RICH IN IRON

RECOMMENDED DAILY ALLOWANCE: FOR GIRLS AND BOYS
13-20, AND WOMEN 18-55, 15 MILLIGRAMS; OTHER ADULTS, 10 MILLIGRAMS

Name of Food and Measure*	Milligrams of Iron
VEGETABLES AND FRUITS	
Raisins, ½ cup	2.6
Beans, dried cooked, ½ cup	2.4
Apricots, cooked, ½ cup	2.3
Prunes, cooked, ½ cup	2.2
Mustard greens, cooked, ½ cup	2.0
Spinach, cooked, ½ cup	1.8
Dates, fresh and dried, ½ cup	1.8
Turnip greens, cooked, ½ cup	1.7
Collards, cooked, ½ cup	1.5
Kale, cooked, ½ cup	1.2
Frozen grapefruit juice (3 ounces)	1.2
Frozen orange juice (3 ounces)	1.0
Lima beans, green, cooked, ½ cup	1.3
Boiled potato in skin, medium	1.0
Mushrooms, cooked, ½ cup	1.0
Broccoli, cooked, ½ cup	1.0
MEATS	
Liver, beef (4 ounces)	8.8
Hamburger (4 ounces)	3.6
Chuck (4 ounces)	3.9
Sirloin (4 ounces)	3.7
Chicken (4 ounces)	2.0
Pork chop (4 ounces)	3.5
Lamb roast (4 ounces)	3.5
Clams (4 ounces)	7.9
Oysters (½ cup)	6.7
OTHER FOODS	
Egg, 1 whole	1.3
Oatmeal, 1 cup cooked	1.7
Shredded wheat biscuit (1 ounce)	1.0
Whole wheat flour, 1 cup	4.0
White flour, enriched, 1 cup	3.2

* Other common foods not listed contain less than 1 milligram of iron
in ½-cup cooked food.

How Much Iron Do You Need Daily?

The National Research Council recommends that boys from 12 to 18 have 18 milligrams of iron daily, and 10 thereafter. Girls need the same from ages 10 to 55, and 10 milligrams thereafter, except in pregnancy and lactation, when they need more.

The table on page 64 shows that iron, like calcium, is not widely distributed in everyday foods. Liver is by far the best source. Meat, green leafy vegetables, and egg yolk also have high iron content.

Eggs Needed in Weight Control

Because of the variety of nutrients, and the low number of calories (75), the egg is an excellent food for those who have a weight problem. Eggs are rich in a high-quality protein, and have only a trace of carbohydrate. The yolk contains fat and fat soluble vitamins A and D, with slightly more unsaturated fatty acids than saturated. Like other animal fats, that of the egg contains cholesterol.

The egg is rich in riboflavin. It contains other B vitamins, but it is low in vitamin C. Eggs contain a trace of many needed nutrients.

Eggs Help the Appearance of Your Skin, Hair, and Nails

Of the many amino acid fragments that make protein, only a few contain sulfur. It happens that the skin, hair, and nails, in order to build their cells, need a protein with sulfur. Just as each girl must be fitted with shoes to fit her particular feet, so each cell must take from the blood plasma (fluid) the nutrients it needs. Thus as the blood comes to your skin, hair, and nails, these cells "pick out" fragments of protein containing sulfur. Eggs contain this type of protein.

Cosmeticians, recognizing this, have made an "egg shampoo." However, the chances of improving your beauty are definitely greater if you eat the egg instead of applying it to the outside of the scalp or hair. One of the greatest elements in beauty is the "glow of health." This comes from within, and is dependent on the food you eat daily.

It is the quality of protein in an egg that makes it a "meat substitute," for eggs, like milk, contain a "complete" protein. Eggs help balance the protein fragments in cereal-breads and vegetables.

The Vitamin D in Eggs Helps Build Teeth and Bones

Vitamin D is quite an important vitamin for the growth and maintenance of bones and teeth. It is especially needed during periods of fast growth, as in the young child and the teen-ager. Unfortunately this vitamin is not widely or richly found in the common foods we eat. Egg yolk is considered one of the best sources, though it takes about 18 egg yolks to give the vitamin D in one teaspoon of cod-liver oil.

Before we had the science of nutrition, rickets, a disease caused by too little vitamin D in the diet or too little sunshine, was a widespread disease in the industrial cities of Europe and the United States. For hundreds of years, this disease crippled both children and adults.

Vitamin D helps the body absorb calcium and build it and other minerals into the bones and teeth. Too little vitamin D retards walking in small children, because the leg bones bend, resulting in bowlegs and knock-knees. Other effects include enlargement of the long end bones at the ankles or wrists, curvature of the spine, or deformity of the chest ("pigeon" chest), which crowds the internal organs. After World War I, many adults in Europe had bone disorders because the diet during the war years was very poor.

In addition, when there is not enough vitamin D in the diet, the teeth of small children come through late and decay early. There is a general lack of vigor, and the muscles and intestinal tract have a loss of tone. Not only is the shape of the bones affected, but also growth is retarded.

In 1922 vitamin D was found to be a separate vitamin, and was given its name. For centuries people had known that cod-liver oil, when taken regularly, could prevent and cure rickets. It is not surprising that vitamin D was first found in cod-liver oil. Later, scientists found it in egg yolk and the cream of milk, and in the oils of seafish such as salmon, tuna, mackerel, sardines, and swordfish. The livers of the halibut and cod fish and of all animals contain a great deal.

This vitamin is also called the "sunshine" vitamin. This is because a fatty substance beneath the skin can produce it when the sun shines directly on the skin. Naturally anything which blocks out the bright rays of the sun, such as clouds, dirty air, and clothing, prevents its formation. This accounts for the fact that in the years when rickets was prevalent, children who lived in the sunny climates were not bothered with this disease. The sunshine helped them use well the calcium in their foods. Though eggs are not equal to cod-liver oil or the livers of animals as a source of vitamin D, they do contain enough of it in the yolk to strengthen the diet in this respect. During periods of rapid growth, young people benefit from including extra vitamin D in the diet.

Since the Eskimo depends on seafish

Why do the hard-cooked eggs make these asparagus-cheese sauce sandwiches a more nourishing dish? What other vegetables could you use with this dish?

An egg dish that could be used at any meal. What would you add to make it a balanced breakfast? lunch? supper?

for a large part of his diet, and the liver is a very desirable food to him, he gets an abundance of vitamin D. This is quite important, for he gets little sunshine and the vitamin D in his food helps him make excellent use of the calcium and other minerals in his diet. Thus he gains strong bones and teeth.

In your social studies course, you may have learned that people from the arctic to the equator use eggs of wild birds and domesticated fowl as a very desirable food. Man learned by experience the worth of an egg, long before the science of nutrition. The pioneers who went West to settle our country took a few chickens, for they knew by experience that eggs help keep the family well.

WORDS TO WORK WITH

Hemoglobin (hē′mô glō′bĭn): the part of the red blood cell which gives the red color to blood, carries oxygen to cells, and carries carbon dioxide (waste) away.

Millimeter (mĭl′ĭ mē′tēr): one thousandth of a meter—equal to 0.03937 of an inch.

Anemia (à nē′mĭ à): a condition in which the red corpuscles of the blood are reduced in number or are deficient in hemoglobin, causing pallor, shortness of breath, and heart palpitations.

THINKING IT OVER

1. The nourishment in an egg can build the body of a chick. How can you make use of this knowledge in your own life?

2. If your blood does not contain enough hemoglobin or red cells, how may this affect your appearance and personality?

3. Why are girls more likely to be anemic than boys? What can you do about this?

4. Why would you consider an egg in the daily diet an important food for those who may have a problem of overweight? Why would it be equally useful for the underweight?

5. Explain how an egg in the daily diet can help the appearance of your skin, hair, and nails.

6. Which do you think will help most to give a shine or luster to your hair—washing your hair with an egg shampoo or eating an egg daily for breakfast? Explain.

7. Why can eggs be eaten as a good alternate for meat?

8. Why do you need vitamin D in the diet, and how can you get this vitamin?

9. How would you summarize the value which an egg has for your health and personal appearance?

PROBLEMS TO SOLVE

1. Checking on the eggs you eat during a week.
   (1) Keep a record of the eggs you eat for one week.
   (2) How many did you eat?
   (3) How were they served, and in which meals?
   (4) Can you improve your meals by using more eggs? If so, how?

2. Learning by seeing.
   (1) Make a trip to the market and study the eggs that are for sale. Note grades, weights, labels, sizes, prices, and other information.

APPLYING WHAT YOU KNOW

1. Prepare eggs in one or more of the following ways, as a part of a balanced breakfast or lunch which you have planned (see recipes in Cookbook):
   (1) Breakfast: Poached; fried; blindfolded; shirred; omelet; scrambled; French toast; popovers.
   (2) Lunch: Creamed eggs with meat, vegetable or cheese; soufflé; spoon bread; baked custard; stuffed eggs; egg salad; egg sandwich.

EVALUATING

1. Did you keep out as much light as possible while cooking your eggs?

2. Was the egg white well done? Was it tough or soft and tender?

3. Starting with poached eggs, what menu would you plan to make a balanced breakfast?

4. How can you improve your method of cooking eggs next time?

HOME EXPERIENCE

With your mother, plan balanced menus for breakfast and lunch for one week, using an egg daily at one meal or the other.

chapter

The Use
of Eggs in Meals

You have learned the reasons why eggs are an important food, and how they can help your health and looks. Now let us consider how to buy and cook eggs and use them in meals.

How to Buy Eggs

Eggs are graded and classified for the market in several different ways. This includes grading for freshness, for size or weight, and for the condition of the shell. Freshness is the most important factor. For your protection and guidance the Federal government has set up standards of freshness for eggs.

A tossed salad with hard cooked eggs provides a low calorie main-dish for lunch. What beverage would you select to make this a balanced lunch?

The different grades of eggs are pictured below. Notice the differences in height of yolk and firmness of white. Since grade does not affect food value, the grade to buy depends on the budget and how the eggs are to be used.

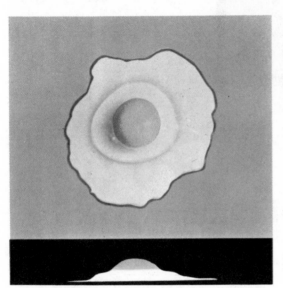

Grade AA

Grade A

Grade B

Grade C

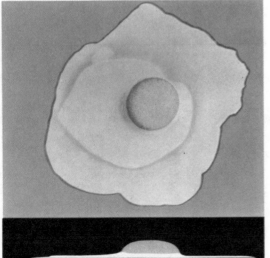

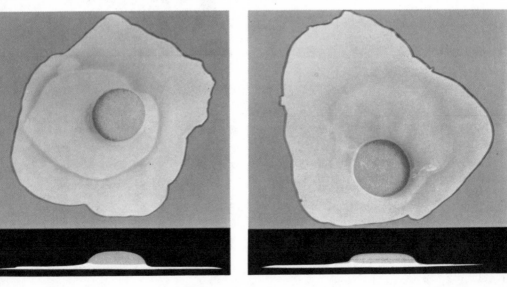

Eggs are graded for freshness by "candling," which is placing the egg in front of a strong beam of light. As indicated in the picture on page 70, the freshest egg has a very firm yolk which is supported by a firm white. The white is so firm that it forms a thicker inner circle to support the yolk, and has a definite outer circle. This may be seen in the candling of an egg.

Fresh eggs have no odor when broken out of the shell. As the egg gets older, its firmness breaks down and the white and yolk spread. In a spoiled egg the yolk and white run together, and the odor is unpleasant. Warm or room temperature affects the freshness of eggs, and that is why eggs should be kept under refrigeration both in the store and at home. When an egg is graded for freshness according to Federal standards, the carton has a shield which reads like this:

U.S. A Grade
Large size
date (   )
Federal State Graded
Passed by (   )

The freshest eggs are graded AA. Next in order is grade A, then grade B, and the lowest grade is C. In the picture you will observe that it is the firmness of the yolk and white which makes the difference in the grade. Grade AA and A are choice for poaching or frying. They also give the most volume in making an angel food cake. But the other grades are quite suitable for cooking in other ways. Fortunately, proper storage will preserve all the most valuable nutrients in an egg for a long period of time. What you pay for freshness in the grade of an egg is a matter of your taste and budget.

There are other factors besides freshness that influence the grade of an egg, such as the color of the shell and its condition. In some cities, white-shell eggs cost more than either brown eggs or eggs with shells of mixed colors. If you wish to use your food money wisely, buy eggs of the color which costs least. Furthermore, an egg with a blood clot or a rough irregular shell may be AA grade in freshness. Since it is not as desirable in appearance, it is placed in a lower grade, and costs less. You can use this knowledge to save money in shopping, for these imperfections in no way affect the food value or flavor of the egg.

Eggs are also classified for the market by size and weight, and these influence the price. The largest or heaviest cost most. As indicated in the pictures on pages 72–73, the largest-size eggs are called "jumbo," and weigh 30 ounces to the carton (net), or per dozen, and this

What contribution do eggs make to this loaf of bread?

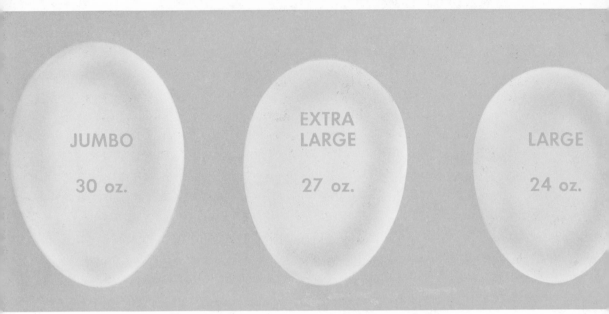

Eggs are classified by size and weight as to number of ounces per dozen to help you buy

classification is graded downward to 15 ounces per dozen for the smallest size.

Supply affects the price of eggs. The largest total supply of eggs is on the market in the spring, and usually the cost is the lowest at this time. In the late summer and early fall the young hens start laying, and then the market is flooded with small and medium-size eggs. These are then your best buy. But by spring these hens are full grown, and are laying large eggs; so you may find large eggs the best buy at that time.

Dried eggs, used extensively in commercial cooking, are less expensive than fresh eggs. If you use them, follow the directions for use given on the package.

How to Store Eggs and Care for Them at Home

Since eggs quickly deteriorate at room temperature, they should always be kept under refrigeration. This ordinarily is between 35 and 45° F., but if eggs are stored just barely above freezing, which is 30° F., for eggs, they may be kept fresh for months. Many of the grade B eggs you buy are kept in commercial storage this way. At the height of the laying season the surplus eggs are stored; later they come to you in an excellent state of freshness, but at a lower price. If you buy grade AA eggs and leave them at room temperature, they deteriorate to a lower grade, and you lose money on your purchase. When using eggs, you should remove from the refrigerator only the number that you need. Egg whites beat to a larger volume when at room temperature. It takes about 45 minutes to bring an egg in its shell to room temperature. But if you wish to hasten this process, separate the white from the yolk and let the white stand till it reaches room temperature.

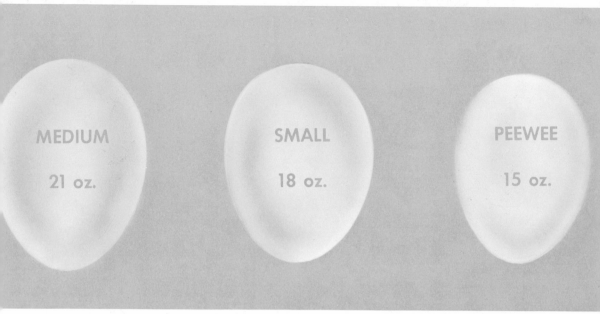

MEDIUM

21 oz.

SMALL

18 oz.

PEEWEE

15 oz.

wisely. The illustration shows actual size of eggs.

If an egg shell is soiled, do not wash it, but wipe with a dry cloth. Nature provides a very thin protective film on the porous egg shell. This film helps prevent the entrance of objectionable odors, flavors, and even bacteria and molds into the egg. The dry unwashed egg will remain in a better state, and thus help save your food money.

If you have left-over egg yolks, store them in the refrigerator in a covered jar, with just enough water to cover them. Stored egg yolks should be used in two or three days. If you wish to store them longer, place them in the freezing compartment without adding the water to cover. Egg whites may be stored in normal refrigerator temperature in a covered jar, and will keep well for a week or 10 days. They may be frozen when broken from the shell. When you are ready to use them, simply bring to room temperature and beat.

You can save time in dish washing by rinsing an egg beater or dish in cold water immediately after it is used. Hot water causes raw egg to stick to the beater.

How to Cook Eggs

The way you cook an egg may determine your enjoyment of it, and the health qualities you get from it. An egg, like milk and meat, is an excellent protein food. Since a high temperature makes protein tough and rubbery, eggs are more delicious when cooked at a low or moderate temperature. There are exceptions to this rule, as in baking popovers. Here you start with a high temperature because steam is used to make the popover rise. When cooking dishes using eggs, you should follow your recipe. The rubbery quality from high temperature shows up more when the egg is cooked alone.

When possible, cook eggs in a covered pan or in the absence of light, for egg

Steps in Making Egg Custard (see recipe, page 376): (1) Heat milk to scalding hot before mixing to save time and cooking fuel. (2) Mix hot milk into other ingredients and pour into custard cups. (3) Set cups in a shallow pan and add boiling water to pan. Bake at 375°F. until custard is firm and a silver knife comes clean when inserted in center. (4) Remove custard from cup with spatula, or serve by placing cup on 5-inch glass plate. (5) Achieve variety by garnishing with fresh fruit in season, chocolate syrup, jelly, or whipped or sour cream.

white is a good source of riboflavin. Eggs are semi-fluid, and, as in the case of milk, when they are cooked in the presence of light there is a greater loss of riboflavin than when they are cooked in a covered pan. An added reason for cooking an egg mixture covered is that there is also a saving of the vitamin C content in the mixture, though eggs themselves contain almost no vitamin C.

Egg whites are 100 percent protein, and the white should be cooked until firm but not hard. The use of raw egg white is undesirable, for it interferes with the use of an important B vitamin, biotin (bī′ō tǐn). A protein in egg white called avidin (ăv′ĭ dǐn) combines with biotin, and the combination cannot be absorbed by the body. This is a loss, for this vitamin helps the body use fat, starch, and sugar in foods. When animals are fed raw egg white, the skin becomes scaly or greasy, skin hemorrhages occur, nervous symptoms and anemia appear, and there is complete loss of hair. But if the egg white is cooked, none of these conditions develop. These are some of the things people have in mind when they say they have an allergy (ăl′ĕr jĭ) to eggs. While it is unlikely that you would eat enough raw egg white to produce a biotin deficiency, it is unnecessary to eat raw eggs. Most recipes which call for raw egg white, such as gelatin and milk desserts, are just as tasty when the egg white is cooked. Cooking the egg also destroys bacteria which raw eggs sometimes contain.

How Eggs Are Used in Cooking

Eggs are used in cooking:

(1) To leaven or raise a mixture, such as bread, cake, or soufflé.

(2) To thicken a mixture, such as custard, cheese sauce, or pudding.

(3) To coat foods, such as croquettes or meat for frying, and to improve the glaze on baked foods, such as pie crust.

(4) To improve the flavor, appearance, and health value of a dish.

When you cook with eggs, as in making a boiled custard, the texture is smoother if first you mix the beaten egg with sugar, flour, and some cold milk before adding it to the hot mixture. If lumps form when the egg yolk mixture is added, these may be reduced or eliminated by beating with a rotary egg beater. Curdling (the formation of small flakes, curds, or lumps) spoils the appearance of a custard mixture, but of course this does not hurt the flavor or food value.

When egg whites are used to leaven a mixture, the aim is to get a large volume. Having egg whites at room temperature and adding salt and cream of tartar help to achieve this result. They make the white firm, and thus it holds more air. If the recipe calls for salt or cream of tartar, add them and beat until the whites stand

The excellent meringue on this Boston chocolate pie is the result of a good technique.

Why does it matter what ingredients you use for cookies? In what ways are these better than plain sugar cookies?

in firm peaks, but are moist. Fold the mixture into the beaten egg whites, and not the other way round. Use a broad spatula with an over-and-under movement, being careful not to over-mix. The lightness of the product depends on not breaking the air cells.

When sugar is added to egg white, as in the case of making meringue, add it gradually, and beat after each addition until it is dissolved. This improves the quality of the meringue.

How Eggs Are Used in Meals

For many Americans, eggs are the main protein dish at breakfast. They are enjoyed with bacon, ham, or sausage at this meal, or because of their high nourishment, they may be eaten alone. Egg yolks are one of the first solid foods given to babies. Eggs are also included in every type of diet for the convalescent. They may be used in many different ways at different meals for almost anyone.

Ways to serve eggs at breakfast are numerous. The most popular way is to fry them. But there are several ways to fry an egg. All the fat may be drained from the skillet, the eggs added with one to two tablespoons of water, the pan covered, the heat lowered, and you get a "blindfolded" egg. It tastes like a fried egg and looks like a poached egg—and has very little added fat. Naturally this method of cooking is desirable, for it keeps the fat and calorie content low. Some people cook fried eggs by dropping the egg into hot fat and flipping the fat over the egg to "blindfold" the yolk. This adds to the fat and calories in the diet and is less popular for this reason. If you like fried eggs, blindfolding by the first method is an ideal way to cook them for flavor and low fat, and to save the riboflavin. They may be fried without fat in the "non-stick" pan.

Shirring eggs is a good way to give them a fried flavor. They are baked in the oven in a hot custard cup or other container that is oiled or circled with bacon. Since they are baked in the absence of light, this is a good way to preserve the riboflavin.

There are two ways to poach eggs. One is in the modern poachers which are sold for this purpose. Here the egg is cooked by steam in a covered pan. Another way is to drop the egg into boiling water that just covers it, place lid on pan, reduce heat, and poach until the white is firm, but not hard.

Soft-cooked (boiled) eggs are also favorites for breakfast, and this is the perfect way to save the riboflavin. You can also add as much or as little fat as you wish when you eat an egg cooked by this method.

When eggs are scrambled, they may be cooked one at a time, or a large amount at a time. If one is cooked at a time, it is done very quickly; and though it is uncovered, the time is so short that there is little loss of riboflavin. But when a large number are scrambled at a time they should be cooked in a covered pan over very low heat and stirred occasionally.

Eggs may be served creamed in many ways at breakfast or at other meals, with or without fish or meat.

Some young people enjoy an egg every morning, and others wish more variety. If you wish to include the egg in a "hidden" dish, popovers, spoon bread, or French toast is a good choice.

Eggs used as a meat substitute occasionally for supper or lunch provide variety at low cost.

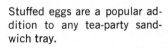

Stuffed eggs are a popular addition to any tea-party sandwich tray.

Eggs are often used as a meat substitute or as the protein dish at lunch when they are not used at breakfast. They may of course be served in any of the ways you enjoy at breakfast time. They may be hard-cooked and served in a cream sauce with Welsh rarebit, cheese fondue, meat, poultry, fish, or vegetables, or a combination of these. Egg is a main ingredient in a soufflé, which may be the main dish for lunch, and a very attractive and tasty dish it is. Spoon bread may also be the main protein dish. Eggs are often stuffed or served as a part of a salad at lunch. They are used in omelets, sandwiches, and sauces.

Eggs are used as a meat substitute for supper, and may be served in any of the above-mentioned ways. In addition they are used with left-over mashed potatoes as "eggs in a nest." The potato is placed in a flat baking dish, and a hole made for each egg. The egg is topped with cheese, and baked until the white is firm. Eggs are also used hard-cooked with spinach or other greens.

Eggs help make some of our most nourishing low-calorie desserts, such as angel food cake, sponge cake, fruit soufflés (such as prune, and apricot), egg custards, floating island, puddings, chiffon pie, and fruit meringues.

In addition, baked foods may be made more nourishing if you add eggs. An egg added to drop biscuits, for instance, makes them more nourishing for bread, dumplings, or deep-dish fruit pie. Eggs in noodles make this product more nourishing than plain spaghetti. Eggs in cake and cookies supply many nutrients besides fat.

When our country was a more rural nation than today, many homemakers were able to add a good-grade protein to the diet through a greater use of eggs in other dishes. Eggs were one of the mainstays of the diet, alongside milk. Even under modern conditions, eggs remain an important food.

WORDS TO WORK WITH

Avidin (ăv′ĭ dĭn): a protein occurring in egg whites.

Allergy (ăl′ẽr jĭ): an excessive sensitiveness to an ordinarily harmless substance such as pollen, hair, fur, or raw egg white.

Biotin (bī′ṓ tĭn): a B vitamin, needed for good health and appearance.

THINKING IT OVER

1. What is the difference between grade A and grade B eggs? Which would you use on a low cost food budget? Why?
2. What are the different things that affect the cost of eggs?
3. How can you use this knowledge to select wisely the eggs you buy?
4. Explain how to care for eggs at home.
5. What should you keep in mind when cooking eggs?
6. How can you use eggs in each of the daily meals?
7. Why is it desirable to use eggs that are cooked rather than raw?
8. Does your study of eggs help you to evaluate recipes more accurately? In what ways?

PROBLEMS TO SOLVE

1. Learning to take a critical view of recipes.
   (1) Look through several cookbooks which your mother may have at home, or which you may find at school. Find recipes using raw eggs, as in mousse, cake icings, eggnogs, floating island, and other dishes.
   (2) How would you change these in view of what you have learned? Check your idea with the teacher and make these changes.
2. Plan menus showing how you might use more than one egg daily during the menstrual period. How might this help you?

APPLYING WHAT YOU KNOW

1. Plan balanced dinner menus using eggs: as a meat substitute for two dinner menus; in desserts for two dinner menus; in salads for one dinner menu; to enrich breads, cakes, and cookies; in soups, cheese dishes, creamed vegetables, or meats to add flavor and nourishment.
2. Prepare and serve as part of a balanced meal one or more of the following dishes (see recipes in Cookbook):
   (1) Eggs with vegetables, such as corn pudding; eggs baked on left-over mashed potatoes; tossed salad with hard-cooked eggs.
   (2) Eggs to stretch meat—creamed beef and hard-cooked eggs; creamed tuna and hard-cooked eggs; creamed chicken or turkey with hard-cooked eggs; ham and egg salad; creole eggs.
   (3) Desserts using the whole egg—floating island, sponge cake, puddings. Desserts using white of egg—prune whip; apricot whip.
   (4) Eggnog made with hot milk served hot or cold for a snack.

EVALUATING

1. Did you practice your new knowledge of food by cooking eggs at a low temperature, and keeping out as much light as possible?
2. In using eggs for cooking, when would you use grade A? grade B? Why?

3. What dishes did you make in which egg was used to raise or leaven? To coat for frying? To thicken?

4. Do you consider a homemaker to be a good manager if she does not put eggs in cooked foods because they are too expensive? Explain your answer.

5. Give examples of how you can use eggs to make mixes better-tasting and more nourishing.

6. How can you judge the true cost of a food?

HOME EXPERIENCE

Talk over with your mother what you have learned about the contributions of eggs to health and appearance, and the various ways you learned to prepare eggs. Plan with her three supper or lunch menus using eggs in different ways. Prepare and serve the egg dish as a part of the balanced meal.

Take to school a favorite recipe of your family which features eggs in a dish suitable for dinner.

Report result of your work to your teacher.

FURTHER READING

Cooking Quality and Flavor of Eggs. Agricultural Information Bulletin 164. U.S.D.A., Washington, D.C., 1956.

Cooking with Dried Eggs. Home and Garden Bulletin 50. U.S.D.A., Washington, D.C., 1956.

Egg and You. Leaflet. Poultry and Egg National Board, 185 North Wabash Ave., Chicago, Ill.

Egg Buying Guide for Consumers. Home and Garden Bulletin 26. U.S.D.A., Washington, D.C., 1954.

Plain and Fancy Ways with Eggs. Poultry and Egg National Board, 185 North Wabash Ave., Chicago, Ill.

Richards Topical Encyclopedia, Volume 9. The Richards Co., Inc., New York, N.Y., 1964.
Poultry and Eggs.

The Versatile Egg, Klippstein. Cornell Extension Bulletin E915. Cornell University, Ithaca, N.Y., 1963.

VISUAL AIDS

Know the Eggs You Buy. (5 min. film, revised, b/w) Agricultural Handbook No. 14. Motion Pictures U.S.D.A., Washington, D.C., 1960.

Know the Eggs You Buy. Poster. 11¾ by 17¼ inches, colored. U.S.D.A. Marketing Service. Poultry Division, Washington, D.C.

Fruits for Any Meal

The Importance
of Citrus Fruits
and Tomatoes in Meals

How Citrus Fruits Helped
Stamp Out Scurvy

All through the Middle Ages, in Europe, scurvy (skûr′vĭ) was a common and terrible disease. It caused the teeth to come loose in their sockets and the gums to swell and bleed, and sometimes there was internal bleeding, or joints became inflamed, swollen, and stiff. A person with scurvy was in such a bad state that the phrase "a scurvy fellow" became insulting.

A British physician writing about it said that scurvy was a part of every disease. When you understand that this disease is caused by lack of a vitamin which is needed for the health of almost every tissue in the body, this statement is no mystery. Furthermore, this vitamin was absent from the main foods many people ate—bread, meats, sweets, and fats.

The name of Captain James Cook, the famous explorer, has gone down in history

Orange juice is a better choice for a cold drink than carbonated beverages. Why?

in a way that might surprise him if he were here today. His intelligent observations led him to believe that scurvy was caused by lack of fresh food. He stocked his ships with fresh fruits and vegetables, at every port, just as he took on fresh water. After he started this practice, there was no more scurvy aboard his ships.

The proof that lack of fresh raw food caused scurvy was first given by Dr. James Lind, a British Navy surgeon, in 1757. He knew by repeated experience that the drugs used by physicians for this disease were worthless. He believed that lack of proper food caused scurvy and decided to try an experiment.

He divided men sick with scurvy into three groups. To the regular diet of the first group he added oranges and lemons. Result: the men were completely cured. To the second group he gave the regular diet plus cider. Result: they improved, but did not recover. To the third group he gave the regular diet plus the drugs recommended by the medical authorities. Result: these men grew worse.

Dr. Lind thus proved: that some unknown nutrient in oranges and lemons could cure scurvy; that a small amount of this nutrient was in cider; but that drugs were worthless in treating this disease. Thus Dr. Lind's experiment helped blot scurvy from the navies of the world. In 1795, the British Admiralty ordered the sailors to drink lemon or lime juice at sea. (English sailors after this were known as "limeys.") Hence by the courage and vision of one doctor, millions who came after him have enjoyed better health.

The Discovery of Vitamin C

Dr. Lind never lived to learn what nutrient in food cured and prevented scurvy. But, in 1931, 174 years after Dr. Lind published his report, an American nutritionist and chemist, Dr. G. C. King, identified the nutrient. It was named ascorbic acid (ă skôr' bĭk) and is also called vitamin C. This discovery has enabled physicians to use pure vitamin C in the treatment of certain conditions. Of course, pure vitamins are no substitute for well-balanced daily meals. We know some nutrients in foods, but year after year scientists are finding others. The foods we

Try these three attractive ways to stuff tomatoes. To help in getting your daily vitamin C, what different fillings might you use to stuff tomatoes for a main dish at lunch?

eat can bring us both the known and the unknown nutrients to keep us feeling well and looking our best.

Vitamin C Can Help Your Health and Appearance

Although scurvy is not a problem for us today, many people do not get as much vitamin C as they need for good vitality. This is reported in diet studies, and by physicians in clinics. Teen-agers are especially low in vitamin C. How may this affect you? While there is still much to learn about it, scientists have found that this vitamin can improve your health in many ways, if you apply what is already known.

For example, vitamin C is especially important in the formation and repair of bones and teeth. Although bones are hard, they are built on a softer structure. In the teeth, this is called *dentine*, which is the part just below the enamel. In the bones, this is called *matrix* and *cartilage* (kär′-tĭ lĭj). When a baby's bones are being made, they are first cartilage, which is a tough elastic tissue or gristle like that found around the joint of a chicken. When there is not enough vitamin C in the daily diet, these structures are not properly formed, and the bones that later develop are weak and porous. Such bones are fragile and break under even a slight pressure. Naturally, you also need this vitamin for good repair of broken bones. The role of vitamin C is to make a glue-like substance that holds the bone cells together firmly. Vitamin C not only helps the structure of your bones and teeth, but also helps you to bend your joints, since it is necessary for the health

Melons are low in calories, delicate in flavor and suitable at any meal. What two vitamins are well supplied in cantaloupes?

and strength of the gristle-like tissue around joints.

The calcium from your milk and the vitamin D from food or sunshine is far better used when there is enough vitamin C in the diet. Orange juice is needed by a baby at an early age for him to grow and stay well. Though mother's milk is four times richer in vitamin C than cows' milk, even breast-fed babies need to have orange juice added to their diet early in life. This is because the need is so great during rapid growth.

Another big job that vitamin C does for you is to make the cells of the soft structures in the body firmer and stronger. Again it helps make a cement-like substance that gives strength to such tissue as the gums around the teeth, the walls of blood vessels, the intestinal tract, and the muscles. Let us take as an example the small blood vessels or capillaries (kăp'-ĭ lĕr ĭ) of the gums. They are firmer and more elastic when the diet contains enough vitamin C. When this vitamin is too low, the gums are weakened, and may bleed easily. When large amounts of orange juice or other foods rich in vitamin C are present in the diet, the condition is corrected.

Thus you can see why physicians often use this vitamin to help strengthen blood vessels and to help the tissues in the body heal faster. Not one food or one vitamin alone but a balance of many are needed to do the variety of building and repair jobs in the body. Vitamin C works best when all the other nutrients are present which are needed to repair or build tissue.

There are many other ways that vitamin C is important to you. You need it to resist colds, for the health of your heart, for the formation of red blood, and for the proper functioning of your glands. When you have sufficient vitamin C in your daily diet, your general vigor, vitality, personality, and good looks are aided.

How Much Vitamin C Do You Need Daily?

From birth to death we need vitamin C. In proportion to body weight, infants need more than adults. Girls from 12–14 years old need 45 milligrams daily; from 14–18, 50 milligrams; after 18, 55 milligrams, except in pregnancy and lactation, when they need more. Boys of 12–18 need 45–55 milligrams; thereafter, up to 60 milligrams daily.

Your need is in relation to your rate of growth, your size, activity, and amount of perspiration. The need is greater during a cold or fever, after surgery, or when there is infection, a wound, or disease.

In the case of vitamin C (and other water-soluble vitamins, such as the B vitamins), if you eat more than you need, it is eliminated quickly and without any difficulty. But if you do not eat enough vitamin C, the body cannot make it or store it, nor can you remain in a healthy state. As you have just seen, too little vitamin C in your daily diet interferes with the growth and repair of all types of cells. They weaken, lose their firm strength, and tend to fall apart.

How to Prepare Foods to Save the Vitamin C

As indicated earlier, vitamin C is one nutrient found to be too low in the diets of many people. Why is this? Probably one important reason is that vitamin C is the most fragile of vitamins. Many people do not know how easily this vitamin can be lost from the high-quality food they may buy. You cannot control the fact that the amount of sunshine such foods as oranges and tomatoes get may affect the amount of vitamin C they contain. But you can control the kind of food you buy, and how it is stored, prepared, cooked, and served in your home. For instance:

(a) Vitamin C is destroyed by the oxygen in the air, especially when a food is chopped or cut into fine pieces. Less is lost when food is frozen or stored at a low temperature as it is in the refrigerator and when it is whole rather than chopped.

PERSIAN

CRANSHAW

CASABA

HONEYDEW

CANTALOUPE

SEEDLESS
WATERMELON

Melons add variety in texture, color, and flavor to any meal.

(b) Vitamin C dissolves in water, and is therefore lost if food soaks or cooks in water and the water goes down the drain. Much vitamin C is lost from food, especially vegetables, in this manner.

(c) Fresh vegetables may lose as much as half their vitamin C in one to two days after they are harvested. This is a great loss for those who do not have a home garden. On the other hand, frozen vegetables lose almost no vitamin C if cooked while frozen and served at once. Foods such as apples that remain in storage several months lose much vitamin C.

(d) Vitamin C may also be lost if soda

is added to a food. Soda is sometimes added to green vegetables by those who are not aware of this fact.

(e) It is quickly lost by contact with copper in a piece of cooking equipment.

(f) It is destroyed by overcooking, or by allowing a food to stand after it is cooked before serving it. To save the vitamin C in fruits and vegetables, prepare them quickly, just before time to serve the meal. This is true whether they are cooked or served in salads.

Thus a food may be of the highest quality when you purchase it, and have some or all of the vitamin C lost by poor practices in preparing, storing, cooking, and serving.

Another reason why many people do not have enough vitamin C is that this vitamin is not stored in the body when you eat a surplus, as is the case with vitamins A and D. This puts a much bigger responsibility on you in planning and preparing meals. It is important for your vitality and your good looks to be generous in including vitamin C-rich foods in your meals every day. What are these foods?

Foods Rich in Vitamin C

Oranges, grapefruit, and other citrus fruits are our most dependable common food for vitamin C. This is a big reason why they should be included in the daily diet. Tomatoes are not so rich (it takes two fresh tomatoes to give the amount of vitamin C found in a fresh orange), but because they are so widely grown they are a most important food for this vitamin. Then too, the natural acid in citrus fruits

FOODS RICH IN VITAMIN C*

GIRLS 12–18 YEARS, 45–50 MILLIGRAMS; 18 UPWARD, 55 MILLIGRAMS
BOYS 12–18 YEARS, 45–55 MILLIGRAMS; 18 UPWARD, 60 MILLIGRAMS

Name of Food and Measure **	Approx. Mgs. of Vitamin C
Orange, whole, medium	77
Orange juice, ½ cup	61
Lemon juice, ½ cup	61
Cantaloupe, ½, 5-inch diameter	59
Strawberries, raw, ½ cup	45
***Turnip greens (properly cooked), ½ cup	44
Grapefruit juice, ½ cup	43
Grapefruit, raw, sections, ½ cup	39
Tomato, raw, medium	35
Canned or cooked, ½ cup	20
Juice, ½ cup	19
Cabbage, raw, ½ cup	25
Pineapple, raw, ½ cup	17
Potato, medium, baked or boiled in skin	17
Turnips, cooked, ½ cup	14
Peas, green, cooked, ½ cup	12
Pineapple juice, ½ cup	11
Watermelon (slice ¾″ x 10″)	10

* Adapted from Handbook No. 8, *Composition of Foods*, U.S.D.A.

** Common foods which do not appear in this table contain less than 10 milligrams vitamin C per serving.

*** Other deep green leafy vegetables compare favorably with turnip greens.

and tomatoes protects the vitamin C from rapid loss. This is true whether the fruit is fresh, frozen, or canned.

You can use this knowledge to save money on your food budget. For instance, in the late summer and fall, the orange crop is at a low point, and the price is high. At this time the tomato crop is at its peak in many parts of the country, and the price is low. Then it is good management to use more tomatoes in meals. and less fresh citrus fruit. Garden-fresh tomatoes and home-canned tomatoes have meant a great deal to many people who grew this fruit, and could not buy citrus fruits. But if you do not raise your own tomatoes, oranges in some form (fresh, frozen, or canned) may give more vitamin C for the money spent. In shopping, keep in mind not only the size, weight, visible quality, and price, but also the amount of vitamin C in each food.

Raw cabbage is a good food for vitamin C. Even the white inner leaves contain it. But when cabbage is cooked, some or all of the vitamin C may be lost. This, and the fact that it tastes good raw, is the reason why coleslaw or cabbage salad is the best way to serve cabbage. Cabbage is inexpensive, widely grown, and available the year round. It should often be included raw at lunch or dinner.

Strawberries and cantaloupes are two excellent foods for vitamin C. One cup of raw strawberries gives 90 milligrams of it. This meets your recommended daily allowance, but if you want to get the best use of this fruit, serve a half-cup with one meal and a half-cup with the next meal. (The yellow melons and red fruits not only are good for vitamin C, but bring vitamin A to your diet too.) Pineapple is a fair source of vitamin C. The guava, mango, papaya, and West Indian cherry are tropical fruits that may be more important to us in the future for their rich supply of this vitamin.

Since it is made in the green leaf, the green leafy vegetables are important for vitamin C, as you will observe in the table on page 88. The amount you get from these vegetables depends on how much and how often you eat them, whether you eat them fresh or frozen, raw or cooked, and whether you prepare and cook them properly or not. (See pages 124-128 on how to do this.) Among other vegetables, potatoes, green peas, turnips, and parsnips are better than average for vitamin C.

Many raw fruits and vegetables contain small amounts of this vitamin, but unless you include a citrus fruit or tomato in your daily diet, it is difficult to meet your need. That is the reason acceptable food guides for nutritional meal planning include at least one serving of citrus fruit daily.

In the next chapter you will learn that nearly all fruits and vegetables are good sources of other vitamins and some of the essential minerals.

WORDS TO WORK WITH

Ascorbic acid (ȧ skôr′bĭk): chemical name for vitamin C.

Cartilage (kär′tĭ lĭj): a tough, elastic tissue; gristle.

Capillary (kăp′ĭ lĕr′ĭ): the smallest of the blood vessels.

Citrus fruit (sĭt′rŭs): fruit high in citric acid, including the orange, lemon, grapefruit, lime, and tangerine. Citric acid gives some protection to vitamin C from loss by heat or by exposure to oxygen in the air.

Scurvy (skûr′vĭ): a disease of the joints, teeth, and blood vessels caused by lack of vitamin C in the diet.

THINKING IT OVER

1. What was the cause of scurvy, and why, during the Middle Ages, was scurvy thought to be a part of every disease?

2. Describe how Dr. Lind proved that scurvy could be cured by better food.

3. Who discovered vitamin C? How has this discovery helped your life?

4. What are the best foods you can eat daily to give you vitamin C?

5. Why is it good to try to include a food rich in vitamin C at each meal? Give examples of how you can do this at different cost levels.

6. Explain the different ways in which you must use proper care to retain the vitamin C content of food from the market to the table.

7. How do you account for the fact that the diets of many teen-agers are far too low in vitamin C? How can this affect their health? Their looks?

PROBLEMS TO SOLVE

1. Checking your food habits for vitamin C in your diet: Make a list of the foods you ate yesterday at meals and between meals. Then answer the following questions:

   (1) Did you eat a food rich in vitamin C at each meal? At a snack? What foods were they? Did you meet your recommended daily need?

   (2) Make a plan to show how you can improve your diet in vitamin C-rich foods.

   (3) Show how you could vary these foods in different seasons.

   (4) How would you vary them to fit different food budgets?

   (5) What foods that are rich in vitamin C would you enjoy eating for snacks?

2. If possible, visit an animal-feeding experiment in your school or community which shows how a diet low in vitamin C affects health. If this is not possible, decide other ways to see this fact proved. Consult pictures in reference books, movies, or slides. Try to present one of these to the class.

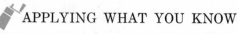APPLYING WHAT YOU KNOW

1. Learning to plan menus and prepare and serve foods rich in vitamin C as part of balanced meals: Plan balanced menus for a day, and prepare one or more of the following to fit into the meals you have planned.

   (1) Whole orange or half grapefruit as a first course for breakfast.

   (2) Fruit cup or fruit salad as a first course using citrus fruit.

   (3) Tomato salad as the main dish at lunch; tomato salad as a part of dinner.

   (4) Fruit juice (citrus), or a mixture with another fruit, or tomato juice or a mixture, as an appetizer.

   (5) Cabbage in combination with fruits as a salad for lunch or dinner.

   (6) Citrus fruit as dessert, or party refreshment.

EVALUATING

1. Discuss how to select, store, prepare, cook, and serve the foods in the menus you have planned in order to retain the most vitamin C.

2. After your meal is served, recount what you actually did, and make a plan to improve your work so that you can save more vitamin C in the food.

HOME EXPERIENCE

With your mother, plan balanced menus for three days using a food rich in vitamin C at each meal. You prepare and serve this food for one meal each day as a part of the whole balanced meal. Report results to your teacher.

10

Other Fruits
in Meals and Snacks

Other Common Fruits We Eat

The most common fruits we eat in addition to the citrus fruits are apples, peaches, pears, apricots, plums, cherries, grapes, berries, pineapples, and bananas.

The *apple* has held first place among fruits throughout history. Like most of our fruits, it came to us from Asia and Europe. There are many varieties of apples, differing in flavor, eating quality, cooking quality, and nourishment. Most people like to buy a general-purpose apple —one that is good to eat raw or to cook in any fashion. Some general-purpose apples are the Northern Spy, Baldwin, Wolf River, Winesap, Wealthy, Jonathan, Ben

Three appetizing ways to use apples—a favorite American fruit.

Apples baked in fresh orange juice. Why are the tops cut off?

Good baking apples are ones that hold their shape well. These include Rome Beauty, Cortland, Greening, Wolf River, and Winesap. Apples are a favorite fruit to eat raw, in sauce, baked, or in pies.

Pears are cousins of apples. There are many varieties. Two popular pears are the Bartlett and the Keiffer. Both have a juicy mellow flavor when ripe. There is the early season Clapp Favorite pear. The Bosc, Comice, and Seckel are mid-season pears. Anjou and Winter Nelis are the varieties from late in the season into spring.

Peaches are a popular fruit either fresh, frozen, canned, or dried. The season for peaches is brief and much of the crop is canned. The peach has many varieties of freestone (a peach which comes loose from the seed) and clingstone (a peach which clings to its seed). The Elberta is a popular freestone peach. White peaches have a delicious flavor, but are not as rich in vitamin A as the yellow ones. Fresh, canned, or frozen peaches contain more vitamin A than dried peaches.

Davis, Grimes Golden, and McIntosh. Favorite eating apples (raw) are the Delicious (red and yellow), Grimes Golden, Gravenstein, Northern Spy, Baldwin, Yellow Newton, Jonathan, and McIntosh.

Peaches, along with pears and some other fruits, are harvested when mature, but ripen after harvest. Both peaches and pears have to be watched carefully as they ripen. The loss by spoilage is rapid if the fruits are not properly sorted and stored.

Apricots are one of the most nourishing of the orchard fruits (fruits that grow on trees). Like the peach, the apricot is excellent for vitamin A. It has a tangy flavor and is far richer in iron than most other fruits. The canned or dried apricot compares favorably to the peach in price.

In the stores you will find both sun-dried and sulfur-dried fruits. Sun drying destroys vitamin A. Sulfur drying de-

Have you tried using apples in stuffing or garnishing meat? What kind of meat is especially tasty with apples?

stroys thiamine (a vitamin we will study later). There is very little thiamine in peaches and apricots and a great deal of vitamin A, so it is better to buy the sulfur-dried apricots and peaches and get this abundance of vitamin A.

Plums are sharp-flavored fruits of summer and early fall. The true plum clings to its seed. The prune-plum is a freestone and the one most used. When this is dried, we buy it as a prune. Prunes, apricots, and raisins are our three best common fruits for iron. These fruits should find their place in your meals often, especially if you are inclined to be anemic.

Prunes are an excellent fruit for a natural laxative. For many people the habit of eating a well-cooked dish of prunes for a bedtime snack is sufficient to correct constipation. The vitamin B content of prunes, the soft undigested roughage, and other nutrients as well aid in this respect. Prune juice can be purchased, but you can save money by making it, and improve the flavor by adding orange peel.

You get more prune and less seed for the money in the large size. Since there is little vitamin A in prunes, but a good deal of thiamine, sun-dried prunes are a better buy than sulfur-dried ones.

Cherries come in sour and sweet varieties. The sweet ones are eaten raw and are used to garnish many foods and drinks. Sour cherries are used for sauces and pies.

Berries are vine or stem fruits. They begin in spring and go through the summer as a delightful fresh fruit. Though highly perishable, they lend themselves to freezing. Today we can enjoy the fresh flavor in a frozen berry right through the winter. Canned, they are not used as widely as some of the other fruits. Berries

Here are five ways to use peaches. Plan a menu that will go well with each. What other ways can you think of to use this delicious fruit?

include: the strawberry, blackberry, dewberry, boysenberry, loganberry, raspberry, youngberry, huckleberry, blueberry, and cranberry.

In the table on page 88, you learned that one cup of strawberries is richer in vitamin C than a whole orange (90 mg of vitamin C compared to 60–75 mg in a medium orange). A cup of raw blackberries will give you between one-third and one-half of your daily recommended amount of vitamin C, and blueberries almost as much. Most berries have a fair share of the B vitamins as well as vitamin C. The cranberry is outstanding among fruits as the best food for iodine, a mineral we need, and often low in the diet.

Melons and grapes are vine fruits of summer and early fall. Each has many varieties. Most of our canned grape juice comes from the purple Concord grape, which is also used for jelly and jam. The dried grape gives us the seedless, seeded, and white raisins, so rich in iron.

Melons add great pleasure to our meals and snacks. Once they were used mostly for snacks. Today they have become a choice food at any meal. Some variety of melon can be purchased in almost any month in the year.

The deep yellow-flesh melons are richest in vitamin A. They are also among the best foods for vitamin C. The most popular and least expensive is the cantaloupe. The cranshaw, muskmelon, and Persian are other yellow melons. The honeydew and casaba have a white-green flesh, and the watermelon a deep red.

The tropical fruits are many. We use only two in large amounts, bananas and pineapples. The avocado, once considered a luxury, is becoming more popular for all.

The *banana* is the only fruit that has a better flavor when harvested green. It is best for eating when the skin is yellow and flecked with brown spots. Until this stage it should be kept out of the refrigerator to ripen. After it is ripe, it is best to store it in the refrigerator until eaten.

The banana is to tropical people what the potato is to those in the temperate zone. A banana has about the same number of calories as a potato, but slightly less minerals and vitamins than the potato. It is a good all-season fruit, and can be quickly and easily digested by people of all ages. It requires no cooking, is sanitary because of its protective skin, and is excellent to eat when traveling.

You can judge a good *pineapple* by the aroma, yellow color, firmness of flesh, and flatness of the eyes. The green leaves pull easily from a ripe pineapple.

The fresh raw flavor of pineapple is tasty in salads and fruit cups. The juice gives tang to many fruit drinks. Canned pineapple adds "zip" to meats, salads, pie, cakes, and cookies.

Marketing for Fruit

To get the best fruit for your money, you should keep the following rules in mind when shopping:

(1) Know what makes *good quality* in each fruit you buy. In general, high quality in fruit means firm, heavy fruit, full of juice. Fruit should be mature (neither too green nor too ripe). Picked too green it will not ripen to a good flavor and it may shrivel. Over-ripe fruit has lost much of its vitamin C; it will spoil quickly, and has a poor flavor. Fruit of high quality has the full and natural

color and flavor of its type. (The color of the skin of the orange does not affect its quality, nor does adding color to the skin.) The best fruit is free of blemishes or rotten spots which hurt flavor or food value. Some skin blemishes such as "scald" in apples are only skin deep. You can often save money by purchasing such fruits. Fruit of good quality has more vitamins, better flavor, and less waste.

Remember that the largest size doesn't mean the best quality. Studies made of oranges, strawberries and tomatoes (a fruit that is used and thought of as a vegetable) indicate that the medium and small sizes are higher in vitamin C than the largest size.

(2) If you use fruits in season as they ripen, they are less expensive, and give a natural variety to your meals. For instance, when oranges are so expensive in the late summer months, use more tomatoes, for they are in abundance then and cost less. By using fruit in season, and the

All canned fruit has a similar texture. Variety comes in combining it with fresh fruit in season.

fruit that grows nearest your home, you can save on the food budget, and get more nourishing and tasty fruit.

(3) Compare the price, flavor, and quality of fresh fruit with those of canned and frozen fruit before you buy. Canned tomatoes may be much cheaper than hot-house tomatoes. Studies show that hot-house tomatoes may be only one-half as rich in vitamin C as garden-ripened ones. If fresh fruit is not of high quality, canned or frozen may be a better choice.

(4) Read labels on canned and frozen fruit. Your government has gone to a great deal of expense to let you know what you are buying in a can. In a modern supermarket, where you serve yourself, the label tells you what the grocer's clerk once told his customers. The law requires the label to contain the following information:

Grade of product (A,B,C)

Name of product and brand (this tells you what it is and who canned it)

Net contents of can in weight or fluid measure.

Name and address of manufacturer or distributor.

In addition, labels may give price and recipes and will state if sugar or other substances are added. Sometimes there is a picture of the fruit.

(5) The best way to buy fresh fruit is by weight. Some fruits are sold by measure or size (pints, quarts, bushels; or small, medium, and large). It is possible to pack fruit so loosely that you are getting from 25 to 33 percent less than an honest full measure. This means you are losing one-fourth to one-third of your money on this purchase. If you buy by

A loaf of quick fruit bread.

Fruit muffins enliven any meal.

Apple crisp, a quick low-calorie type pie.

Oatmeal cookies served with fruit.

Prunes and apricots make delicious soufflés.

Peaches top this upside-down cake.

measure, look the fruit over carefully. Is it firmly packed? Is the quality uniform throughout, or do you find moldy, over-ripe, or decayed fruit beneath the surface?

(6) You have a right to look carefully to see that you are getting firm, good quality fruit. But over-handling, squeezing, and bruising fruit causes it to spoil more quickly. You are overstepping your rights in doing this. Keep in mind that the cost of all spoiled fruit is added to the price you pay. It is to your financial interest to be considerate in handling fresh fruits.

(7) You can probably save money and obtain better-quality fruit if you shop in person. You can then take advantage of the best fruit on the market.

(8) Take a second look at "bargain basket" fruits before you buy them. Too often they are old fruit that the store wishes to dispose of before further loss.

(9) Watch for sales of canned fruit. Often stores will run a sale on one fruit or vegetable at a time. If you know the brand and the quality of each, then buy and save money. Stores sometimes sell a "leader" for cost or a few cents under cost. The purpose is to bring you into the store, where you will do all your shopping. Plan your food budget so that you can take advantage of these sales.

Such sales often come just before the new crop of that food is canned. For instance, an advertisement in late August might read:

Our finest quality applesauce
4 (14 oz. cans) for 45¢
lowest price in years

A homemaker who knows this brand to be one of high quality for which she usually pays 29¢ for two cans sees a bargain.

Apple pie is a favorite dessert for guests or the family.

On four cans she saves 13¢. This may seem very small to you. But if she uses at least two cans a week, this adds up to a real saving in a year. Lots of such little savings during the year can add up to many dollars! By good management you can have more fruit at less cost.

Storing Fruit

Fresh fruit should be stored in the refrigerator. All fruit, except berries, should be washed before being stored. Berries should be washed just before you use them, to prevent rapid spoiling and loss of vitamins. Many people store citrus fruits and apples in a cool cellar. This is better than a warm kitchen, but not as good as a cool refrigerator. Cold delays the ripening process and loss of vitamin C.

Why does cottage cheese improve fruit salad so that it is a desirable main dish for lunch?

Preparing and Cooking Fruit

Most fruits and some vegetables are sprayed to kill insects and prevent disease. This gives us more food and a better diet, but not if we eat the spray! Fruits that are eaten raw or cooked in skins should be thoroughly washed and dried first. This frees the fruit of dirt and removes any remaining spray or fallout.

The Federal government has passed laws to protect us from sprayed fruit that is shipped from one state to another. But if you buy locally grown fruit, which does not come under the Federal law, you are dependent on your state and local laws to protect you, and on your own knowledge. Fruits with heavy skins, such as apples and pears, can and should be thoroughly scrubbed before they are eaten raw or are cooked. The grey residue which you may see at the stem or blossom end of fruit may be spray. Cut this part away before eating or cooking the fruit.

Cooking fruit is a simple matter. Here are a few suggestions that may help you:

(1) When possible, cook fruits in their skins and natural juice. Apples, apricots, and pears lend themselves to being cooked in the skins, and berries cook easily in their own juice. The skin helps retain the natural flavor, adds color, and helps retain more minerals, vitamins, and amino acids. Peeling causes some loss of these "protective" nutrients. If you peel fruit, use a sharp knife, and cut off the peel as thinly as possible. Sieving fruit causes increased loss of vitamin C, but there is less loss if the fruit is sieved when cool. It is also more desirable to add sugar to fruit sauce when it is cool.

(2) Some homemakers place peeled fruit in water to prevent it from turning

To prevent their odor from being absorbed by other foods, fruits with a strong aroma, such as pineapple and cantaloupe, should be wrapped tightly in a paper or plastic bag before being placed in the refrigerator.

Frozen fruit should be stored immediately in a freezer or the freezing compartment of the refrigerator. The best temperature is 0°F or lower. They should not be thawed until ready to use, and then should be used immediately. The texture of frozen fruit breaks down quickly after thawing. But even more important is the very rapid loss of vitamin C. It is better to serve fruit partially frozen than over-thawed for flavor and for vitamins.

Dried fruit should be stored in its sealed container in a cool, dry place. Wash dried fruit before eating or cooking it. Sulfur-dried fruit should be washed quickly in boiling water.

dark, not knowing that this causes loss of water-soluble vitamins, minerals, and natural sugars. There are better ways to prevent fruit from darkening when peeled. One way is by dipping the fruit in lemon juice. This prevents discoloring and slows loss of vitamin C. Another way is to employ a commercial product which uses citric acid and vitamin C to prevent discoloring. It is not necessary to use either of these methods when making an apple pie. If you peel the apples, slice them directly into the pie, and bake it immediately, or refrigerate or freeze the pie until ready to bake, then there is little darkening of the fruit.

(3) Cook fruits in as little water as possible. Berries and rhubarb require no water, but cook in their own juice. Other fruits require very little. If fruits are cooked in a pressure saucepan, the pressure has to come barely to 15 pounds until their tissue is softened. If you are cooking by the waterless cooking method (see pages 124-126), cover the pan and cook until just tender. If dried fruit is soaked in water, the fruit should be cooked in the same water. Dried fruit is especially tender and delicious when cooked in the pressure saucepan.

(4) Canned fruits are ready to serve. It causes further loss of vitamins and softens the texture to cook them again. All of the juice should be used in order to get all of the nutrients from the fruit. If you do not serve the juice with the fruit, use it as the liquid in making Jell-O or with a cake mix. If you wish low-calorie fruit, buy the canned fruit in light-sugar syrup. Fruits canned in heavy syrup retain their shape better, but they cost more and the extra sugar adds more calories to the diet.

(5) Cooked or opened canned fruit should be stored in covered containers in the refrigerator. It is perfectly safe to store left-over canned fruit in the can, but cover it tightly. To store fruit juice, use a jar just large enough. This helps prevent oxygen from destroying vitamin C.

(6) Canned or frozen fruit juice should be opened and mixed just before serving. Vitamin C is lost faster in left-over fresh or frozen juice than in left-over canned juice. This is because cooking destroys enzymes (ĕn′zīm), and enzyme action hastens the loss of vitamin C. Remember to squeeze only the amount of fresh juice, and mix only the amount of frozen, that you will drink. It is better to cover the remaining frozen juice in its can and store in the freezer.

How to Use Fruit in Meals and Snacks

Raw fruit is excellent either at a meal or for a snack. Raw fruits require little time or energy for preparation; many fruits have the most delicate flavor when raw; the texture of raw fruit is firm and gives contrast to the soft food of which we eat so much; the color adds beauty; and you are likely to get more minerals and vitamins when the fruit is raw than when it is cooked. A raw fruit requires no sugar, or very little, and has fewer calories than sweetened fruit. This is important to those who watch weight.

It is fashionable in our country today, just as it has been in Europe for a long time, to serve a bowl of fresh fruit for dessert, with or without cheese.

Fruit is the perfect dessert for a picnic, school lunch, or snack. Fresh fruit or juice

What background knowledge do you need to make wise decisions in shopping for fresh fruits? frozen? canned? dried?

is a low-calorie snack food that is good for both vigor and figure.

Some fruits need to be cooked—for example, rhubarb, green apples, and usually cranberries. Canned, stewed, or baked fruits may be served plain or with cream for breakfast or lunch. Canned fruit may be used with left-over cake and topped with ice cream for a quick and tasty shortcake.

In desserts, fruits are used in upside-down cake, fruit cake, fruit pies, cobblers, ice cream, gelatin, fruit cookies, breakfast rings, sherbets, mousse (mo͞os), and as

COMPARISON OF VITAMIN C IN COMMERCIALLY CANNED JUICES

MILLIGRAMS PER 3½ OUNCES OF JUICE. THE SECOND COLUMN SHOWS THE INCREASE WHEN VITAMIN C IS ADDED DURING PROCESSING OF JUICE.

Apple	0.2	3.6
Grape	0.0	4.7
Tomato	2.5	32.0
Pineapple	5.4	18.0
Grapefruit	10.0	49.0
Orange	9.7	70.0

Source: U. S. Department of Agriculture.

simple fresh fruit, with cheese or without.

Fruits are used in a variety of ways as appetizers: juice, fruit cup, melon slice, or fruit kabobs. In the main part of the meal, fruit may be served as: a salad, in breads, sauces, salad dressing, stuffing, jelly, preserves, pickles; or a large fruit salad with cottage cheese makes a low-calorie main course.

Summary of Fruit in Our Meals

Fruit, an expensive but delicious food, adds much to the pleasure of eating. Because of their high and dependable vitamin C, which we need every day, our most important fruits are the citrus fruits (oranges, grapefruit) and tomatoes.

Vitamin C is quickly and easily destroyed by oxygen, especially when heated, and it dissolves in water like sugar. Unless you are aware of its fragile nature, you can destroy it by the way you prepare food—as when you soak it in cold water to "crisp" it, let it stand in water to keep it from turning dark, or drain off the water in which a fruit is cooked or canned. Since this vitamin is not stored in the body to any extent and is needed constantly, it is well to have a food rich in vitamin C in each meal. You should therefore keep this in mind when you plan meals. A generous use of fruits helps balance the low vitamin C content of cereal-bread, meat, eggs, and milk.

The values of fruits are greater than just their content of vitamin C. Fruits provide other vitamins and minerals which help keep the "tone" of your body in a healthy state, and your vitality high.

WORDS TO WORK WITH

Enzyme (ĕn′zīm): a substance which splits sugar, starch, protein, and fat into smaller parts and makes digestion possible.

Mousse (mo͞os): a frozen or refrigerated dessert, usually made with gelatin.

THINKING IT OVER

1. What are the most common fruits you eat? How often do you eat fruit at meals? For snacks?

2. Which fruits do you like best? Why?

3. Which are the most needed fruits? What can they contribute to your appearance and health?

4. When you go to buy fruits, what are the qualities you look for to obtain a high-grade fruit?

5. Why do we thoroughly wash fruit before we eat it raw or cook it?

6. How can you be sure that specials in canned fruits represent savings?

7. What are the advantages in buying fruit by weight? In season? When it is locally grown?

8. Why is it better to serve fruit raw if possible? When fruit is peeled, why should the peelings be thin?

9. What fruits besides citrus fruits and tomatoes are rich in vitamin C?

10. How can you plan meals to include two fruits daily, even on a low food budget? Give an example.

PROBLEMS TO SOLVE

1. Learning by seeing and doing: Make a trip to a supermarket to see and study the fresh, canned, frozen, and dried fruit.
   (1) Choose several fruits that you often eat or should eat, and compare prices, flavor, color, texture, and nutritive values of the fresh, canned, frozen, and dried forms.
   (2) Compare the cost of in-season fruit in these different forms with that of out-of-season fruit.
2. Evaluating what you have learned:
   (1) Which fruits would you buy and how much of each to meet your family's needs for three days?
   (2) Plan three days of balanced menus using the fruits you have chosen each day.
   (3) What was the cost of your fruit for each day? How could you bring down the cost? What fruits would you choose if you had more money to spend? Which would give you the best balanced meals and why? Does spending more for fruit mean that you are better fed? Explain.

APPLYING WHAT YOU KNOW

1. Prepare fruit in one or more of the following ways.

(1) Bake apples; make apple sauce, cooking fruit in skins.
(2) Make a quick fruit pudding, using one of these: canned cherries, canned apricots, canned apple sauce.
(3) Make an upside-down cake, using canned fruit—pineapple, peaches, or apricots.
(4) Prepare raw fruit for breakfast, lunch, and dinner in one of the following ways: first course, salad, dessert, fruit punch.
(5) Decide which fruits are most suitable for snacks and how to use them.
(6) Plan balanced meals or snacks in which you use the fruit you have prepared.

EVALUATING

1. Did your work meet the standards you have learned for buying, preparing, cooking, and serving food—for health value, flavor, and appearance?
2. Was the money, energy, and time spent reasonable in amount?

HOME EXPERIENCE

With your mother, plan a balanced meal using a fruit dish you learned to prepare and serve at school. Prepare and serve this fruit yourself as a part of the meal.

FURTHER READING

Apples—A Favorite Food, Dunn. Cornell Extension Bulletin E 973. Cornell University, Ithaca, N.Y., 1963.

Chiquita Banana Cookbook. United Fruit Co., Pier 3, North River, New York 6, N.Y.

Cranberry Dishes. National Cranberry Association, Hanson, Mass.

Fruit and Vegetable Buying Guide. Home and Garden Bulletin 21. U.S.D.A., Washington, D.C., 1952.

Good Housekeeping New Picture Cookery. Good Housekeeping Book Division, New York, N.Y., 1966.

How to Choose and Use Grapefruit. Leaflet Pa 161. Extension Service from the Land Grant College in your state.

How to Choose and Use Oranges. Leaflet Pa 162. Extension Service from the Land Grant College in your state.

How to Choose and Use Peaches. Leaflet Pa 158. Extension Service from the Land Grant College in your state.

Nutritive Value of California Prunes, 3rd ed. California Prune Advisory Board, San Francisco, Calif., 1955.

Richards Topical Encyclopedia, Volume 9. The Richards Co., Inc., New York, N.Y., 1964.
   a.   Where Our Berries Come From.
   b.   A Famous Family of Fruits.
   c.   A Fruit That Many People Live On.

VISUAL AIDS

An Apple a Day. (5½ min. film, color and b/w) U.S.D.A., Washington, D.C., 1952.

Good Things Come in Pears. (5½ min. film, color and b/w) U.S.D.A., Washington, D.C., 1952.

It's a Peach. (6 min. film, color and b/w) U.S.D.A., Washington, D.C., 1952.

Something You Didn't Eat. A Walt Disney cartoon showing early discoveries of how important citrus fruit is to the cure of scurvy, and whole grains for the cure of beri-beri; results of a poor diet on modern people; and ways of securing a good diet.

Balance Your Breakfast, Balance Your Day

11

Planning, Preparing, and Serving Breakfast

A Good Breakfast Gives a Good Start for the Day

Breakfast is an important meal. It is perhaps the most important of all. After the night's rest, your body is naturally refreshed, and the nerves and muscles are relaxed, but it takes food to give you the strength for work or play. Breakfast comes after 12 or 13 hours without food— it is a "break" from the longest "fast" we have

This breakfast has less than one-third of the calories needed daily by a boy or girl 12 to 18 years old, but it has a fair share of essential nutrients.

What are the advantages in using dry milk to make cocoa for breakfast?

In a study in Connecticut, it was found that more young people missed breakfast than any other meal. And among 9000 high school juniors and seniors in New Jersey, one-fourth of the girls and one-seventh of the boys had eaten no breakfast the day before the survey was made. What can you learn from these studies that may help you have a more adequate breakfast every morning? How can a good breakfast help your day, and your life?

Why You Need a Balanced Breakfast

By eating a good breakfast you end your long fast and provide nutrients to meet demands of the new day. A good, balanced breakfast gives you strength right up to lunch time. This helps prevent a feeling of nervousness which teachers recognize in pupils who skip breakfast or eat a poor one. It improves your disposition, thus influencing how well you are liked by friends and teachers. It increases your ability to get your work done, which may affect your class standing.

between meals. People who have a lot to do count on getting a great deal of their difficult tasks done in the morning. For the energy to meet this challenge, a good, balanced breakfast is necessary.

In Montana, a diet study of 15-year-old high school boys and girls and of college freshmen has shown that those who ate a good breakfast were among those who had an adequate diet from their other meals as well. Those who ate no breakfast, or ate a poor one, did not meet their nutritional needs for the day.

Studies in Iowa showed that breakfast was the poorest meal in the day in meeting the health needs of school children. They also indicated that as children grow older, this meal is likely to become poorer, and that girls have poorer breakfasts than boys. In Iowa, as in Montana, the children who had poor breakfasts were likely to have a poor diet for the whole day.

If you skip breakfast, you go four or five more hours without a meal. This forces your body to call on reserves to "keep you going." Thus you are breaking down your body instead of building it up. You are forcing your body to take calcium from the bones or teeth to meet your immediate need, instead of storing calcium for reserve. Your body is taking vitamins wherever they are stored. But, as in the case of vitamin C, some nutrients are stored in very small amounts. Your health and your looks are gradually affected if you don't supply what you need at regular meals. This does not happen in just one part of your body, but in many.

The studies mentioned before showed that often those who skipped breakfast did not eat a good food for vitamin C in the whole day. In fact, they had a difficult time getting as much calcium, vitamin C, riboflavin, thiamine, and other nutrients as they needed.

The idea that skipping breakfast helps one lose weight is mistaken. Just the opposite is true, with adults as well as teen-agers. The reason for this was brought out by a group of men studied at Rutgers University. When they skipped breakfast or ate a poor one, they got a mid-morning "slump," which caused them to eat sweets. This, in turn, took away their appetite for a good, balanced lunch. These men were missing breakfast, often missing lunch, but getting fatter and becoming more poorly nourished every day.

You may have heard the discussion on TV by a panel of teen-age boys and girls on the question "How Do Eating Habits Affect Teen-agers?" One boy said, "The worst habit of teen-agers is to skip breakfast, for we make up for this with a candy bar later in the morning. This gives us a lift (calories), but not what we need for health." The others heartily agreed, and one girl added that the girls she knew who missed breakfast or ate a poor one had more trouble with overweight than those who ate a good one.

There is also no truth in the idea that you do not have enough time to eat breakfast. We all have the same amount of time. How you manage your time is something for you to decide. You can make your decision either thoughtfully or by neglect. To have a good breakfast, you may have to get up 20 or 30 minutes earlier in the morning. You may feel that you need the extra sleep more than you need the good breakfast. It is doubtful if the few extra minutes of sleep will benefit you as much as a well-balanced breakfast. Indeed, those who do eat a good breakfast are so "sold" on the idea that they gladly make the effort to have one. This is because they know that they have more vitality for the morning, and they feel that over the long pull they will feel better and become more attractive persons.

Under what circumstances would you need both cereal and an egg for breakfast?

What You Can Do About Breakfast

One of the many wonderful things that come in your teens is that you become a young adult. This brings privileges and responsibilities. To prepare or help prepare a good breakfast every morning is a privilege as well as a responsibility. By planning ahead with your family, you can all enjoy a well-balanced breakfast.

In a California study, among the reasons given by teen-agers for skipping breakfast were that breakfast was not ready, and that there was no one to eat it with! By planning breakfast, you can in most cases be ready in time for the family to eat it together. As indicated above, to plan, prepare, and serve a well-balanced breakfast for yourself and your family is to improve the quality of your life in many ways. It is a social pleasure to be with your family at a good meal before you each depart for the day. Eating good food together as a family brings happiness that is deeper than the enjoyment given by the food as such.

How to Plan a Good Breakfast Menu

There are many different combinations of food which can make a tasty and well-balanced breakfast. Here are some basic principles to guide you in planning a good breakfast menu at different cost levels.

(1) A well-balanced breakfast menu should meet between one-fourth and one-third of your total day's need for vitamins, minerals, protein, and calories. If it does this, the remainder of the day's menus are easier to plan.

(2) The choice of food for breakfast should be in balance with what you will eat for lunch, dinner, and a snack (if you have one), and can be varied from day to day when you think and plan ahead.

(3) Breakfast should use a fair portion of the day's food money.

(4) The menu for breakfast should be one that you can prepare and serve in the amount of time available, and with the equipment you have.

(5) The foods in the breakfast menu should "go together" to give a balance in flavor as well as in nourishment.

(6) The menu should please the taste of your family as far as possible.

Types of Breakfasts

Since a light breakfast of toast or sweet rolls, coffee, and juice is not adequate for anyone, we shall consider only two types of breakfast—the medium and the hearty.

The medium type of breakfast is most suited to the kind of lives most of us live, regardless of age. It and the hearty type should include the following standard nutrients: *a good protein food; a food rich in vitamin C; a food rich in calcium; foods containing B vitamins, especially riboflavin and thiamine; and enough calories to meet your need for energy.* How do we translate this into foods?

> *Medium Breakfast*
> *Fruit* (orange, grapefruit, tomato, or other vitamin C-rich food)
> *Egg* (or lean meat or both; or whole grain or enriched cereal)
> *Bread* (whole grain or enriched)
> *Butter* (or fortified margarine or other fat)
> *Milk*

This breakfast is well suited to those who are reasonably active during the morning but not engaged in strenuous labor or exercise. If you establish the habit of eating this type of breakfast every day, you will be fortifying yourself with the strength found in food to give sparkle to your morning hours.

A hearty breakfast follows the same pattern as the medium, but you add more calories by one-half to double. For in-

Steps in Making a Quick Coffee Cake (see recipe, page 406): (1) Preheat oven to 375°F. Sift dry ingredients into mixing bowl and blend thoroughly. (2) Add other ingredients and mix until smooth. (3) Spread dough evenly in 9-inch oiled pie pan, using a spatula. (4) Spread dough with topping of choice and bake 25 minutes or until done. (5) Cut coffee cake and serve warm or cool for breakfast or dessert.

stance, you might have both an orange and a dish of prunes or stewed apricots; or cereal, eggs, and toast. You might eat two eggs with meat or potatoes; or hot cakes plus eggs and meat; or more milk or cheese with eggs; or simply more bread and butter. Although jam supplies few needed nutrients, it could be added for calories and flavor. The hearty breakfast is suited to those who do strenuous labor or exercise, or to teen-age boys who are growing rapidly.

One may have a wide variety of food in the medium breakfast as long as the portions are small and the calories do not exceed your need. If your budget allows meat for only one meal during the day, it is more satisfactory to use eggs as the protein food for breakfast and serve meat at dinner. An alternate protein food for breakfast is cereal served with a generous portion of milk. Naturally, if cereal is cooked in milk, it is far more nourishing in protein and in other needed nutrients than either dry cereal or cereal cooked in water, and this will help delay mid-morning hunger.

Marketing and Management of Food for Breakfast

Since this is the first meal you have studied, let us consider some points in management that can help you with all meals. Your market list should, of course, be for all meals, not just one. It should also cover as long a period as is possible in view of the amount of storage space available, and the money and time you have to use.

(1) Choose the time to do your big marketing when the most "specials" or bargains are on the market. The newspaper or other sources of news and the experience of your mother in shopping can help guide you here. Shop around to find where you can make the best use of your food money, and go to that store at a time of day when it is likely to be least crowded. This will save time and fatigue.

(2) Make your market list by checking your staples, such as salt, flour, sugar, and the like. Keep a pad in the kitchen and write down items that you need as the food gets low. Buy to replace before you are out of an item. It is a big waste of time, energy, and money to run to the store for one or two items. Your market list should be completed on the basis of what you have in reserve, and the menus you have made for the week.

(3) Use your money wisely in buying food. One important way is by planning your meals first. Keep in mind the health needs of all members of the family and, as far as possible, their personal food likes. A food budget sets a limit to what you can spend. Impulsive buying at the store

Why are fruits so important in normal meals? In reducing diets?

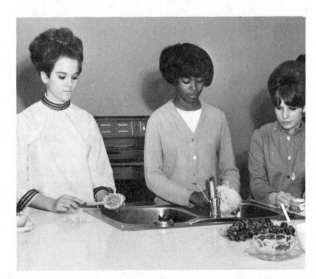

EXAMPLE OF A MARKET LIST FOR FOOD
(to check before marketing)

MILK PRODUCTS (if fluid milk is delivered)

Dry milk solids
Evaporated milk
Condensed milk
Cheddar-type cheese
Cottage cheese
Blue cheese
Ice cream

EGGS

Grade A eggs
Grade B eggs

FRUITS

Fresh oranges or grapefruit
Canned or frozen citrus juice
Lemons
Tomatoes—fresh, canned, or juice
Fresh fruit in season
Dried apricots, prunes, raisins, or other dried fruit

VEGETABLES

Fresh salad greens (the best in season for the money)
Celery
Carrots
Onions
Cabbage (best variety in season)
Potatoes, white (and yellow if in season)
Green leafy vegetables to cook—fresh, frozen, or canned
Other vegetables—in season, fresh, frozen, or canned
Dried or canned beans, peas, or lentils

Keep a pad and pencil handy in the kitchen to make a list of foods needed each day as you find you are running low. This can save time and energy in the number of trips to market.

MEATS

Lean meat—beef, lamb, pork, or veal, cut and grade to fit your budget
Fish—fresh, canned, or frozen
Liver, heart, brains, kidney, or other variety meat
Poultry

CEREAL-BREAD

Ready-cooked whole grain or enriched bread
Flour—enriched or whole grain or both, all-purpose
Mixes if desired
Ready-to-bake products if desired
Yellow corn meal
Breakfast cereal to cook
Whole grain or enriched ready-to-eat cereal

FATS-SUGARS

Butter or margarine
Vegetable oil or other fat of choice
Fat meat for seasoning if desired
Ready-cooked cakes, pies, or cookies
White sugar
Brown sugar
Syrup
Dark molasses
Honey
Jelly or jam

MISCELLANEOUS

Tea, coffee, cocoa
Salt, pepper, spices, extracts, herbs
Wax paper, foil, paper towel
Vinegar, mayonnaise, French dressing
Soap, detergents, cleaning powder
Related products needed for cooking and serving food

can lead to waste of money. Don't buy too much, especially perishables, which may deteriorate before they can be used.

But take advantage of bargains if they fall within your real needs. For instance, day-old bread is as nourishing as fresh bread, and usually costs less. Dried and evaporated milk and grade B eggs are nourishing and less expensive for cooking. You may be able to fill your vitamin C need for breakfast for less money through canned or frozen orange juice at some seasons and fresh oranges at others. Keep in mind that it takes twice as many tomatoes as oranges to meet your vitamin C need. Figure this in cost when you use tomatoes as an alternate for oranges.

Have you tried to make popovers? They are a delicious way to eat a "hidden" egg.

If your food budget is low, remember that you will have more money to spend if you make your own hot breads instead of buying the ready-mix or frozen or other commercially prepared ones. Furthermore, you can make your breads more nourishing if you prepare them yourself. In some stores, broken pieces of bacon sell for about half as much as the regular kind. If it is lean, it is a good buy and will add flavor to a low-cost breakfast, but not enough protein to be considered a meat. Its value lies in flavor and fat content.

(4) Select recipes that are easy to prepare and are nourishing. Let us consider some principles concerning recipes that will help you in planning all your meals.

(a) By planning your menus in advance, you can take time to select a good recipe for each dish. The recipe goes right to the heart of the meal. All that you have learned about nutrition may be wasted by a poorly chosen recipe. Read your recipe carefully and critically.

(b) The ingredients in a recipe should be healthful and in proper proportion to one another. For instance, if the proportion of flour to liquid is not right, the dish will not turn out well. And if the recipe calls for 1½ cups of sugar when only 1 cup is needed, you are hurt twice—once in the poor dish, and again in adding over 400 "empty" calories you may not need.

(c) The directions for a recipe should be clearly written and easy to follow.

(d) The directions should be in keeping with our modern knowledge of nutrition and food chemistry.

(e) The measurements should be standard.

(f) The equipment needed to prepare the recipe should be in the average home.

(g) Cooking temperature should be stated; also the number of servings.

(h) Use recipes that have been tested by qualified people, until you are experienced enough to create your own.

(i) The total ingredients in a recipe should not cost more than your food budget can allow for that dish in the meal. Here is an example of how this can affect you. A young couple invited a friend from another land to prepare a special meal from her country, but they did not go over the ingredients in the recipes beforehand. When the food was purchased and the meal prepared, it far exceeded their budget and worked a hardship on them. This could have been avoided by planning properly ahead of time.

Before you go shopping for food, check whether the menus you have planned can be prepared in the amount of time available. You need about one hour to prepare a breakfast with popovers, because it takes so long for them to bake. If you fry sausages, you will need more time than if you fry bacon. Muffins take more time than toast.

The unseen work of planning and marketing contributes immeasurably to the success of a meal.

Management of Work and Time in Preparing Breakfast

Experienced homemakers have a work plan that is carefully timed, whether it is written or not. To save confusion and give yourself a feeling of confidence, write out a complete plan of all steps in preparing and serving breakfast. Consider these items in writing down your work plan:

(1) Set the hour for breakfast as a starting point.

(2) Divide your plan into three parts: (a) work to do the night before; (b) the actual preparation of breakfast; (c) cleaning up after breakfast.

(3) If other members of the family are to help you, assign various tasks to them and be sure each understands what he or she is to do and when it is to be done.

(4) Choose a menu that meets all the tests for a good breakfast and that you know how to prepare in every part.

(5) Allow enough time for each task. Rushing causes accidents and often wastes money, as well as taking extra time and energy to clean up the accident.

(6) Think of the different jobs to be done at each work period, and dovetail these; that is, fit different jobs into a smooth whole as you work. For instance, when you go to the refrigerator, take a tray and get everything you need at one trip. Or when you start to set the table, assemble all of the dishes and the silver, and take as much on a tray at one time as you can comfortably. Seeing what can be done at the same time, and doing it, yields expert results.

(7) Keep your work area clean as you work. Dispose of the garbage properly and keep the sink, table tops, and stove top neat, clean, and as orderly as possible. Return perishable foods such as milk to the refrigerator promptly after use.

(8) Give a five-minute warning for your meal. If you cook eggs for breakfast, don't start them until near the time they are needed.

(9) When you call the family to the table, have the meal ready. This encourages the family to come promptly.

Now let us take a menu that you have learned to prepare in its separate parts and put it together. Then you can see how *work* and *time* can be *arranged* to give a good result. If you think and plan and work ahead as shown below, this menu can be prepared in 20 minutes without rushing.

Breakfast Menu of Moderate Cost
One-half grapefruit
Blindfolded eggs   (crisp bacon if desired)
Whole wheat or enriched toast
Butter or margarine   Plum jam
Milk   Coffee (adults)

Schedule for Preparing and Serving Breakfast

(1) AFTER DINNER
1. Arrange dining area attractively (see Chapter 25).
2. Place centerpiece on table and set table (see Chapter 25).
3. Place on the table the following: salt, pepper, hot pad for coffee pot, and cups and saucers, carrying these on a tray at one time.
4. In kitchen, place on tray number of glasses needed for milk.
5. Place five-inch plates on table for grapefruit.
6. Assemble in proper places the coffee pot, grapefruit knife, skillet and tight fitting lid, saucer for breaking eggs, and cookie sheet for making broiler toast (if this method of toasting is used).

(2) BEFORE BREAKFAST (Breakfast served at 7:30)

7:05   Personal preparation:
   1. Arrange hair neatly.
   2. Put on clean apron.
   3. Wash hands and clean nails.
   4. Go to kitchen.

7:10   Dovetailing:
   1. Remove and place on a tray margarine or butter, jam, eggs, grapefruit from refrigerator.
   2. Measure coffee and water for coffee, and start in the way your family makes coffee.
   3. Light oven (or place bread in toaster).
   4. If toast is to be made in stove, place proper amount of bread on cookie sheet for toast, butter it, and set in broiler, leaving door open until toast is brown.
   5. Turn out fire of broiler, leaving toast in broiler.
   6. Place plates for eggs in oven to warm.

An easy-to-prepare, nutritious breakfast that helps keep these high school leaders attractive in person, and personality.

7:20 Prepare grapefruit and set on plates on the table.

7:25 Give first call for breakfast. Pour milk and set on table. Place just enough butter or bacon fat in skillet to grease (and no surplus). Turn on heat under skillet.

7:29 Break eggs one at a time into saucer, and slip into skillet. Add 2 tablespoons of water, cover tightly, turn heat low.

7:30 Call breakfast. Serve eggs on warm plates, and serve toast in a covered napkin to keep it warm. (For service of meals and table manners, see Chapter 25).

(3) AFTER BREAKFAST
1. Clear table, and put away leftovers.
2. Rinse dishes and stack, and clean off table top.
3. Wash dishes later if there is not time.

THINKING IT OVER

1. In your opinion, why is breakfast such an important meal?

2. Why do you think some young people skip breakfast? How may this affect their looks, health, efficiency—physically, mentally, and socially?

3. What can you do to help yourself and your family have a well-balanced breakfast every morning?

4. What is a well-balanced breakfast menu? What do you need to keep in mind in planning a well-balanced breakfast?

5. Why is a light breakfast not suitable for anyone? What is the difference between a medium and a hearty breakfast? Which type do you need?

6. Explain how wise marketing for breakfast can help you with other meals in the day.

7. What points would you keep in mind in marketing for the family food? Explain how adequate information about the health values in different foods can help you save money in marketing.

8. Why is the selection of the recipe so important to the health value of the meal? To its appearance and taste? How can you decide whether a recipe is a good one or a poor one?

9. Explain how you would organize your work and time to prepare breakfast on a school morning. A Saturday or Sunday morning.

PROBLEMS TO SOLVE

1. Discuss your goals in learning to plan, prepare, and serve breakfast.

2. Plan a menu for a breakfast which you might prepare and serve to your family at school, keeping in mind and practicing all that you have learned.
   (1) How might this menu be adjusted to serve your family at home? Guests?
   (2) If you had less money to spend, how would you change the menu and still meet the health needs and the tastes of your family?
   (3) If you had more money to spend, show how you could improve your menu.
   (4) If you do not have the equipment you need, what could be used as a substitute?
   (5) Make a plan showing what you will do, who will do each task, and the timing for the work. When your plan is finished, check each step to see if you have everything, and if you can improve it. Check the plan as you follow it, and make notes of how it works out.

APPLYING WHAT YOU KNOW

1. Prepare and serve your family a balanced breakfast which you have planned.

 EVALUATING

1. Did each dish in the menus you planned taste good? Did the foods go together in flavor? In nourishment?
2. Did you practice what you learned in regard to saving the nutrients in the foods you prepared and meeting your health needs with the money you could afford?

3. Was your meal attractively and properly served? Did you practice good manners?
4. Thinking through what you did and how you did it, can you make a plan to improve your breakfast menu, and the use of your time and energy?

 HOME EXPERIENCE

Discuss with your mother what you have learned concerning breakfast. With her, make a plan for a balanced menu for a week-end breakfast which you can prepare and serve for the family. Report results to your teacher.

FURTHER READING

Better Homes and Gardens New Cookbook. Meredith Press, Des Moines, Iowa, 1968.

Eat a Good Breakfast to Start a Good Day. Leaflet 268. U.S.D.A., Washington, D.C., 1959.

Encyclopedia of Cooking, Meta Givens. J. G. Ferguson and Associates, Chicago, Ill., 1955.

Family Fare: Food Management and Recipes. U.S.D.A., Washington, D.C., 1968.

Family Meals at Low Costs. U.S.D.A., Washington, D.C., 1962.

VISUAL AIDS

Better Breakfasts, U.S.A., a 16 mm color film on health and nutrition for intermediate and junior high school students. It emphasizes the importance of an adequate breakfast for teen-agers and tells the story of breakfast cereals and their nutritional value. The film is available free to educational libraries. Additional prints may be obtained at cost from the Cereal Institute, Inc., 135 La Salle Street, Chicago, Illinois 60603.

Food Models (for planning menus). National Dairy Council, Chicago, Ill. MB 196.

Visual Foods. Philadelphia Dairy Council, Philadelphia, Pa.

Which Breakfast Is Yours? (poster) National Dairy Council, Chicago, Ill.

Why Eat a Good Breakfast? Film strip. Full color, 34 frames with captions. Based on the Iowa Breakfast Studies. Available at cost from Midwest Film Studios, 6808 North Clark Street, Chicago, Ill.

unit **6**

You and Your Vegetables at Mealtime

How to Buy, Prepare, and Cook Vegetables

The Management of Vegetables in Your Meals

At few points in the management of family meals are more mistakes made than with vegetables. The troubles may begin at the market. Today you do not often have a clerk to tell you the name of the many vegetables displayed in the modern supermarket. Nor do you have someone to tell you how to cook a new vegetable, if you should buy it. There are vegetables from all over the United States, and we are importing vegetables from other countries as well. Vegetables may be bought frozen, canned, dried, pickled, and fresh in almost every market today.

A good vegetable soup made from high-quality vegetables is nourishing and inexpensive.

Most vegetables are important, but some are far more important than others in what they contribute to your health and your looks. You are likely to make poor choices in buying vegetables if you do not know the food values to be found in each one. This should be considered along with their cost and their flavor. Studies show that families eat far too few green leafy and yellow vegetables, yet these are among the best for health. Some home-makers do not try new vegetables because they do not know how to cook them. How, then, can they ever know if they like them?

One of the purposes of this unit is to help you become acquainted with a wide variety of vegetables. You will learn how to buy them and how to plan and cook balanced meals using them. While you stay at home, you can become something of a world traveler in the use of vegetables in your meals, for most of our vegetables originated in Asia and Europe. In this unit you will learn how to cook vegetables so that they taste good, look good, and retain as much of their health values as possible. This will help you to enjoy your meals more now, and to widen your acquaintance with vegetables so that you can do a better job in feeding the family when you have your own home.

How to Market for Vegetables

All that you have learned about marketing for other foods will help you market for vegetables. But in buying vegetables there are some special things you need to consider.

(1) Make your market list for vegetables on the basis of the meals you have planned. In planning your meals, keep in mind the food you have on hand, the different needs and likes of your family, the season of the year, and the health values in different foods, as well as the budget. Here is an example of how background knowledge helped Nancy shop for her mother.

Nancy and her mother made the meal plans and list of foods needed. Nancy did the shopping. The list had "one quart of Brussels sprouts," but Nancy noticed that the Brussels sprouts looked old. They had been trimmed and put back in the box. The tips of some leaves looked black. Also water was being sprayed over the boxes. It was running through the sprouts, carrying away nutritionally valuable vitamins and minerals.

Nancy turned the Brussels sprouts down as a very poor buy, even at 35¢ a quart, and bought fresh and crisp kale that was two pounds for 35¢.

The romaine lettuce, which was on her list, she found to be wilted and the leaves brown at the edges. She looked at the heads of iceberg lettuce. Although iceberg is the most popular variety, she knew this lettuce, which was more white than green, would not be rich in either vitamins or minerals. But large bunches of fresh escarole seemed to be of first quality and were less expensive than the romaine. She got twice as much lettuce by weight as the romaine she had intended to buy, and it was more nourishing and tasty than the iceberg lettuce.

The next item on her list was "two pounds of fresh green beans." She looked at the basket of green beans sitting in the sun. They were limp, bruised, and pale-colored. She looked at canned beans and frozen beans, read the labels, and remembered how each of these looked and tasted when cooked. The frozen green beans cost a little more, but her family liked the flavor and color. She reasoned there was no waste and they would save time and energy in preparing and cooking, as compared with the fresh ones. She knew that they were frozen at the peak of their maturity, and had the best food value under these circumstances. She bought them.

Instead of buying hothouse variety fresh tomatoes to use in Spanish rice, she went to the canned foods section of the store and selected grade C canned tomatoes. Her knowledge of food values and grades helped her save money and get more vitamin C in this choice.

The trust which Nancy's mother had placed in her was justified. This high school girl was a very fine manager of family food. With enough background information she was freed from following a list blindly. She used her knowledge to make quick and wise decisions in view of market conditions. This helped every member of the family. This type of experience will help Nancy when she has her own home.

Vegetables can be used in many ways to add interest and flavor to a luncheon or buffet supper for family or guests.

(2) When you buy fresh vegetables, select high quality. High quality fresh vegetables are firm, crisp, tender, and of equal maturity, and the color is good for its kind. Green vegetables should have a deep green color, and not a faded-out green. Wilting and black or brown edges indicate low quality, as do spoiled sections or bad spots. Fresh vegetables should look fresh—and good enough to eat raw.

(3) Figure out how soon you will use a fresh vegetable, and don't over-buy. Much money is wasted by buying more fresh vegetables than a family can eat immediately or store properly to maintain their food value.

Many people in Europe shop for fresh vegetables every day. This is not necessary in our country because of superior facilities for transporting vegetables to market and for storing them at home. Once a week is often enough to shop for fresh food if you have adequate refrigeration. Fresh perishable vegetables should be properly cooked or stored as soon as possible after being purchased.

(4) The price of fresh vegetables varies with the season, the locality, and the abundance of the crop. You can save money and have a wider variety of food by planning your meals to use the vegetables as they come in season. That is one reason why it is wise to shop personally for perishable vegetables. You can keep up with the changes in market variety, quality, and prices.

(5) In deciding whether it is wisest to use fresh, frozen, canned, or dried vegetables, you must keep in mind what you learned in the unit on fruits, and an understanding of what follows in the remaining chapters in this unit will be helpful too. Vegetables are frozen or canned in peak condition. You can look at the fresh vegetable and judge the quality on this point, comparing it to other methods of preparation. The freezing process for quick-frozen foods causes almost no loss in vitamins. This method of preparing vegetables for the market most closely resembles gathering vegetables fresh from your own garden The proper canning of vegetables causes no greater loss of vitamins than cooking fresh ones properly at home. Dried vegetables show a greater loss in vitamins.

Besides keeping these things in mind, make a study for yourself. Count the number of servings you get for the same amount of money in fresh, frozen, and canned food of a given variety. Compare flavor, food value, and appearance of the vegetable, as well as cost. Take into account the time, energy, and fuel saved by using one kind instead of another. When you have considered all of these points, you can make a wise choice on which is the best buy.

How to Prepare Vegetables for Cooking

When you have done a good job buying vegetables, it is important to get them to the table in peak condition. Here are some suggestions to help you.

(1) Use first the more perishable vegetables, such as leafy greens. Mushrooms should be cooked immediately. Even one day of standing causes spoilage. Root vegetables are not as perishable and can be held until the more perishable ones are used. For flavor and nutrients, the best time to cook a fresh vegetable is as

soon as it is picked from the garden. Since most of us get our fresh food from a market, prompt cooking is even more important.

(2) In washing vegetables, fill the sink with cold water first, then wash. This is to save vitamins and minerals from loss by soaking. Thorough washing removes not only dirt, but any remaining spray. This is better accomplished if a small amount of vegetable is washed and dried at a time. If you wrap green leafy vegetables in a clean towel, it absorbs remaining water. Then remove from towel and store in a plastic bag in the hydrator (vegetable container) of the refrigerator.

(3) In preparing vegetables to cook, leave the skins on, if possible. Otherwise, pare as thin as you can in order to save vitamins and minerals. The less chopping, the more vitamins and minerals remain in a vegetable. Shell peas or lima beans, or shuck corn, just before cooking. If you wish shelled peas and beans, buy frozen or canned, rather than the ones shelled in the store. Prepare fresh vegetables for cooking just before time to cook and serve the meal. All of these steps save vitamins for which you have paid.

How to Cook Vegetables

The aim in cooking vegetables is to produce a dish that is as attractive, delicious, and nourishing as possible. While it is important to eat some raw vegetables, it is not an easy matter for us to eat as many vegetables as we need if we eat all of them raw. Cooking reduces the bulk, softens fiber, and aids in the digestion, absorption, and the use of more vegetables in the diet.

There are two basic methods of cooking vegetables: by moist heat and by dry heat. Moist heat is used in cooking by steam in a pressure saucepan; in "waterless" cooking; in boiling; in frying; and in cooking by steam in casserole dishes. Dry heat is used in baking and broiling.

Each of these methods is well suited to certain types of vegetables. Baking is a good method for some vegetables. There is naturally less loss of the flavor and nutrients in baking than when vegetables are peeled and boiled. Vegetables such as potatoes, onions, and winter squash are delicious when baked in the skins. Tomatoes, eggplant, potatoes, and mushrooms are suited to broiling.

If you wish to achieve the stated aims for cooking vegetables, which method would you choose? Boiling is the method chosen by most homemakers in the past. It has been severely criticized as "the biggest murderer of vitamins, minerals, and flavor." This is because homemakers use too much water in boiling the vegetable, and often pour it down the drain. Lost: much of the health value and flavor! You can do better than this.

A good method in boiling is "waterless" cooking. Actually water is used, but just enough to produce steam to soften the fiber in the vegetable and reduce its bulk (in the case of green leafy vegetables). It can be very satisfactory if properly done.

(1) Use a firm, thick, but light saucepan with a handle and a tight-fitting lid. It should be a type which keeps out light and distributes heat evenly.

(2) Use as small an amount of *boiling water* as possible. The aim is to have no more than one or two tablespoonfuls left when the vegetable is tender.

TIME TABLE FOR COOKING FRESH VEGETABLES, AND AMOUNTS TO BUY*
(boiling or waterless cooking)**

Name	Approximate Time After Vegetable Starts to Boil (Minutes)	Approximate Number of Servings in 1 lb.
GREEN LEAFY VEGETABLES		
Beet tops	5-12	3
Broccoli	5-13	3
Brussels sprouts	10-12	5
Cabbage (shredded)	3-5	4
Chard	8-15	3
Collards	8-15	3
Dandelion	10-20	3
Kale	8-15	3
Mustard	15-25	3
Spinach	2-5	3
Turnip tops	8-25	3
OTHER VEGETABLES		
Asparagus	10-12	3
Beans, green lima in pod	20-30	1½
Beans, green snap	10-20	4
Beets, whole new	50-90	3
Carrots, young whole	15-20	3
Carrots, sliced	8-15	3-4
Cauliflower, small sections	5-8	3-4
Corn on Cob, 4 ears	1-2	4
Okra, whole	8-12	4
Onions, whole small	10-20	4
Peas, green, in pod	5-15	2
Parsnips, whole	15-25	4
quartered	7-15	4
Potatoes, whole	25-45	3
quartered	10-15	3
Sweet potatoes	25-35	3
Rutabaga, diced	20-30	3
Squash, summer, diced	8-10	3
winter	30-40	3
Tomatoes, quartered	5-8	3
Turnips, whole	30-40	3
quartered	15-25	3

*Time required to cook vegetables varies with size, tenderness of vegetable, amount cooked, kind of utensil used, and tightness of lid. Cook vegetables the least amount of time possible to make them tender, and use the least amount of water.

** Follow directions on the package for cooking frozen vegetables.

For use of *pressure* saucepan in cooking vegetables, follow the directions that come with the pan. Stop the time of cooking at once when the timer indicates it is done. Do this by running cold water over the lid to reduce the pressure.

Canned vegetables are already cooked. Remove liquid and boil it to reduce volume by one-half to two-thirds, then add vegetable and heat but do not boil.

(3) Cover pan after boiling water is added to vegetable.

(4) Cook until just tender and with firm texture by bringing vegetable to boil quickly with high heat, then reducing heat to a simmer.

(5) Serve hot, at once, and use all remaining vegetable water as a part of each serving. If no water remains in pan, add about one tablespoon. Rinse this over bottom of the pan and pour over the vegetable. This is to remove any minerals or vitamins that might cling to the bottom of the dry pan.

The *pressure saucepan* is excellent for cooking vegetables by steam. It takes much less fuel, time, and energy and saves the green color, firm texture, vitamins, minerals, and natural sugars, thus giving a better flavor. There are no disadvantages if the pressure saucepan is properly used. But if the vegetable is cooked too long, all of the above values may be lost.

The directions given on the pressure recipe-book are simple. You can easily learn to operate the pan properly. Briefly this is how:

(1) Place a small amount of water in pan (amount depends on kind and quantity of vegetable).

(2) Place rack in pan, bring water to boil, and add vegetables.

(3) Lock handle in place, and bring food to boil until steam escapes in steady stream from vent pipe.

(4) Place vent weight over vent pipe, and allow pressure to rise to 15 pounds on pressure indicator. (Studies show that in cooking vegetables no more vitamins are lost at 15 pounds pressure than at 5 pounds. This is because pressure cooking is done so quickly.)

(5) *Stay in the kitchen* and watch the cooker until desired pressure is reached. Then set timer, or carefully time with your clock. Such vegetables as green beans, green peas, asparagus, spinach, and green lima beans, require only a few seconds to cook. To save color when cooking a green vegetable, lower the pressure quickly by running a stream of cold water on the lid. Let the pressure go down before removing the vent weight.

(6) Serve at once with remaining vegetable water.

The pressure saucepan is one cooking utensil that lets the busy homemaker scoff at time. With it you can get a complete and balanced dinner in 30 to 40 minutes. For example: broil a steak, hamburger, or fish; cook carrots in pressure saucepan, and set aside in covered bowl; cook potatoes whole in skins; make a tossed salad or slaw; serve milk, bread, butter or margarine, and for dessert a canned or fresh fruit.

How to Save Color in Cooking Vegetables

Green is the color most treasured in fresh vegetables, and the easiest lost. Vegetables are more appetizing when a bright green, but unless the vegetables are overcooked, loss of color does not relate to loss of vitamins. This green color is due to the presence of chlorophyll (klō′rŏ fĭl) and it accompanies high vitamin and mineral content. When vegetables are heated very hot and for too long, acids inside the vegetables are released and turn the deep green color to an olive green. This can happen very rapidly.

This California teacher is demonstrating the use of local vegetables in a tossed salad (see recipe, page 390). In what ways do raw vegetables help your appearance? Your health? Which varieties of lettuce can you choose that are higher in vitamins C and A?

When the pressure cooker is properly used, color is retained. The vegetable does not get hot enough inside to release the acids.

There are two other ways to save green color without great loss of vitamins. One is to avoid overcooking. The other is to bring the vegetable to a boil quickly, if the waterless cooking method is used, then set the lid slightly ajar. The acids will escape into the air. Stir the vegetables once or twice during the cooking period to let acids escape and then replace the cover. Some homemakers add soda to preserve the green color, not knowing that soda destroys vitamin C and thiamine.

The red color in cabbage and beets is made more red by adding vinegar while cooking. But adding vinegar to a green vegetable immediately turns it olive green.

Other Ways to Cook Vegetables

We have already discussed the basic method of cooking vegetables by steam in the waterless cooker or the pressure saucepan. Here are some other ways that are occasionally used.

(1) *Broiling* is usually for meat, but some vegetables can be broiled. These include green or ripe tomatoes; raw or cooked potato or onion slices, mushrooms, eggplant, and green pepper. Shish Kebob, a Near East dish, is made by simply broiling meat and vegetables together on a skewer or stick. It is a delicious combination, especially for outdoor cooking.

The method for broiling is to season the food and brush each side with melted butter or oil. Then place the broiler about three inches from the broiling heat. Brown on one side, turn and brown on the other, and serve at once.

(2) *Panning* of vegetables is simply sautéing in a small amount of fat in a covered pan and cooking the vegetable in its own juices. This is an excellent way to cook vegetables to save the nutrients. It is fast and gives fine flavor and color to the food. It is a favorite method used in the orient and the Near East. The foods used in Shish Kebob (for instance, in Turkey) are also used in Gardener's Kebob by panning them together instead of broiling.

Panning is a quick way to cook many fresh or frozen vegetables to retain crisp texture, color, vitamins and minerals.

Panning is suited to almost any fresh or frozen vegetable (see page 393). Often several vegetables are used for panning, plus a little meat. This is a way to make meat go a long way. If properly planned and carried out, panning can give a good one-dish meal and saves vitamins and minerals.

The method is to use a skillet that suits the amount to be cooked and that has a tight-fitting lid. Place a small amount of fat in the pan, let it melt, and add vegetable pieces. Mix the vegetable thoroughly until all sides of the pieces are lightly covered with fat. This coating helps retain the vitamins and minerals and improves flavor. Season to taste, and cover. When steam begins to rise, turn down the heat and smmer until just tender (5 to 7 minutes). Serve at once.

(3) *Frying* vegetables can be done in two ways. One is frying in a small amount of fat, as in panning. This is suited to potatoes, eggplant, onion, squash, and croquettes. The method is to use a small amount of fat in a skillet. It is heated hot but not burning. The food is browned in an open skillet, turned and browned on the other side, then served at once. Fried food has a poor flavor if not served at once.

The other way is frying in deep fat; it is used mostly for potatoes and onions. This method is discussed in the study of fat in Chapter 23.

Seasoning of Vegetables

Good seasoning cannot make up for poor cooking, but it can add a lot to good cooking. Salt is of course the most important seasoning for vegetables, along with fat. (Iodized salt brings an added nutrient needed by the body.) Then come pepper (white and black) and paprika. Next we have the many herbs, such as:

parsley	garlic
mint	chives
horseradish	chervil
mustard	caraway seeds
dill	celery seed
hot and sweet peppers	mace
celery leaves	bay leaf
onions	rosemary

One teaspoon of fresh chopped herbs equals a half-teaspoon of the dried leaves, or a quarter-teaspoon of the powder.

Many young married girls today are more experimental with herbs than their mothers were. A set of different herbs is a choice wedding gift that brings showers of thanks from the bride.

In seasoning vegetables you can let your imagination go—to create a new flavor. You will need to experiment to find just the right amount and kind of herb that tastes best with each vegetable, but use a light touch. Seasoning, like perfume, should be used sparingly. Your aim is to create a delicate flavor that can hardly be analyzed! You will be surprised at what a tiny pinch of an herb can do to improve the flavor of carrots, cabbage, cauliflower, and turnips, as well as any of the greens. Fresh herbs are most desirable, though the dried leaves and powder are also good. Seasoning is a skill that you must develop for yourself. Cook vegetables properly, then season them to suit your taste.

Cooking Equipment

Good cooking equipment is important for health. It is more important to have the right cooking equipment for vegetables than to have the latest stove model. Poor cooking utensils cause loss of flavor and nutrients in vegetables. If you use good equipment you can also save time and energy in preparing food. Good cooking equipment need not be the most expensive, but should include as a minimum the following, and meet these standards.

(1) A set of three saucepans of graduated size. Handy sizes include 1 quart, 1½ to 2 quart, and 3 to 4 quart; there should also be a ten-inch skillet with lid. These should have handles that are removable, so that the pan can convert into a casserole. They should be made of heavy enough material to prevent warping and to spread heat evenly on bottom, sides, and top. They should have tight-fitting lids which do not admit light.

(2) Small equipment should include: two sharp paring knives, one butcher knife, knife sharpener, peeler, vegetable brush, spatula, wooden spoon, egg beater, big fork, slotted spoon, timer, can opener, chopping board, and covered refrigerator dishes.

(3) One each of these: set of mixing bowls, set of measuring cups, set of measuring spoons, colander, food chopper, grater, potato masher, tea kettle, 1- to 1½-quart casserole, 2- to 2½-quart covered casserole, set of baking pans, pot holders, tea towels, and plastic bags for vegetables.

(4) One pressure saucepan of the size best suited to your family. If you are buying a new pressure saucepan, take a look at the automatic ones. They have heat unit, pressure and time control, and automatic valve for letting out excess steam.

WORDS TO WORK WITH

Chlorophyll (klō′rŏ fĭl): green coloring matter in plants.

Iodized salt: salt treated with iodine to supplement needed minerals. (See page 245.)

THINKING IT OVER

1. Why is the management of vegetables in our meals so important?

2. Give examples of how you can save money in shopping for vegetables if you know food values.

3. Why was Nancy able to change her mind so quickly about the best buy in vegetables? Do you think the changes were for the good? Why?

4. Describe the best way to wash and put away fresh vegetables.

5. Why should vegetables not be soaked in water? Do you think many people soak vegetables? Why should the water be dried from green leaves before refrigerating them?

6. When is the best time to cook vegetables for a meal? How can poor timing affect color, flavor, and nutrients?

7. Describe how to cook vegetables properly by the boiling or waterless cooking method. The pressure cooking method.

8. Why is a small amount of water desirable in cooking vegetables?

9. What health values may go down the drain if you pour off the vegetable water?

10. What is a desirable way to save the green color in cooking vegetables? Why not use soda? Does loss of color mean loss of vitamins? Explain.

11. In what ways can poor methods of cooking vegetables hurt your health and looks? Your food budget?

PROBLEMS TO SOLVE

1. Learning cooking equipment by seeing.
   (1) With your class or your mother, or alone, make a trip to a good department or hardware store to study cooking equipment. Observe:
       (a) The variety and price of equipment available.
       (b) The different uses that can be made of each piece.
       (c) Sizes of equipment to fit needs of different families.
   (2) Pool results of your studies as a class, decide which type you would select

if you needed this equipment now, and give reasons.

APPLYING WHAT YOU KNOW

1. Learning to use different equipment in cooking vegetables.
   (1) Select a vegetable that you enjoy eating and cook part by the waterless cooking method and some in the pressure saucepan. Take all points you have learned into consideration when you compare results.
   (2) Select a vegetable which you have never eaten and prepare by the two above methods, comparing results.

2. Plan menus for two balanced dinners, including the vegetable you selected.

EVALUATING

1. Which method of cooking gave the best color, texture, flavor?

2. Which method saved the most nutrients? The most fuel? The most money?

3. Was your vegetable tender by each method of cooking? Was it overcooked?

4. Was the seasoning well blended in each method used? Did the vegetable taste good?

5. Which method do you think you used more successfully? Is this your fault or the fault of the method? Can you make a plan to get better results next time?

HOME EXPERIENCE

Discuss with your mother what you have learned, and if possible make a plan to buy any new cooking equipment your family needs. Plan a balanced meal including the vegetable you learned to prepare. Prepare and serve this vegetable as a part of the family meal. Report results to your teacher.

The Importance of
Green Leafy Vegetables

Vegetables, with fruits and cereal-grains, make up the plant foods in our diet. The various kinds of vegetables have much in common, yet each makes its own distinct contribution to our meals.

Why Variety in Vegetables Is Important

Almost no other food group can give such great variety to meals as vegetables. They give variety in *color*, and thus make meals much more attractive. They give variety in *texture* and *flavor*, adding enjoyment to eating. While all the common

What varieties of cabbage are in this picture? Which varieties are missing? How many have you eaten?

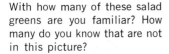

With how many of these salad greens are you familiar? How many do you know that are not in this picture?

vegetables are good foods, some are far more important to your health and looks than others. Approximately 200 kinds of vegetables are grown in the United States. How many of these can you name when you see them? How many have you eaten? How many can you cook so that they are tasty and attractive and retain as much nourishment as possible? Do you know which are the most important for your health and looks?

We think of our country as one with abundant food, and that is correct. But unless you as an individual make a wise use of this food you do not profit from it. Of all food groups, vegetables are least liked by children. We each have to learn to like different vegetables, and we usually like what we are used to eating. A study in one of our rich agricultural states, for instance, showed that 90 per-cent of the students ate these seven vegetables: potatoes, carrots, lettuce, cabbage, peas, tomatoes, and celery. While these are fine, cabbage is the only green leafy vegetable in the group to cook. The reason given for not eating a wider variety of vegetables was not so much that they disliked others, but that they had not tasted them. By including a variety of the important vegetables in your meals regularly, you can acquire a taste for them all, and in so doing, improve your personal vitality and better your appearance.

The greatest contribution vegetables (and fruits) make to your health and appearance is through the vitamins and minerals they contain. As you go forward in this unit, you will learn to prepare and serve a variety of important vegetables.

Vegetables Help Keep Your Body Chemistry in Balance

Vegetables and fruits as a whole help keep the chemistry of the body on the alkaline side—and that is the state of the normal healthy body. Alkaline is the opposite of acid. When you are in good health, you are equipped to use efficiently the food you eat, whether it is acid- or alkaline-forming. It is important that you understand this, for much misinformation is put out that tends to create a fear that you may not be getting the alkaline foods you need, and should take some special product to make up for this lack. What are the facts?

Here is what is meant by the alkaline or acid effect of foods. The alkaline- or acid-forming substances in foods are minerals. These minerals remain after food is burned in the body. Those that produce acid are found in the rich protein foods such as meat and eggs. The foods containing minerals, such as calcium, which produce alkaline effect when burned by the body, are milk, vegetables, and fruits.

If you eat the balanced diet recommended on pages 14–15, your meals will supply more foods that give alkaline elements than acid ones. You cannot tell whether a food is acid or alkaline by taste. Oranges, grapefruit, lemons, and apples taste sour, and you might think that these would give an acid reaction in the body. This is not the case. They are alkaline. Therefore when you hear a person say he cannot eat oranges or apples because they are acid-forming, you can be sure that this statement is not based on facts. It would be more accurate if the person said he could not eat meat because it is acid-

What are the advantages in bringing the salad bowl to the table and adding the salad dressing there?

forming. Both statements are misleading, however, because of the body's great ability to maintain the proper chemical balance between acid and alkaline foods.

There are a few fruits that are acid-forming, such as plums, prunes, and cranberries. In general, though, vegetables and fruits are quite important in your diet to give the proper minerals to balance the meat and eggs you eat. If you really need an alkalizing product, you should see your physician.

The minerals and vitamins found in the vegetables (and fruits) which you eat also assist in the normal elimination of waste. This is partly due to the fact that they help build healthy soft tissue in the long digestive tract, thus assisting in a more vigorous movement of the waste products. Then too, the soft undigested bulk of vegetables and fruits also forms a "roughage" (rŭf'ĭj). This bulky material helps push the waste through the intestinal tract, aiding in normal elimination. Vegetables and fruits also promote good hygiene in the intestinal tract. As a whole they are weak in protein, and should be eaten in a balanced diet with milk, eggs, and meat to help offset this weakness. Some of these foods are high in calories, but most are low. Fat content is low. Let us now look more closely at the differences in a variety of common vegetables.

Green Leafy Vegetables Are Tops, Yellow Ones Are Next

You have learned that some nutrients in plants are made in the leaves. As you study the tables on food values, you will notice that the green leafy vegetables stand highest in most of the vitamins and minerals in which your diet is likely to be low. There are at least a dozen deep-green leafy vegetables that may be cooked, and as many that may be used raw in salads. Yet in diet studies it has been found that people do not eat as many green leafy or yellow vegetables as they need.

A cartoonist called our attention to the great health values found in the green leafy vegetables. No matter how difficult the task, when Popeye ate his spinach, his strength was equal to the challenge. Many boys must have learned to like spinach through the example of Popeye. While he didn't have the same appeal to girls, they did get the idea that spinach had something to offer. And if it had so much,

In the bowl are basic ingredients for tossed salad. How can you vary these ingredients to make a main-dish salad?

then why not other green leafy vegetables too! As a matter of fact, other green leafy vegetables are more valuable than spinach, as you shall soon see.

It is in the green leaf of the plant that vitamins are made. Here minerals are also richly established. The leaf also makes sugars, starches, and amino acids. It does this with the help of nutrients which the roots take up from the soil and pass to the leaf through the stem. With water and sunshine and nutrients from the soil, the green leaf performs a miracle in growth. Understanding this helps you see the great importance of including green leafy vegetables in your diet.

The big contribution of the green leafy vegetables and the yellow vegetables and fruits (and also certain red and dark-colored ones) is in the yellow coloring matter referred to as carotene (kăr′ŏ tēn). This substance is partially converted by the body into vitamin A. (However, some yellow coloring is not due to this substance, for instance the yellow in oranges and rutabagas.)

We need the green leafy and yellow vegetables to add vitamin A to our diet. A half-cup serving of kale, turnip greens, collards, or other green leafy vegetables can add between 4000 and 5000 units of vitamin A to your diet. A half-cup of tomato juice adds 1000, and a half-cup of cooked apricots can add about 4275 units. One deep yellow sweet potato can add 11,000 units or more, and a half-cup of cooked carrots 7500 units. Thus we see that vitamin A is all around us in the green leafy and yellow vegetables and fruits. You simply need to be aware of this fact, and plan your meals and snacks to include a generous amount of these foods every day. Unlike vitamin C, vitamin A is stored in the body, and it is not necessary to have it in every meal. Yet diet studies repeatedly show that teenagers and others do not have enough vitamin A in their diets to supply the quantity recommended for health.

Aside from citrus fruits and tomatoes, the green leafy vegetables are also one of our best sources of vitamin C. (As you recall, there is often too little of this vitamin in the diet.) One-half cup of cooked broccoli, for instance, gives 65 milligrams of vitamin C when properly cooked. Turnip greens, kale, the cabbage family, and other green leafy vegetables are also quite high in vitamin C. Of course this vitamin (as well as other water-soluble vitamins) is lost in cooking water. It is destroyed by oxygen from standing after the vegetables are chopped or by standing after they are cooked. Vitamin C and thiamine are destroyed by adding soda.

In addition, green leafy vegetables (along with the dried bean group) are the best of the vegetables for the B vitamins. This makes them even more important to us, since there are often not enough B vitamins in the diet.

The green leafy vegetables contribute three minerals that may not be well represented in your diet—iron, calcium, and magnesium.

The newly recommended B vitamin *folacin*, which helps build red blood cells, is also found in leafy green vegetables.

These vegetables are of particular importance to those who have a weight-control problem. They are low in calories, but high in essential vitamins and minerals. They help your general vitality and appearance, as well as your figure.

Kinds of Green Leafy and Yellow Vegetables

Some green leafy and yellow vegetables can be eaten raw daily. But you can eat more if you cook some of these vegetables and serve them as a part of the meal.

The cabbage family is the largest in this group. There is the white head cabbage, kale, broccoli, collards, green savoy cabbage, Brussels sprouts, purple cabbage, and an important cabbage product, sauerkraut. Cauliflower and kohlrabi also belong to this family, though they are not of the green leafy variety.

Cabbage is inexpensive, hardy, and is easily grown in a wide variety of climates. It can be purchased in some form in almost any food store at any season of the year in our country. The health values described above for the green leafy vegetable can be claimed by most cabbages.

Members of the cabbage family have had a bad reputation in the past, and many people claim they do not like them. This is because they have been so poorly cooked. The overcooking of any member of the cabbage family produces an unpleasant aroma, flavor, texture, and color. But when properly cooked, the cabbages make attractive and delicious dishes. When you have learned to cook these vegetables correctly, you will enjoy the flavor, add variety to your meals, and enrich the health value of your diet.

Other green leafy vegetables to cook include turnip greens, mustard greens, celery tops to mix with other greens, and onion blades. All of these greens as well as those in the cabbage family are delicious when cooked with a ham hock, fat pork, or minced bacon and onion. Greens go especially well with ham, pork chops, pork roast, or any other form of pork. However, they are also tasty with any meat you enjoy.

There is a group of green leafy vegetables—spinach, beet tops, chard, and wild greens—which contains oxalic acid. Unfortunately for us, this substance combines with calcium and is insoluble in the digestive tract. It therefore interferes with the absorption and use of calcium. This naturally makes these greens less valuable to us than the others mentioned above. However, if you place a clean egg shell in the pan when you are cooking one of these greens, the calcium from the egg shell tends to "tie up" the oxalic acid, thus

Brussels sprouts—a winter green vegetable often served for family or holiday dinner.

making the vegetable a more desirable food.

The green leafy vegetables which we eat raw are especially important for vitamin C, but because they are so bulky raw, we cannot eat as much. For instance, a large salad of leaf lettuce makes only about one-quarter cup when this is wilted in hot fat and vinegar.

The salad greens include green leaf lettuce of different varieties, Boston lettuce, curly endive or chicory, escarole, romaine, iceberg lettuce, Chinese cabbage, white cabbage, purple cabbage, celery leaves, onion blades, chives, parsley, and watercress. Then there are many other vegetables that may be combined with these greens to make interesting salads for flavor, texture, and color and to add a variety of nutrients. These include tomatoes, carrots, celery stalks, onions, radishes, green and red bell peppers, cucumbers, green fresh peas, cauliflower, grated beets, green beans, spinach, and broccoli.

For a discussion on how to buy, prepare, and cook vegetables, see the preceding chapter.

The Vegetable Salad

For many people in the past, salad did not bring a rich supply of vitamin C to the diet. Some ate only relishes, such as pickles and olives or potato and macaroni salad. Today, however, the green salad is widely accepted as an important part of lunch and dinner.

These meals are more satisfying when they include the firm texture and bright color of a salad. There are many different types of salads, using only vegetables, or vegetables and fruits, or these foods combined with cheese, meat, fish, or poultry. The salad can and should be an excellent source of vitamin C. By using greens, tomatoes, and other vegetables in season, you can achieve variety and make the best use of your money.

Salads are sometimes used as a first course or appetizer. Usually this is a combination of citrus fruits with other fruits, served on a bed of green lettuce or watercress. Often melon is used, alone or in combination with other fruits. When the salad is served as the first course, you do not usually serve another raw food. Sometimes, however, you might also have a plate of celery, radishes, and the like.

Salad may be served as the main dish at lunch, and is then often referred to as "chef's salad bowl." When it is the main dish, it should contain about two ounces of cheese, meat, fish, or poultry per serving to meet the need for protein. Stuffed or chopped eggs may also be used for protein in the main dish salad. There are many types of main dish salads. One is with fruits (fresh, canned, frozen) combined with lettuce. This salad can have a mound of cottage cheese in the center for protein; or toasted cheese sandwiches can be served with it. An exotic type of fruit salad is avocado stuffed with a mixture of crab, lobster, or shrimp, and served with a garnish of lime on a bed of green lettuce or watercress.

The salad is more attractive and tasty if you combine at least two types of lettuce. Iceberg lettuce is the least nourishing of the lettuces (when the leaves are white), yet it is most widely used. Improvement is being made in growing greener iceberg lettuce. If you especially like the flavor of iceberg, try other kinds of lettuce with it, and you will find the flavor and appearance improved.

Most often the salad accompanies the main meal. It may be a combination of vegetables and fruits, or either alone, or a bowl of raw vegetables such as carrot sticks or celery. When the salad is a part of the meal, it should blend in color and texture and bring out the flavor of the meal. It may be served from a bowl, or on a five- or seven-inch salad plate.

A salad is often served with a beverage and a small hot bread or cracker or other type of bread as the refreshment for a party. Fruit or gelatin salads are favorites but many other kinds may be served. Many people who understand food values prefer a salad to an over-sweet or fat dessert as a party refreshment. Indeed, one way to have your refreshments highly appreciated is to serve an attractive, tasty salad which your friends can count as meeting part of their total nutritive need for the day. A salad for dessert is usually served on a seven-inch plate, which is large enough that no ingredients spill over.

A well-chosen, well-prepared salad can enliven a meal or a party. It can give a bright note of color to carry out a color scheme you may have. It can give the firm texture we enjoy in contrast to so much soft food we eat. It can add a tangy flavor to a meal that might otherwise be too mild. Some hostesses are famous for their excellent salads. How can you achieve this result?

What Makes a Good Salad?

No dish tastes any better than the ingredients which make it. This is especially true of the salad. To make a good salad:

(1) Select green lettuce and other ingredients of high quality. The ingredients should be fresh, crisp, and properly washed and dried so that they are clean but no water clings, and they should be cold.

(2) Prepare the salad (except gelatin) just before serving. Raw vegetables and fruits which are cut, chopped, or shredded and left standing at room temperature lose vitamin C rapidly. If it is necessary to prepare ingredients by chopping ahead of time, cover with foil or similar material and place in the refrigerator. Break or cut ingredients in bite sizes. Use ingredients whose flavors blend together. Do not let vegetables stand in cold water to "freshen," as this leaches out, or dissolves, water-soluble vitamins, minerals, and natural sugars into the water.

(3) Combine a variety of vegetables or fruits to achieve quite different flavors. Two or three types of lettuce with a little grated onion give a simple but tasty and nourishing salad, especially if you use a nippy salad dressing. When green lettuce is not available or is too expensive, use cabbage. It combines well with either fruits or vegetables. For instance, with vegetables these combinations are possible at different seasons of the year: cabbage, onion, tomato; same plus bell pepper; same plus radishes; same plus celery; same plus cucumber; same plus carrot; or omit tomato from any of the above when it is not available.

Cabbage makes an excellent salad when combined with fruits, such as pineapple (fresh or canned), apple, orange, tangerine, grapefruit, grapes, banana. Celery or carrots may also be added to any of these combinations you enjoy. If you have not experimented with cabbage salad using fruit, you may be surprised at the excellent dishes you can turn out.

Enlarge your taste for salads by starting with the foods you do enjoy and adding others to them.

(4) If the ingredients are of high quality, then the salad dressing, if properly chosen, can blend the flavors and heighten the delicious taste of your salad. The French type of dressing is often preferred for green lettuce or combination salad. Sour cream, mayonnaise, and boiled salad dressings are good with fruit, and may be used effectively with vegetables. There are many variations of these basic dressings. Experiment and find the one for you.

Use enough dressing to blend the ingredients, but do not use more than is needed to accomplish this goal. Keep in mind that one tablespoon of oil or mayonnaise gives 100 calories, and that your salad combination of vegetables may contain no more than 15 calories. "Hidden" calories are often added to the diet through excess use of salad dressing. For those who have a weight-control problem, it might be well to use only lemon juice for the dressing, or use an oil dressing of one part oil to two parts lemon juice, which gives less calories than the usual dressing. Different types of vinegar also give variety in making the salad dressing.

(5) Experiment with herbs and seasonings in making salads and salad dressing. Try various combinations until you find just the blend that suits your taste. Onion and garlic can be used in small amounts to improve the flavor of either a fruit or a vegetable salad.

Here is an oil base which one homemaker finds exciting in a salad: In a pint

Cooking Green Leafy Vegetables (see recipe, page 391): (1) Broccoli cooks more evenly if the stems are split. (2) Spinach in season. (3) Young beet tops with the young beets.

Green leafy vegetables are highest in most of the vitamins and minerals in which the diet is likely to be low.

jar mix 1 cup of vegetable oil, 3 pieces of cinnamon bark, 1 crushed clove of garlic, 1 tablespoon grated onion, 1 teaspoon dry mustard, ¼ teaspoon celery seeds, 1 teaspoon salt, ¼ teaspoon basil, ¼ pound of minced blue cheese. Cover and let stand 24 hours before using. Store in the refrigerator. When ready to use, combine in equal parts with lemon juice or tarragon, wine, or cider vinegar, using only 1 tablespoon at a time for small amounts until you get the proper proportion. If you prefer a lower-calorie and more tart dressing, use 2 tablespoons of vinegar or lemon juice to one of oil.

If you make this dressing or one of your own favorite combination, it will add an individual flavor to your salads, and save you time and money.

(6) Keep fresh fruits such as apples and pears from turning dark after they are peeled by dipping in lemon juice; or use a commercial product which is sold at drugstores and some grocery stores for this purpose. Then store the fruit in the refrigerator until you are ready to use it.

(7) Unpeeled tomatoes may be used in salads if the skin is firm and smooth. If you wish to peel tomatoes, put them in boiling water for about 30 seconds or until the skin slips when pricked. Then plunge them into cold water, dry, and store in the refrigerator until ready to use. The skin slips off smoothly and evenly. This is

called "blanching," and may also be used effectively for peaches, if they are ripe. If you peel vegetables for salads, peel thinly with either a very sharp knife or a peeler, for as you learned in the preceding chapter, many of the best nutrients lie just beneath the skins.

(8) If some members of your family cannot eat the coarse, rough vegetables for a period, grind such foods as cabbage and carrots, mix with pineapple, gelatin, and mayonnaise, and make a delicious, nourishing salad that may be eaten by almost anyone.

The green leafy and yellow vegetables are important in your diet. You will be well repaid in the pleasure of eating and in more permanent benefits in health and personal attractiveness, if you learn to use them daily.

WORDS TO WORK WITH

Alkaline (ăl′ka lĭn): pertaining to a soluble salt or mineral obtained when plants are burned (outside or inside the body). The normal chemistry of the blood is slightly alkaline.

Carotene (kăr′ŏ tēn): a substance found in plants (usually associated with yellow and green ones), out of which the body can make vitamin A. It is also called *provitamin A.*

Folacin (fō′la sĭn): a B vitamin essential for normal red blood and life.

Roughage (rŭf′ĭj): soft bulk left over after the digestion and absorption of fruits, vegetables, and cereal-bread.

THINKING IT OVER

1. In what ways do vegetables make a meal more appetizing?

2. Which vegetables do you like best? Which least? About how many servings of vegetables do you eat daily?

3. How often do you eat green leafy vegetables? Yellow ones? Salads?

4. Why are green leafy vegetables so important, and why are the yellow and red vegetables and fruits so important? How can you use this knowledge to help you plan your meals more wisely?

5. Do you eat more vegetables fresh, frozen, canned, or dried?

6. What are the advantages of the cooked vegetable over the raw? The raw over the cooked? Why do we need both?

7. Look at the charts on pages 44 and 88. On the basis of what you have learned in this unit and preceding ones, explain how the use of the recommended vegetables and fruits daily might help you reach your goals for health and beauty.

8. How do vegetables and fruits assist in normal elimination? How do they help to keep the chemistry of the blood on the alkaline side? How do they help maintain good intestinal hygiene?

9. Describe the best way to prepare and serve a salad. How may salads be used in balanced meals, and what type of dressing is best suited to different kinds of salad?

PROBLEMS TO SOLVE

1. Learning to improve your food habits.
   (1) Keep a record of the food you eat for

one week, and check how often you had a green leafy vegetable; a yellow vegetable or fruit; a salad.

(2) What were they, and how were they served?

(3) Do you need to include more? Can you make a plan for improvement?

2. Marketing for green and yellow vegetables.

(1) Make a trip to the market and prepare a list of the fresh green vegetables available at this season in your market. How will this change with other seasons? How does the quantity of vegetables available for the market affect the price?

(2) What fresh yellow vegetables are available at this season?

(3) Compare the variety and cost of the fresh foods you have seen with those of canned and frozen foods. Decide which would be the best buy for the vegetables you wish to purchase. What will influence your decision?

APPLYING WHAT YOU KNOW

1. Planning menus using green and yellow vegetables and salads.

(1) Plan three balanced dinner menus in which you use a different cooked green leafy vegetable each day; plan three dinner menus using a different cooked yellow vegetable each day.

(2) Plan menus in which a salad is used for a first course for dinner; as the main dish at noon; as an accompaniment to the main part of the meal at dinner; as a party refreshment.

2. Preparing and cooking vegetables as part of the balanced menus you have planned.

(1) Select and cook one or more of these by either the pressure saucepan method or waterless cooking: white cabbage, purple cabbage, kale, broccoli, Brussels sprouts, or collards.

(2) Use different seasonings in cooking turnip greens, mustard greens, or any of the cabbage family, and compare flavors.

(3) Cook carrots and try different seasonings such as mint leaves (dried or fresh), grated onion, orange peel, and honey.

(4) Prepare as many different types of salads as time permits, using the vegetables and fruits in season.

EVALUATING

1. Did the vegetable retain its color by each method of cooking?

2. Was it tender in texture but not mushy?

3. How much water was left by each method?

4. Was the vegetable tasty, with seasoning well blended?

5. How can you do better when you use each method again?

HOME EXPERIENCE

With your mother's help, plan three balanced dinners for your family.

Use a vegetable cooked by one method at one dinner and by another method at the second meal. Serve a salad at the third meal. Prepare the vegetable each time yourself and serve it as a part of these meals. Report results to your teacher.

Other Vegetables
for Lunch and Dinner

How Do Vegetables Compare in Food Values?

The most important vegetables from the standpoint of health are green leafy and yellow vegetables, tomatoes, potatoes (yellow and white), raw cabbage, dried beans, peas, and lentils. These vegetables give much nourishment in relation to their cost. They should be frequently used in meals.

There are many other vegetables that give your meals variety in flavor, texture, color, and nourishment. Learn to cook these, and use them in season. In addition to the leaves of plants, we eat stems, roots, tubers, flowers, and seeds.

Carrots, once called "rabbit food," are now popular with all age groups. How much vitamin A does ½ cup cooked carrots yield? raw?

The Most Popular Vegetables Are Also Nourishing Ones

Popular vegetables include green peas, green beans, corn, and potatoes. We eat them fresh, canned, frozen, and dried. Green peas and green beans compare favorably to the green leafy vegetables in nourishment, and corn is a good alternate for potatoes.

Stem Vegetables

Many vegetables fall into two classes. Corn is an example because it is both a stem vegetable and a seed. The fact that it can produce a new plant indicates that it is a nourishing food. Fresh corn on the cob is delicious, but it is frequently overcooked. Hybrid sweet corn should be boiled only one minute for the best flavor. Other stem vegetables include celery, asparagus, and kohlrabi of the cabbage family. Asparagus is a stem often used for special dinners, banquets, and luncheons. It has spears (tight little leaves) along the stem, which should be thoroughly scrubbed to remove the sand that gets caught there. Some people prefer to scrape off these spears.

Celery stems and leaves are excellent for seasoning vegetables and meat. They blend with greens, peas, tomatoes, and all green or dried beans to give a delightful flavor. They add flavor to soups, stews, Spanish rice, and macaroni dishes. Celery is most often used raw in sticks three to six inches long as a food to eat with the fingers, or it is chopped and used in salads.

Pascal celery which is tender and green, is more nourishing than white celery. The stems should be washed thoroughly, but not scraped. Trim only the bruised and brown spots, and use every leaf that is not spoiled. The green leaves and green stem are the most nourishing parts.

Mushrooms, another stem vegetable, add interesting texture to soups, creamed dishes, soufflés, and meat, and contain a worthwhile amount of iron. However, they are highly perishable, and should be used the day purchased.

Flower and Fruit Vegetables

Botanists classify some vegetables as flower clusters, such as broccoli, and some as fruits, such as tomatoes. Cauliflower, truly a "flower" vegetable, is nourishing

Green beans can be prepared and cooked in a variety of ways: (1) French cut beans. What other ways would you cut beans for variety? (2) Green beans cooked with small white onions. They are also tasty combined with small potatoes or okra. (3) Canned beans with a sauce of sour cream, grated onion, and Parmesan cheese.

and reasonably priced. Use it frequently in season either in salads or raw along with celery, carrot sticks, or other "finger foods." It is tasty when cooked plain and seasoned with sour cream and raw grated onion, and superior when served with the sharp cheese sauce you learned to make in your study of milk.

Eggplant, all types of summer squash, yellow winter squash, cucumber, okra, pumpkin, and bell peppers begin as flowers and develop into fruits. You will remember the high vitamin C content of bell peppers, and the high vitamin A content of the yellow squash and pumpkin.

Okra, a deep green vegetable most popular in the Southern part of our country, is as tasty when frozen as when fresh. It requires only a few minutes to cook and is delicious served with butter, salt, and pepper. It combines well with other foods in soups and combination dishes with chicken and fish.

Root and Tuber Vegetables

The root and tuber vegetables are popular and important. These include white potato, sweet potato, onion, garlic, and carrots.

In addition there are beets, parsnips, and white and yellow turnips (the yellow turnip is also known as rutabaga). The root vegetables as a group are high in starch. Parsnips are about equal to potatoes in calories and should be used as an alternate for potatoes.

Frozen Vegetables

Frozen vegetables have many of the qualities we enjoy in garden-fresh vegetables. Freezing of food is a highly perfected science today. Vegetables are harvested at the peak of maturity, and quickly frozen to retain their fresh color, flavor, and nourishment. When frozen vegetables are kept frozen until they go into your saucepan in the kitchen, you have the benefit of fresh garden vegetables without the labor of trimming and cleaning them. Indeed, one of the big points in favor of frozen vegetables is the time, energy, and fuel they save in cooking, but that is not all.

With frozen foods, fresh vegetables are always in season. Often frozen vegetables

Steps in Preparing Corn on the Cob: (1) Season and wrap in foil. (2) Cook in pressure saucepan at 15 pounds pressure for 30 seconds, or boil for 1 minute. (3) Serve quickly to retain warmth and flavor.

are of much higher quality for flavor and nutrients than so-called "fresh" vegetables which were harvested several days before reaching your table.

Many highly perishable vegetables are frozen today. Among the green leafy vegetables you can buy frozen turnip greens, collards, kale, broccoli, Brussels sprouts, spinach, and mustard greens. Then there are other frozen green vegetables, such as green peas, green and yellow beans, okra, and asparagus. There are mixed vegetables, cauliflower, carrots, potatoes (cooked and frozen), squash, artichoke hearts, and many others. If you do not see these vegetables in the store, ask your grocer to order them, for they are available.

In buying frozen vegetables, read the label. The standards have not yet been as widely set for frozen foods as for canned ones, but the weight, the price, and the name of the processor are on the package. You will also find directions for cooking. Look over a package of frozen food; if it shows signs of having thawed and been refrozen, it is not a good buy. Thawed vegetables lose vitamin C very quickly, and enzymes go to work to cause fast spoilage. A frozen food that has an "off" odor should be discarded. Store frozen food in the freezing unit of the refrigerator as soon as you bring it home from the market.

To cook frozen vegetables, remove from the refrigerator and place in saucepan at once. To thaw before cooking may cause loss of vitamin C. Frozen vegetables require very little water and very little time to cook. In the pressure saucepan, a vegetable such as frozen peas is tender by the time the pressure reaches 15 pounds.

Steps in Cooking Beets: (1) Scrub clean and cut stems, leaving about 3 inches: place in pressure saucepan with 1½ cups of water and cook according to the timetable on page 125. (2) Peel and store in refrigerator until ready to use. (3) Here the beets are seasoned with raw onion rings, lemon juice, marjoram leaves, and pepper. In what other ways might they be served?

Cook until just tender and no more. Then serve the vegetable at once to enjoy the most nourishment and best flavor.

Canned Vegetables

It is quite a fascinating experience to go through the canned vegetable department of a modern supermarket. You can find almost any variety of vegetable from our country, and many from other lands. Since the introduction of modern commercial canning, the human diet has been greatly improved. Canned food has many advantages. It is completely sterilized, that is, all bacteria, molds, and yeasts have been destroyed. It will keep indefinitely without spoiling until the can is opened. Canned food is easy to store, and easy to transport. It is cooked and ready to serve with only heating and seasoning.

The acids which cause a bright green vegetable to turn an olive green cannot escape in canning; so canned green vegetables are not as attractive as the fresh and frozen. To some people this is a disadvantage. Also the texture of canned vegetables is sometimes softer than some people prefer. However, these two factors affect only the appearance and texture of the vegetable, and not the food value.

Foods are canned at the height of maturity. This is exactly the right time for the best flavor and nourishment. If a field of peas is just past the peak, for instance, a canner with high standards will pass this crop over and use it for seed. The canning industry uses modern scientific knowledge to bring you a canned vegetable that is carefully tended from the selection of the seed to the rapid harvest and immediate canning. Steps are now taken to save even more nutrients. For instance, cans are shaken while being heated. This distributes the heat fast and cuts down the time of cooking, thus saving more vitamins. Canned food got a bad reputation at one time because of its low vitamin C content. But with our knowledge of balancing the diet today, and improved methods of canning, this criticism is no longer so serious.

The canning industry has done much to bring the homemaker a high-quality, nourishing product, but the homemaker may further destroy the vitamin C and other nutrients by overcooking the food or by pouring the water from the can down the drain.

To save health values in your vegetables, open the can just before using it, heat without boiling, and serve at once. The vegetable water may be saved and used in a number of ways. Here are a few suggestions:

(1) Serve vegetable juice with vegetable.

(2) Drain juice from can into sauce pan, and boil until about one-third cup remains. Add vegetable, season, heat, and serve.

(3) Brown an onion with minced bacon, add 1½ tablespoons of flour, and add vegetable water and evaporated milk to make one cup. Cook until smooth, then add vegetable, season, heat, and serve.

(4) To vegetable sauce add one cup grated sharp cheese.

(5) Add the vegetable juice to soup or gravy.

(6) Mix the vegetable juice with tomato juice and add grated onion and lemon juice. Chill and serve as an appetizer.

Butternut squash, a deep yellow autumn and winter vegetable that is rich in vitamin A, may be cooked in many different ways. How many have you tried?

The canners are doing a good job for us today, and you can give your family variety in flavor and nourishment through properly prepared canned vegetables.

Dried Vegetables

Beans, peas, and lentils are the chief dried vegetables we use. But we may soon eat more dried foods, for a freeze-dry method is being perfected to improve them so as to compare with fresh food. It is possible that this new method of dehydrating (dē hī′drāt) food may greatly change our cooking habits. The old-fashioned method of drying food lost vitamins. Scientists are trying to save the vitamins by this new method. You may wish to follow the work of scientists as they report their studies of food.

One piece of pumpkin pie supplies about one-third of your recommended daily need for vitamin A (recipe p. 398).

(7) Use the vegetable water as the liquid to make a vegetable gelatin salad.

(8) Cook other vegetables in the juice —for instance, raw carrots in the juice from canned peas, green beans, or asparagus.

Learn to read labels in buying vegetables, and observe which brand has the most solid food in proportion to liquid. Measure each after opening a can. You may find that a brand which sells for less costs you more money for the same weight, for it may contain more water in proportion to food. You will have to learn this by experience. Then you can know which brand gives you the most for your money. In buying a new brand, try one can until you learn what you are getting.

Mushrooms stuffed with potted ham and broiled make a quick and easy appetizer or a tasty garnish for a green vegetable.

WORDS TO WORK WITH

Dehydrate (dē hī′drāt): to preserve food and reduce the bulk and size by reducing water content.

THINKING IT OVER

1. Which vegetables in the following groups have you eaten: leaf, root, tuber, flower, stem, seed? Underscore the ones you like best in each group. Put a circle around the ones you like least. Are these circled vegetables important to your health and looks. Can you substitute in each group an equally good one that you do like? Could you learn to cook a vegetable of the group you like least in a way that would enable you to enjoy eating it?

2. Explain when either canned or frozen vegetables might be a "better buy" than the fresh ones.

3. How may the vitamins and minerals in canned vegetables be saved and used?

4. What can guide you in making wise choices of the canned and frozen vegetables?

5. Thinking of what you learned in preceding chapters, describe and rate the different ways to cook fresh, frozen, and dried vegetables, and how to prepare canned vegetables. Which methods do you put first? Which second? Why?

6. Keeping in mind what you learned about marketing in preceding units, how can you make the wisest choices in buying canned vegetables?

7. Explain how seasonings can make a big difference in cooking vegetables, and the use you get from them. Which seasonings have you tried? Which would you like to try?

8. What are the most important things that you have learned in your study of vegetables?

9. How can you use what you learned to help your life now? To help you when you have a home of your own?

PROBLEMS TO SOLVE

1. Learning by seeing.
   (1) Make a trip to the market to compare the quality and price of root vegetables, stem vegetables, flower vegetables, and seed vegetables.
       (a) At which season does the fresh vegetable have the best quality and lowest price?
       (b) How does the price of the fresh compare with canned?
       (c) How many of these vegetables do you find frozen? How do they compare with fresh and canned in price per serving?
   (2) In view of what you have learned, how can you make the best use of your food money in buying different types of these vegetables?

2. Planning menus using a variety of vegetables.
   (1) Plan three balanced luncheon menus in which you use a vegetable that you have not eaten before.
   (2) Plan four balanced dinner menus in which you use vegetables that you have not eaten before; or use vegetables with which you are familiar but cook them in a new way.

3. Make a plan to use a variety of vegetables as they come in season.

4. Make a habit of looking at vegetables when you go to the market, and learn

what the new ones are and how to cook and serve them in meals.

APPLYING WHAT YOU KNOW

Here are some suggestions to help you get better acquainted with many vegetables.

Look in the vegetable section of the Cookbook, pages 385-399, and learn to cook as many vegetables as you can.

1. Prepare canned green peas or green beans and frozen green peas or beans. Compare cost per serving, appearance, taste, and time and energy used.

2. Make a corn pudding from cream-style canned corn. If fresh corn is in season, cook it on the cob, as you have learned.

3. Prepare, cook, and serve asparagus (fresh, canned, or frozen); celery; okra.

4. Prepare, cook, and serve one or more: cauliflower, eggplant, summer squash.

5. Prepare, cook and serve one or more of these root and tuber vegetables: baked onions in skins, carrots, parsnips, turnips, rutabagas, beets.

6. Plan balanced dinner menus for one week, using the vegetables you have learned to cook.

7. Prepare, cook, and serve a balanced dinner, using what you have learned about vegetables.

EVALUATING

1. Did you make the best use of your knowledge of how to buy, prepare, cook, and serve vegetables?

2. Did the vegetables look good and taste good, and did you eat all of your serving?

3. Was your work organized to make the best use of your time and energy?

4. Were you able to stay within your food budget and still include the balance of vegetables you need in meals? How did the cost of canned and frozen vegetables compare? The flavor and appearance?

5. Can you make a plan to improve your use of vegetables, and put it into practice?

HOME EXPERIENCE

With your mother, plan a balanced dinner using some of the vegetables you have learned to cook. Prepare and serve the vegetables as a part of this family meal. Report results to your teacher.

15

The Place
of Potatoes in Your Meals

The Contribution of Potatoes to Your Health, Appearance, and Food Budget

The white potato is the most popular vegetable in America and Europe. In 1960, the world production total was 627 billion pounds. Yet it has been in our diet for only about 400 years. Why has the potato become such an important food to us in such a relatively short time?

Part of the answer is that potatoes are easily and quickly grown, and in a temperate climate two crops may be grown in a season. They yield a large return on the money spent, and do not require expensive soil or equipment. In fact, a person can grow potatoes by cultivating them

New potatoes yield more vitamin C than old ones. A small whole boiled or baked potato has 90 calories. 8 pieces of French fries contain 155 calories. Why?

with a hoe. On the basis of a 15-year study of the retail cost of potatoes recently reported by the Federal government, it was found that during that period a serving of one medium-sized potato was the lowest in price of any vegetable. The cost of potatoes varies with the season and with the volume on the market as well as the variety. Considering its nutrients, this is a low-cost vegetable which is mild in flavor, and can be eaten regularly without becoming tiresome.

It was the widespread use of the white potato in Europe which helped wipe out scurvy. Aside from the green leafy vegetables and tomatoes, the potato (both white and yellow) is one of the best of our cooked vegetables for vitamin C. A medium-size potato boiled in the skin, or baked and the skin eaten, may contain about one-half as much vitamin C as a medium-size raw tomato, or one-fourth as much as an orange.

R. H. Dana describes in *Two Years Before the Mast* how the raw potato helped save the lives of the men on his ship. He left college to go to sea in the days of the sailing vessels. There was an outbreak of scurvy on ship. The men were unable to walk or even eat. Then they met a ship from the Bahamas, loaded with raw onions and potatoes. The men ate these foods raw, and were cured. Dana tells how some could not chew the food because their gums were so swollen and inflamed and their teeth so loose in the sockets. But when other men scraped the juice from the potato and onion, and poured it into their mouths, they too were healed. They would not let these foods be cooked, for they knew cooked food would not cure scurvy.

This dramatic experience shows how important potatoes are for vitamin C. It also suggests how important it is to cook potatoes properly. We will consider this point later, for even today many people do not prepare and cook potatoes in a way that saves the most nourishment.

Potatoes, both white and yellow, have a fair amount of the B vitamins. One medium-size potato boiled in its skin will supply about 30 percent of the vitamin C recommended by the National Research Council as a daily allowance for a 25-year-old man, and 8 to 10 percent of the thiamine and niacin needed. It also meets about 4 percent of the daily riboflavin needed. Thus it was not only the vitamin C content which helped make the potato popular in Europe and America; people learned by experience that when their diet included potatoes they stayed healthier. No doubt, this was partly due to the B vitamins, which were so poorly represented in so many foods they ate.

The sweet potato is one of the best yellow foods for vitamin A, and it is far superior to the white potato in this respect. The deeper the color, the richer the vitamin A. One large deep-yellow potato gives around 11,000 units of vitamin A. Including this potato in your diets especially during the winter months, is of importance in helping protect you from respiratory diseases and infections.

Another reason why it is important to include a serving of potato (either white or yellow) in the daily diet is the amount of iron it contains. You recall that the iron content is one reason for including an egg yolk in the diet of babies. A medium-size potato boiled in the skin gives about as much iron as the yolk of

Sauces add zest. Bowls, left to right, contain Russian dressing for green salad; barbecue sauce for chicken or other meat; Hollandaise for cauliflower, other cabbages, or asparagus; cheese sauce for fish, vegetables or meat, as Welsh rarebit, or for au gratin dishes. Dish at left bottom holds ice cream with chocolate sauce. What other dishes besides those shown would be improved with these sauces? (See Cookbook, pages 427-430.)

an egg, as much as 2 ounces of canned pork luncheon meat, and more than the average serving of fish.

Next to dry beans, peas, lentils, and nuts, the potato is the most important vegetable for protein. It is as important for protein as it is for carbohydrates. Yet most people think of the potato as only a source of energy. A medium-size potato boiled in the skin meets 4 percent of the recommended daily protein allowance for a man 25 years old; and it also meets 4 percent of his need for calories. Though the amount of protein is small, it is of high quality. Many people in some sections of our country eat potatoes, and corn in some form, every day. Scientists have found that the protein in potatoes balances the weakness of the protein in corn. Thus on a low-cost diet, corn bread and potatoes in the same meal balance each other in protein. Both are improved when the meal includes some milk, meat, or eggs.

Some people leave the potato out of their meals because they think it is fattening. This is an unfair conclusion, not based on fact. A medium-size potato boiled or baked in the skin has only 100 calories. You get that many from two slices of bacon, a good-size apple, orange, or banana, or a half of a large grapefruit. And you get more than that from a piece of fudge candy or a bottle of soda water. It is not the potato that is fattening, but the amount of gravy, or butter that you add to it. Keep the potato in your daily diet, but use less fat on it. This will help your figure, and your health, as well as your food budget.

While spaghetti and white rice are used as potato alternates to vary the diet, they are not equal to potatoes in food value. They are weaker in vitamin C and some other nutrients. They may be used for variety, but not to push potatoes out of your meals. The unpeeled potato contains

Baked sweet potatoes served with pork and apples.

Add chopped raw green leaf vegetable, to make a new dish of mashed potatoes. How many other ways can nourishing mashed potatoes add variety to our meals?

its original nourishment. Both white rice and macaroni products are refined foods. Brown rice contains its original nourishment and is a better alternate for potatoes than polished white rice. The potato is approximately 78 percent water, and 18.4 percent carbohydrate. But the tiny parts, such as its 2.2 percent protein, and its 1 percent minerals, and the vitamins which do not show in the percentage tables, make the calories in potatoes valuable. Few foods give so much nourishment for so little money as potatoes. They may be eaten by the young and the old, and by the rich and the poor, to yield good returns in health, appearance, and economy.

How to Buy Potatoes

When you buy potatoes, there are several things to keep in mind. Allow about one pound, or 3 medium-size potatoes, for three servings. Remember that freshly dug potatoes contain more vitamin C than older ones. For instance, about one-half the vitamin C is lost in three months of storage, and two-thirds is lost in six months. People who have home gardens and dig potatoes at need enjoy the highest amount of vitamin C and of fine flavor.

Potatoes may have red or white skins, and are graded for the market by sorting for size, shape, defects, and cleanliness. A medium-size potato is usually the best buy. It is 2½ to 3 inches in diameter for the round type, and will weigh from 4 to 10 ounces for the long type. A potato of good quality (Grade A) is firm, smooth, free from serious defects, reasonably clean, and has shallow eyes. The skin should be bright, with no discolorations. Take a good look at potatoes that are reduced in price for a "special" sale. These are often not bargains. Wilted or leathery potatoes; decayed potatoes showing skin cuts or bruises; or potatoes with small brown- or black-lined holes are all of low quality. They may have been frozen or improperly stored, or be partially rotten. The brown- and black-lined holes indicate wireworms, and this may cause great waste and a

This attractive vegetable plate, when combined with whole grain or enriched bread, milk, and custard or cheese for dessert, makes a well-balanced vegetable meal.

poor flavor. Potatoes of low quality are not a "good buy."

Potatoes vary in cost according to the amount you purchase, the abundance of the supply, the nearness to the place where they are produced, whether you buy them fresh, canned, frozen, or dried, and the quality. If you plan to buy a large amount of raw potatoes at one time, select the type you wish and first buy a trial amount to see if you like the texture and the way the potato cooks. Most Americans prefer a mealy textured potato. But this quality varies among potatoes of the same variety, and even from the same hill. It is therefore difficult to predict cooking quality of potatoes by variety.

Storing

Potatoes should be stored in a cool (50° to 60° F), dark, fairly moist place. The green color on potatoes is caused by light resulting from poor storage. The green is toxic and bitter; therefore, discard it. It is wise buying to purchase only the amount of potatoes which you can properly store, and which you can use before deterioration. The longer potatoes are stored, the more mealiness they lose and the soggier they become. The flavor and the food value are better when potatoes are freshly dug than when they are held in storage. If freshly dug potatoes are not properly matured, they spoil more rapidly than mature ones. It might be worthwhile to buy new potatoes in smaller amounts until you see how they keep in storage.

Cooking and Use of Potatoes in Meal Planning

Throughout this discussion the value of the potato has been based on cooking it in the skin. This is because research shows that the most nutrients are saved when the potato is cooked that way. If it is cooked in the skin in the pressure saucepan, or by the waterless cooking method, its thin skin may easily be peeled away,

Parsnips, a nourishing winter vegetable may be used as an alternate for potatoes. Compare the nutrients by using the table on page 458. Parsnips are delicious with meat.

leaving most of the nutrients. Baking is also effective if you eat the whole skin, but not if you leave it.

In preparing potatoes to cook, always scrub the skins thoroughly. If there are green spots, decay, or other serious defects, cut these away, and discard. If the potato is to be pared before cooking, pare it with as thin a peeling as possible. The new potato may be scraped, removing only the thin skin. Although it takes longer to cook the whole potato, it has a mealier texture than cut potatoes.

The darkening of potatoes after cooking has no effect on flavor or nutritive value, but it is not attractive. Darkening after cooking may be avoided in some varieties by adding a small amount of lemon juice, vinegar, or cream of tartar to the cooking water.

If it is necessary to pare potatoes and leave them for a few hours before cooking, place in a plastic bag, wrap firmly, and store in the vegetable box of the refrigerator. Then there is very little discoloring. Mashing or whipping potatoes is one of the favorite ways Americans enjoy them. Unfortunately, whipping air into potatoes increases the loss of vitamin C. This loss is less if the potato is first boiled in its jacket, and then peeled and mashed. When you serve mashed potatoes, be sure to include a vitamin C-rich food in the meal, such as a raw salad.

Potatoes should be served immediately when they are done. Standing after cooking causes rapid loss of vitamin C. Furthermore, it is better to cook fresh the amount of potatoes that you need for each meal. Warmed-over or second cooking of potatoes greatly increases the loss of vitamin C, and of flavor as well. The directions in Chapter 12 for cooking vegetables should be followed for potatoes. There is less loss of vitamins if left-over potatoes are frozen until ready to use, and thawed just before cooking.

Many "convenience" forms of dehydrated potatoes are on the market. Read the label to see whether vitamin C is added, for much is lost in drying. (See recipes in the Cookbook section for ways of using potatoes to give tasty variety to the diet.)

THINKING IT OVER

1. Why do some people think they should avoid eating potatoes? Is this fair to the potato? To the family food budget? Why?

2. Using the table on page 452, compare the calories in potato with those in banana, orange, apple, bacon, candy, and soda water, cookie, cake, doughnut, pizza.

3. Why does the potato give so much in nourishment in relation to its cost and the calories it contains?

4. How do sweet and white potatoes compare in food value?

5. Is a sweet potato a better alternate for the white potato than macaroni or white rice? Explain your answer by using the table on page 452.

6. What nutrients may be lost if the water in which potatoes are soaked or cooked is thrown away?

7. What is the best way to cook potatoes? The second best? Why?

8. Thinking of what you have learned, how could you use the water in which potatoes are cooked?

9. What points do you need to remember when you buy potatoes? When you store them at home?

10. If you have to pare potatoes ahead of the meal, where and how should you store them until they are ready to cook?

11. Explain how to cook potatoes: (1) in the skins; (2) pared and cooked by the water-less cooking method; (3) pared and cooked by the pressure saucepan method.

12. Why are potatoes important in your daily diet? Under what circumstances would you include them more than once daily?

PROBLEMS TO SOLVE

1. By eliminating one dish in the following meals, you will balance the meal. Can you do this?

A.

Tomato juice
Liver and bacon
Mashed potatoes   Macaroni salad
Purple cabbage
Bread   Butter or margarine
Cherry pie
Milk

B.

Pot roast of beef, gravy
Carrot sticks   Mashed potatoes
Baked sweet potatoes
Bread   Butter or margarine
Canned apricots   Cookie
Milk

C.

Golden fried chicken, gravy
Baked potatoes   Buttered rice
Green tossed salad
Bread   Butter or margarine
Fresh peaches and cream
Milk

2. In a good reference book, look up the history of the potato.
3. Marketing.
   (1) Study different grades and prices of white and yellow potatoes in your market. Report results of your findings to the class.
   (2) In what different ways can you buy canned potatoes? How do the prices compare with prices of fresh potatoes?
   (3) In what different ways can you buy frozen potatoes? How do their prices compare with the canned and fresh potatoes?
   (4) What type of potato now in your market is the best buy? Why?

APPLYING WHAT YOU KNOW

1. Planning menus using potatoes: Plan a week of balanced menus using potatoes as a part of a balanced meal for your family each day.
2. Preparing and cooking potatoes (see recipes in Cookbook, pages 396-397): Prepare and cook potatoes in one or more of the following ways:
   (1) Bake white or yellow potatoes in skins in the oven.
   (2) Cook in skins in pressure saucepan for 5 minutes, and finish baking in the oven.

   (3) Cook in skins in pressure saucepan or by waterless cooking, season white potatoes with sour cream mixed with chives or butter and grated onion, and serve in skins. Peel when cooked and push through potato ricer; or mash.
   (4) Pare potatoes with peeler or sharp knife and cube to cook for a quick meal in waterless cooker (5 to 8 minutes) or pressure saucepan (1 to 2 minutes). Season and serve with all of juice.
   (5) Scalloped potatoes.

EVALUATING

1. How do you decide which potatoes to buy and how often to use them in meals?
2. How do you decide the best way to prepare and cook potatoes? Is this a wise decision? Why?
3. Did you make good use of your time and energy in your work?
4. Why is it better to cook potatoes as you need them?

HOME EXPERIENCE

Using what you have learned, cook and serve potatoes as a part of a balanced family meal at home. Report results to your teacher.

16

How to Use
Dried Legumes
and Nuts in Your Diet

Dried Legumes and Nuts
Have a Long History

Beans, peas, lentils, and nuts go by the family name of "legumes" (lĕg'ūm). Historians tell us that lentils were included in the diet of man 15,000 years before Christ. The navy bean got its name because it was frequently used by military groups as an important part of their diet. Dried beans and peas cooked in open pots over campfires helped give the pioneer strength to push West and settle our country. Nuts were an important part of the American Indian's diet before and

Beans (and cereal) have provided a major portion of the protein in the diets of many developing nations including our own. How many varieties of beans have you cooked?

after the coming of the white man. Primitive people in many countries have for centuries eaten nuts—a clean food, rich in protein and fat. Why has this group of foods played such an important role in the history of man?

Why Dried Beans, Peas, Lentils, and Peanuts Are Good Foods

These foods are rich in protein, and, when balanced with other foods, can be used as a substitute for meat. In many parts of the world, people eat them every day.

This plant group has two distinctions. First, it is the only group that gives nourishment back to the soil. Legumes take nitrogen from the soil and make protein. They return nitrogen to the soil when their vines and roots are plowed into it.

Second, these foods, like cereal grains, are the seed of the plant. Nature stores in the seed the variety of nutrients needed to carry on the life of each plant, and protein is quite important for this purpose.

Soy beans have the only complete protein in plants. Other legumes lack "essential" amino acids and need to be eaten with milk, cheese, eggs, or meat (see Chapter 6). Even a small amount of meat as in chili con carne, for example, helps make the protein in beans more useful to us. So does the egg in bean and egg salad. Whole wheat bread contains the amino acids which beans lack and gives an inexpensive combination for nutritional balance; but bread and beans are a better protein combination when some milk, cheese, meat or egg is eaten with the meal.

Dried beans, peas, lentils, and nuts supply important amounts of both calcium and iron in the diet. The iron is of more importance. One-half cup of dried cooked beans, for instance, gives as much iron as a large hamburger, and almost as much as two eggs. A cup of cooked beans meets about one-third of your daily need for iron.

You recall that leafy vegetables are the best in the vegetable group for iron and calcium. It is good to include a leafy vegetable in a meal containing beans. The contrast in texture and color is good. The calorie content of green vegetables is low, and that of beans is high, and this balances. But best of all, you will combine their minerals, vitamins, and amino acids. For while the amount of protein in green vegetables is low, the quality is high. That means the protein is well used by the body. As in other vegetables, the fat content is low in beans.

Unless your food budget is very low, or your activity very high, you do not need both potatoes and bread in a meal that has beans as a meat substitute.

Dried beans, peas, nuts, and lentils are also important in giving us a wide range of B vitamins. They are especially rich in the three in which our diets are most likely to be low—riboflavin, thiamine, and niacin.

Legumes lack vitamins A and C, which is why the armies and navies of the world faced health problems when beans and cereals were a major part of their diet. This is also a good reason why you need a cooked green leafy or yellow vegetable and a raw salad with a meal that has beans as the main dish. The raw onion is a favorite vegetable for flavor contrast with beans. It pulls more than its weight in providing vitamin C, especially when you eat the green blades.

Kinds of Beans and Peas

Probably the most popular bean in our country is the *pea bean*, also known as the *navy bean*. This is the bean used for the famous New England baked beans. It is also boiled with either fat pork meat or a ham hock for seasoning.

The *red bean*, or *kidney bean*, is preferred in Mexico and some parts of the Southern U.S. Puerto Ricans eat this bean with rice as the main dish. Beans and polished white rice do not make an adequate meal. But if milk (or cheese), a green vegetable, and tomatoes or an orange are added, this is a well-balanced meal. If the rice is brown, the meal is more nourishing.

The *black-eyed pea* is tasty both green and dried. It is usually cooked with ham or bacon.

Lima and *black beans* and *chick peas* are used along with other varieties, but are not the national dish for any group.

Lentils and *split peas* are more popular in Europe than in America. They cook more easily than the dried bean and in this respect are less expensive. They are excellent in soups. Since the protein is not complete, they are more nourishing with a little meat or a few sliced frankfurters. To get a good, balanced lunch, when bean soup is the main dish, you need whole grain or enriched bread, milk, and a good food for vitamin C, either a raw vegetable salad or fruit. Cheese, cheese cake, or a custard is a good choice for dessert.

The *soy bean* is a favorite bean in the Orient. Although it has been used for livestock food in our country for many years, we do not eat many soy beans.

However, the soy bean is an excellent food. It contains all of the essential amino acids we need (and you recall this is what makes a complete protein food). It contains no carbohydrate and can be eaten by diabetics. It is richer in iron and calcium than any other bean. Then too, it has large amounts of some B vitamins, and is the only legume, except the green split pea, containing vitamin A. In the Orient, the people have a tradition of sprouting the soy bean and other dry beans by placing them in pans of water. When the sprouts appear, they use the bean and sprout as food. This practice has probably resulted in better health for millions of people, for the bean sprout contains vitamin C, and the dry legumes lack it. You can buy canned bean sprouts at your local grocery.

Soy beans are canned and are also used for salad oil, soy bean flour, and prepared cereals. Soy bean flour is used to make bread more nourishing. We should get better acquainted with this bean and use it in our meals.

Use of Peanuts in Your Diet

Nuts are a good protein food, and high in fat. Peanuts are the most important. We grow around two billion pounds of them in the United States annually. Strictly speaking, though, the peanut is not a true nut, but a bean that turns its blossom down into the soil, and grows underground. Peanuts are roasted and sold on the streets. They are a popular food at the zoo. We eat peanut butter sandwiches for lunch and snacks.

The peanut is a good meat substitute, as a protein food. There is more protein in a pound of shelled peanuts (117 grams) than in a pound of sirloin beef (80 grams). Five tablespoons of peanut butter gives the same amount of protein as in a large hamburger (3½ ounces). But the protein in the meat is of higher quality.

A peanut butter sandwich with a ripe tomato, a few leaves of green lettuce, a glass of milk, and a dish of stewed fruit or a milk dessert makes a tasty, nourishing, and quick lunch for home or school.

A bag of peanuts and an orange make a good snack to put in your pocket for a long hike. Peanuts and peanut butter sandwiches are nutritious snacks for car travelers who may have long waits between good places to eat.

The wider use of peanuts could greatly improve the health of millions of people in parts of the world where there is not enough protein in the diet. This is particularly true of those who do not use much meat, milk, or cheese.

Other Nuts Are Also Good Foods

Other nuts are good foods when used as a planned part of the meal. Almonds, for instance, are richer in calcium and iron than dried beans and peas. California is an important state for growing almonds and walnuts commercially. Pecans are widely grown in Texas and many other southern states. Southern states also grow peanuts. Besides these, other nuts used for food are filberts, Brazil nuts, cashews, and pistachio nuts. The almond and coconut are not true nuts. The almond is a pit of a fruit related to a peach. Walnuts contain more polyunsaturated fat than other nuts (see Chapter 23).

With the exception of peanuts, nuts are used as occasional foods and for flavoring in most of our diets. They are high in

calories due to the high fat content which you may wish to look up in the table on page 459. One ounce of peanuts contains 170 calories, and the other common nuts contain a little more. If nuts are simply one element in the plan of a balanced meal, this may not be too important. However, if they are eaten generously as a snack food in addition to a meal, you need to watch the amount you eat, lest you gain unwanted weight. One cup of nuts in a pecan pie adds 750 calories. But divided between seven people this delicious pie may be used as dessert and fit into a well-planned meal. Nuts with fresh fruit make an excellent dessert.

How to Buy Dried Beans, Peas, and Lentils

We mentioned earlier that you can save close to 20 percent on the food budget with adequate information about the values in food and with experience in marketing and cooking. A saving can be made even in buying beans. Beans, peas, lentils, and nuts are easy to grow, transport, and store, and the price does not go up and down suddenly as with some foods. The saving on these foods comes in the form in which you buy them and how you use them in meals. As indicated, these foods are an adequate meat substitute when used in a meal with milk, cheese, or eggs. For instance, if you use beans only once each week as a meat substitute, you might save from 30 to over 50 cents per serving. A pound of dried beans costs from 15 to 25 cents and will give seven to nine servings when cooked. A pound can of cooked beans costs about half as much as a pound of dried beans, but yields only two servings.

When you cook the beans yourself, you can achieve variety in seasoning flavor. With proper equipment it is a simple matter to cook dried beans, peas, and lentils and get delicious results.

How to Cook Dried Beans, Peas, and Lentils

Busy homemakers are always looking for short cuts to save time in cooking. Some have added soda to dry beans to hasten the cooking, not knowing that soda destroys thiamine. Others use the canned beans from the supermarket shelf because they are ready to serve. Time is a precious commodity. However, you need to think through what you are sacrificing for time saved, and how much money you are spending for that saving. Almost anyone will be repaid in the pleasure of eating, and in addition save money, if she will learn and practice a good short cut for cooking dried beans. There are two ways to do this without the necessity of adding soda. The first steps are the same for each method.

Using the pressure saucepan is the quickest and most economical way to cook dried beans. But the following method can also be used with a saucepan that has a tight-fitting lid. (This is called the *"preboil and soak" method.*)

(1) Look beans over for bits of stones, dirt, or hulls.

(2) Wash, and place in pan in which they will be cooked.

(3) Add two cups of water per cup of beans for cooking in pressure saucepan, or three cups of water for boiling.

(4) If you use a pressure saucepan, it should be only one-third full, counting beans and water.

A quick low cost main dish for lunch or dinner is a casserole of left-over beans (or canned) with chunks of ham, topped with apple slices. With fresh coleslaw and milk added to this meal, it is well balanced.

(5) Bring to boil, and boil two minutes. Do this after breakfast and let soak until time to cook dinner, or at least one hour. The purpose of the two-minute boiling is to hasten the softening of the bean. It helps the bean to absorb more water faster, and also helps keep the skins from breaking.

(6) When you are ready to cook the beans, add seasoning of your choice. Standard seasoning is one teaspoon of salt and one tablespoon of fat per cup of dry beans. With different kinds of beans, try different seasonings, such as onion, garlic, dry mustard, celery leaves. A ham hock, or bacon chunks that are scored (sliced), is a choice seasoning. For good flavor, it is important to season beans before you cook them. The fat helps hold down foaming during cooking. This is important in the pressure saucepan.

(7) Always cook beans in the water in which they have been soaked. This saves money as it does not waste health values in the beans.

(8) *If beans are to be boiled*, cook in a utensil with a tight-fitting lid. Bring to boil, lower fire to simmer, and cook covered until done (about $2\frac{1}{2}$ to 3 hours).

(9) *If beans are to be cooked in a pressure saucepan*, prepare as for boiling, using the correct amount of water and seasoning. When pressure pan is no more than one-third full, adjust lid. Then:

(a) Heat slowly to boiling.
(b) Let steam escape for one minute.
(c) Place vent cover on lid.
(d) Heat slowly until pressure rises to 15 pounds, and adjust heat to hold pressure.
(e) Start counting time.
(f) Hold pressure five minutes at 15 pounds for all beans except pinto and navy; for navy and pinto beans hold pressure at 15 pounds for 10 minutes.
(g) Turn off heat. (Do not open vent until pressure returns to normal.)

This process takes about 30 minutes.

(10) Serve hot as a part of a balanced meal.

If you use the pressure saucepan, you save 140 to 150 minutes (about $2\frac{1}{2}$ hours) in cooking time over the boiling method. This is a short cut that saves more than time. It also saves fuel, energy, money, and nourishment, and is very tasty.

Planning a Vegetable Plate

Some people do not think of the nutritional value when they start to plan a vegetable plate. They follow such rules as including a fresh, frozen, or canned vegetable in a vegetable plate. Others follow the rule of color and texture contrast. It is a fine thing to keep these things in mind, but they are not adequate to guide you in planning a balanced vegetable plate. How, then, can you begin? Begin just as you would with any meal, with one exception. In a vegetable plate you do not use meat, and you must be sure to include a good protein food. Apply these principles:

(1) Choose the protein food first. Among vegetables, this can be beans, peas, lentils, or nuts, as a substitute for meat. To balance a vegetable protein without meat, it is well to include some milk, cheese, or eggs in your menu. Since legumes lack vitamin C, you also need a vitamin C-rich food. In a vegetable plate you need other vegetables, and you may need bread and table fat, to make the meal satisfying and healthful.

(2) Keep in mind the seasonal freshness of different vegetables and use the ones that fit your need at the price you can afford. You may wish to use some vegetables fresh, such as green lettuce, tomatoes, carrots, or potatoes; some frozen, such as green peas, beans, Brussels sprouts, or okra; some canned, such as beets, sauerkraut, or corn; and some dried, such as beans.

(3) You will want your vegetable plate to be attractive, and tasty as well as nourishing. Keep in mind the color and texture contrasts that are attractive on the same plate. Here are a few examples of vegetable plates that combine good nutritional balance with color and texture contrast to give a tasty and attractive meal:

(a) Pea-beans and ham hock, turnip greens, baked sweet potatoes, table fat, finger salad (such as radishes and green onions), bread if desired, milk, and canned peaches with a scoop of ice cream, or apple pie with sharp cheese.

(b) Lentil or bean soup, buttered minted carrots, baked potato, tossed green salad, table fat, whole grain or enriched bread if desired, milk, pecan pie.

(c) Black-eyed peas, buttered frozen or fresh okra, scalloped potatoes, lettuce, tomato-onion salad, table fat, whole grain or enriched bread if desired, milk, prune or apricot whip.

(d) Stuffed tomato salad—whole tomato stuffed with a mixture of red beans, pickle, diced celery, and grated onion on a bed of green lettuce garnished with hard-cooked eggs, plus hot corn sticks, table fat, milk, and deep dish cherry pie with sharp cheese.

(e) Baked beans, sautéed sliced eggplant with paprika, cabbage, carrot and pineapple salad, brown bread or corn sticks, table fat, milk, and baked custard.

(f) Cheese soufflé, buttered frozen peas, potatoes cooked in their skins and topped with paprika, cabbage-pear-orange salad, milk, gingerbread topped with applesauce.

(g) Lima beans, corn on the cob, mashed carrots, sliced tomatoes on green lettuce, bread and table fat if desired, milk, fresh peaches with angel cake.

(h) Cauliflower with cheese sauce and cooked red beans, boiled potatoes in the skin with parsley-butter sauce, kale or spinach, carrot and green pepper sticks, milk, banana nut bread.

In planning vegetable plate meals, you will see that the reason vegetarians (those who eat only plant foods) get along as well as they do is that they also eat cheese, milk, and eggs which balance the weakness of the protein found in beans, nuts, and other foods in the vegetable diet.

Summary of Vegetables

In his satire *Animal Farm*, George Orwell makes the point that while all animals are equal, some are more equal than others. It is said that all vegetables are important, but now you are aware that some vegetables are far more important than others. The dark green and deep yellow vegetables (and fruits), tomatoes, potatoes (both white and sweet), and the legumes—beans, peas and lentils—are among our most important vegetables. This is because they contain a variety of nutrients we need, and are not expensive.

The contribution of vegetables (and fruits) to our diet is not only the wide variety they give in flavor, color, and texture, but also the large amounts of vitamins and minerals which they contain. Thus they help build new cell tissues, such as red blood cells. They help regulate body processes, by keeping the chemistry in proper balance, aiding in the normal elimination of waste, and promoting good intestinal hygiene. While they carry their share of protein and calories, they are quite important in planning low-calorie, low-fat diets. This is because they give so many needed nutrients in proportion to their calories. Many vegetables may be eaten raw, and can bring important amounts of vitamin C to the diet, but we eat most of our vegetables cooked.

The preparation and cooking of vegetables may greatly alter their health values. This affects what you actually get for your money in buying them. It is important to buy, store, prepare, and cook vegetables in ways that will retain the most nourishment and flavor possible. Vitamins, minerals, and sugars may be lost by soaking or cooking vegetables in large amounts of water and pouring this water down the drain. Oxygen destroys vitamin C after a vegetable is gathered. This can happen wherever the vegetable is exposed to air, such as in the market, in the kitchen, and when the food is cooked and waiting to be eaten. But there is less loss at low temperature, and none when vegetables are frozen. The drying of vege-tables causes further loss of nutrients. Reports indicate that if vegetables are cooked in the absence of light, more ribo-flavin is retained. Frozen and canned vege-tables may often be a better buy than "fresh" vegetables which actually are not fresh. Plan your meals to include a variety of vegetables, and prepare these foods in ways that will save the most nourishment and flavor. Then you will use your food money wisely, for vegetables can give a sparkle to your life, and make you a more attractive person.

WORDS TO WORK WITH

Legume (lĕg'ūm): the fruit or seed of a pod-bearing plant, such as beans, peas, lentils, and peanuts. Legumes are a rich source of protein for man and animals, and they are further useful in returning nitrogen to the soil.

THINKING IT OVER

1. In what ways do the legumes—dried beans, peas, lentils, and peanuts—resemble cereal grains?

2. What are the important contributions which this group of vegetables makes to your meals and to your health?

3. In which vitamins are these foods especially low, and why is it desirable to include milk, cheese, or eggs in the meal also when legumes are used as a meat substitute?

4. How has the nutritional weakness of beans affected the health of the world? How has their nutritional strength affected the life of man? How is it that people in the Orient get more nourishment from beans than we do?

5. What are the common varieties of beans, peas, and nuts, and which do you prefer? Which have you eaten?

6. Explain why peanuts could improve the health of people in parts of the world where they do not have much animal food. Why do you suppose more peanuts are not used in these countries as human food?

7. Explain how to cook dried beans by the short cut methods. Which is preferred? Explain your answer.

8. What would guide you in planning balanced vegetable plates? Give an example.

9. Explain how you can save money on the food budget by using beans once a week as a meat substitute.

PROBLEMS TO SOLVE

1. Marketing.
   (1) If you could spend only $1.00 per person each day for all food, what

kind of beans would you buy—dried or canned? Why?

(2) If canned beans were on sale, how would you decide whether they were a bargain or not? Are dried or cooked beans better for your quick meal shelf? What would you have on reserve? Why?

2. Planning menus.

(1) Plan three balanced lunch menus using the following main dishes: lentil or bean soup, baked beans, bean salad.

(2) Plan three balanced dinner vegetable plates using beans as the meat substitute.

3. Look up the story of the peanut in a good reference book.

APPLYING WHAT YOU KNOW

Cooking beans.

(1) Boil and soak beans or lentils for cooking by the short cut method, then finish cooking in a pressure saucepan. (Since this will take longer than a class period, one class or the teacher ahead of you can take the first step, and you can finish cooking their beans. You can prepare, boil, and soak for another class.)

(2) Let different "families" try various types of seasoning, such as ham bone, fat pork, bacon, and bacon drippings; and try onion, a clove of garlic, celery tops, mustard, celery seeds, or other herbs of your choice.

(3) Have a tasting evaluation of the beans you have cooked. Let each family taste its own and those prepared by other families.

2. Prepare a dessert using nuts.

EVALUATING

1. Why did you cook the beans in the water in which they soaked? Why is seasoning added before cooking?

2. Why is it not desirable to add soda in cooking beans?

3. If you followed the directions exactly for cooking by the precook and soak method, you would have got perfect results. Were your results perfect? How would you judge perfectly cooked beans?

4. How much did the bean dish cost per person? How does this compare with hamburger? With sirloin steak? With pork chop? With liver?

5. Why do you need milk or cheese or eggs and whole grain bread in a meal that has beans as the main protein food?

6. Why do you need tomatoes or a green leafy or yellow vegetable, when beans are the main dish?

HOME EXPERIENCE

Discuss with your mother what you have learned about beans. Plan a Saturday night supper in which beans are used as a meat substitute in a balanced meal. Prepare and serve this dish as a part of the family meal. Report results to your teacher.

FURTHER READING

Conserving the Nutritive Values in Foods. Home and Garden Bulletin 90. U.S.D.A. Washington, D.C., 1963.

Dry Beans, Peas, Lentils . . . Modern Cookery. Leaflet 326. U.S.D.A., Washington, D.C., 1957.

Fruit and Vegetable Buying Guide for Consumers. Home and Garden Bulletin 21. U.S.D.A., Washington, D.C., 1955.

Green Vegetables for Good Eating. Home and Garden Bulletin 41. U.S.D.A., Washington, D.C., 1954.

Home Canning of Fruits and Vegetables, Wood. Cornell Extension Bulletin E792. Cornell University, Ithaca, N.Y.

Home Freezers, Their Selection and Use. Home and Garden Bulletin 48. U.S.D.A., Washington, D.C., 1956.

Home Storage of Fruits and Vegetables. U.S.D.A., Washington, D.C., 1960.

How to Cook Vegetables, Williams. Cornell Extension Bulletin E883. Cornell University, Ithaca, N.Y.

Legumes in Human Nutrition. Columbia University Press, International Documents Service, New York, N.Y., 1964.

Peanut and Peanut Butter Recipes. Home and Garden Bulletin 36. U.S.D.A., Washington, D.C., 1954.

Potatoes—Facts for Consumer Education. U.S.D.A., Washington, D.C., 1957.

Potatoes in Popular Ways. Home and Garden Bulletin 55. U.S.D.A., Washington, D.C., 1957.

Read the Label on Foods, Drugs, Devices, and Cosmetics. Miscellaneous Pub. 3, Revision No. 2, U.S. Department of Health, Education, and Welfare. Washington, D.C., 1951.

Richards Topical Encyclopedia. Volume 9. The Richards Co., Inc., New York, N.Y., 1964.

Root Vegetables in Everyday Meals. Home and Garden Bulletin 33. U.S.D.A., Washington, D.C., 1953.

Storing Perishable Food in the Home. Home and Garden Bulletin 78. U.S.D.A., Washington, D.C., 1961.

Tips on Selecting Fruit and Vegetables. U.S.D.A., Washington, D.C., 1961.

Tomatoes on Your Table. U.S.D.A., Washington, D.C., 1961.

Vegetables-Consumer Quality, Yield, and Preparation Time of Various Market Forms. U.S.D.A., Washington, D.C., 1962.

VISUAL AIDS

Ahead of 'em All (cabbage). (5½ min. film, color and b/w; released 1952)

Fourteen Carrots. (5 min. film, color and b/w; released 1952)

Onions and More Onions. (4½ min. film, color and b/w; released 1952)

It's a Snap (beans). (5½ min. film, color and b/w; released 1952)

Potatoes Are Appealing. (5 min. film, color; also b/w; released 1952)

All of these films from T.V. Film Consumer Education Series, U.S.D.A., Washington, D.C.

Cereal-Bread
in Your Diet

17

Cereal-Bread and Its Contribution to Your Meals

Cereal-Bread Is the Most Used Food in Our Diet

There is a story behind the word "cereal."

The Romans believed in a great earth-goddess who watched over the grains they cultivated for food. Her name was Ceres. Through the influence of Latin upon the English language, she gave her name to the grains of which she was the symbol. In the United States, "cereal" often means any breakfast food made from grain; but this is a later and narrower meaning. Its more general meaning is "any grain that is used for food."

High in nutrients, low in calories, a snack of cereal and milk is a sound eating practice for teen-agers in the family.

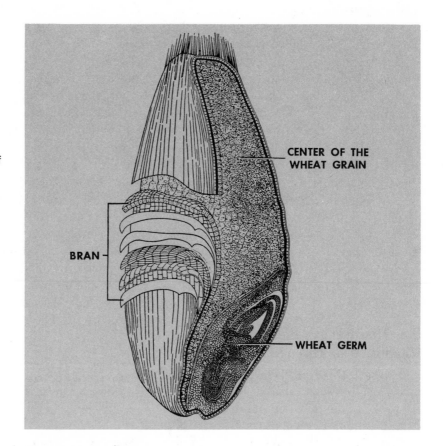

Structural drawing of a grain of wheat.

CENTER OF THE WHEAT GRAIN

BRAN

WHEAT GERM

The most common cereal grains are wheat, rice, corn, oats, rye, barley, and buckwheat. Throughout recorded history, millions of people have relied on these as a basic part of the diet. In Asia, rice is the main article of food. In the United States and elsewhere in the Western world, no other cereal matches the importance of wheat.

Cereals came to be leaned upon so heavily because they are easily grown in most climates, inexpensive, and easy to transport and store, and their mild flavor helps them fit into any meal. From the earliest times they have been within the reach of the average man. The beginnings of civilization are closely associated with the cultivation of grains for food.

Cereals gained their historic importance because the whole grain was used. The grain of wheat (or any cereal) is the seed of that plant. Just as the egg nourishes and in fact becomes the chick, so the grain produces the new offspring—the baby plant— and feeds it until it can grow roots and leaves. It is not surprising, then, that all cereals are similarly rich in nutrients, and high in energy. They all have the job of producing a new life.

But cereals lose some of their food-value when white flour and white cereals are made. The whole grain is broken down and the outer coverings and germ are removed. It has been popular to throw away some of the darker parts of the whole-wheat flour since the time of the

Egyptians, but the greater whiteness comes through a sacrifice of nutritional values. The full story of what happens in creating white flour will be told later in this unit.

Meanwhile, the popular phrase "the staff of life" could easily suggest that bread made from whole-grain cereals provides all the nutrients the body requires. This is not true. No food is perfect and whole grain bread, when it stands alone, is less well balanced in protein than milk, meat, or eggs. It is when eaten with other foods, and especially with milk, that bread makes its finest contribution to our diet.

The Discovery of the First Vitamin Was Through a Cereal

Between 1878 and 1883 the Japanese navy lost between 20 and 40 percent of its men by death from the disease beriberi (bĕr′ĭ bĕr′ĭ). This death rate disturbed Takaki, the physician in charge. The science of bacteriology was just coming into its own then, and if you didn't know what caused a disease you put the blame on a germ or unsanitary conditions.

Takaki knew his ships were as clean as the British ships, yet the British men did not die of beriberi. What made this difference? He thought it was the lack of some food the body needed, and not a germ. He persuaded authorities to let him try an experiment.

Two shiploads of men went on a nine-month cruise. Ship One had the usual diet of white polished rice. On this ship 169 cases of beriberi developed, with 25 deaths.

Ship Two had a similar crew and went over the same route for the same time.

Their sanitary conditions were the same, but there was one big difference. On Ship Two the sailors were given less rice to eat. Added to this smaller amount of rice was some barley, vegetables, meat, and condensed milk. Only 14 men on this ship had beriberi—and they all were men who did not eat their portion of the new foods because they didn't like them!

Because of this experiment Takaki was able to change the diet and, as a result, beriberi practically disappeared in the Japanese navy. You might think that all of the Orient would be cheered by this good news and would make use of it, but this was not the case. The medical profession in the Orient was divided in its

Adequate measuring equipment is essential for success in cooking. For good results in baking, always sift the flour before measuring. Level with a spatula for accurate measurement.

opinion. The majority of doctors still believed beriberi was caused by poor sanitary conditions or infections, and people continued to die from this disease.

In 1897, a Dutch physician in the East Indies named Eijkman had many people coming to him with beriberi. He found the same symptoms over and over—weakness, dizziness, fatigue, no appetite, digestive troubles, lameness in the feet and legs. He concluded the germ theory did not explain this type of sickness, for he could find no germs. Then he made a brilliant discovery that marked the beginning of our knowledge that a poor diet caused beriberi and a better diet could cure it.

His patients included many types, but he noticed all of them ate white rice—the whole grain stripped of its outer layers and its germ. This white rice was preferred largely on account of its white color and fluffy texture. In contrast to this, he noticed that prisoners, who were fed plain natural brown rice that had not been milled, escaped this sickness. Eijkman believed that some unknown nutrient which the body needed for health and life was in the outer layers of the rice and its germ, which were being removed by the milling. So he tried an experiment.

Dr. Eijkman fed two kinds of diets to two different groups of birds. One group had white polished rice and the other had whole grain natural brown rice. In twenty days the birds eating the white rice were showing some of the same symptoms as his patients. Those fed brown rice were like the prisoners, healthy and strong!

To be more sure of what this seemed to tell him, he changed the white-rice diet. The dark outer layers and germ which had

Hot muffins can provide vitamin B and a delightful accent to any meal. Fluted paper cups save dishwashing and enhance appearance.

been removed from the white rice were added to the diet of the sick birds. Almost at once the sick birds started to recover. Something in the dark layer of the grain and germ gave them health and vitality!

It was this work that led to the discovery of vitamin B[1], later known as thiamine (thī′a mēn). Thanks to the progress of science, thiamine has become a household word. We know that its presence in food is essential for growth, a normal appetite, healthy nerve tissue, healthy tone

and action of the digestive tract, and good body coordination.

Thiamine, along with riboflavin, another B vitamin (see pages 35–41) helps the body use the starch, sugar, and fat in the food we eat. When these B vitamins are absent these nutrients are not properly "burned," or utilized.

What Foods Supply Thiamine?

The whole-grain, dark cereals are among our best natural foods for thiamine. Wheat, barley, and oats are about twice as rich in it as rice. This is one reason we need to eat a variety of cereal grains. Lean pork and especially liver are excellent sources of thiamine. Kidney, heart, eggs, mature dried peas, beans, and green leafy vegetables are also valuable for adding thiamine to the diet.

What Does Cereal-Bread Contribute to Your Meals?

If we could have only two foods to eat, whole-grain cereal-bread with milk would probably be the best combination. But bread alone, or bread with butter, jam, and tea or coffee, cannot do the job.

A study made in an industrial part of England at the turn of the twentieth century showed this. Many families were eating a diet of bread, jam, and tea and little more. Such families lost a fourth of their babies and small children. The teenage boys and girls were five inches shorter than other children of the same age who had a better diet. They had stunted bodies, bowed legs, decayed teeth, and sallow cheeks, and as one writer said, "The hair of these girls is a scanty crop. When tied back, it is simply a wisp and looks like a rat's tail." Yet it may surprise you to know that even today many elderly people (and some not so elderly) eat far too much bread, butter, jam, and coffee. Cereal-bread is not a good enough food to take the major place in the diet, but when the whole-grain or enriched products are eaten in balance with other foods, they make a major contribution to our food supply.

Cereals contain about 75 percent carbohydrate by weight. This makes them an abundant and quick source of low-cost energy. Then too, we can eat cereal or bread day after day without becoming weary of its taste. These are additional reasons why a large part of the world gets a great amount of its calories from cereal-bread.

Although there has been a steady decline in the use of cereal-bread in the United States recently, we still get about

Steps in Making Muffins (see recipe, page 402): (1) Preheat oven to 400°F and lightly oil muffin pans. Sift dry ingredients and add liquid ingredients. (3) Mix until dry ingredients are just moistened. Do not overmix. (4) Fill muffin pan two-thirds full of batter and bake until done (about 20 to 25 minutes). (5) Remove from pan and serve hot as part of any meal.

30 percent of our calories from cereals and bread. The Food and Agricultural Organization of the United Nations recommends that more land should be used to grow cereal grains and to provide milk, and less land to supply meat, especially in areas where food resources are very limited. It takes seven calories of grain to make one calorie of meat. Bread and milk give a better food combination for health than bread and meat. This combination also costs less, which is important for people all over the world.

Another reason cereal-bread has been a great food through the ages is that it contains 9 to 16 percent protein by weight. Eight to 12 percent of the calories in cereal-bread come from protein. This is not far from the recommended 10 to 15 percent of calories which should come from protein foods. A "complete" protein food such as milk, eggs, or meat in the same meal helps the body use the protein in cereal-bread more efficiently. If the English children referred to had only used a quart of milk with their bread each day, what a big difference it could have made in their health and looks!

Whole-grain cereals are an excellent source of iron. This, along with its protein, B vitamins, and high energy content, is a reason bread became known as "the staff of life." The people in middle Europe who ate "the dark loaf" had the nourishment to keep their red blood in a healthy state. When the whole grain was stripped of its bran and germ, almost three-fourths of the iron was lost. The poor of Asia, who could not afford the white, refined rice, ate the iron-rich brown and lived!

The whole-grain cereals are one of our best foods for B vitamins. About 22 percent of the thiamine we need daily comes from whole-grain or enriched cereals (which we shall presently explain). They supply about 9 percent of the riboflavin and a considerable amount of niacin. The B vitamins are five times as rich in the germ as in the bran (the outer covering removed to make white flour). And if any vitamin A is present, it is in the fat of the germ. This is also where vitamin E is found.

Cereal grains contain no vitamin C or D and, with the exception of yellow corn meal, no vitamin A. They are also low in calcium. These are other reasons why the English children on the white bread and sugar diet were in such a low state of health and looked so old and stunted. They lacked essential vitamins, minerals, and proteins.

During World War II, the British government required that bread be made of the whole grains, and it is well known that that country had healthy babies and growing children during this period.

Why Are White Cereal-Breads Preferred by Many People?

The fact that 97 percent of the flour used in our country is white shows how much it is preferred. Why is this?

Many people prefer the white color in bread and cereal, somehow associating white with purity. Of course color has nothing to do with purity. The clearest water may be swarming with deadly bacteria.

Then too, during hard times millions of people lived on dark bread and little more. For some, the dark loaf suggests poverty. The ruling and rich were the first to have the white loaf. When the French and Swiss millers made it possible for every man to eat the bread of the rich, every man wanted that bread! For man did not know he was making his health poorer by this choice.

White flour keeps better because fat is removed in the germ. It is from the germ, rich in many nutrients, that the new plant

Biscuits topping a meat-vegetable pie help make left-overs delicious and nutritious.

is made. This is what the grain weevil (bug) eats to support his own life! Also, in hot weather the fat causes the flour to have an "old" or "rancid" taste. Those who buy and sell large amounts of the whole grain risk greater loss. Ordinarily it is difficult to find whole grain (Graham) flour on the market in the summer.

Then there is the texture of white bread compared with that of the heavier whole grain. The gluten (glo͞o′tĕn) in white flour is the chief protein. It is a weak protein for health, but a strong one for giving baked foods, such as bread and cake, a spongy light texture that is a joy to the baker or cook.

On the other hand, the grain used in white, fine-texture bread has less and poorer-quality protein, and less iron and B vitamins than the whole grain. What has been done to correct this weakness in such an important food?

Scrapple is left-over cereal chilled in a mold with diced meat. Delicious when browned.

Enrichment of Bread

During World War II our leaders were concerned for our health. We had a war to win, and we needed to be well and strong to win it. Studies showed that a large number of people were not eating the food they needed for good health. One step to try to improve this was the daily food guide called the "Basic 7." This was not enough. A boost in essential nutrients was needed in some basic food.

Bread, scientists pointed out, is important in the diet and especially in low-cost diets. It is easy to "enrich" bread with some of the nutrients removed in making it white. Nutritionists pointed out that the whole grains were the food that had been known as the "staff of life." They cited experiments which showed that white bread, when used as the only protein in the diet, did not support growth of the young, but that under exactly the same conditions whole grain supported good growth. It was decided that four important nutrients (but not protein) removed in making white flour should be put back.

A Federal law was passed in 1943 to enrich white-flour with thiamine, riboflavin, niacin, and iron. These nutrients are also added to some cereals that are spoken of as "restored." The flour companies cooperated in this program to the extent that some have also added two nutrients which are low in white flour but not required by law to be added. These are calcium and vitamin D.

AMOUNTS OF SIX NUTRIENTS IN ONE POUND OF DIFFERENT TYPES OF FLOUR*

Kind of Flour	Protein grams	Calcium mg.	Iron mg.	Thiamine mg.	Riboflavin mg.	Niacin mg.
Whole Wheat: 100%	60.3	186	15.0	2.49	0.54	19.7
Not Enriched White: Family or all-purpose	47.6	73	3.6	.28	.21	4.1
Enriched White: Family or all-purpose	47.6	73	13.0	2.00	1.20	16.0

* Adapted from Handbook 8, *Composition of Foods,* U.S.D.A.

In the table above you see a comparison of six important nutrients for health found in one pound of (a) whole wheat, (b) enriched, and (c) not enriched white flour. Notice that whole wheat is superior in five of the six nutrients over the enriched flour. Also observe how greatly superior the enriched is over the unenriched.

Since 97 percent of the flour used in our country is white, you can see that the enrichment of flour brings an enormous improvement to the diets of many people. Indeed, nutrition clinics report that since the enrichment of white flour, diseases and physical defects caused by lack of vitamin B have practically disappeared. This has helped those with a lower income more than those with a higher income.

At the end of World War II, Federal requirement for the enrichment of cereal-breads was dropped. Some states have passed laws requiring enrichment, but not all. In some states where there is no such law, some bakers voluntarily enrich bread.

If you bake bread at home, you can make it more nourishing by using such ingredients as whole grain flour, dry milk, brewer's yeast, wheat germ, eggs, and dark molasses. Special breads have been developed that are much richer in nu-

trients we need than ordinary bread. Such breads are used in hospitals, schools, and other institutions. Many of these recipes also use 10 percent soy flour.

Many people use unenriched white rice. What are they getting for their money from this, in comparison with the brown, whole-grain rice? They get a white color compared with a cream one. They get a lighter, fluffier texture compared with a firmer, slightly smaller grain of rice. The

Chicken curry with rice is a favorite dish from India.

flavor of the white rice is quite mild, and that of the brown is somewhat nutty. Those who eat brown rice claim that it has a superior flavor. But these are not the most important points. Brown rice has four times as much calcium as white rice, more than seven times as much iron, and five times as much thiamine.

Keep in mind that the "enrichment" of cereal-breads in any form has greatly improved health. We do need the nutrients that are put back into the white, refined products. But also keep in mind that both the known and the unknown nutrients can help you when you eat the natural whole-grain cereal-breads. These facts can guide you in planning meals, and in buying the food that makes your meals. Such a small item as the difference in the nourishment of the bread you eat can add up over the years, to make a difference in your vitality and appearance.

 WORDS TO WORK WITH

Beriberi (bĕr′ĭ bĕr′ĭ): a disease caused by inadequate amounts of thiamine in the diet.

Enriched: the term used when thiamine, riboflavin, niacin, and iron have been added to flour.

Fortified: the term used when a nutrient has been added to a food, such as vitamin A to margarine, iodine to salt, etc.

Gluten (gloo′tĕn): soft, spongy substance in wheat that gives lightness to the texture of breads and baked foods.

Restored: the replacement of nutrients for the enrichment of cereals.

Thiamine (thī′á mĕn): the first B vitamin to be discovered, found in the polishings of brown rice. It is necessary in the diet to prevent or cure the disease beriberi, and for general health.

 THINKING IT OVER

1. Why is a food (such as cereal-grain or an egg) that can make a new life so important for human food?

2. Why do milk and whole grain bread make a good food combination in the same meal? How can you use this knowledge to plan better meals?

3. What causes the disease beriberi? How did Takaki lead the way in showing that diet is related to disease?

4. Describe how Dr. Eijkman proved that brown rice contained a nutrient which was lost in making white rice. What was this nutrient?

5. What are the contributions that cereal-bread makes to our meals?

6. Why is white bread more popular than whole wheat? Do you think most people know the reasons why whole-grain cereals and breads are better for health and appearance?

7. Explain what is meant by the terms "enriched," "restored," "fortified."

8. How can you add nourishment to bread when you bake it at home?

9. What is the best choice in bread or cereal, the white enriched or the whole grain? Give reasons for your answer.

10. Does your state have a law requiring the enrichment of bread and flour?

APPLYING WHAT YOU KNOW

1. Cooking cereals in different ways.
   (1) Select two different cereals that give high nourishment for the money spent, and prepare one as a part of a balanced breakfast, and the other as a part of a Sunday night supper that would follow a hearty dinner at noon.
   (2) Plan menus in which these cereals will help make a balanced meal.
2. Making your own ready-mix.
   (1) Study the recipes for biscuits, whole wheat muffins, corn muffins, and pancakes. Decide how you can make a mix for each, and how you would store it.
   (2) Select a type of mix you would like to prepare, and make it. Write and place on your container a label telling what is in the mix and what is to be added.
3. Select a muffin recipe and make muffins as the bread for a balanced breakfast or lunch. Discuss what you need to keep in mind to make a high-quality muffin.
4. In what ways can you use left-over bread? Select one way and make a dish using left-over bread, serving this as part of a balanced meal.

PROBLEMS TO SOLVE

1. Make a trip to the market to see and compare the way various cereal-bread products are packaged and sold. Observe the following:
   (1) Variety of cereals to cook—find what the label tells you that can help you make a wise selection: weight, size of container, cost, kind of cereal.
   (2) Variety of ready-to-eat cereals—read label and note weight, size of container, cost, kind of cereal.

   (3) Variety of ready-mix quick breads—note what the label tells you that can help you make a wise decision in what to buy: weight, cost, and what you have to add to it.
   (4) Variety of ready-to-use quick breads—observe same information as above.
2. Make an exhibit of a variety of the cereal-breads you found in your market, and discuss what you are getting in relation to the cost of different types of products. Consider time, energy, money, taste, and nutritional value.
3. Plan four days of balanced menus, showing how you would use in different meals the foods you have decided to buy.
4. Look up the story of the cereal grains in a good reference book, and report what you find to the class.

EVALUATING

1. Under what circumstances would you cook extra cereal for breakfast, and how would you store and use the left-over cereal?
2. Under what circumstances would you buy ready-prepared cereal? Ready-prepared mix for quick breads? Ready-made quick breads?
3. What are the advantages in making your own mixes? Your own bread? Are there any disadvantages? What?
4. In what different ways can you serve cereal or bread in each meal?

HOME EXPERIENCE

Discuss with your mother what you have learned about cereal-bread. With her, plan menus for three balanced meals using cereal or quick bread in some form. Prepare and serve the cereal or bread as a part of these meals. Report results to your teacher.

18

Buying, Preparing, and Using Cereal-Bread

Our Daily Need of Cereal-Bread

The amount of cereal-bread which should be included in the daily diet varies with different families, and with individuals within each family.

The less you have to spend, the more important bread and milk are to keep your diet well balanced. When people in Europe lived mostly on bread, they ate two pounds or more per person daily. (One pound of bread gives about 1200 calories.) With the foods we have available, bread should be part of a balanced diet, but not too prominent.

Your need of bread or cereal also relates to how fast you are growing, your size,

weight, and activity, and the other foods you eat. A baby on a milk diet soon needs cereal to add calories. A teen-ager who is growing very fast and thus gaining weight, may eat the recommended daily diet, with six slices of bread a day, plus

A variety of rolls may be made from basic bread dough. Here are some you will learn to make. (See steps on pages 190 and 192-3.)

cereal, and not gain too much weight. An adult who has his growth may gain excess weight if he eats that much bread or cereal, plus the other foods he needs.

But bread is not fattening when used in your meals in balance. One slice of bread has between 45 and 55 calories. It is what you put on bread that so often makes it fattening. You can eat about four slices of bread a day for the same number of calories in one candy bar.

Getting the Most for Your Money in Buying Cereal-Bread

You get the most nourishment for the money spent when you buy *whole grain* breads or cereals. The second-best buy is the "enriched," "restored," or "converted"; and you get the least for your money in the plain white, "patent" flour, processed cereal or bread.

Read the label on any cereal-bread product before you buy it. The label helps you understand what you are buying, by listing the price, the weight, whether coloring or preservative has been added, percentage of whole grain, and the nutrients added for enrichment. The label helps you understand what you are buying. Take the matter of color. Dark bread sometimes is dark not from the whole grain flour, but from added coloring! Some very dark bread may have very little whole grain flour. Yellow color in noodles may come from coloring instead of eggs.

Buy bread and cereals by weight, and not by the size of the loaf or package. Size can be misleading. For instance, a one-pound loaf of whole-wheat bread may be one-third smaller than a one-pound loaf of some types of white bread. You are not getting more food in the big loaf, even though it looks as if you are.

Similarly, in prepared cereals, also look at the weight. A puffed cereal may be in a box three to seven times larger than a box of compact cereal, yet the weight may be greater in the smaller box. Sometimes a big box may be only two-thirds full. Some of the cost of cereal may be going into prizes and the size of the box. By checking what you get for your money, you can make wiser decisions.

Cooked cereals are less expensive than prepared cereals, weight for weight. The volume looks bigger in the prepared ones. However, it takes $1\frac{1}{4}$ cups of corn flakes to give one ounce, but only three tablespoons of corn meal; or $2\frac{1}{4}$ cups of puffed cereal compared with two tablespoons of the uncooked cereal.

You can save money by buying day-old bread and baked goods. They are nourishing, and when rolls are reheated they seem fresh. In some cities it is necessary to get to the store early if you want to get this less expensive bread.

Here are some examples of commercial breads designed to *save time* for the busy homemaker. Remember that you pay for this service, and that the products may be less nourishing than breads you can make.

Baked products—ready to serve
Partially baked products—baking to be completed at home.
Frozen baked products—to unwrap, thaw, and warm if desired.
Frozen prepared bread—to bake at home.
Canned prepared biscuits—to bake before serving.
Prepared mix—add liquid and eggs, mix, and bake before serving.

Buying in quantity saves money if you have suitable storage space. One pound of flour costs more than a fifth of the cost of five pounds. Five pounds costs more per pound than fifty. But if you do not use much flour and have poor storage space, it is wasteful to buy larger amounts than you can store. Sometimes real savings can be made in buying baked goods to put in the deep freezer, if you own one.

Shopping for bread should be done along with that for other foods. It is wasteful of time and energy to make a trip to the store for only a loaf of bread. Check the· sale foods in cereal-bread products before you buy. For instance, when a company is introducing a new product, the store may run a "special" on it. Or a company may run a special on a regular product for a day. If you know the quality of this product and need it, buy it "on special," and save.

The Use of Cereal-Bread in Our Meals

The variety of cereal-breads we can use in meals is almost endless. For example, there are cereals to cook made from wheat, rice, corn, and oats. Many variations of these foods are in prepared cereals.

Cereal cooked in water is an ancient way to use the cereal grains. In our country we eat cooked cereal mainly for breakfast. But in the Orient, people eat boiled rice at every meal. The British Isles and parts of Europe have been carried through hard times more than once by a generous use of oatmeal porridge. Oatmeal retains most of the bran and germ when it is processed. The American Indian boiled whole crushed corn in a pot, as well as

making bread of it and baking it on hot rocks. Processed corn meal today, however, has no germ and little bran but in some states it is enriched. Bulgur, made from the whole cracked wheat, may be used as an alternate in almost any recipe where rice is used. This has long been a favorite food used by Turks, Arabs, Armenians, and some Europeans. It is a tasty and nourishing way to use wheat.

Cereals are clean and do not need to be washed before cooking. Some vitamins can be lost by overwashing rice. Cereals should be cooked in just enough water so that all is absorbed. Cereals such as rice and macaroni products which are cooked in large amounts of water and drained, lose nourishment.

Cooked cereal is usually served with sugar and cream. If it is whole-grain or enriched and is cooked with inexpensive but highly nourishing dried milk, you have an excellent dish. By adding raisins or other dried fruit, you can add still more nourishment. Served with a citrus fruit or other food rich in vitamin C, along with a glass of milk, such cereal makes one of the least expensive and best-balanced meals. This is a typical breakfast for many in America.

To save time, some homemakers cook more cereal at once than is immediately needed. If you try this, there are several ways you can make good use of what remains: (a) Left-over cereal can be reheated in hot milk in the top of the double boiler or over direct low heat. Heat the milk first, then drop in the cereal, cover, and get the remainder of breakfast, letting the cereal heat slowly until breakfast is ready. Left-over cereal reheated in this way has a smooth texture and pleasant

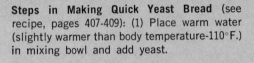

Steps in Making Quick Yeast Bread (see recipe, pages 407-409): (1) Place warm water (slightly warmer than body temperature-110°F.) in mixing bowl and add yeast.

(2) Add sugar, salt, oil, dry milk, and eggs and beat until batter drops from spoon. Add half the flour and beat 2 minutes. Work in remaining flour 1 cup at a time until a soft dough is formed. Turn onto lightly floured board.

(5) Fold dough under, divide, and shape into loaves the length of the pan and one-half the depth. Fold dough over on itself, pressing firmly to a smooth loaf.

(6) Place loaf in oiled pan, brush top with oil, cover, and set in warm place until double in bulk (about 50 minutes).

186

(3) Knead by folding under until soft and smooth. Clean mixing bowl, oil it, and return dough to bowl. Oil dough lightly, cover, and set in warm place until double in bulk (about 1 hour).

(4) After dough doubles in bulk, fold under, oil top, and let rise until double in bulk again (about 45 minutes).

Preheat oven to 400°F. Place pans in center of oven and bake for 15 minutes. Reduce to 350°F and bake 30 to 35 minutes, or il done.

(8) Remove bread from pan by loosening with spatula and cool on rack. Brush crust with melted fat and cover with clean towel for a few minutes to soften crust. Serve warm; or cool, wrap, and store.

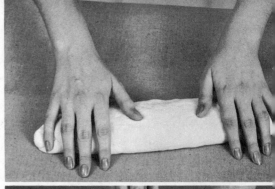

flavor. Dried fruit used with it improves in flavor with standing in the refrigerator and being reheated. (b) Pour hot left-over cereal into a mold. Store in refrigerator. Slice it and brown in a small amount of fat. Serve this with syrup or honey, as you would French toast. If chopped meat is added to hot corn mush and molded, you have scrapple. (c) Left-over oatmeal or whole wheat makes yeast bread more tasty if added to the dough. (d) Left-over rice is used in various Spanish-rice dishes, with red beans, with left-over meat, fish, or poultry, and in rice puddings.

Prepared cereals belong to the modern age of processed foods. They are made of wheat, corn, oats, and rice. Small amounts of buckwheat and soy beans are added to some cereals. Ready-to-eat cereals may be whole-grain, enriched, or refined. Any vitamins, minerals, or proteins added to cereal can be found listed on the box, under "ingredients." Salt, sugar, malt, honey, and other flavorings are used in the processing. The ready-to-eat cereal is pre-cooked and rolled, shredded, puffed, or flaked. It can be bought in individual servings and in medium-size and large boxes. As the volume you buy increases, the relative cost declines.

Prepared cereals are used for lunch and supper dishes but they are most popular for breakfast, especially in the warm summer months. If you eat the whole grain or "restored" ones and use generous milk and fruit, ·you have a nourishing, quick meal. But you pay more for prepared than for cooked cereal.

Macaroni, spaghetti, and noodle products are all about equal in nourishment. They all come from the hard durum wheat, which is high in a tough protein

Steps in Making French Bread: (1) Shape yeast dough into desired size for French bread. (2) Place loaf on lightly oiled cookie sheet, cut gashes at 2-inch intervals across the top, and bake as for bread. To glaze top, brush with egg yolk mixed with 2 table-spoons of water. (3) Serve hot or cool as part of a balanced meal.

that holds its shape. They are processed in different shapes to give variety, and noodles usually have eggs added. These products are popular as a main dish for lunch and dinner. They are made from the starchy part of the wheat grain and need to be balanced with meat or cheese, green and yellow vegetables, tomatoes or green salad, fruit, and milk.

Quick breads get their name because they are quick and easy to make. Among the quick breads are pancakes, popovers, waffles, muffins, drop biscuits, rolled biscuits, quick loaf bread, and coffee cakes. Yeast bread is made into loaves and into many varieties of rolls and coffee cakes. Quick breads are leavened with baking powder, soda, eggs, and steam. Compared to the old-fashioned yeast bread, with its long process of preparation, they give the homemaker a quick way to add a tasty lift to a meal. Furthermore, they can be nourishing when properly made.

Quick bread mixtures fall into three patterns: (a) *Pour batters* are used for popovers, pancakes, and waffles. These are thin batters, using about one cup of liquid to one cup of flour. (b) *Drop batters* are used for drop biscuits, muffins, loaf breads, and coffee cakes. These are thick batters, using about a half-cup of liquid to one cup of flour. (c) *Dough that is soft but can be rolled* is used in making biscuits, cobbler dough, and dumplings. The principle to follow here is to use about one-third cup liquid to one cup flour. These measurements vary with the kind of flour used. An all-purpose or family flour needs more liquid than pastry flour. You can make a better product by noticing the thickness of your batter or dough

and adding the last flour or liquid cautiously.

The ingredients in quick breads are: flour, liquid, fat, sugar, eggs, a leavening agent, and flavoring.

To make good quick breads, start with a good recipe, and mix quickly, for over-mixing develops the gluten in the flour and causes "tunnels" and coarseness in the bread. There are two methods of mixing: by adding the dry ingredients to the liquid, or the liquid to the dry. Follow your recipe. Bake quick breads just before serving, remove from pans, and serve hot. If you have a good recipe and follow it accurately, you will have good results.

Yeast bread has the same ingredients as quick bread, except that the leavening agent is yeast, and one allows approximately three cups of flour per cup of liquid in making it. When the word "bread" is used, it means for most people a bread leavened with yeast. Yeast bread is the most-used bread for breakfast toast. It is widely used at lunch in sandwiches. At dinner we see it in many different types of hot and cold rolls and loaf breads. The yeast coffee cake and the doughnut are special breakfast breads, and are more cake than bread, owing to the large amount of sugar and fat used.

Making Quick Breads and Yeast Breads

(1) *Wheat flour* is a basic ingredient in bread. This is because wheat contains a protein, gluten (glōō′těn), which develops an elastic quality in the presence of liquid and holds the carbon dioxide (kär′bŏn dī ŏk′sīd) gas to make a light bread.

In making bread with other grains, such as cornmeal or rye, wheat flour must also be in the recipe to supply the needed gluten to make a light product.

There are several varieties of wheat flour, used for different kinds of baking: (a) Whole wheat, or Graham (named for a man who opposed white flour and got the whole grain back on the market), contains the whole grain of wheat with its bran and germ, ground into a fine flour. (b) Plain white flour (enriched and unenriched) is made of the center starchy part of the wheat grain, called "endosperm." (See diagram, page 173). White flour can be bought bleached or unbleached. If the flour is unbleached, this is stated on the label. It is slightly more yellow, but is the natural white flour. Bleached white flour is made whiter than the natural by the use of chemical bleaches. (c) Self-rising flour contains salt and a leavening agent. When you use this flour, be sure to follow the directions on the package. (d) "Wondra" flour is a trade name for a lump-proof flour that disperses instantly when mixed with cold liquid. It does not lump or pack. It costs about two cents per pound more than regular enriched all-purpose flour. (e) Self-sifted enriched all-purpose flour may pack and require sifting, despite the claims. It costs no more than regular flour. Often flours packaged and sold under the special name of the specific chain store cost a few cents per pound less than other brands.

Flour also varies according to the kind of wheat from which it is made. The hard red winter and spring wheats give hard strong flour used by bakers for yeast bread. This *hard wheat flour* has more gluten and gives a stronger framework to make the bread light and spongy. *Durum wheat* also produces a strong flour that is high in proteins, and it is used in macaroni products.

Soft wheat flour is made from red winter wheats and white spring and winter wheats. It is less rich in protein (8–11 percent against 12–16 percent for hard wheat), and its weaker gluten gives finer texture to cakes and quick breads.

Steps in Making Crescent Rolls: (1) Preheat oven to 425°F. Divide basic yeast dough into small portions. (2) Roll dough into circle about ¼ inch thick and brush with melted fat. (3) Cut dough into center, fastening securely by pressing. Place with center points down on oiled cookie sheet and let rise until double in bulk (about 30 minutes). Bake for about 12 minutes until golden brown.

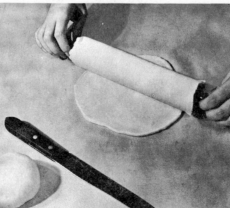

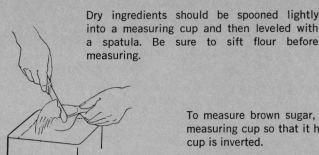

Dry ingredients should be spooned lightly into a measuring cup and then leveled with a spatula. Be sure to sift flour before measuring.

To measure brown sugar, pack it tightly in a measuring cup so that it holds its shape when cup is inverted.

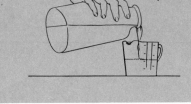

Measure liquids in a liquid-type measuring cup. Be sure that the cup is level.

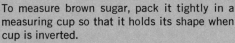

Measure spoonfuls of liquid ingredients over empty dishes; measuring over other ingredients is too risky.

All-purpose or family flour is a blend of these two and, as the name suggests, can be used for any purpose.

Sift white flour *before measuring*. Spoon it into the cup lightly and then level with a spatula (see diagram). But do not sift whole wheat or graham flour, or stone-ground cornmeal before measuring. To sift and throw away the siftings is to throw away a good part of the flour or meal. Stir it with a fork and spoon into a cup without sifting. Keep it stored in a tight container, so that it will stay clean.

(2) *Liquids* are essential to bind and blend the different ingredients together. Liquid dissolves the sugar, starts the action of the leavening agent, and combines with flour to start the development of the gluten. The one most frequently used in making bread is milk. Milk gives bread more nourishment, a better brown crust, and a more tender moist crumb, and helps it keep a fresh taste longer than when water is used as liquid. Milk contains nutrients that offset the weaknesses of flour, and therefore a nutritious bread results.

Measure liquids accurately (see diagram). Too much liquid makes the product too thin, causes it to take longer to cook, with more likelihood of burning, and produces a tighter texture. Too little liquid produces a coarser-grained, drier, tougher product.

(3) *Leavening agents* are gaseous substances which raise and lighten a dough or batter. They give a porous quality to baked food, increasing the volume during baking and improving the texture. There are three leavening agents: air, steam, and carbon dioxide.

It is customary to use the term *leaven* (lĕv′ĕn) in flour mixtures such as quick breads, yeast breads, or cakes. Here carbon dioxide is the leavening agent, and it is produced when baking powder, soda, or yeast is used in the mixture.

There are three types of *baking powder*, and the amount used varies according to the type. The tartrate and phosphate baking powders require the most per cup of flour, because of the fact that the action begins to take place as soon as the powder is mixed with the liquid. The double-action baking powder is called S.A.S. (standing for sodium aluminum sulphate). It has a double action. That means some of its leavening takes place as soon as it is mixed with liquid and some takes place at oven temperature. Follow the directions on the baking powder can and in your recipes for use of baking powder. (See recommended amounts on page 354.) Keep baking powder cans tightly closed to prevent lumping and loss of strength. Discard lumpy baking powder.

Soda was used for leavening long before baking powder. It reacts with buttermilk or sour milk or molasses to form carbon dioxide gas, which leavens. Use a half-teaspoon of soda per cup of sour milk or molasses. (You can make sour milk by adding two tablespoons of lemon juice to one cup of milk.) Soda does not have as much leavening power as baking powder. If you use too much soda, it ruins the taste, affects the color, and tends to destroy thiamine in the bread. Studies of bread enriched with thiamine show loss of this nutrient when soda is added. Many old-fashioned recipes using large amounts of soda for cookies and chocolate cake need to be revised. Measure baking powder and soda accurately in a measuring spoon, and level with a spatula.

Steam is used to leaven popovers. You need to have a thin batter and high heat. The heat raises the batter in the first part of cooking and sets the egg and flour cells firmly to form a thin outer crust. Then the heat is reduced to finish cooking. The center is now hollow. In a good popover you have a tasty, crusty shell, and little more, but it is quite nourishing.

When the *whites of eggs* are beaten separately and folded in after mixing a batter, as in waffles, they help leaven and give a lighter, finer, crisper texture.

Yeast is the leavening agent used to make breads, rolls, breakfast cakes, and raised doughnuts. Unlike baking powder and soda, yeast is an excellent food. It is composed of living yeast plants and is rich in B vitamins and protein.

Our ancestors observed that when they ate bread leavened with yeast they seemed to be healthier than when they ate bread leavened with soda or baking powder. Until quite recently some people had a deep prejudice against quick breads. Some blamed the leavening and others blamed the hot temperature for inferior-

Knots, or breadsticks, are appropriate with meals of lasagne or spaghetti.

ity. Neither is at fault. With our better knowledge of food we find that it is not the leavening or the temperature in the quick breads which makes them show up more poorly over the long run. It is the yeast in the yeast bread that brings added B vitamins! Over a long period these extra B vitamins every day add up to an increase in vitality and vigor that may be noticeable. People do look better and feel better when they get enough B vitamins.

There are two types of yeast in common use today. One is the granular dry form, which requires no refrigeration before use. The other is a compressed damp cake, which requires storage in the refrigerator.

Yeast needs liquid, sugar, and a warm temperature to grow new yeast plants and form the gas that the gluten holds to lighten the bread.

Some homemakers hesitate to make yeast bread because of *kneading*. To knead dough, pull the outer edge up and fold it down, pushing it gently into the mass with the heel of the hand until it forms a smooth ball. Kneading develops the gluten, a protein that gives the attractive fine grain to yeast bread, but it is not necessary to knead bread for a good flavor. By using more yeast (which is an advantage for health), you can make quick yeast bread without kneading. This dough will keep in the refrigerator for a week at a time. You can bake fresh hot bread or rolls as you wish.

(4) *Fat* of your choice is used in making bread, and should be measured accurately in graduated measuring cups. (See diagram page 191.) Fat improves the flavor, makes the crumb more tender, and increases browning. Butter and margarine add vitamin A. Recent studies seem to indicate that the vegetable oils are the most desirable for the health of the blood vessels. (See Chapter 23.)

(5) *Sugar* adds flavor, improves texture, increases browning, and provides

Clover leaf rolls are popular for lunch or dinner.

To make quick clover leaf rolls, shape dough in ball and clip with shears to one-third of the depth.

food to enable the yeast plants to ferment or multiply, thus making the bread light in texture. Dark brown sugar, molasses, or honey is used instead of white sugar in some breads to give a good flavor, and dark molasses adds iron. Sugar does not need to be sifted before measuring unless it has lumps. Brown sugar is packed into the cup when measured.

(6) *Eggs* combine well with flour to hold the gas in a batter or dough. They also add color, flavor, and nourishment.

(7) *Flavorings* go into all baked products. Salt is our chief flavoring. This nutrient is a mineral that forms a part of the body fluids, and man has a great craving for it. It brings out the natural flavor of many foods, including bread. Salt also prevents the yeast plants from growing too fast and toughens the gluten in the flour and the protein in egg white.

There are other flavorings used in breads, such as nuts, fruits, cheese, spices, and extracts. These give variety, and some improve the nourishment.

What Makes Good Quality in Bread ?

Each type of quick bread and yeast bread has its own standard for quality. But certain standards can be applied to all bread.

The color of the crust should be golden brown, except for whole wheat, which should be dark brown. Bread should be light in texture, with a tender, moist crumb. The shape and grain should be characteristic of its type. The flavor of bread should be mellow, mild, and pleasant. Quick breads and rolls should be served hot. Loaf bread and breakfast breads may be served hot or cool.

The Storage of Cereal-Bread Products

It is of great importance to store cereal-breads properly. Any opened package of cereal must be closed so that insects or rodents cannot get into it. In areas where these pests cause trouble, store dry flour and all opened cereals in closed containers with tight-fitting lids, or in tight jars.

Partially cooked or frozen breads should be stored in the freezer at 0° or lower. If bread is purchased on sale in large amounts, or if the homemaker prepares and bakes a large amount at a time to save money and time for a later period, store this in the freezer. If the bread is perfectly wrapped and sealed and is stored immediately, it is as good as fresh when used later.

When small amounts of bread are made at a time, store in a clean bread box. Bread boxes should be washed with soda and sunned every week if possible. Bread picks up odors quickly, and fresh bread is spoiled in flavor by an old odor in the bread box. Furthermore, mold sets in faster on bread if the bread box is not clean. Place the bread box in a cool part of the kitchen.

If bread is not used quickly, wrap it well and store it in the refrigerator. This retards mold, especially in hot weather. The bread becomes firmer in texture when stored in the refrigerator, but this does not hurt the food value or flavor.

Use of Left-Over Bread

There is no need to throw out bread that has not been eaten when fresh. Ways you can make good use of it are given on page 196 and are shown opposite.

Using Left-Over Bread: (1) Cut stale bread in cubes for soft bread crumbs to be used in stuffings, fondue, or white sauce.

(2) Run bread through food chopper and store in covered jar to be used for topping casserole dishes.

(3) Use bread cubes or crumbs to make a stuffing for poultry, fish, meat or vegetable (see recipe, page 432).

(1) Place left-over quick breads or rolls in a pan and sprinkle with water. Cover and heat in a moderate oven for 10 to 12 minutes. Serve at once.

(2) Split, butter, and toast left-over muffins, biscuits, corn bread, and rolls.

(3) Use left-over biscuits and corn-bread, and old yeast bread and rolls, in dressing for meat, fish, or poultry.

(4) Dry out yeast bread and roll it into bread crumbs. Store in tight jars in the refrigerator for casserole toppings.

(5) Use any kind of left-over bread with milk, eggs, brown sugar, dried fruits, and nuts to make bread pudding.

Value of Homemade Bread

Homemade yeast bread, and quick breads, can be among the most economical, healthful, and tasty foods in your diet. When you make the bread yourself, you know what you are getting. You can "enrich" it with eggs, dry milk, and other nutrients your family needs. The aroma of homemade yeast bread is one of the most delightful among foods. The flavor of homemade bread adds great pleasure to any meal. It can lift an ordinary meal to one that is something special. Many homemakers make their own bread simply because the family enjoys it so much. Vary the bread you use in meals to add interest and nourishment to your diet. Studies show that the choice of bread influences people's preferences in regard to other foods at a meal. For instance, when corn bread is served, more vegetables are eaten than when biscuits are served. With biscuits, people tend to prefer more butter, jam, honey, and sweets and they eat less of the vegetables.

 WORDS TO WORK WITH

Carbon dioxide (kär′bŏn dī ŏk′sīd): a gas produced by the action of a leavening agent in the presence of liquid.

Gluten (glo͞o′tĕn): a protein, found in wheat, that helps produce a yeast bread of desirable light texture.

Leaven (lĕv′ĕn): to raise or lighten a dough or batter by gas produced from the fermentation of yeast or from baking powder or soda in the presence of liquid.

Knead (nēd): to work and press dough into a mass by folding it over on itself.

THINKING IT OVER

1. What determines the amount of bread you need to eat daily?

2. Why should you spend more money for bread and milk than for meat and bread on a low-cost diet?

3. Why do people think bread is fattening when one slice has only 45 to 55 calories?

4. How many slices of bread could you eat for the number of calories in a candy bar? What does bread give you which you don't get in candy?

5. Which type of bread or cereal gives you the most health for your money—whole grain, white enriched, or white unen-

riched? Cooked or prepared? Why is this?

6. Explain what the label on cereal-bread products tells and how you can save money by reading the label before you buy.

7. Why should you buy whole grain bread by the label instead of the color? Why purchase baked products by weight instead of size?

8. In what different ways can you serve cereal or bread at breakfast, lunch, and dinner? When is bread or cereal the main dish?

9. What are the ingredients in bread? Explain how each ingredient helps make a good bread. How do you judge a good bread?

10. How can making bread at home improve the pleasure and nourishment in your meals? How does your choice of bread in a meal influence your health and looks?

11. Explain what good quality is in quick breads; in yeast breads.

12. How would you store left-over bread? How could you use it in meals?

PROBLEMS TO SOLVE

1. Make a trip to your market and compare the flour products available, by reading what is on the label, and using your general knowledge. Look for white "patent" flour, white "enriched" flour, bleached white flour, unbleached white flour, non-lumping flour, whole wheat flour, buckwheat flour, cornmeal, soy flour, other flour. Using what you have learned, discuss and decide which you would buy to use most wisely the food money for your family.

2. Study the labels and compare the following short cuts in breads for the family:

types, prices, ingredients, weight, and cost of (1) fresh-baked bread; (2) partially baked bread products; (3) frozen ready-baked products; (4) canned bread to bake; (5) canned ready-to-eat bread; (6) prepared mixes to which liquid and egg is to be added; (7) prepared mixes to which only liquid is to be added.

(1) As a class, pool the results of your study, and evaluate what you learned. Consider time and energy saved in the different types of products in relation to the total cost, food value, taste, and attractiveness.

(2) How do you rate each of these products in comparison with those that are homemade?

(3) Which would you use on a low-cost food budget? A moderate one? A liberal one?

(4) What points can guide you in deciding what is the "best buy" in bread or cereal?

3. Study recipes for baking different types of bread.

(1) What nutrients are added by dry milk solids? By eggs?

(2) Which type of bread would you make if you wished to increase the B vitamins?

APPLYING WHAT YOU KNOW

1. Learning to make yeast bread by the quick method. (This process is learned by cooperating with other classes.)

(1) Mix yeast bread by the quick method, and store in the refrigerator.

(2) Using bread that has been prepared ahead by another class fold it under and let it rise.

(3) At the following lesson bake bread that has been set to rise by another class, and serve it as a part of a balanced meal.

2. Plan balanced menus for one week for your family, using some form of yeast bread in each meal and showing a variety of nutritious ways in which it can be used.

3. Plan three supper or luncheon menus using left-over bread or cereal as a part of the balanced meal.

4. Plan and prepare one supper or luncheon menu using macaroni or spaghetti as a part of the balanced meal; plan and prepare one using brown rice.

 HOME EXPERIENCE

Discuss with your mother what you have learned about yeast bread. Plan a balanced dinner menu including hot quick rolls or bread. You prepare and serve the bread. Report results to your teacher.

 FURTHER READING

Baked Products: Consumer Quality, Composition, and Preparation Time of Various Market Forms, R. H. Mathews, E. W. Murphy, A. C. Marsh, and E. S. Dawson. Home Economics Research Report No. 22, 39 pp., illustrated. July, 1963.

Cereals and Pasta in Family Meals. Home and Garden Bulletin 150, U.S.D.A., Washington, D.C., 1968.

Cooking with Rice. U.S.D.A., Washington, D.C., 1956.

"Developing Bread of Higher Nutritional Value," V. B. Parks, E. M. Hewston, *et al., Journal of American Dietetic Association,* 30:245–250 (March, 1954).

Enriched Bread. Leaflet. American Institute of Baking, Chicago, Ill., 1957.

Exploring Home and Family Living, 3rd ed., Henrietta Fleck and Louise Fernandez. Prentice-Hall, Inc., Englewood Cliffs, N.J., 1971.

"Food and Drug Administration Program," E. M. Nelson. (Reprinted by U.S. Dept. of Health, Education, and Welfare from *Public Health Service Reports,* June, 1956.)

Redi Wheat: A New Canned Cooked Bulgur. U.S.D.A., Washington, D.C., 1963.

Spice Cookbook, Avanelle Day and Lillie Stuckey. David White Company, New York, N.Y., 1964.

Yeast Bread and Rolls. Dudgeon and Dunn. Cornell Extension Bulletin E 888. Cornell University, Ithaca, N.Y., 1963.

VISUAL AIDS

A Kernel of Wheat. Poster. Wheat Flour Institute, Chicago, Ill.

Better Breakfasts U.S.A. Film. Tells the story of breakfast cereals. (For further description see page 118.) 1964.

Grains—Origin of Breakfast Cereals. Poster showing barley, corn, oats, rice and wheat. Cereal Institute, Inc., 135 LaSalle Street, Chicago, Ill.

Something You Didn't Eat (see page 104 for description).

unit **8**

Balance Your Lunch

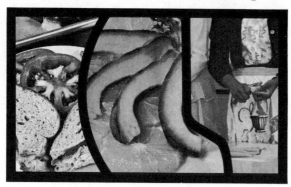

Lunch at
School or at Home

Vegetable plates plus milk provide a nourishing hot lunch with low calories. (If you add dessert to this type menu, it can also be used for dinner.) What other combinations would you enjoy?

Why Is Lunch So Important?

Did you ever stop to think that you eat most of your lunches at school for twelve years of your life? This adds up to over 2000 lunches—for each pupil in our schools! Since about one-third of the day's total food is consumed at lunch, our government wisely sees that helping its "growing" population nutritionally will better the health of its people generally.

Our national government—and many states, counties, and local communities as well—spend money to plan balanced lunch menus and supplies surplus foods free or at low cost for school lunches.

Studies show that a good lunch maintains efficiency in the afternoon; so in helping to provide good food for its pupils, the government also helps them get the most from their education.

Teen-age girls, according to studies, have the poorest food habits of any group. Their diets are too low in vitamins A and C, riboflavin, thiamine, calcium, iron, and sometimes calories.

Many teen-age boys and girls do not know how to select a balanced meal. How can you be guided in choosing a good lunch, away from home or at home?

How to Choose Your Lunch at School

When you pick up the tray and start down the cafeteria line, you are on your own. There are several things to remember when you start to select your lunch: (a) Keep in mind the amount of money you can spend. (b) Think of what you ate for breakfast and what you will probably have for dinner. Your lunch needs are influenced by the other meals of the day. (c) Think of what foods you need in a balanced lunch. (d) Choose a medium lunch or a hearty one according to your activity and rate of growth.

Guide for a Balanced Lunch

(1) *Choose a good protein food.* This can be eggs (if you did not eat one for breakfast), lean meat, fish, poultry, or cheese. It can be a meat substitute of lower protein value, such as dried beans, peas, or peanut butter.

(2) *Choose a good food for vitamin C.* You recall that foods rich in this vitamin are oranges, grapefruit, tangerines, tomatoes, raw cabbage, green lettuce, cooked green leafy vegetables, green or red peppers, cantaloupes, and strawberries. Almost all raw fruits and vegetables contain some vitamin C. This is a big reason why raw salad or raw fruit is desirable at lunch.

When you have lunch in a public restaurant, observe whether the menu contains a vitamin C-rich food, and include one as appetizer, salad, or dessert.

(3) *Choose a good calcium food,* such as milk or cheese. Remember that when you skip milk and choose another beverage, you are probably losing on your day's

This fish vegetable chowder is an excellent main dish for lunch. How can you achieve variety in soup?

Panned cabbage and ham give a different and nourishing main dish for lunch.

supply of calcium, riboflavin, protein, and vitamin A. Soda water and fruit-flavored drinks yield water, sugar, flavoring, and perhaps a stimulant, which add up only to "empty calories."

(4) *Choose other foods to meet your need for calories.* Keep in mind that the best foods for calories are the ones that also carry vitamins, minerals, and proteins.

If your school cooperates with the Federal government's school lunch program, you may have one or two different combinations of food from which to choose a balanced plate lunch. The "Type A" lunch is recommended by the government and it includes a variety of foods that come under the pattern suggested here.

When You Bring Your Lunch from Home

Some young people prefer to bring part or all of their lunch from home. Let us

202

consider how to put a packed lunch together.

(1) What goes into the lunch box meal? A hot food tastes good and often helps us enjoy lunch, but it is not the temperature of the food that nourishes. A well-selected lunch box meal, even if it is all cold, can be as good as, or better than, a poorly chosen, poorly cooked hot lunch.

(a) *Bread,* usually for a sandwich, gives variety in taste and nourishment, and supplies energy. Poultry and ham are tasty on rye bread. Roast beef, cheese, variety meats, and peanut butter combine well with whole wheat. Homemade quick loaf bread and yeast bread give a cold lunch a big boost in flavor.

The sandwich filling can supply a complete protein, such as lean meat, poultry, fish, eggs, or cheese. Peanut butter or baked beans may be used as an alternate if you also have milk in the meal.

(b) *Milk,* either brought from home or bought at school, is part of a good lunch box meal, for reasons mentioned in Chapters 1 to 6.

(c) Fresh, crisp *green lettuce* watercress, celery tops, green peppers, fresh to-

What meats can be used in a Shepherd's Pie? Why would you not put much potato, rice, or macaroni in such a stew as this?

matoes, and carrot sticks give contrast in texture and add nourishment to the sandwich. (See Chapters 9, 13, and 14.)

(d) *Dessert* for the packed lunch, then, can be fresh fruit in season, firm cakes, cookies, and sweet breads. Raw fruit can climax a meal; add vitamins and minerals, and help cleanse the teeth.

Variety of food is possible in the packed lunch. Even a baked egg custard may be used in the packed lunch for dessert. There are easily two dozen different excellent protein combinations for sandwich fillings, all of which are tasty. Think of the many breads, types of lettuce, and various fruits you have in season. With milk as a dependable beverage, you can have a delicious and nourishing packed lunch with some variety every day.

(2) *Packing the lunch* is simple with modern equipment. By planning ahead, you can make a dozen sandwiches from left-over turkey, ham, roast beef, or lamb, almost as easily as one, if you have a freezer. Make the sandwiches as if you were to eat them immediately. Then cut and wrap each just as you want it. Be sure that it is perfectly sealed. Place in freezer and remove each day as needed.

A paper napkin and a penknife are a help in eating a large tomato, a juicy pear, or an orange. Tangerines are an excellent lunch box fruit because their distinct sections are easy to manage. Apples, avocados, bananas and small fruits such as grapes, plums, cherries, and apricots also help balance a lunch.

(3) *Good table manners* should be observed at school whether you bring your lunch or buy it. Such little things as chewing with your lips closed, not taking large bites, and not talking with your

Sandwiches in the Luncheon: (1) Hot open sandwiches with vegetables can be nourishing and low in calories. (2) Sandwiches are a favorite as the main dish for lunch. Why is this sandwich a good choice? (3) A lunch packed at home can be tasty and nourishing.

Salads for Luncheon: A well-selected and well-prepared fruit salad is perfect for luncheon from the standpoint of flavor, appearance, low calorie content, and nutritive value. Salads can be used as main dishes, as accompaniments to the main dish, or as salad-desserts. How would you use the salads pictured here?

mouth too full of food mark the well-bred young person. Bad eating manners make one unpopular at home or away from home. On the other hand, good manners bring respect from others and greatly help your own self-respect. (See Chapter 25.)

Preparing Lunch at Home

Lunch can be at its best when prepared and served at home. Lunch is usually a smaller meal than dinner, though some families eat their dinner or larger meal at noon. The pattern is the same, regardless of what you call it. The menu is determined by the principles you have just considered. If the family works or exercises strenuously, lunch should be hearty like dinner. Otherwise a medium lunch is appropriate.

Lunch is a time to use up left-over food, if there is any. But this takes good planning.

The *main dish* for lunch at home is usually your complete protein dish; it may be the hot dish, or it may be a chef's salad bowl (see page 413). Casserole dishes are popular for lunch because they enable you to use up left-overs in a tasty, attractive manner. For instance, left-over rice makes an excellent Spanish rice, when combined with left-over ground beef (or hamburger) and onions, celery, green pepper, and tomatoes. This may be topped with cheese and browned in the oven, or mixed and cooked on top of the stove.

Left-over poultry, fish, or any other kind of meat may be combined with sauce, browned in the oven, and served as the main protein dish at lunch or supper. Chicken or turkey may be creamed and served on toast "a la king." If broccoli is first placed on the toast and then the creamed chicken, followed by sharp cheese, and this is browned in the oven on the platter on which it will be served, you have "Chicken Divine."

Macaroni and cheese is a popular luncheon casserole main dish. It is even more tasty and nourishing if you add diced onion, celery and celery leaves, and carrots to the macaroni while it is cooking. When cheese sauce is added to this and it is browned in the oven, it gives an attractive and tangy main dish that is also inexpensive and nourishing.

Lasagna is a more expensive main dish which is attractive and delicious. It is a good choice to serve for guests at lunch or supper. It uses a variety of cheese, and is one of the most nourishing of the macaroni dishes.

If you review the units on milk and eggs, you will find many ways in which to use cheese, milk, and eggs as the main dish at lunch.

Waffles and creamed dried beef make a main dish for lunch that is sufficiently attractive for guests at a brunch. Creamed chicken may be used instead of dried beef. Variety at lunch may be secured by using different types of bread with a creamed meat and vegetable, and by adding herbs and seasoning. For instance, a teaspoon of curry powder added to creamed tuna fish served on toasted squares of corn-bread gives quite a different dish from the same creamed tuna served over rice. Add sliced stuffed olives, and you have a dish of even greater distinction.

In Chapter 16, you will find a discussion of the place of dried beans, peas, and nuts in your meals. Lunch time is an excellent occasion to use baked beans,

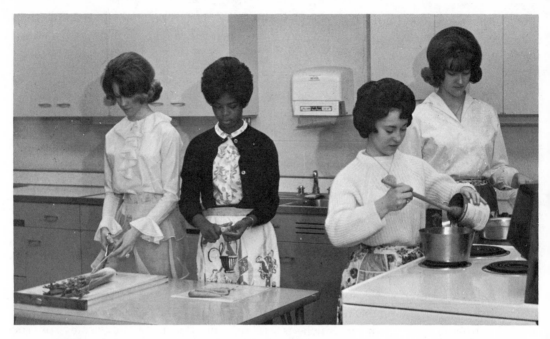

These girls are preparing a vegetable-beef soup for lunch. What ingredients might they use?

Delightful lunch. One tomato supplies nearly half your recommended daily need of vitamin C.

bean soup, or bean casserole or salad as the main dish. Peanut butter may be used as an alternate for meat.

Balancing the Protein

Whatever the main protein dish for lunch, balance the remainder by following the guide for a good lunch. How does this work out? If you select baked beans as your main dish, for instance, you can balance this meal with coleslaw or a green salad, hot corn sticks, milk, and canned or fresh fruit or a milk dessert.

If your main dish is macaroni and cheese, you might serve sliced tomatoes (when they are in season) as the salad, or during the winter months serve a cabbage-apple-and-celery salad. Add milk for a beverage and a deep dish fruit pie or fresh fruit for dessert.

If a more hearty lunch is desired, serve a green or yellow cooked vegetable, such as green peas, green beans, asparagus, or broccoli, when you have a creamed meat; or green leafy vegetables such as turnip greens, collards, kale, or mustard greens with baked beans; or any cooked vegetable with a cheese or egg dish.

Milk is the most suitable beverage for lunch at school or at home, because it contains so much that you need to supply you with strength for the afternoon.

The *extra calories* for lunch at home can come in the form of hot breads to enliven the meal. A simple lunch becomes something special when hot biscuits are served with a creamed meat dish or Welsh rarebit. Corn sticks give contrast in texture and flavor and add their own mellow taste with a mixed vegetable, meat, and cheese salad as the main dish or with bean soup. Serve brown bread with baked beans and homemade yeast bread or rolls with any menu. It takes only a few minutes for this special touch if you plan ahead.

Extra calories may also come through dessert. Your choice depends on the main dish, salad, and bread. If weight control is a problem, fruit makes a good dessert. If you use a high-calorie dessert, have a nourishing but low-calorie main dish.

The time required for preparing lunch at home should be short. Since marketing was discussed in Chapter 12, you know how to do this for lunch and probably you have been practicing it.

Serving lunch should not take much time. Simplicity and informality should be the theme, whether the meal is served at the dining table or on a tray in your favorite place. As you develop the habit

After-lunch chores. Homemaking training begins early.

Egg custard is a favorite luncheon dessert.

of eating a well-balanced, nourishing lunch, such substitutes as a bag of potato chips, cookies, candy, or an ice cream bar, will not satisfy you.

Sharing Responsibility at Luncheon

On week ends and during vacations you might work out a plan with your mother for preparing lunch. This is a good time to take more responsibility for a meal. Not only will it help her, but it will help you. It is by applying what you learn in the preparation and service of meals that you gain skill and confidence. Then your imagination and creative ability can grow. This is when you begin to experience the rich pleasures of homemaking.

THINKING IT OVER

1. Why is the government so interested in good school lunches?

2. What nutrients are often inadequate in the diets of teen-agers? Do you think their selection of lunches has anything to do with this?

3. Which types of food are missing when calcium content is too low? Riboflavin? Thiamine? Vitamin C?

4. What points do you keep in mind when you select a lunch away from home?

5. Do you buy your lunch at school, bring it from home, or bring a part and buy a part? What are the advantages of each?

6. Why is a light lunch not adequate for the average person? Who needs a medium lunch? A hearty lunch? What is the difference?

7. Give an example of a well-balanced medium lunch you might select at the school cafeteria; one you bring from home.

8. Explain how you would plan, prepare, and serve a balanced lunch at home. How would you change this plan for a larger food budget? A smaller one?

9. If you bring your lunch from home, do you think you should take responsibility for preparing it? Why?

10. In what ways will it help you now and in the future to take some responsibility in preparing lunch for the family on week ends and during vacations?

PROBLEMS TO SOLVE

1. With your class or family group, plan a project to teach children in an elementary school how to select a well-balanced lunch.
   (1) Decide what you will present to guide them.
   (2) Select pictures, posters, slides, or other illustrative material.
   (3) Select suitable stories or reading material.

(4) Decide on an activity with food.

(5) If possible, bring experimental animals to show how food makes a difference in health and looks.

2. Compare the American type of lunch with the lunch menus of other nations. Choose nationalities represented in your class or community.

3. Demonstrate packing a lunch.

APPLYING WHAT YOU KNOW

1. Planning luncheon menus: Plan one balanced luncheon menu beginning with the following dishes.

(1) Vegetable plate.
   (a) Using cheese as the main dish and protein food.
   (b) Using dried beans as the protein food.
   (c) Using nuts as the protein food.
   (d) Using eggs as the protein food.

(2) Making the main dish from leftovers to save money and time.
   (a) Rice, ground beef, and vegetables.
   (b) Left-over baked ham.
   (c) Left-over fish.

(3) Soup as the protein food and the main dish.
   (a) Vegetable-meat soup.
   (b) Bean or lentil soup.
   (c) Clam or fish chowder.

(4) Salad as the main dish.
   (a) Cottage cheese salad.
   (b) Bean salad.
   (c) Potato, egg, and ham salad.

(5) Sandwiches as the main dish.
   (a) Cheese.

(b) Meat, fish, or poultry.

(c) Peanut butter.

2. Preparing a lunch: Select a menu you have planned, and prepare a lunch. Study your motions in performing each task. Take notes and see if you can make a plan to save steps and time. If time permits, prepare each type of lunch you have studied—that is, a packed lunch, one you could make at home, and one you could choose away from home.

3. Collect luncheon menus from restaurants, tea rooms, and hotels. Discuss these menus to see if they meet with the standards for a good lunch. Compare the prices with what it would cost you to prepare the food at home. What needed nutrient is most likely to be lacking or poorly represented? How do you account for this?

EVALUATING

1. Which of the luncheon menus that you planned would be most suitable for a packed lunch? For preparing at home?

2. How could you vary the cost up and down in the luncheons you planned?

3. Which would you serve at different seasons?

4. Make a plan to improve your work. How can you save time and energy?

HOME EXPERIENCE

Prepare and serve a balanced luncheon at home with your mother's approval. Report results to your teacher.

FURTHER READING

Better Homes and Gardens New Cook Book. Meredith Press, Des Moines, Iowa, 1962.

Casserole Cook Book, John and Marie Roberson. Prentice-Hall, Inc., Englewood Cliffs, N.J., 1952.

Family Fare—Food Management and Recipes. Home and Garden Bulletin 1, U.S.D.A., Washington, D.C., 1968.

Family Meals and Hospitality, Dora S. Lewis, Gladys C. Peckham, Helen S. Hovey. The Macmillan Co., New York, N.Y., 1960.

The Large Type Cook Book, Avanelle S. Day. David White Company, New York, N.Y., 1968.

Meal Planning Guides, Dudgeon. Cornell Extension Bulletin E 921. Cornell University, Ithaca, N.Y., 1960.

Milk Consumption by Children at School and at Home in Relation to Special Milk Program. U.S.D.A., Washington, D.C., 1960.

National School Lunch Program: Fifteen Years of Progress 1947–1961. U.S.D.A., Washington, D.C., 1961.

Nutrition and Healthy Growth. Dept. of Health, Education, and Welfare, Washington, D.C., 1955.

Principles of Good Nutrition. Public Health Service, Dept. of Health, Education, and Welfare, Washington, D.C., 1957.

Special School Milk Program in Los Angeles, Calif. U.S.D.A., Marketing Research Division, Washington, D.C., 1957.

VISUAL AIDS

Films

Kids Must Eat. (15 min. film, b/w) A radio quiz unrehearsed. U.S.D.A., Washington, D.C.

Posters

A Glamorous Miss Picks a Lunch Like This. Poster. National Dairy Council, Chicago, Ill.

Handbook of Agricultural Charts. Agricultural Handbook 258. U.S.D.A., Agricultural Research Service. Washington, D.C.

Milk Packs a Punch with Every Lunch. Poster. National Dairy Council, Chicago, Ill.

unit **9**

Meat in Your Menus

The Proper Place
of Meat in Your Meals

What Does Meat Contribute to Your Daily Diet?

Meat or a meat substitute is the first food a homemaker selects when she starts to plan a meal. Meat has been a popular food throughout the recorded history of man. People learned by experience that they felt better when they ate meat—that is, all types of animal meat, poultry, fish, shell fish, and glandular meats, such as liver. Modern knowledge of food gives us the reasons.

Wherever man has lived he has made use of the meat near him. Those who lived by the water ate fish. Those who lived inland ate animals and poultry. Today in the United States we can have almost any kind of meat we choose at any season of the year. This can be a fine thing for our enjoyment of eating and our health. What contribution does meat make to your meals? And what role does it play in giving them balance?

For a quick meal, broil a slice of cured, tenderized ham with pineapple.

Meat in a meal stimulates your appetite and helps you enjoy the whole meal more. Some nations eat very little meat. But every nation has a dish of vegetables or cereal that uses a little meat to give flavor, to the main dish. Hungarian goulash, chili con carne, Irish stew, and the many delightful and delicious Chinese dishes are examples.

Meat gives a complete protein that is well used by the body for growth and health. Four ounces of cooked meat daily meets about a third of the 58–62 grams of protein a teen-age girl requires, and about one-fourth of the 75–85 grams of protein needed by a teen-age boy. Before nutrition became a science, there was a folk belief that "to build muscles you must eat muscle meat." Like so many folk beliefs, this contains an element of truth, but not the whole truth. You need some meat daily, but the diet is better balanced in vitamins and minerals if some of your protein comes from other foods.

Milk, cheese, and eggs build muscles just as well as meat, and often at much less expense. For instance, a large glass of milk, or 1½ ounces of cheese, gives as much protein as a lamb chop or two ounces of luncheon meat. But meat helps make better use of the vegetables in your diet and it makes the meal more appetizing.

When the diet does not contain enough complete protein, you recall, this stunts growth, weaken muscles, affects red blood cells and lowers resistance to infections. The strictly vegetarian diet (consisting only of plant foods) is discouraged mainly because of these bad results from the lack of adequate protein. Most vegetarians, however, also eat cheese, eggs, and milk, which provide high quality protein that balances the weakness of vegetable protein.

Meat helps build red blood, through the iron and copper it contains. Lean meat and shell fish are good blood builders, but liver is best of all. (Liver gives so much to the diet we shall consider it at length in another chapter.) Four ounces of lean meat supplies between one-fifth and one-fourth of your daily need of iron. Compare meat with other foods (see table on page 64). You will note that a half-cup of cooked dried beans, spinach, or mustard greens contains more iron than a very large hamburger (four ounces), or four ounces of sirloin beef; and two slices of whole wheat bread give as much iron as a lamb chop. However, the iron in animal foods such as meat, eggs, milk, and cheese is more completely absorbed by the body than iron from plant foods. You need both.

Lean meat gives us multiple B vitamins. You have learned in Chapters 4 and 17 of the health values of riboflavin and thiamine. These and other B-vitamins are found in meat, and account in part for the feeling of well being you get from eating it. We will mention only two of the most important here, niacin and vitamin B₁₂.

Niacin (nī'a sĭn), found in meat, is a very important B vitamin. An exciting discovery concerning this vitamin was made in the United States. A physician, Dr. Joseph Goldberger, had a theory that pellagra (pĕ lă'gra) was caused by a poor diet, and that a good diet would cure it. Other physicians did not agree with this point of view, so in 1915 he tested his theory. He knew what the people who had pellagra ate. He used volunteer prisoners as human subjects for the experiment. Their reward was a pardon when the experiment was over. Dr. Goldberger fed these men corn bread, grits, white bread, white rice, cane syrup, sugar, sweet potatoes, and pork fat, with a small amount of turnip greens, cabbage, and collards. They got pellagra, just as did those who lived on this diet outside prison. When they were placed on a good diet of fresh meat, milk, fresh vegetables, and fruits, they completely recovered!

Other scientists were working on this problem. They found in fresh meat, milk, green leafy vegetables, and yeast, the nutrient which prevented and cured pellagra: a B vitamin, later named niacin. (However, while niacin can cure pellagra, those who had this disease needed a better diet in general, and not just one pure vitamin.)

Niacin has been called the "personality" vitamin. Lack of it disturbs the memory and causes people to be afraid, anxious, suspicious, depressed, and confused. The astonishing thing is that when the diet is changed to include fresh meat, milk, fresh vegetables, and fruits (foods rich in niacin) the whole personality also changes! The person's mind is clearer, and he has courage and confidence again.

Vitamin B_{12}, another of the essential vitamins in the B complex, is found in red meat (especially liver) and is important in building red blood cells. It has proved a great blessing in the hands of physicians. Through the use of this vitamin, people with even the serious disease *pernicious anemia* can live normal lives.

These are all excellent reasons for including some meat in your daily meals.

How to Use Meat to Help Balance the Daily Diet

Meat is low in calcium and vitamins A and C. This works no hardship, as long as you include in the daily diet the milk or cheese to supply calcium, and the fruits and green leafy and yellow vegetables to supply vitamins A and C. But if meat pushes these foods out by taking too much of the food dollar, this throws your diet off balance in meeting your total health needs.

The iron and B vitamins are found in the lean of meat, and not the fat. In buying some meats you are buying a great deal of fat. If your income is high, you can afford it. But on a low income, watch small items like this. Money is more wisely spent for your figure and your health on lean rather than on fat meat.

Also, the bacterial reaction in the intestinal tract is not as healthy when meat forms too large a part of the diet. But this disadvantage does not arise if meat is eaten with the proper amounts of milk, vegetables and fruits that promote good intestinal hygiene.

The body needs a certain amount of protein daily. When you eat more meat than you need to build and repair cells, the excess protein is burned as is a carbohydrate food, or it is changed into fat and stored in the body as fat. Starches and sugar are much less expensive sources of calories for energy than protein.

A Department of Agriculture Study of families in all regions of our country in 1965 shows that we are spending more on meat and less on milk and milk products, vegetables, fruits, flour, and cereals than we were in 1955. Though the values in meat are great, should we eat so much

A boned rolled roast is economical and easy to cook. Heat pre-cooked vegetables in juice of meat just before serving.

of it that there is not enough money for the other foods we need? No, because a well-balanced diet that includes all the recommended vitamins and minerals is necessary.

If your income is high enough to provide also all of the vegetables, fruits, milk, and eggs that you need in addition to meat, you can spend whatever you wish on meat and be well fed. But on a lower income, if you spend such a great deal of money for meat, then you may fall short on other foods you need to maintain your life at a high level of vitality. If your daily diet includes the variety and amounts of foods recommended in the table on page 12, it contains the following: 3 to 4 ounces of meat, 1 quart of milk (and possibly some milk in cheese, ice cream, and cooked foods), 1 egg, 3 servings or more of bread-cereal, and 4 servings or more of vegetables and fruits. The proteins in these foods add up to give a generous amount for a teen-ager. Furthermore, this gives you a variety of minerals,

vitamins, and other nutrients needed. Your goal in meal planning is to have a balance—not too much or too little of any one food.

Kinds of Meat

The kind of meat people eat is usually related to the amount of money they have to spend on food, and to their family customs. There is a wide variety of meat available in the modern market. It is good to broaden your acquaintance with meat, and learn to use different kinds and different grades and cuts in your meals.

(1) Red meats, which are animal meats, include:

(a) *Beef*, which is the mature cow or steer, and the first choice of most Americans. (*Veal* is the meat of a calf under three months of age. It has less fat than beef, and a paler color.)

(b) *Lamb*, the meat of young sheep. Spring lamb is up to six months, and lamb up to 14 months of age. *Mutton* is the older sheep. Lamb has the more delicate flavor and is preferred by Americans to mutton.

(c) *Pork*, the meat of the hog. Usually the pig (young of the hog) is allowed to mature before it is used for meat. The color of cooked fresh pork is light gray. Pork is the highest in thiamine of any meat (except glandular organs), and it is excellent in other B vitamins.

(2) *Poultry* includes chicken, turkey, goose, duck, capon, squab, guinea, and some wild game. Birds and fowls have been an important part of man's diet through recorded history, from the Arctic regions to the tropics. The fowl and the egg have been standby protein foods for many people all over the world. This is partly because poultry is so easily and quickly raised.

(3) *Organ meats* are sometimes called "variety meats." These include liver (of first importance), heart, kidney, spleen, brains, sweetbread, and tripe. Tongue is also included in this group, though it is not an organ. These meats are highly nourishing in vitamins and minerals as well as protein.

(4) *Fish* includes fresh water fish, sea fish, and shell fish.

How to Buy Meat Wisely

What you have learned about marketing in the preceding chapters can help you in shopping for meat. In buying meat, the cut part of the animal and grade tenderness are important in relation to price.

(1) The amount of money you can spend on all food should be considered when you buy meat for the family. Buy enough meat so that every member has the amount recommended for the day—but fit this into your total food needs. If your food budget is low, you may need to give thought to the less expensive cuts that give the most lean meat for the money spent. You will probably buy good grade instead of prime grade, for the former costs less and gives more protein and less fat for the money. Allow about one-fourth to one-third pound of *lean meat* per person.

(2) Consider the waste when selecting meat. Bone and fat can greatly increase price, because you must buy more to supply the amount of desired protein. Fish such as haddock, halibut, or swordfish have little fat and bone. Liver and heart contain little fat, and no bone. Poultry

Pan frying liver French style—roll meat in your favorite marinating sauce, then flour, brown in fat over low heat on each side and serve hot at once.

has a great deal of bone but is low in fat. It takes a three-pound chicken to feed three or four people, but only a pound of fish fillet or liver.

(3) A good manager can save money through buying larger amounts of meat than she immediately needs and freezing the surplus. Suppose pork chops are 90 cents a pound, but a loin pork roast is only 59 cents a pound. If you have adequate freezing or storage space, you can buy a large roast, have part of it cut into chops, and freeze them for later use. Apply the same principle with a beef roast or leg of lamb. Have steaks cut off the beef roast. Have the leg of lamb cut into chops and steaks, and roast only a part of it. Often you can buy a whole ham at a saving. Have it cut in half, and freeze ham steaks, or a half of it. Have the shank bone cut off and use it in cooking beans or green vegetables.

Buying in quantity for less, and freezing the surplus, saves a great deal of money on the meat budget.

(4) Compare the cost of ready-prepared meats with what you get. Some are quite expensive. You can buy a pound of hamburger for the cost of one-third pound of some luncheon meats. Cold cuts save time and labor, but you pay for this service. Some cold cuts have cereal added. Read the label to see what you are getting.

If you have the time, you can learn to make your own cold cuts. They cost less, and may be more nourishing. For instance, homemade liver loaf or liver paté, sliced thin, makes a delicious delicacy for lunch, dinner, or parties. Sliced home-baked ham tastes better and costs as much as 50 percent less than cold cut baked ham. A lean piece of boiled shank or beef tongue is an inexpensive but delicious cold cut you can prepare easily.

(5) Save money by using more often the meat that is in the peak of season. Then it is the least expensive.

(6) Remember to include organ meats such as liver in the diet at least once each week. Organ meats give a variety of nutrients to enrich your diet, and at low cost. Learn to cook these meats properly and you will enjoy them.

(7) When planning your week's menus, remember that fish is as complete a protein as meat (and lower in fat and price). Include seafood at least once each week.

These suggestions may help you in shopping for meat, but you will learn more as you shop.

How to Store and Care for Meat

The care of meat in the home is as important as the care of milk. All kinds of meat, even cooked meat, spoil quickly.

Fresh raw meat should be unwrapped and placed in wax paper so that a little air can get into it, but not enough to dry out the meat. Store fresh raw meat in the coldest part of the refrigerator. This is usually in the meat keeper beneath the ice chest.

Either use fresh fish the day you buy it, or wrap it firmly in foil and freeze it. Fish has a strong odor and can spoil the flavor of other foods in the refrigerator unless firmly wrapped to keep in the odor.

Poultry spoils quickly and should be purchased when you are ready to use it or can freeze it for future use. Cook leftover bones of poultry in the pressure saucepan and make soup. This makes use of the rich minerals in the bones and adds flavor to soup.

Store left-over cooked meat in covered dishes or wrap and place in the coldest part of the refrigerator. Use left-over poultry within a day or two, or freeze it.

Frozen meat should be stored at 0° F or lower until ready to use. Thawed meat should be used without re-freezing. Do not throw away the juice that runs out of meat in storage. Save it and add it to the meat during the last few minutes of cooking. It is nourishing, and gives flavor.

In the next chapter you will learn ways to cook different kinds of meats and how to judge the grades of meat. This will help in the use of your food money, and in planning and cooking meals.

WORDS TO WORK WITH

Pellagra (pĕ lă′grȧ): a disease caused by a diet deficient in fresh lean meat, milk, and fresh vegetables.

Niacin (nī′ȧ sĭn): a B vitamin essential for life; cures or prevents pellagra.

THINKING IT OVER

1. What does meat contribute to your health?
2. How can you decide whether you are spending too much or too little of your food dollar for meat?
3. Why is "taste" alone not the best guide for the amount of meat to include in the daily diet? How can you be guided?
4. What are the different kinds of animal meat we eat? Poultry? Fish?
5. What minerals and which B vitamins in meat help build red blood?
6. How did Dr. Goldberger prove that pellagra is caused by a poor diet?
7. What points would you keep in mind in planning your menus and buying the meat your family needs for a week?
8. What is the best way to care for and store meat at home?

APPLYING WHAT YOU KNOW

1. Checking on the meat you eat, and evaluating your food habits.
   (1) Keep a record of the food you eat for one week.
   (a) Did you have a serving of lean meat each day? More often?
   (b) Did you have sea food at least once during the week? Liver?
   (2) How do you rate? Make a plan to improve the variety of meat you eat.
2. Selecting meat for balanced meals.
   (1) Plan balanced meals for one week for your family using a different meat each day.
   (2) Select a meat and prepare it for one or more of these meals (see Cookbook for recipes): breakfast; lunch; dinner.
   (3) Show how you could reduce the cost of the meals you planned by selecting a different meat. How could you increase the cost by a different selection?

HOME EXPERIENCE

With your mother, plan a balanced meal including a meat dish you learned to make at school. Prepare and serve this dish as a part of the meal for the family. Report results to your teacher.

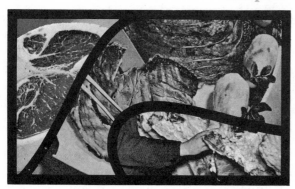

21

How To Select, Cook, and Serve Meat in Balanced Meals

Know Quality in Meat Before Buying

When you can judge quality in meat, it helps you get better meat and to save money in buying it. In the large supermarket today, meat is packaged, like so many other foods. You no longer have the help of the butcher to guide you. The meat is labeled and priced, but you need to understand what the label means, and what the cut and grade indicates, if you are to make wise selections. Let us see, then, what makes good quality in meat, and how to use different grades in preparing meals.

There are two to four parts in meat— lean muscle, connective tissue, fat, and bone.

Rolled roast, browned potatoes, green beans, and fresh tomatoes.

The lean muscle is most important. It is made of long, tiny fibers; and it is muscle fibers which contain the protein, minerals, and vitamins. Here we find the good flavor as well as nourishment.

Connective tissue holds the muscle fibers together in little strips. It is elastic. In the best meat the connective tissue is white, and when cooked, it becomes soft and tender. In undernourished or old animals the connective tissue may be more yellow in color than white. Then it is tough and makes meat tough. Long slow simmering, or cooking in the pressure saucepan, can soften this tissue.

Fat is a large part of meat. Less is found in the white meat of poultry and most varieties of fish than in animal meats. There is little fat in liver. In mature meat, a layer of fat usually covers the outside of the cut. The fat helps hold in the juices when the meat is cooked, and makes it tender and tasty. You can tell the meat of young animals and poultry because it lacks this outside fat, as a rule. In the best grades of beef, the fat is interspersed with the lean. This is called "marbling," and makes meat more tender, juicy, and delicious. It costs more to produce this type of beef, and we pay more for it. Many cuts of beef, veal, lamb, and pork are quite lean. A 3½-ounce serving of the lean cuts averages about 200 calories.

Bone is a part of some cuts of meat. It is prized for flavor in soups. Primitive people who did not have milk or cheese in the diet depended on bones to supply calcium. Vilhjalmur Stefansson, the Arctic explorer, who survived in a good state of health on an all-meat diet, did not do this on choice cuts alone. He ate bones (cooked soft), skin, liver and other organs, fat, bone marrow, and other parts of an animal, fish, or fowl. The bone marrow, where the red blood cells are made, is a choice tidbit in flavor and nourishment.

In judging the quality of meat, then, these are the things to keep in mind: (a) Meat should have a good odor and color for its kind. (b) The lean tissue should be firm and fresh-looking. (c) The connective tissue should be white and not too prominent. (d) Fat around the outside of pieces such as leg of lamb, beef roast, or ham is desirable; and beef should have some marbling of fat. If the fat is yellowish, it indicates a more mature animal. (The animal has lived long enough after growth was completed to store some carotene in the fat.) Keeping the basic structure of meat in mind helps you when you go to buy it.

Government Standards Help Guide You in Buying Meat

As in the case of milk, the Federal government has set high standards for health and cleanliness of meat. Meat is inspected by the Federal Government before it is released for the market. A trained person inspects the live animals before they are slaughtered. The meat is also inspected afterwards. The animals and the people who handle meat must be clean and free from disease, and the packing plant must have high standards of health and cleanliness. A plant that does not meet these high standards is closed until it meets them. Animals that show signs of diseases are discarded and are not used for food. If meat passes all health and cleanliness tests, it is stamped by the inspector with a purple ink. You may have

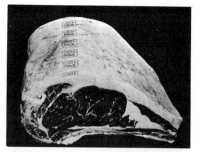

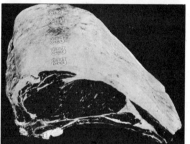

Why does the Federal Government inspect and grade meat? How do these different grades in a standing rib roast guide you in marketing? (1) Prime. (2) Choice. (3) Good. (4) Standard or Commercial. (5) Utility.

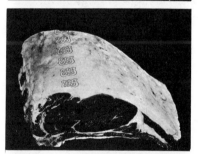

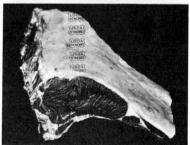

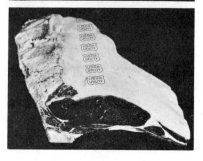

seen this stamp, "U. S. INSPECTED AND PASSED." The ink is harmless, as it is made from vegetable coloring. Poultry is not as widely inspected as meat. The mark is usually a metal clip on the wing. Eighty percent of U. S. meat is Federally inspected. Some states and cities have their own inspection laws. The remainder of the meat is slaughtered on the farm. If you do not slaughter your own animals, it is wise to buy inspected meat.

The Federal Department of Agriculture has set standards for different *grades of meat*. This too is a great help and protection to the buyer. Some meat packers hire government graders to grade their meat. Others train and use their own men. Grading is not compulsory. But since it helps fix price and shows the customer different qualities, most packers like to grade meat.

Meat is priced according to grade. Naturally, the higher grades are more expensive. Grades not only tell price; they indicate how to cook the meat and what flavor to expect. You can save money in buying meat if you understand the meaning of grades.

The illustrations on page 221 show the differences in grades of meat. Taking beef (which is most graded) as an example, prime is the highest quality and has the highest price. As the grades go down so do the prices until you reach utility grade.

Grades of Meat

Prime beef is from a young steer of heavy, broad type. The lean shows more marbling than do other grades. Prime is the juiciest, the most tender, and the quickest and easiest to cook. It is also the highest priced.

Choice is the next grade. It comes from young but mature cattle, not quite so big and broad, nor is there as much marbling in the meat. If properly cooked, it can taste as good as prime, and is preferred by many.

Good grade is from the same high-quality, fully grown but young steers and heifers. The animals are smaller in size and there is less marbling of fat in the lean. Because of less fat and more lean or protein, this grade is preferred by many home makers. It can be cooked with full flavor but is not as juicy as the two more expensive grades.

Standard or *commercial* is from older but good animals. The meat is rougher, more uneven, and the lean looks coarser in texture. It may be marbled or not, depending on the animal. The color is slightly dark red to darker red, as compared with a brighter red color in the above grades. The fat is also more yellow. This grade is commonly used for stews, soups, and other forms of braising meat.

Utility grade is from "skinny" animals —both young and old. The fat varies from none in young animals to soft in older ones. The cut surface of the meat is watery in young animals to firm but coarse in older ones. This is the lowest grade sold in retail stores and requires moisture in cooking. There is a lower grade called "cutter and canner." It is used for processed meat, and you buy it in cold cuts, cured or canned.

Buy meat, then, by the grade you want and can afford. Keep in mind that the lower grades may have more protein per pound than the higher grades, because there is less fat. Also remember that the vitamins and minerals are found in the lean part. It is the flavor, juiciness, and ease in cooking that change with grade, and not the food value. A less expensive cut of meat may be more nourishing than a more expensive grade, and as tasty, if you know how to cook it properly.

The Principles of Cooking Meat and How to Serve It

In cooking meat your goal is: (a) to produce a tender, juicy dish full of flavor; (b) to save the most nutrients possible (but to pour off the excess fat); and (c) to spend as little money, time, and energy as possible. To accomplish this is

to practice good cooking and good management.

These goals can easily be reached if you keep in mind the tenderness of different cuts. *The most tender cuts of meat come from the part of the animal or fowl which is least used or exercised.* Since these are fewer and most prized, they cost more. The less tender cuts come from the part of the animal most used, such as the legs and neck. Study the meat charts in this chapter to learn the common cuts you may buy. When you have the tender cuts and less tender cuts clearly in mind, you know what to buy and about what to pay.

There are two ways to cook meat—by dry heat and moist heat:

(1) *Tender cuts* are cooked in dry heat —i.e., roasted; or broiled in their own juices, under a flame or on charcoal; or pan-broiled. These methods are quick and easy and the result is delicious, when the cooking is properly done.

(2) *Less tender cuts* are cooked in moist heat. This is done by *braising,* which is used for pot roasts, Swiss steaks, and stews. *Cooking in liquid* is suited to pot roasts and soups.

A low *temperature* is the key to success in cooking meat. This is true whether you roast, broil, fry, or cook in liquid. You may have seen a big plump roast go into a hot oven (at 450°F) and come out a

Roast all meat at low temperature to save volume, nutrients, and juicy flavor. The roast above shrank 2 pounds 2 ounces when roasted at 350°F to an internal temperature of 160°F. A roast of the same size and weight lost 3 pounds 8 ounces when cooked at 450°F to the same internal temperature.

shriveled roast! The higher the temperature, the greater the shrinkage. As indicated in the pictures on page 223, 15 to 20 percent is lost by shrinkage at a high temperature. Low cooking temperature also saves time and energy, for you do not have to watch the meat or baste it. Then too, meat has a better flavor, is more tender, and carves better because the muscle fibers and juice hold together better when cooked at a low temperature.

A *meat thermometer* is desirable equipment for cooking meat. If there is no meat thermometer in your home, give your mother one for a Christmas present. Then help her use it! The inside temperature of meat will always indicate when the meat is done. You need a thermometer to tell you this. You can guess it by the oven temperature and the time of cooking per pound, but this guide is only approximate. It takes more minutes per pound for a thick chunky roast than a thin, spread-out one. Also, the more fat a piece of meat has, the faster it cooks. Your time table can't tell you that, but a thermometer can. To get the desired rare, medium, or well-done flavor you like, use a thermometer for best results.

Cook pork well done. This is because nearly all pork contains the parasite (păr′ȧ sīt) trichina (trĭ kī′nȧ). It can be killed at 140°F, but a temperature of 185°F at the center of cooked pork is recommended for a margin of safety. When this temperature is reached, the pink is all gone from the meat. Pink pork is not a food to eat. Trichinosis (trĭk′ĭ nō′sĭs), a disease of tendons and muscles, develops from eating undercooked pork. A meat thermometer can protect health in this respect.

BEEF

Porterhouse steak

Sirloin steak

Round steak

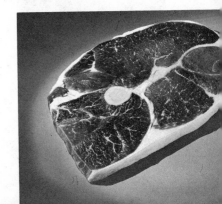

BEEF CHART

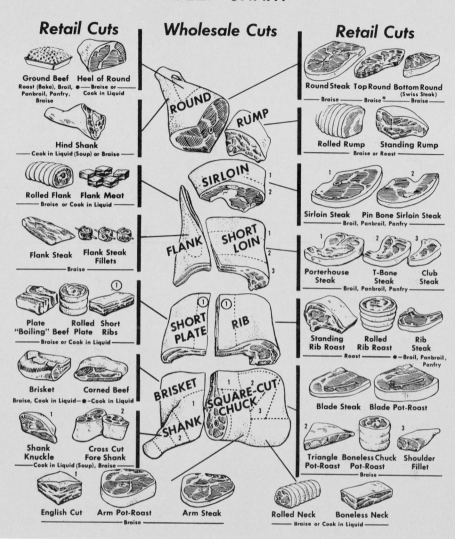

Retail Cuts

Ground Beef — Roast (Bake), Broil, Panbroil, Panfry, Braise

Heel of Round — Braise or Cook in Liquid

Hind Shank — Cook in Liquid (Soup) or Braise

Rolled Flank   Flank Meat — Braise or Cook in Liquid

Flank Steak   Flank Steak Fillets — Braise

Plate "Boiling" Beef   Rolled Short Plate   Ribs — Braise or Cook in Liquid

Brisket   Corned Beef — Braise, Cook in Liquid — Cook in Liquid

Shank Knuckle   Cross Cut Fore Shank — Cook in Liquid (Soup), Braise

English Cut   Arm Pot-Roast   Arm Steak — Braise

Wholesale Cuts

ROUND, RUMP, SIRLOIN, FLANK, SHORT LOIN, SHORT PLATE, RIB, BRISKET, SQUARE-CUT CHUCK, SHANK

Retail Cuts

Round Steak   Top Round   Bottom Round (Swiss Steak) — Braise — Braise* — Braise

Rolled Rump   Standing Rump — Braise or Roast

Sirloin Steak   Pin Bone Sirloin Steak — Broil, Panbroil, Panfry

Porterhouse Steak   T-Bone Steak   Club Steak — Broil, Panbroil, Panfry

Standing Rib Roast   Rolled Rib Roast   Rib Steak — Roast — Broil, Panbroil, Panfry

Blade Steak   Blade Pot-Roast

Triangle Pot-Roast   Boneless Chuck Pot-Roast   Shoulder Fillet — Braise

Rolled Neck   Boneless Neck — Braise or Cook in Liquid

Standing rib roast

Rump roast

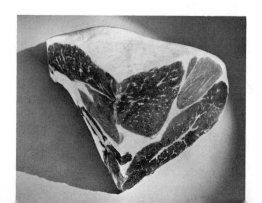

Pork is one of our best meats but it must be cooked well enough to kill this parasite. It is richer in the B vitamin thiamine than any other meat except liver. And pork liver is the richest of all livers. It has a variety of other B vitamins likely to be missing from our diets.

Ways to Cook Meat — Tender Cuts

(1) *Roasting* in dry heat is an excellent way to cook any tender cut of beef, veal, lamb, pork, or poultry. To cook a tender roast:

(a) Set oven at desired temperature and turn on to preheat as you prepare roast. The new method of roasting meat is to use a very low temperature, the value of which is illustrated in the pictures on page 223. In general, roast the better grades and cuts of meat at 300° to 325°. Cheaper grades, such as "good," and cuts such as chuck can be roasted without adding any water if a lower temperature—such as 175° to 200°—is used. Low temperature produces a roast that is juicy and delicious in flavor with a minimum of shrinkage.

(b) Season to taste. Salt penetrates only one-half inch on a roast. It causes loss of some juices by drawing them out. For this reason, you may prefer to salt meat when it is done. But rub the outside of the roast with any herb or seasoning of your choice.

(c) Place roast on rack in shallow pan with fat side up. The rack helps keep the temperature even. A roast sitting in hot fat cooks faster than one on a rack. The fat which surrounds the meat should be left on, to hold in the juices and give a better flavor. If a roast is lacking fat, use

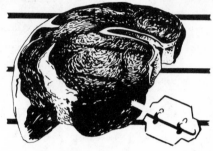

For best results, use meat thermometer. Place roast on a rack in a shallow pan to cook evenly with little loss of juice.

bacon strips or brush with oil, to hold in juices and prevent drying.

(d) Cut a hole for the meat thermometer in thickest part of meat and insert thermometer. Take care it does not touch bone or fat.

(e) A meat thermometer is the most accurate measure for doneness. Insert it before placing roast in oven. Place bulb in thickest part of the meat so as not to touch either fat or bone. Roast meat until thermometer indicates the doneness you desire—rare, medium, or well done. Then remove roast from oven at once. (The internal heat continues to cook a roast outside the oven.)

(f) Serve meat on a hot platter with vegetables as part of a balanced meal. Proper service adds beauty and appetite appeal to a meal. Parsley, green lettuce, green pepper, watercress, crab apples, spiced apricots, orange slices, and some other fruits are suitable to garnish meat.

(2) *Broiling* over live coals was the way primitive man cooked meat. We have not found a tastier way to cook tender meat. In fact, today many families own portable broilers and roll them into the yard or onto the terrace, or cook meat over charcoal right in the living room.

The more usual way is to broil in the broiling compartment of your stove, or pan broil on top of the stove.

Meats suitable for broiling are: beef, lamb, ham, poultry, fish, bacon, and sausage. Fresh pork and veal are usually not broiled. Broiled meat has a better flavor if cut thick. Steaks and chops should be at least one inch thick, ham a half-inch. The thick parts of chicken, such as breast, drumsticks, and thighs, are choice for broiling. Any type of thick fish is excellent. Meats broil well if naturally tender or "tenderized." Tougher cuts of meat can be broiled when the meat is tenderized. To broil meat inside the stove:

(a) Light broiler or turn on oven regulator to 350°F. Do not preheat broiler, for this roasts the meat.

(b) Season, omitting salt.

(c) Place meat on broiler rack pan. Meat should be 2½ to three inches below flame. Turn flame low. If you use electricity, you may need to place broiler five inches below heat and turn heat off for a few seconds at intervals. *Leave oven door open while broiling.* Though the heat is near your meat, it should be low enough to prevent curling, smoking, or burning.

(d) When one side is brown, season it with salt and herbs of your choice. If you wish heavier brown, sear meat quickly with a higher heat for the first minute or two then reduce heat.

(e) Turn meat and brown the other side. When brown, season and serve on a hot plate or platter.

(f) Doneness in a thick steak is most accurately determined by use of a thermometer. Insert it in the middle of the steak and parallel to it, before meat is placed in broiler. Place the reading side down, so that you can watch it during the last half of broiling, when the meat is turned.

Broiling good meat requires constant attention. Heat must be adjusted by hand. If you do not have a thermometer, only experience can guide you in knowing when the meat is done to your taste.

(top) From one cut of rump: Steaks and a juicy roast. (below) How can you produce a tender steak from a cut of round?

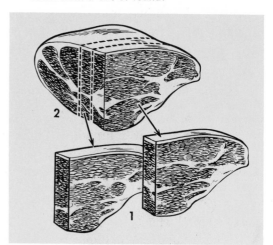

Broiling a good steak is an art you can learn—try it.

(3) *Pan broiling* is a popular quick way to cook tender steaks or chops. Any of the meats mentioned for broiling may be used. This is how to do it:

(a) Use a heavy skillet or griddle, according to the amount to be pan broiled. If searing is desired, heat skillet about as hot as for pancakes, but not smoking. This hastens the cooking.

(b) Place meat on a lightly greased skillet or griddle, but with no standing fat. The meat for pan broiling should be tender and well marbled to cook in its own juice.

(c) Turn heat low and cook slowly until meat is browned on one side. Pour off fat when meat is ready to turn. This prevents the meat from cooking too fast.

(d) A gradual browning is better than searing. If meat is turned occasionally, it will be brown by the time it is done.

(e) Follow directions for seasoning as given above.

(f) Be careful not to overcook. Rare meat can be cooked as perfectly by pan broiling as by oven broiling. You have to watch it, and turn it more frequently. The turning helps hold the temperature down, and keeps the meat more tender.

(g) Never cover meat or add water or any liquid when pan broiling. To cover it or add liquid means you are braising it. This is quite another dish!

Ways to Cook Meat — Less Tender Cuts

A thick chuck steak from a good beef is about as tasty a meat as a person could desire. Yet this is a less tender, less expensive cut, which may be broiled.

VEAL

Loin chop

Rib chop

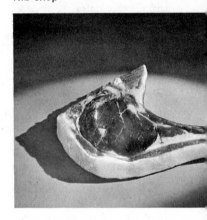

Round steak (veal cutlet)

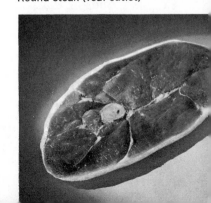

VEAL CHART

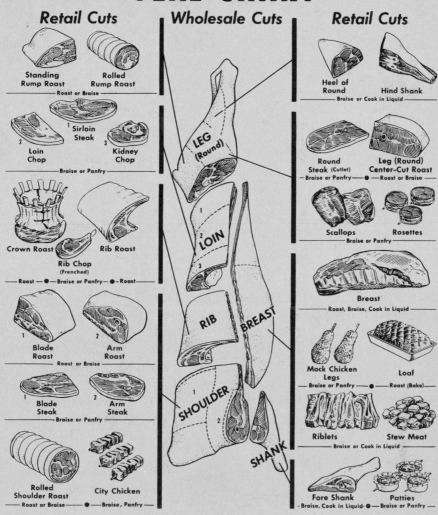

Retail Cuts

Standing Rump Roast Rolled Rump Roast
— Roast or Braise —

2 Loin Chop 1 Sirloin Steak 3 Kidney Chop
— Braise or Panfry —

Crown Roast Rib Roast
Rib Chop (Frenched)
— Roast — ● — Braise or Panfry — ● — Roast —

1 Blade Roast 2 Arm Roast
— Roast or Braise —

1 Blade Steak 2 Arm Steak
— Braise or Panfry —

Rolled Shoulder Roast City Chicken
— Roast or Braise — ● — Braise, Panfry —

Wholesale Cuts

LEG (Round)

LOIN

RIB BREAST

SHOULDER

SHANK

Retail Cuts

Heel of Round Hind Shank
— Braise or Cook in Liquid —

Round Steak (Cutlet) Leg (Round) Center-Cut Roast
— Braise or Panfry — ● — Roast or Braise —

Scallops Rosettes
— Braise or Panfry —

Breast
— Roast, Braise, Cook in Liquid —

Mock Chicken Legs Loaf
— Braise or Panfry — ● — Roast (Bake) —

Riblets Stew Meat
— Braise or Cook in Liquid —

Fore Shank Patties
- Braise, Cook in Liquid- ● — Braise or Panfry —

Rolled shoulder

Shank

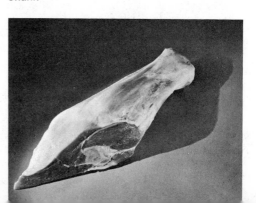

(1) *Tenderizing* meat is not new. For hundreds of years homemakers have *pounded* meat. This breaks down the connective tissue that makes meat tough. It also softens coarse lean that has little fat. Today you can buy a gadget with sharp spikes to tenderize meat, instead of using a rock or a hammer!

Another way to tenderize meat is by adding *vinegar, lemon juice,* or *wine* while cooking. These do not detract from the flavor, but soften the tough connective tissue. The French are experts in this.

Then there are *tenderizers* on the market today which can be sprinkled over meat. By enzyme-like action, these make tough meat tender. Natives who ate the papaya fruit in the tropics pointed the way for us to tenderize meat by this means. They found that the juice of the yellow, melon-like papaya tenderized tough meat. They rubbed this juice into the toughest meat and made it so tender it melted in their mouths!

Chemists went to work, and found that this juice contains a substance similar to

Why is it good management to buy a large roast and use part of it for chops?

A tender, juicy standing rib roast of beef cooked rare.

pepsin, a digestive juice in the intestinal tract. This substance is now made and sold as a meat tenderizer.

Many people prefer the flavor of meat cooked by dry heat such as roasting or broiling. Also it is likely that more vitamins are retained by quick broiling than by longer methods of cooking.

Here are some cuts that have been cooked with moisture in the past, but that can be broiled or roasted when tenderized: chuck roast (also known as blade roast) and steak; arm steak or roast (also known as chuck roast); short ribs (usually used for soup and stew); flank steak; heel of round; rump steak; shoulder rolled roast and steak. Less tender cuts of meat may also be roasted in dry heat, if cooked at a very low temperature (175–200°F) until they are done.

Despite the advantages of cooking meat in its own juices, between 50 and 75 percent of meat is cooked in moisture, so let us see how this is done.

(2) *Braising* is using moisture, either liquid or steam, to make meat tender. This is used for pork chops, veal, pork liver, fowl, and the less tender cuts of beef just mentioned. To braise:

(a) Choose a heavy utensil. Brown meat in fat evenly on all sides, at a low temperature. (If you wish deep brown, roll meat in flour.)

(b) Season meat thoroughly on all sides with salt and add any herbs you like. In moist cooking, the seasoning penetrates the meat. Herbs used for meat include garlic, chives, onion, celery, sage, thyme,

FRESH PORK

Loin chops

Rib chops

Loin roast center rib cut

CURED PORK

Sliced bacon

Smoked shoulder butt

Smoked picnic shoulder

PORK CHART

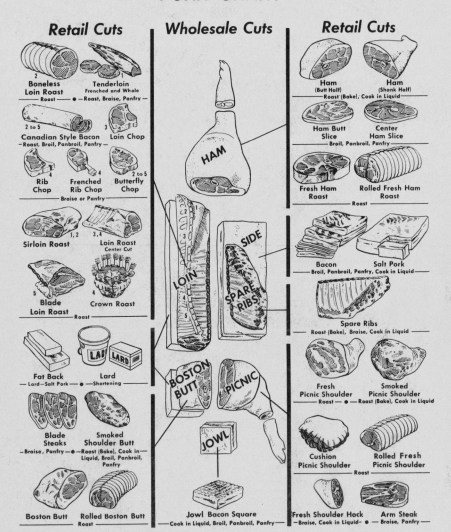

Retail Cuts

Boneless Loin Roast — Roast —
Tenderloin Frenched and Whole — Roast, Braise, Panfry —

Canadian Style Bacon — Roast, Broil, Panbroil, Panfry —
Loin Chop

Rib Chop
Frenched Rib Chop
Butterfly Chop — Braise or Panfry —

Sirloin Roast
Loin Roast Center Cut — Roast —

Blade Loin Roast
Crown Roast

Fat Back — Lard—Salt Pork —
Lard — Shortening —

Blade Steaks — Braise, Panfry —
Smoked Shoulder Butt — Roast (Bake), Cook in Liquid, Broil, Panbroil, Panfry —

Boston Butt
Rolled Boston Butt — Roast —

Wholesale Cuts

HAM

LOIN

SIDE

SPARE RIBS

BOSTON BUTT

PICNIC

JOWL

Retail Cuts

Ham (Butt Half) — Roast (Bake), Cook in Liquid —
Ham (Shank Half)

Ham Butt Slice
Center Ham Slice — Broil, Panbroil, Panfry —

Fresh Ham Roast
Rolled Fresh Ham Roast — Roast —

Bacon
Salt Pork — Broil, Panbroil, Panfry, Cook in Liquid —

Spare Ribs — Roast (Bake), Braise, Cook in Liquid —

Fresh Picnic Shoulder — Roast —
Smoked Picnic Shoulder — Roast (Bake), Cook in Liquid —

Cushion Picnic Shoulder
Rolled Fresh Picnic Shoulder — Roast —

Fresh Shoulder Hock — Braise, Cook in Liquid —
Arm Steak — Braise, Panfry —

Jowl Bacon Square — Cook in Liquid, Broil, Panbroil, Panfry —

Shank half of ham

Smoked ham, butt half

All pork must be thoroughly cooked to destroy harmful parasites. Using a thermometer takes the guesswork out of cooking pork.

bay leaf, caraway seeds, parsley, pepper, paprika, chili powder, mustard, horse-radish, basil and many others.

(c) Add a small amount of liquid if you wish, but it is not essential. Liquid can be vegetable juice, sour cream, wine, lemon juice, vinegar, soup stock, or water.

(d) Cover with tight-fitting lid, for the steam must be held in to soften the tough connective tissue. Steam is the tenderizer.

(e) Simmer—which is just below boiling (185°F)—until tender.

(f) If vegetables are to be added, prepare and add them during the last few minutes of cooking. The time depends on the kind of vegetables and whether they are whole or diced.

Several kinds of meat broiled together for a cookout.

(g) Remove fat and measure back one tablespoon for each cup of sauce. Thicken juice in braised meat with one to two tablespoons of flour per cup of liquid to make gravy.

(h) Use all of the drippings (except fat) in which braised meat is cooked. Some of the minerals and water-soluble vitamins are in the bottom of the pan, and the drippings are quite tasty.

(3) *Pan frying* is a good method for cooking less tender cuts that have been pounded or cubed, or meat that has been ground. This is done by cooking meat in a small amount of fat. Another name for this method is sautéing (sô tā′ĭng). (If the meat is completely covered with fat, it is called *deep-fat frying*.) This method is used for less tender steak, chops, ground meat, and mature poultry. To pan fry:

(a) Use a heavy skillet and place fat about ½″ deep in it. Pork chops are so fat they do not need added fat for pan frying. If the meat is seasoned and rolled in flour, or dipped in egg and then in crumbs, this forms a coating on the outside to hold in vitamins and minerals. Meat prepared with crumbs is called "breaded."

(b) If meat is not coated with flour or breaded, season it after browning.

(c) Do not cover meat unless you wish to braise it. This loses the crispness and is not frying.

(d) Cook at moderate to low temperature. Fried meat is not as tender as braised or broiled. Crispness is gained at a higher temperature and the price paid is a slightly tougher meat.

(e) If you do not have a thermometer, cut a gash in the meat to determine when it is done. Be sure that no pink shows in pork chops or cutlet. A thermometer is not practical with thin-cut meat in frying.

There are other ways to cook meat, but these are the principal ones.

Meat in Meals

You learned in the pattern for planning meals that homemakers usually begin planning a meal with either meat or some other protein dish. One of the things that the study of nutrition has taught us is the importance of adequate protein in the daily diet, and lean meat is an important food in this respect. In this chapter you have learned of the wide variety of meats available for daily meals by using different kinds and cuts of meat and various ways of cooking and serving these. In general, it is a wise use of food money to use large amounts of the meat which is in season

LAMB

Loin chops

Rib chops

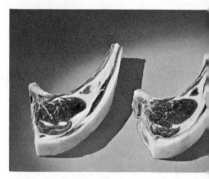

Shoulder chops

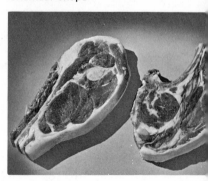

Leg

LAMB CHART

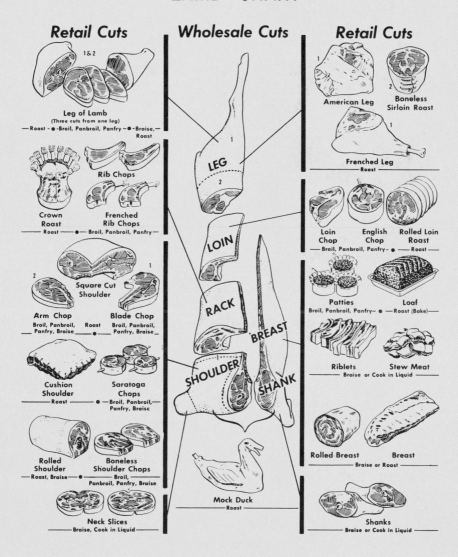

Retail Cuts

Leg of Lamb
(Three cuts from one leg)
— Roast - ●-Broil, Panbroil, Panfry -●-Braise,—
Roast

Rib Chops

Crown Roast
— Roast - ●— Broil, Panbroil, Panfry —

Frenched Rib Chops

Square Cut Shoulder

Arm Chop
Broil, Panbroil,
Panfry, Braise

Blade Chop
Broil, Panbroil,
Panfry, Braise

Roast ●

Cushion Shoulder
— Roast —

Saratoga Chops
●—Broil, Panbroil,—
Panfry, Braise

Rolled Shoulder
— Roast, Braise - ●—

Boneless Shoulder Chops
—— Broil,
Panbroil, Panfry, Braise

Neck Slices
— Braise, Cook in Liquid ——

Wholesale Cuts

LEG

LOIN

RACK

BREAST

SHOULDER

SHANK

Mock Duck
— Roast —

Retail Cuts

American Leg

Boneless Sirloin Roast

Frenched Leg
— Roast —

Loin Chop

English Chop
— Broil, Panbroil, Panfry— ●

Rolled Loin Roast
— Roast —

Patties
Broil, Panbroil, Panfry— ●

Loaf
— Roast (Bake)—

Riblets

Stew Meat
— Braise or Cook in Liquid —

Rolled Breast

Breast
— Braise or Roast —

Shanks
— Braise or Cook in Liquid —

Shanks

Riblets for lamb stew

The pleasing combination of colors and the variety of texture and flavor make this meal especially inviting.

and lower in cost, rather than making menus and buying meat without considering this factor. Almost any type of meat adds to the appeal of a meal.

In the next chapter you will learn that further variety and nourishment may be added to your daily diet through the use of poultry and fish of different kinds, and organ meats. These are important meats too, because they are high in protein and low in fat, and many kinds are low or moderate in cost.

WORDS TO WORK WITH

Parasite (păr′a sīt): a plant or animal that lives on or gets its food from another.

Trichina (trĭ kī′na): a small, slender worm that is a parasite in the hog, other animals, and man.

Trichinosis (trĭk′ĭ nō′sĭs): a disease of the intestines, muscles, and tendons, caused by the parasite trichina.

THINKING IT OVER

1. What are the different cuts of meat? How can this knowledge help you in buying meat?

2. Explain how the government protects your health by inspecting meat.

3. Is poultry inspected as thoroughly as other meats? Where do you look for the inspection clip on poultry?

4. How can you determine the cuts of meat which are most tender?

5. How can knowing the grades of meat help you to manage money and to feed your family the meat they need?

6. Do the less expensive grades have as much nourishment as the more expensive? Explain.

7. What are your goals in cooking meat? How can you reach these goals?

8. How would you cook the tender cuts of meat? Why?

9. What methods are used to cook the less tender cuts of meat? Why?

10. In cooking meat, what temperature gives the best flavor, volume, and nourishment? How can a meat thermometer help you cook meat?

11. Why should pork always be cooked well done? In what way is pork superior to other meats?

12. Explain how to roast, broil, and braise meat.

PROBLEMS TO SOLVE

1. Relating your study of meat to your study of milk and other foods.
   (1) Examine a long soup bone that has been split down the center and a joint bone. Note the bone marrow, cartilage, and calcium splinters.
   (2) Discuss:
       (a) The value of the calcium splinters in the large end bones. If they are not present, what does this tell you?
       (b) The minerals and vitamins needed to make the red blood cells in the bone marrow.
       (c) Why bones should be thoroughly cooked in a pressure saucepan as the first step in making a good soup.
       (d) How meat and milk help each other make a better diet.

2. Marketing and evaluating: If possible, go with your family group to the meat market, or with your mother, or alone. The purpose is: (1) to study the inspection marks on meat and poultry; (2) to see the different grades of meat; (3) to see the different cuts. Also take note of the following:
   (a) Variety of fresh meat on the market.
   (b) Which kind of meat is most expensive at this season.
   (c) Which is least expensive.
   (d) The range in price for different grades.

(e) The difference in price for various cuts.
(f) What is on the label for packaged meat.

APPLYING WHAT YOU KNOW

1. Using a soup bone and marrow and a less expensive cut of meat, make one or more of these soups.
   (1) Beef heart soup. (Recipe, page 412.)
   (2) Beef vegetable soup.

2. Plan a balanced luncheon using the beef heart soup, and a balanced dinner using the beef vegetable soup.
   (1) Decide how a well-made soup can be used to save time for a busy homemaker.
   (2) Decide how to plan your work to save motions and fatigue in preparing the soup.
   (3) Figure the cost of soup per serving.
   (4) Compare with other types of prepared soup in cost, nourishment, and flavor.

3. Broiling meat.
   (1) Decide the tender cuts of meat to broil, and the less tender cuts.
   (2) Choose one of each, if possible, and broil according to what you have learned.
   (3) Plan three balanced dinners, using low-cost, moderate-cost, and higher-cost meats to broil.
       (a) Have family groups in the class try different methods of tenderizing meat.
       (b) Compare results in flavor, appearance, food values, and cost.

HOME EXPERIENCE

With your mother, plan two balanced dinners using the meats you have learned to cook at school. Prepare and serve the meat dish as part of the family meal. Report results to your teacher.

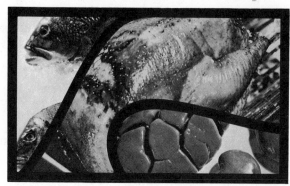

22

Poultry, Fish, Liver, and Other Meats in Your Meals

Poultry in Your Meals

Birds, both large and small, have been an important part of man's diet for thousands of years, all over the world. This is not only because of the rich nourishment in the meat, but also in the eggs, the value of which you learned in Unit III. The table on page 452 shows that canned boned chicken has more protein per unit of weight than other meats. Poultry contains a variety of the minerals and vitamins found in other meats, and is especially good for young children and the elderly because of its low fat and high protein content.

Kinds of Poultry

The most common commercial varieties of poultry are chicken, turkey, duck, and

Broilers, roasting chickens, and young ducks or turkeys are delicious when broiled in an electric rotisserie or on a cookout.

capon. The chicken has been most popular. But with the improved breeding of the wide-breasted turkey, this bird's popularity has been increasing, and it is the first-choice meat for national holidays such as Thanksgiving and Christmas.

A Guide to Help You Buy Poultry

There are several things to consider in making the wisest choice of poultry. When you buy poultry that has been inspected and graded, you are helped by marks that assure you that at the time of inspection, the bird was healthy and wholesome for food.

U.S. Grade A birds have a broad breast, and the legs are "meaty." There is a good layer of fat beneath the skin, and the birds have no defects. They're also clean and free of pin feathers.

U.S. Grade B birds are as healthy as grade A, but have less meat on the breasts and legs. They may have minor bruises or deformities that affect the appearance but not the flavor or health value.

U.S. Grade C birds have less meat on the breast and legs and usually less fat than the other two grades. They may have broken bones, deformities, and pin feathers. They are healthy, but less at-

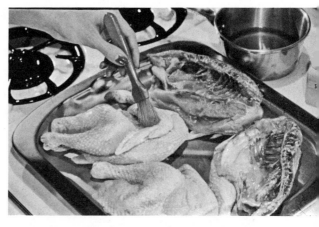

Fryers and broilers are delicious. Season with herbs of choice, brush each side with fat, and broil on each side for about 15 minutes.

tractive and "meaty." If the difference in price between grade C and grade B is only one or two cents per pound, then the higher-grade bird is the better buy. You will need to read the labels and compare the cost to the amount of meat on the different grades of bird. Keep in mind that the bones weigh about the same, regardless of grade.

Fresh poultry is not as widely inspected and graded as other kinds of meat. When you are buying fresh poultry, try to select birds that have been inspected and graded. Canned and frozen poultry has

This inspection mark may be used only on poultry that has been examined by a Government inspector and passed as wholesome food. This mark does not indicate quality.

The grade mark means that poultry has been graded for quality. It may be used only if a bird already carries the inspection mark.

The grade and inspection mark means that poultry has been graded for quality and also passed as wholesome food.

Steps in Frying Chicken: (1) Cut chicken in pieces and wash and dry. Roll in seasoned flour or shake a few pieces at a time in bag of seasoned flour. (2) Place in skillet with ¼ inch of hot fat. Cover and cook slowly on one side until golden brown. (3) Turn chicken, cover skillet, and cook until golden brown.

to pass inspection before processing. If you read the label on packaged products, you know what you are getting.

How Poultry May Be Purchased, and the Effect on Cost

In some small towns and rural areas you may purchase live poultry and dress it yourself. Many markets still sell poultry with only the feathers removed. Today it is more common to find poultry on the market that is "dressed" or "drawn" and ready to cook. This means that the feathers, head, feet, and entrails or viscera were removed from the bird at once after it was slaughtered.

In deciding which is the most economical buy in fresh poultry, you will find that live poultry costs least, and dressed ready-to-cook poultry costs most. Keep in mind that one-fourth of the weight of a live chicken and one-sixth of that of a turkey is lost as waste. Thus you may be paying very little for the time saved in preparing a bird to cook, if you buy the ready-to-cook bird. On this point you will have to study the market price and the amount of time you have, to decide which is the better buy for you. You can afford to pay one-third to one-fifth more per pound for ready-to-eat poultry.

In figuring price, you consider not only the grade, and the way the bird is marketed, and its weight, but the age and sex. These two factors affect tenderness and juiciness. Poultry under 16 weeks of age is classified as *broiler* or *fryer*. It is tender, and cooks quickly. Mature but young poultry is classed as *roaster*. Old hens and roosters are classed as *fowls,* or *stewing chickens,* and have more fat than

Turkey is the first-choice meat for national holidays.

young poultry. Turkeys are also classed as hen (the more juicy and tender) or tom turkeys.

Poultry that is canned, frozen, or prepared fresh and ready-to-eat is quickly and thoroughly cleaned as soon as it is slaughtered. It is weighed, packaged, labeled, and refrigerated at once, if it is to be sold fresh. If it is to be frozen, it is frozen at once. Poultry for canning is canned at once.

Storage of Poultry

Poultry is a highly perishable food, and fresh or cooked poultry should be stored in the refrigerator (between 35 and 38° F). Remove the paper or cellophane wrapping in which poultry comes, and wrap loosely to store. If you cannot use the fresh or cooked poultry within two or three days, wrap it properly to seal out air, and store in the freezing unit of your refrigerator. Store cooked poultry of any kind in a covered container.

If you buy frozen poultry, store it in the freezer while frozen, and do not thaw until you are ready to use it. Frozen poultry is clean and ready to cook, and should not be washed. It will retain its freshness for many months if it is stored at 0° F or lower.

Steps in Stuffing Poultry for Roasting: (1) Use prepared stuffing of choice (recipe, page 432), stuff neck end loosely. (2) Fasten neck skin with skewer and place wings to back or tie flat against sides with a string around the bird. (3) Stuff tail end loosely and put rest of stuffing in pan to bake.

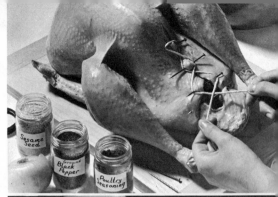

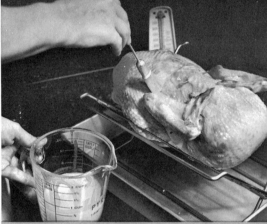

(4) Secure stuffing with skewers and string. (5) Brush bird on one side with seasoned fat, place on rack of roasting pan, and bake at 325°F. (6) Roast until well done (second joint is loose when pressed against the bird), meat is soft and tender, and color is golden brown.

How to Cook Poultry

Poultry is cooked just as other meats—the tender cuts by dry heat as in broiling and roasting, and the less tender cuts by stewing or braising. (See discussion of how to cook meat, pages 222–236, and recipes on pages 410–426.)

Why Fish Is So Important in Our Meals

In the Middle Ages, educated leaders noticed that the people who lived near the sea and regularly ate the fish from the sea did not get the disease called goiter (goi'tẽr). On the other hand, goiter was common among the people who lived inland. This was especially true of women. Goiter is a disease of the thyroid (thī'roid) gland, and this gland must have iodine to do its job properly. It is the thyroid gland which masterminds, as it were, the use of the food we eat. Thyroxine (thī rŏk'sēn), made by the thyroid gland, circulates in the blood to do this job. *Iodine* is needed to make thyroxine. Naturally when the food you eat daily does not contain enough to meet this need, your body does the best it can without it. What happens? The thyroid gland enlarges in an effort to do the job, and this condition is known as simple goiter.

Inland soil has lost some of its minerals because of rains and other factors. Iodine seems to be one mineral that is lacking in much of the inland soil. Vegetables and fruits that are grown near the ocean contain, as a rule, more iodine. Cranberries grown in sea bogs are an example of a fruit rich in iodine.

In an effort to meet the need for this nutrient, iodine has been added to com-

To stew less tender chicken, place in pressure saucepan or kettle and add water. Add herbs and seasoning to taste. Cover and cook in pressure saucepan 20 minutes at 15 pounds pressure, or simmer 2 to 4 hours, depending on size and age of bird. When tender, remove chicken and cook dumplings, spaghetti, or rice in broth.

mon table salt. But only about half of the homemakers select iodized salt.

Sea food included in the diet regularly supplies the needed iodine, and the inlander is no longer handicapped in this respect. The frozen food and canning industries have brought a great variety of sea food to each one of us, regardless of whether we live in California or Maine or in the Midwest. We can now have sea food every week of the year.

Sea food, like other meats, ranges in price from inexpensive to expensive. And, as with other meats, the inexpensive varieties are just as nourishing as the more costly. Lobster, shrimp, and crab are examples of the more expensive seafish. Codfish, mackerel, haddock, and sea perch are examples of the less expensive. There is a wide variety in between.

Aside from iodine, the nutritional value of sea food is high, and the cost is low considering what you get for your money. You get a high-protein food that is quite low in fat, and therefore low in calories. Seafood contains a variety of other minerals and vitamins. It is a tender, tasty food that can be cooked quickly and easily, and can add wide variety to the flavor of the diet. When you learn how to buy many kinds of sea food and use it in different ways, your meals will have more variety and interest. You will also be able to save on your food budget, and at the same time feed your family well.

How to Buy Fish

In buying fresh fish of any variety, there are no government grades and inspection marks to guide you. But by learning to judge the quality of fish, you can make wise decisions in buying it.

How many of these fish can you identify? How many kinds have you eaten?

Fish is marketed fresh, frozen, canned, smoked, and dried. Dried fish is heavily salted and has to be soaked and boiled in water, and some nourishment is lost. With the newer methods of freezing and canning, old-fashioned drying of fish is less important today than formerly. But new techniques are being used to preserve food by drying, and when perfected, these may well rank with freezing and canning.

Salmon, tuna, and sardines are popular canned seafood. The cost of these depends on the grade. Red salmon costs more than pink, though it is no more nourishing. The small sardine, as a rule, is more expensive than the larger. The dark meat of the tuna may cost less than the white. Your personal taste and budget will influence which choice to make.

You can judge quality in fresh fish by several factors:

(1) The odor should be fresh and typical of the fish. Stale fish develops an offensive odor.

(2) If the fish is whole, look at its eyes. They should be bright, clear, and bulging. The gills should be free of slime.

(3) The flesh of a fresh fish is firm, and springs back fast when pressed by the finger. This is not the case with stale fish.

Antibiotics (ăn′tĭ bī ŏt′ĭk) have been used by some commercial companies to keep fish (and poultry) fresh longer. Studies indicate that the growth of bacteria which spoils meat is slowed down by it. This may have wide use in the future. Investigations are under way to further this method of retaining freshness in meat, and to see how this may affect health.

Frozen fish can be bought in two ways. One is over the counter from the butcher.

HOW TO BUY FRESH OR FROZEN FISH

STEAKS

Ready-to-cook cross-sections or slices of a large dressed fish, such as halibut, haddock, or swordfish. There is usually one small part of the backbone in this type of fish. Buy ⅓ pound per serving.

WHOLE OR ROUND FISH

Sold as they come from the water. They must be scaled and eviscerated (entrails removed) before cooking. Allow ¾ to 1 pound per serving.

FILLETS

Ready-to-cook boneless sides, cut lengthwise and away from the backbone and rib bones. Buy ⅓ pound per serving.

DRAWN FISH

Entrails removed and usually scaled. The head, tail, and fins may also be removed. Allow ¾ pound per serving.

FISH STICKS

Boneless pieces cut in uniform size from steaks or fillets. They are cooked and then frozen and are ready to eat when thawed and heated in the oven.

DRESSED FISH

Entrails, scales, head, tail, and fins removed. They are ready for the pan as purchased. Allow ⅓ to ½ pound per serving.

SHELLFISH

Fish such as lobsters, crabs, clams, and oysters that are sold alive in the shell. Lobsters and crabs may be bought boiled in the shell. Shellfish may also be purchased shucked (removed from the shell) either fresh, frozen, or canned.

To preserve quality in this fish, keep it frozen until you are ready to use it.

The other type of frozen fish is packaged, and is sold in the frozen food container at the market. By reading the label you can see exactly what you are getting and how much it costs in relation to other kinds of frozen fish. Remember that price does not indicate either nourishment or quality. It indicates the scarcity of the fish, or the difficulty in catching and processing it.

Frozen fish is often fresher than "fresh" fish. Today much of the freezing of fish takes place on boats, right where the fish is caught. Actually the fish is out of the sea and into your pan! The freshness is frozen in and held until you thaw and cook the fish. Frozen cooked fish may also be purchased.

How much fish to buy is a question that puzzles young homemakers. Allow one-third pound per person, for steaks or fillets of cod, swordfish, haddock, halibut, sole, and the like. Since there is much waste in whole fish, either fresh or frozen, buy about three-fourths to one pound per person. Americans usually discard head, viscera, tail, and fins but the Eskimos and other primitive people eat them, reserving these choice bits (rich in minerals and vitamins) for children, expectant mothers, and the sick.

Care of Fish

Wash fresh fish thoroughly, but do not soak. Dry thoroughly on absorbent paper. Wrap so that no odor comes from the package, and store in the coldest part of the refrigerator. Buy fresh fish on the day your fish market has the freshest and the best variety. Use or freeze it promptly.

Do not wash packaged frozen fish, but place in the freezer as is. Frozen fish sold over the counter should be wrapped in wax paper or foil, thoroughly, and stored in the freezer. It may be quickly washed and dried before cooking.

To thaw frozen fish, place it on the lower shelf of the refrigerator, and let it thaw gradually. It cooks more evenly when thawed. Packaged frozen fish may be cooked directly from the frozen state. This takes longer, and you have to see that it is cooked in the middle. If you are stuffing a fish, it is better to thaw it first.

How to Cook Fish

Fish, unlike red meats and poultry, is naturally tender. The connective tissue is very slight and delicate. In cooking fish, we wish to prevent the connective tissue from breaking down. This holds in the vitamins, minerals, and flavor along with the juice.

Keep in mind that fish is protein food, and has much less fat than red meats. The fat fish include shad, mackerel, herring, and lake trout; these average 7 to 10 percent fat, and salmon 14 percent. Other fish average only 1 percent or less. Well-marbled beef, on the other hand, has 33 percent fat, and a ham may have as much as 50 percent fat (but of course one does not have to eat the surplus fat that is around the outside of red meat).

You can see that in fish you get more protein and less fat. This is good for your pocketbook, your health, and your figure!

Cook fish at a *low* temperature (300° to 325° F) to preserve the flavor, shape, juices, and nourishment. Fish cooked at this temperature does not give off the offensive fish odor which causes many to dislike cooking it. If you can smell fish odor, it is your cue to turn down the heat.

Methods of cooking fish are the same as for meat: broiling, baking, frying, and steaming or broiling.

Frying is a popular way to cook fish. When properly done, this gives a good flavor and preserves the nutrients. One way to fry fish is to coat it with egg, then roll it in meal, flour, or bread crumbs, and fry in *deep* fat. If the fat is about 350° F and surrounds the fish, it cooks the fish in three to five minutes. Drain the fish on absorbent paper and serve hot.

Broiling fish is like broiling any meat. You use fish about one inch thick. Be-

cause fish is lacking in fat, brush it with oil if desired. Paprika helps fish to brown. Broil it eight minutes on one side; turn with a pancake turner and broil seven minutes on the other side. It is done when the flesh is tender but firm when pierced with a fork. A thicker piece or frozen fish would take a few minutes longer. (See recipes for marinate sauce pages 424 and 429.)

Baking fish is another favorite way. Bake it stuffed, or bake it in milk or a sauce of your choice. Keep the heat low (300° to 325° F). To brown fish, season it with paprika and set it under the broiler.

Fish is usually *boiled* for soup and chowder. However, as in the case of beef or poultry soup, the nutrients which come out in the water are used.

How to Use Fish in Meals

Our New England forebears ate fish for breakfast instead of the ham and eggs preferred by their Western relatives. Both are a good protein food. Which you serve is a matter of taste and purse, but variety makes meals more interesting and gives different nutrients. Fish for breakfast is usually served in a creamed dish, smoked, or broiled.

Lunch is an excellent time to use fish— in soup or chowder, a creamed dish, a salad, or broiled. Fish plus a green salad, whole grain or enriched bread, and milk, with a dessert of your choice, gives a balanced lunch.

Left-over fish is often served in a creamed dish at lunch, including vegetables such as green peas, green beans, or corn; or with fresh chopped vegetables such as onion, tomato, and green pepper. Since milk is used in making the cream

Why is it important to include fish in meals frequently? What varieties are shown here? Have you eaten all of them? Cooked them?

A wide selection of fish may be used for fish loaf—(see recipe on page 424).

sauce, you have a more nourishing dish than fish alone.

Tuna, salmon, and other fish are used to make a main dish salad for lunch. Celery, tomato, green pepper, and green lettuce, and other vegetables, along with hard-cooked eggs, are used with fish for salad. A glass of milk, whole grain or enriched bread, and a dessert would nicely balance this type of menu.

Lobster, crab, and shrimp are used in salads, and these, along with oysters, are served for a first course at a dinner. The clam is a less expensive shellfish that should be used frequently in low-cost meals. It is delicious when added to potato soup.

Use fish as an alternate with red meat or poultry at least once each week. With fish as your protein food, build your menu around it. Choose potato or brown rice; a green or yellow vegetable; a salad; whole grain or enriched bread and butter; milk; and a dessert of your choice.

Seasoning fish is a delicate matter. Your aim is to bring out its natural flavor. Plain lemon or lime juice is excellent for this purpose. (It is surprising what the juice of a lime can do to improve the flavor of fish.) In addition these juices add vitamin

C and balance the weakness of fish in this vitamin. Tartar sauce is enjoyed by many and easy to prepare, (but lacking in vitamin C). Look at the sauces for fish in cookbooks and try some or create your own.

Liver, the Most Nourishing Meat

(1) Dr. Weston A. Price, in his study of the diets of people in different parts of the world, found that the tall men (Neurs) of the upper Nile valley, even in the 20th century, worship the liver. In the South Pacific he learned from the King of the Fiji Islanders that these cannibals were primarily interested in the vitamin-loaded livers of their victims! They believe that the soul of man is in his liver, and his physical and spiritual growth depends on eating liver.

(2) All through this book you have learned that liver is a superior food in one vitamin after another, and in the minerals iron and copper. It even contains some vitamin C, a vitamin that is lacking in other meat. Except for calcium and phosphorous, liver is a place of deposit or reserve for vitamins and minerals. This organ acts as a sort of banker. We carry

on a checking account, as it were, with the liver. Little wonder the primitive people took care that every member of the family had a serving of liver when an animal was killed! The sick, the young, the old, and the expectant and nursing mother were given liver.

With better knowledge of food, we know why liver is so important to us. One four-ounce serving gives you excellent protein, and low fat. It gives over 60,000 units of vitamin A, a fine boost to our diet's content of a vitamin that is often poorly represented. It gives 10 milligrams of iron (your daily teen-age need is 15). It provides more than double the recommended amount of riboflavin and meets your need for niacin. It is the richest food source of vitamin B_{12} and other B vitamin nutrients. You have learned how all of these nutrients improve the way you look and the way you feel. Liver is a safety food that helps make up for weaknesses in your diet. You should include it in your meals at least once each week.

Liver is cooked the same as other meats. Calf's and lamb's liver is broiled; pork and beef liver is braised. Homemade liver loaf or pâté is a delicacy for a family meal or a party. A great variety of liverwursts are on the market. The Germans are famous for liverwursts, and we are getting imports, as well as home varieties. Try liver sausage or liverwurst as a sandwich filling for your lunch occasionally.

Other Variety Meats

Heart is similar to liver in nourishment. There are many ways to use heart in meals. One way is to make it a part of vegetable beef soup (see recipe, page

Livers: (top) veal and pork; (bottom) beef and lamb.

Hearts: (left to right) lamb, pork, veal, and beef.

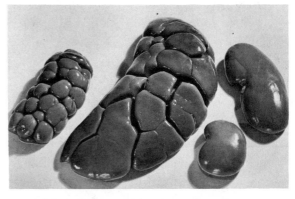

Kidney: (left to right) veal, beef, lamb, and pork.

Sweetbreads: (left to right) lamb, veal, and beef.

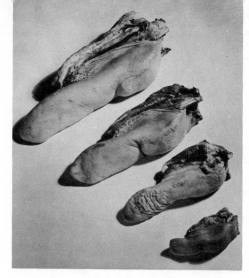

Tongues: (left to right) beef, veal, pork, and lamb.

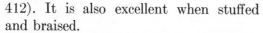

Brains: (left to right) lamb, pork, veal, and beef.

412). It is also excellent when stuffed and braised.

Kidney is a choice meat in Europe, and is tasty when properly prepared. Snip off the white tubing before the kidney ever touches water. Then wash kidneys thoroughly, and use either a little vinegar or lemon juice in the water in which they are cooked. If they are broiled, squeeze lemon juice over the kidneys and use low heat. If kidneys cook too long or too fast, they give off an offensive odor of ammonia. Lemon or vinegar neutralizes the ammonia.

Sweetbreads—thymus (thī′mŭs) glands —and *brains* are choice variety meats. They are delicious when properly prepared, and are excellent as the protein dish for luncheon or dinner.

Tripe is the honeycombed second stomach of a cow. It contains nutrients that make it desirable as a food. If ground in a food chopper it is excellent in soups, such as pepper pot. It can also be breaded and fried, or broiled or baked.

These are the principal organ meats. They are a "good buy." They give meals variety in flavor, and offer nutrients that give sparkle to your looks and add to your feeling of well being.

WORDS TO WORK WITH

Antibiotic (ăn′tĭ bī ŏt′ĭk): a substance which combats bacteria.

Goiter (goi′tẽr): an enlargement of the thyroid gland.

Thymus (thī′mŭs): an edible gland in lambs and calves, which is called *sweetbread*.

Thyroid (thī′roid): an important large gland in the neck.

Thyroxine (thī rŏk′sēn): a substance made by the thyroid gland, from iodine and other nutrients, which is essential for health.

THINKING IT OVER

1. Why is sea food needed in your diet regularly? What kinds are available, and in what different ways can you buy sea food?
2. How can you judge good quality in fresh fish? Frozen fish? Poultry?
3. Explain how to care for and store different kinds of fish and poultry.
4. Why is fish an excellent protein food for weight watchers? How does the fat in fish compare with that in other meats?
5. How would you use fish at breakfast, lunch, and dinner in balanced meals?
6. Explain the different ways to cook poultry. What is the best temperature?
7. What does liver give to your diet that can help your appearance and your vitality?
8. How often do you eat liver? How can it be used at dinner and lunch?
9. What are the other organ meats, and why are they important?
10. What do we mean by keeping the meat in our meals in balance with the total money spent on food?

PROBLEMS TO SOLVE

1. Learning by seeing.
   (1) If possible, visit a meat-packing plant.
   (2) Arrange to have organ meats in class: tripe, kidney, brain, liver, heart.
   (3) Give a demonstration to show how to snip white tubes from kidney; separate covering sheath from brain; examine heart and liver.
   (4) Freeze these meats and, at another period, learn to cook one or more of them.
   (5) Find recipes you would like to use to cook each of these.

2. Discuss:
   (1) The superstition that milk and fish should not be eaten together.
   (2) Other superstitions connected with foods.
   (3) How scientific knowledge of food frees us from superstitions.

APPLYING WHAT YOU KNOW

1. Learning to cook meat in different ways: If time permits, cook one or more of these meat dishes by the methods you have learned. (For recipes, see the Cookbook.)
   (1) Panbroil or braise: beef, lamb, or pork liver.
   (2) Pan fry or broil fish.
   (3) Make a meat loaf of liver. (p. 426)
   (4) Make a beef-heart soup, using pressure saucepan to save time. (p. 412)

2. Plan menus for one week, using the amount of meat you need in each day. Include liver and sea food at least once.

EVALUATING

1. What changes would you make to decrease the cost of meat in the meals you planned? What selections would increase cost?
2. Are you using enough meat? Too much? How would you judge this?
3. Do the foods you have planned for meals taste good together? Look attractive together? Balance in nutrients?
4. What garnish would you use with fish and poultry, and how would you serve these?
5. Where did you waste motion in your work, from marketing and planning the meals to serving and cleaning up? Did your food preparation give a good result? Make a plan for improvement.
6. What dessert would be a good choice when you serve fish or liver?

HOME EXPERIENCE

You can show imagination in your cooking by getting acquainted with many new meats. With your mother, plan balanced dinners, using fish, liver, and poultry (one each day). Prepare and serve the meat as a part of a balanced family meal.

FURTHER READING

Basic Fish Cookery. Test Kitchen Series No. 2. Fish and Wildlife Service, U.S. Dept. of the Interior, Washington, D.C., 1956.

Beef and Veal in Family Meals. Home and Garden Bulletin 118, U.S.D.A., Washington, D.C., 1967.

Fresh and Frozen Fish Buying Manual. Circular 20, Fish and Wildlife Service, U.S. Dept. of the Interior. Washington, D.C., 1954.

How to Buy Poultry. Home and Garden Bulletin 157, U.S.D.A., Washington, D.C., 1968.

Lamb in Family Meals. Home and Garden Bulletin 124, U.S.D.A., Washington, D.C., 1967.

Meat Carving Made Easy. National Livestock and Meat Board, Chicago, Ill.

Meat for Thrifty Meals. Home and Garden Bulletin 27. U.S.D.A., Washington, D.C., 1953.

Modern Meat Cookbook, Jeanette Frank. Dell Publishing Co., Inc., New York, N.Y.

Pork . . . Facts for Consumer Education. Bulletin 109. U.S.D.A., Washington, D.C., 1954.

Poultry Buying Guides for Consumer. Home and Garden Bulletin 34. U.S.D.A., Washington, D.C.. 1953.

Poultry in Family Meals. Home and Garden Bulletin 110, U.S.D.A., Washington, D.C., 1967.

Turkey on the Table the Year Round. Home and Garden Bulletin 45. U.S.D.A., Washington, D.C., 1954.

USDA Poultry Inspection: A Consumer's Safeguard. U.S.D.A., Washington, D.C., 1959.

U.S. Grades for Beef. U.S.D.A., Washington, D.C., 1960.

VISUAL AIDS

Fishery Motion Picture Leaflet 452. Bureau of Commercial Fisheries, Fish and Wildlife Service, U.S. Dept. of the Interior, Washington, D.C.

It's Carving Time. (TV $4\frac{3}{4}$ min., color; also b/w; 1956) Motion Pictures U.S.D.A., Agricultural Handbook No. 14, Washington, D.C.

Know the Poultry You Buy. (4 min. film, color; also b/w; 1956) Motion Pictures U.S.D.A., Agricultural Handbook No. 14, Washington, D.C.

Make Mine Chicken. (TV, 4 min. color; also b/w; 1957) Motion Pictures U.S.D.A., Agricultural Handbook No. 14, Washington, D.C.

Fats and Sugars
in Your Diet

The Place
of Fat in Your Diet

The Contribution of Fat to Your Diet

There is a folk belief that wild animals were first tamed for their meat and milk. According to the noted geographer Professor Carl O. Sauer, this is not the case— wild animals were first hunted and tamed for their fat. Why was fat so important in the diet of primitive man? It was important for the same reasons fat is important to us today, and some additional reasons.

(1) Fat is the most concentrated form of food. It gives 2¼ times as much fuel or energy (calories) as any other type of nutrient (that is, a gram of fat gives 9 calories, whereas a gram of either protein or carbohydrate yields only 4 calories).

An attractive pie or cake may be used as a centerpiece, and then as dessert.

To primitive man this was important. It kept him warm longer and he didn't have to eat as much. It was a "storehouse" of energy. He could call on this reserve when food was low. Our need is not the same today.

(2) Fat not only gives more calories, weight for weight, but it is more slowly digested than protein, starches, or sugars. For this reason it has "staying" power. If you pour heavy cream over your cereal at breakfast, it "stays" with you longer than if you use skim milk. Fat helps hold off the feeling of hunger. Even weight-control diets need some fat.

(3) Fat helps in normal elimination.

(4) Some fat is needed to pad us against shock of movement, and insulate us against sudden change of temperature, especially cold. This was far more important to primitive man than to us, though we also need a bit of fat to support our organs, such as kidneys.

(5) We like and want fat in our meals, because it makes food taste better. Compare the flavor of hot biscuits with and without butter. Think how beans, turnip greens, or kale would taste if not seasoned with suitable fat. It is fat that gives crispness to fried foods and tenderness to pastries. Fat is about as important as salt in bringing out the flavor of vegetables. People who can't eat fat for medical reasons often complain of the tasteless-ness of their meals.

(6) Fat can affect your personal appearance, for it helps your skin and hair. Too little fat in the diet over a long period may cause eczema and a dry, rough skin.

Some fats—cream, wheat germ, egg yolk, some animal and fish liver oils, and poultry fat—bring to your diet the much-needed fat-soluble vitamins A, D, E, and K, and assist in their absorption.

Vitamin E, a newly recommended daily nutrient, prevents blood disorders and prevents destruction of some other nutrients by oxygen. Vegetable oils are our richest food source. Vitamin E has health values for lower animals; research will clarify further its value to human beings.

Fats in Relation to Health

Fats, however, can be harmful. Many of the recipes in this book call for non-fat dry milk instead of milk with cream, and use vegetable oil instead of firm fats. This is done to help you apply what scientists are learning about fats—at the point where it counts, in your meals and snacks. In this book much less fat is used in recipes than is usually found.

While we need more scientific research for a complete picture, the evidence points to a relation between coronary heart disease and the *kind* and *amount* of *fat* in the diet. In the past, physicians observed a relation between coronary heart disease and cholesterol (kō lĕs′ tēr ōl) level in the blood. Present research indicates that it is the *firm fats* containing *saturated fatty acids* which are related to cholesterol deposits in the blood vessels. The villain seems to be the saturated fatty acids in the diet rather than cholesterol as such. Cholesterol is a waxy fat-like substance found in animal fat. It is needed for many body functions and can be made by the body. In fact, the amount of cholesterol in the diet is small compared with the amount the body produces. Research indicates that when the diet contains unsaturated fatty acids high in linoleic (lĭn ō lāy'ĭc) acid, then cholesterol in the body is at a lower level.

There are, then, two kinds of fat in the diet, liquid oils and firm fats. A major portion of most liquid fats consists of "unsaturated" fatty acids. (They have fewer hydrogen atoms and, therefore, have small molecules.) The firm fats contain a larger amount of "saturated" fatty acids. (These have a longer chain of hydrogen atoms and larger molecules than the unsaturated fatty acids.)

If you turn to the drawings on page 6, you can see in the middle right picture many of the oils containing the unsaturated fatty acids. These are more easily oxidized (burned) by the body and are associated with a lower cholesterol level in the blood. Hence they—the vegetable and fish oils—are more favorable fats for your health.

The picture in the middle left of page 7 shows the firm fats which contain saturated fatty acids. Use these with restraint, but do not completely eliminate them from the diet because some carry other nutrients you need, such as vitamin A.

You may wonder why the shortenings and margarine are classified as saturated fats since they are made from unsaturated vegetable oils. The process of changing an oil to a plastic firm fat is called *hydrogenation* (hī drŏ jĕn ā' shŭn). This processing changes not only the appearance of the fat, but its chemistry too. The oils take on more hydrogen atoms, form larger molecules, and so become saturated fats. Margarine is processed to resemble butter in appearance, flavor, texture, and nutritive value. Since it costs less than butter, it is frequently used as a substitute for it. Other fats containing saturated fatty

acids include lard, the "hydrogenated" shortenings, chocolate, coconut oil, and the fats in pork, beef, and lamb.

Fats which fall into an intermediate position between the two types of fat include: olive oil, peanut oil, fat in egg and poultry fat.

The next picture, middle right of page 7, shows fats "hidden" in food. The animal fats—beef, pork, lamb, and cream—contain saturated fatty acids. The plant foods —seeds, nuts, and whole grains—contain oils with unsaturated fatty acids.

Using Fats Intelligently

This knowledge has great importance for the homemaker. How can you use it to help your life now and your future family? Try to understand in which group the particular fats are classified and use them or reduce their use in accordance with your needs. Remember that the most favorable fats for your health are, generally, the vegetable oils, fish oils, and seafoods. You will find corn oil, cottonseed oil, soy oil, and safflower oil on your grocer's shelf. These are tops. There is no need to pay a fancy price for fancy oils you may hear advertised.

Even if this new nutritional knowledge were not available, it would still be desirable to avoid overeating of fat, for a lower fat content not only helps the heart, but helps control weight. (For a full discussion of overweight, see pages 306–312.) Too much fat in the diet may come from poor choice of food in meals or snacks, or from poor cooking, or both. For instance, here are some of the ways people add excess fat calories to the diet: (a) by not pouring off fat when making gravy; (b) by eating a great deal of fried food; (c) by frequently eating pies, cakes, and pastries; (d) by use of excess butter on bread and other foods; (e) by use of excess cream and ice cream; (f) by use of excess mayonnaise or other oily salad dressing; (g) by use of excess fat in seasoning vegetables; (h) by using excess fat in making bread; (i) by adding fat to stewed fruits; (j) by eating visible fat on meats; (k) by eating nuts, pastries, and chocolate between meals.

Perhaps no one is a victim of all of these poor practices, but many people are victims of half of them or more.

We are aware of the fat we eat if we eat it on bread, or as cream, but we are not always so aware of the fat that is in the food we eat. Here are two examples.

You learned in your study of meat that many popular cuts have fat interspersed with lean. Let us see how this works out for the fat content of your diet. If you will turn to page 459 in the appendix, you will see that a three-ounce hamburger yields 245 calories, and that 21 grams is protein and 17 grams is fat. (Some other cuts of meat have more fat than hamburger.) You recall that a gram of protein yields 4 calories and a gram of fat yields 9 calories. You can therefore find the number of calories in a three-ounce hamburger which come from protein by multiplying $4 \times 21 = 84$ calories from protein, and the number from fat by multiplying $9 \times 17 = 153$ calories from fat.

The standard two-crust pie recipe calls for 2/3-cup of fat. You will observe in the table on page 460 that one cup of cooking fat (vegetable oil) contains 1770 calories. Hence, two-thirds cup of any kind of fat adds well over 1000 calories to the pie. If the pie is cut in six pieces, each person is getting close to 200 calories from the fat in the crust alone. Thus we see that fat sneaks into the diet in many unnoticed ways.

Research indicates many Americans eat too much fat, with 40 percent or more of their calories coming from it. Nutritionists consider that 25 to 30 percent of the total calories from fat would be more desirable. You can figure the percentage of fat in your diet by using the formula given and the table on page 452.

The Care of Fat and Its Use in Cooking

Since fat is used in so many ways in cooking, let us consider these. Fat is used for frying food, to improve flavor, texture, and appearance. There are two types of frying. You have learned about pan-frying or sautéing in your study of vegetables. Deep fat frying is quite another technique. We shall discuss it briefly. But first let us take a look at a few things that may help you use fat more wisely in cooking.

(1) Any fat used as a food should be fresh and pleasant to smell and taste. Rancid (răn′sīd) or stale fat can spoil the flavor of a dish. (Butter and the vegetable oils are more likely to become rancid than other fats.) After fats are opened they should be stored in the refrigerator. This includes bacon or meat drippings. If meat is properly cooked at a low temperature, the fat is clean and clear. In your study of meat you learned to remove fat from the pan, and to save the brown drippings for their vitamins and minerals. They are associated with the juice in the meat and remain in the bottom of the pan.

TEMPERATURE FOR DEEP FAT FRYING*

Type of Product	Temperature of Fat (Degrees F)	Time to Brown One Inch Bread Cube in Hot Fat
Doughnuts Fritters Oysters, scallops Soft shell crabs Fish	350 to 375	60 seconds
Croquettes Eggplant Onions	375 to 385	40 seconds
French fried potatoes	385 to 395	20 seconds

Handbook of Food Preparation. American Home Economics Association, Washington, D.C., 1964.

(2) In frying foods, see that the fat does not burn. The appearance of a white or blue smoke or an unpleasant odor indicates the fat is burning. Deep frying is the cooking of food by submerging in hot fat. A thermometer should be used to judge the correct temperature. Tests done to find the best temperature for frying indicate 365° F as a good temperature. But this can vary from 350° to 395° F, depending on the food, for deep frying.

(3) When you deep fry, use a wire basket or sieve to lower the food into the fat; the food should be dry. The temperature should be exactly right when the food is placed in the fat. (If you do not have a thermometer, use the practical test given in the table shown above. The fat should be only one-half the depth of the pan, to prevent bubbling over. Fry only a small amount at a time, to insure quick cooking and even browning. The food is done when golden brown. It should be drained on absorbent paper. If it is not burned, strain leftover fat through a cheese cloth in a sieve, and store in a covered container in the refrigerator for re-use.

Precautions to observe when deep frying are: Keep the fire low; you have an inflammable pot of oil above a fire. (In an electric fryer, the fire is hidden and there is automatic temperature control.) Be sure the handle of the fryer is over the stove and not sticking out where it might cause an accident. Hot fat is almost twice as damaging as hot water, because it can reach such high temperatures. (Boiling water is 212° F. We fry at 365° F.) If you do not have *adequate equipment*, do not try to deep fry.

(4) Since we tend to eat too much fat food, it is well to cook most food by other methods. Everyone enjoys fried food occasionally; but make it a special treat rather than a regular method of cooking. The potato illustrates how fast calories are added by frying. One potato gives 90 calories when baked, but when it is French fried it gives 393. If you eat the same potato fried into potato chips it gives 544 calories. If you are concerned with overweight, you can make good use of this knowledge.

The standard for a deep-fried food is: golden brown color; crisp, tender texture; fat only on the surface, and not soaked through; delicate flavor of the natural food. If you use a good method of frying throughout, very little fat penetrates beyond the outer surface of the food. The vitamins and minerals are reasonably well retained in fried foods.

How to Use Fat in Your Meals

Go over the points listed on pages 258–259, and see how you can eliminate excess fat. It may be that you will only need to cut down on fatty foods for snacks, and take milk, fruit juice, or fruit. By such a change you may also gain extra minerals and vitamins in your daily diet. It may be that you need only to watch at meals the amount of salad dressing, sauces, gravies, butter (on bread and potatoes), and pastries that you eat.

Here are some hints on how to make sure your diet includes enough fat, but not too much:

(1) Avoid eating a large amount of fat at any meal. Eat it as it occurs naturally in the foods you need daily (such as milk, eggs, and meat) instead of in rich foods.

(2) In cooking, season food with just enough fat to give a good flavor, and no more. (The recipes given in the cookbook section of this book follow that principle.)

(3) Add visible fats to your foods sparingly—such as butter or margarine on bread and on potatoes. If you tend to eat too much fat, use whole or skim milk on cereals instead of cream and eat more yellow and green vegetables.

(4) Use vegetable oils when possible instead of firm fats.

(5) Make a habit of eating fruits for snacks and desserts. Aside from olives and avocados, they contain no fat and provide many nutrients you need for health and beauty. If you can form the habit now of controlling the fat you eat daily, the benefits will apply for the present and also for your future life. Overweight is one of the big health problems for adults.

Pastry

Americans like pie—and their favorite dessert is probably apple pie. Once it was the dessert of fall and winter. Now it is eaten the year round.

Fruit pies, with cherry next to apple are the most popular. (See pages 91–95 for the variety of fruits to use in pies.) There are many ways to make fruit pies, such as the standard two-crust, latticed top, deep dish, cobbler, fruit dumpling, and shortcake. The last four of these may be made with a low-fat biscuit-type dough.

Other kinds of pies are cream and chiffon. The cream fillings for pies include vanilla, coconut, pineapple, butterscotch, chocolate, and custard. This type of pie

differs from the fruit pie in having only a bottom crust, and the crust is baked first except for custard.

In the cream type of pie, the filling is made separately of milk, eggs, sugar, butter, a thickening agent such as corn-starch, flour, or tapioca, and flavoring. This is cooked in the top of a double boiler until it is smooth and firm and the taste of cornstarch, if used, is gone. Then it is poured into the baked pie shell, meringue is added, and the meringue is browned. (See Cookbook page 438 for exact method.)

Chiffon pies use gelatin to give a thick, firm filling. The lemon chiffon is most famous, but pumpkin, chocolate, and butterscotch are favorites too. The chiffon pie may be made without gelatin, by use of egg whites to give the high fluff. Some recipes call for raw egg white in chiffon pies. Find a recipe for this type of pie that doesn't use raw eggs (see page 441), as they interfere with the use of a B vita-min. Chiffon has less fat than cream pie.

Meringues are used on cream filling pies with one crust. Here are some points to guide you in making meringues: (a) Egg whites give the biggest volume when beaten at room temperature. (b) Add salt or cream of tartar to increase volume and help egg whites hold air. (c) Recent research shows that $2\frac{1}{2}$ tablespoons of sugar for each egg white is about right to give the best meringue. Too little gives less tenderness; too much causes it to be syrupy or gummy. (d) Sugar is added gradually so that it can all be dissolved, giving a better texture to the meringue. (e) Beat until the meringue stands in peaks, but is not dry. (f) Pile meringue onto hot pie filling and be sure it seals with edge of crust to prevent shrinking. Swirl it to give decorative effect. (g) Bake at 400° F for eight to ten minutes, or until golden brown. (Research indicates that high temperature for a short baking gives a more tender meringue. Be careful not to overcook, as this causes toughness and shrinkage.)

The *pie crust* is a key to your success as a pie maker. A tough crust can spoil the best filling. Four ingredients make a pie crust: flour, fat, liquid, and salt. Then there is crumb crust, made from crushed graham, vanilla, or ginger wafers, which is an alternate for pastry crust and has less fat.

Pastry dough is made with firm fats or oils. All-purpose flour is preferred to pas-

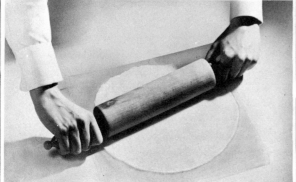

try flour, and whole wheat flour gives a different, nutty-flavored crust with added nourishment. Fat is usually cut into the flour to a coarse blend. A cold liquid mixed quickly gives best results. Add the last of the liquid cautiously. Chill dough before rolling, if there is time; this gives a more flaky crust. If you roll dough between sheets of slightly oiled wax paper, you will have no trouble with sticking, provided you have measured and mixed your pastry accurately. Lift the top sheet of paper, turn over other sheet with crust attached, and place the crust over the pie plate or on top of the pie. This reduces handling and prevents breaking.

Baking time depends on the type of pie. Pie shells are baked in a hot oven at 425° to 450° F. Soggy crust on fruit pies is due to baking at too low a temperature. Fruit pies should be baked at 425° to 450° F. Most fruit pies cook in 45 to 55 minutes. Apple may take 60 minutes. The outer edges of the pie shell will not burn at this high temperature, if you place aluminum foil over the top. Remove it 15 minutes before the pie is done.

Storing pies is not a big problem, for they are usually quickly eaten. Chiffon and cream pies are stored in the refrigera-

Steps in Making Pastry: (1) Sift dry ingredients together in mixing bowl. (2) Cut in fat and add cold liquid gradually, mixing lightly with a fork. (3) Shape pastry into firm ball and divide for a two-crust pie. Chill in refrigerator if time permits. (4) Roll pastry between two pieces of wax paper (for ease in handling) from center out. It should form a circle 1 inch larger than pan and be ⅛ inch thick. (5) Remove top piece of wax paper. Place pastry over pan and press firmly in place. Remove wax paper, and fill crust with fruit. Repeat process for top crust, making a design in the pastry to let steam escape. Press crusts together with tines of fork or flute the edges. (6) To make individual shells, shape dough over muffin tins and bake at 450°F until brown (10-12 minutes).

A one-crust pie. What are your favorite fillings for one-crust pies?

tor. Pies may be cooked or prepared ready to cook, carefully sealed, and stored in the deep freeze. Frozen baked pies taste better if warmed before eating. Fruit pies may be topped with ¾-cup grated cheese and warmed.

Pies are served on a pie plate and eaten with a fork, unless pouring cream is added. Then a spoon is used. Fruit pies are frequently served with sharp cheese or ice cream. Pie with ice cream is called "pie a la mode."

The Place of Pies in Meals

From our discussion of fat (and sugar, which follows) you see that the calorie content of a piece of pie is high. Pie is not a good choice for dessert with a heavy meal. Choose pie for dessert when the amount of fat, starch, and sugar in the remainder of the meal is small. If you do this, you can have pie occasionally and control your weight too. Fortunately the vegetables, fruits, and milk which we need are not high in calories. When you serve as the meat, liver or fish which is low in fat, that is a good time to have pie for dessert.

Eating is a pleasure when foods are served in proper balance. But there is a sting in the pleasure of eating if the foods we enjoy bring us overweight and lowered health.

 WORDS TO WORK WITH

Cholesterol (kō lĕs′tĕr ōl): a waxy, fat-like, substance present in many foods, especially in animal fats. It can also be made by the body.

Hydrogenation (hī drŏj′ĕ nā shŭn): the processing of oils to make them firm.

Linoleic (lĭn ō lā′ĭc): the most healthful, smallest unsaturated fatty acid, essential for life.

THINKING IT OVER

1. Why is fat called the most concentrated food? How does it help your looks and your health?

2. In what ways may too much fat be harmful?

3. Explain the ways in which fat adds up in your meals by poor choice of foods and poor cooking. Give examples.

4. What is the best way to include the fat you need in your meals?

5. What are the foods for snacks that add fat calories fast? Compare the calories in a soda with those in an eight-ounce glass of milk. Compare them with those in the juice of one orange.

6. What steps can you take to lower the amount of fat in your diet, if necessary?

7. What are the important points to keep in mind when cooking with fat? In using fat foods in meals?

PROBLEMS TO SOLVE

1. Keep a record of the food you eat at meals and between meals for two days. Does this represent what you have been eating recently? Check each food for fat content by the table on page 452, and find out how much fat you are eating daily. You can do this by using the formula given on page 259 and with the aid of the table. Can you decide how much fat you ate at each meal? Between meals? Total for the day?

2. Make an exhibit of different types of fats.
   (1) Discuss the advantages and disadvantages of each type.
   (2) From what is each fat made?
   (3) Why is it important to know the different types of fats?

APPLYING WHAT YOU KNOW

1. Planning menus.
   (1) Plan balanced menus for three days. Underline the foods which are high in fat which you can see. Underline twice the foods which are high in "hidden" fat.
   (2) Show how you could get the fat too high by changing only one food. Show how you could lower the fat in the meals you planned.
   (3) Do the same for snacks.

2. Preparing desserts using fats: If time permits, make a pie crust and prepare one or more of the following pies.
   (1) Deep dish fruit pie.
   (2) Cream pie with meringue.
   (3) Chiffon pie.

3. Serve dessert in an appropriate dish and with appropriate silver.

EVALUATING

1. If weight control is a problem, what type of pie would you choose? Why? What would you serve in a meal with pie?

2. Thinking through what is in each type of pie, which do you think is most nourishing? Explain your answer.

3. Do you see ways to prevent there being too much fat in your meals and snacks? What are they?

HOME EXPERIENCE

With your mother, plan a balanced meal in which you use the dessert you learned to make at school. Prepare and serve this as a part of the meal. Report your results to your teacher.

24

The Place of Sugar in Your Diet

Sugar's Contributions to Your Diet

Sugar has one of the most attractive flavors in food. It is sugar the bee seeks in the flower. It is sugar in fruit which causes us to prefer it above vegetables, and it is sugar in peas, carrots, sweet corn, sweet potatoes, winter squash, and other vegetables which gives the extraordinarily good flavor. Sugar appeals to our taste and makes our diet more satisfying.

Sugar, along with starch, is a carbohydrate. White sugar is 100 percent carbohydrate, giving nothing but energy or calories. It is sometimes referred to as having "empty" calories. Carbohydrates supply the largest share of calories in the average diet—in some parts of the world as much as 90 percent.

Sugar gives the quickest energy of any food, requiring slight digestion and pass-

Ice cream and cake are traditional refreshments for a birthday. Serve angel food or sponge cake with low-fat ice cream to control calories.

ing almost at once into the blood stream. From sugar we feel an immediate "lift," because it gives such quick energy. This can work for us when properly used. However, if over-used, by our depending on candy or sweet soda water for quick energy, this can work against health and looks.

Eating concentrated sweets is not the best way to satisfy hunger. Milk will also give a "quick lift," and will provide nutrients that add immeasurably to your health and other goals—as does the sugar from fruit or fruit juice. It is the nutrients from these foods that help maintain your "pep" and good looks.

Sugar (like starch) helps the body use the fat in food more efficiently. That is why it is said that "fat burns in the fire of carbohydrate." Fat and carbohydrates work together—another example of this teamwork is that the B vitamins help "burn" carbohydrate and fat foods.

Why Too Much Sugar in the Diet May Be Harmful

We eat more sugar today than we did a hundred years ago. Americans in 1957 averaged eating two-thirds cup of sugar per day (97.1 pounds per person per year). This is about 500 calories per day. In 1820 it was only 8 pounds a year per person. This is an enormous increase (1100) percent). How may it affect us?

(1) Eating too many sweets, especially between meals, can cause loss of appetite for the foods you need at mealtime.

(2) Irritation in the digestive tract may result from eating too large amounts of sugar.

(3) Eating too much sugar can have a harmful effect on your teeth, in two ways.

Bacteria act on food that clings to the teeth, producing acids. This may cause enamel to dissolve. Then if your diet includes so many sweets that they replace the milk, fruits, vegetables, and other foods out of which teeth are built, the teeth are weakened for lack of needed nutrients, and decay results.

One study made several years ago showed that 95 percent of the young people who had reached 15 years of age in our country had defective teeth. This was also the chief physical defect of the young men examined for military service in the World Wars. An Ohio dentist became so concerned about widespread tooth decay that he made a study of different types of people in various parts of the world. He found that where people ate natural foods in sufficient amounts, the condition of the teeth was excellent. But where a large part of the diet consisted of highly refined foods such as white sugar, white flour, and white rice, teeth were defective. Other studies of controlled diets have shown that when the food is improved to furnish the nutrients needed to build teeth, there is a decrease in cavities.

(4) The overeating of sugar usually leads to overweight. (For further discussion of control of weight, see Chapter 27.) When you eat more concentrated sweets than you need for your daily activity, the excess calories are changed and stored as body fat.

The Place of Sugar in a Balanced Diet

The place for sugar in the balanced diet is in meals, and not between them. A sweet food at the end of the meal for dessert is satisfying. You have then eaten the meat, vegetables, fruits, milk, and bread you need to supply the "protective" vitamins, minerals, and protein. A sweet gives a feeling of completeness and enjoyment as a climax to the meal.

Keep in mind the dessert when you plan the meal. For instance, if you wish a high-calorie sweet dessert, hold down on excess starchy and sweet foods in the main meal. Some homemakers give their families far too much starch and sugar in one meal. Here is an example:

For dinner one family had glazed ham, candied sweet potatoes, corn on the cob, lima beans, bread, butter, chocolate pie, and coffee. You see at once that this meal is too high in starch and sugar. It does not have enough calcium (milk) or vitamin C (raw vegetable, fruit, citrus fruit, or tomato). Yet it is not unlike many meals that are considered "good" by many families. Let us see how this menu could be improved to supply a variety of

the nutrients you need, without producing overweight.

Dinner Heavy in Starch and Sugar

Glazed ham

Candied sweet potatoes   Corn

Lima beans

Bread   Butter

Chocolate pie

Coffee

Improved

Broiled ham

Baked sweet potatoes   Green beans

Tossed green salad

Bread and Butter (if desired)

Chocolate pudding

Milk

When eating a sweet snack food such as cookies, cake, or any pastry, remember that sugar needs B vitamins in order to be used well. Drink a glass of milk with your sweet snack.

Teach yourself to use less sugar on foods such as cereals and fruits, and in

The same recipe in pans of three different sizes. What happens in baking when the pan is too small? too large? See further discussion on page 271.

PAN— too small   PAN— just right   PAN— too large

Use the correct size of pan for quality in baking. All of these pans are standard sizes. (See recipe pages 354 and 433-41.)

beverages. Many pie recipes call for more sugar than is needed. Experiment with sugar in pies and see if you can use less. Buy canned fruits in light syrup instead of heavy to save money and to get fewer calories. If you have a habit of over-eating sweets, you should change it. Save your concentrated sweet for dessert. When there is enough milk, vegetables, fruits, and meats in the diet, there is less craving for sweets. There is a place for sweet desserts in your daily diet; but you will look and feel better if you use them in their proper place.

Sweets for Dessert — Cakes

The cake is the symbol of perfection in cooking. This is partly because its taste is so satisfying. It requires great skill and art to turn out a beautiful and delicious cake that melts in the mouth, but you can achieve this distinction with practice. Many hostesses are known for a famous cake recipe. From the ancient Chinese all through the early civilized world, the cake was used in religious and state celebrations. Today the cake is still used to celebrate a birthday, or to serve as the food highlight at a wedding reception.

The ingredients that make this delicious and attractive food are as follows: (a) Sugar gives flavor, helps the cake to brown, improves the texture, and adds calories (770 per cup). (b) Fat improves flavor, texture, keeping quality, and browning. One cup of fat yields approximately 1635 to 1985 calories.* (c) Flour gives the framework to the cake. There are two kinds of flour used in cakes. "Cake flour," because it is made of soft wheat with a weak protein, gives a good cake a finer texture. The other type is a "blended," "all-purpose," or "family" flour; use two tablespoons less of this for each cup in the recipe unless the recipe states "all-purpose" flour. The protein is stronger in a blended flour. (d) Eggs add tenderness, color, improve texture, lightness, and give greater nourishment.

* One cup of margarine yields 1635 calories. One cup of lard or vegetable oil yields 1985 calories. Hence ⅞ cup of the latter equals one cup of butter or margarine.

TEMPERATURE AND TIME USED IN BAKING*

Type of Product	Oven Temperature (Degrees F)	Baking Time (Minutes)
BREADS		
Biscuits	425 to 450	10 to 15
Corn bread	400 to 425	30 to 40
Cream puffs	375	60
Muffins	400 to 425	20 to 25
Popovers	375	60
Quick loaf breads	350 to 375	60 to 75
Yeast bread	400	30 to 40
Yeast rolls, plain	400 to 425	15 to 25
Yeast rolls, sweet	375	20 to 30
CAKES WITH FAT		
Cup	350 to 375	15 to 25
Layer	350 to 375	20 to 35
Loaf	350	45 to 60
CAKES WITHOUT FAT		
Angel food and sponge	350 to 375	30 to 45
COOKIES		
Drop	350 to 400	8 to 15
Rolled	375	8 to 10
EGG, MEAT, MILK, AND CHEESE DISHES		
Cheese soufflé (baked in a pan of hot water)	350	30 to 60
Custard, plain, corn, etc. (baked in a pan of hot water)	350	30 to 60
Macaroni and cheese	350	25 to 30
Meat loaf	300	60 to 90
Meat pie	400	25 to 30
Scalloped potatoes	350	60
PASTRY		
One-crust pie (custard type), unbaked shell	400 to 425	30 to 40
Meringue or cooked filling in prebaked shell	350 or 425 to 450	12 to 15 or 4 to 4½
Shell only	450	10 to 12
Two-crust pies with uncooked filling	400 to 425	45 to 55
Two-crust pies with cooked filling	425 to 450	30 to 45

For packaged mixes, follow directions on label.

* *Handbook of Food Preparation.* American Home Economics Association, Washington, D.C., 1964.

(e) Liquid is the binder of all ingredients. Milk adds to the nourishment and keeps a cake more moist than water does. (f) Leavening agents include baking powder, soda, and egg white for butter cakes, and egg whites plus air for angel or sponge cakes. The leavening agent causes the cake to rise, improving its looks, taste, and texture. (g) Flavoring is the last delicate touch to blend the whole flavor of the cake and give it individuality. Flavoring should be delicately added. Too much spoils a good cake. Too little fails to bring out the mellow flavor. The common flavorings are vanilla, almond, orange, and lemon. These are called "extracts," and there are many other extracts on the market. The common spices used in cakes are ginger, cinnamon, cloves, nutmeg, and allspice. Nuts, chocolate, and fruits are also used to add flavor. A cake is no better than the ingredients that make it.

The *method of mixing cakes* shows a homemaker's skill, for different results are often achieved with exactly the same ingredients. How you mix a cake depends on the type of cake. There are three types: (a) butter cake, (b) sponge cake, (c) chiffon cake.

There are two methods of making a butter cake. The *standard method* is to mix butter and sugar together until the mixture is light and fluffy like cold cream. Then the eggs are added and mixed. The flour is sifted with dry ingredients and added in four parts, alternating with the liquid, which is added in three parts. You start by adding flour and end with flour. The flavoring is added, and egg whites are folded in last, if they are beaten separately. A butter cake is baked at 375°F

in layers and takes about 25 minutes. Experiments show that the time required to mix the standard butter cake by hand is about 18 minutes, compared with six minutes for the commercial "ready-mix" butter cake. The standard method gives an excellent cake in appearance and taste.

Experimenters in cooking have found a new and *quick method* of making butter cakes. This method takes little equipment and little time and gives good results.

Here are the steps in the *quick method:* In one mixing bowl sift together all measured dry ingredients. Add shortening and a part of milk and mix at medium speed for two minutes; add eggs, remaining milk, and flavoring and mix 2 minutes by electric mixer or 300 strokes by hand. With an electric mixer it is ready to bake with four minutes of mixing.

When you use this method, be sure that the recipe is worked out for the quick method. You cannot use it on a standard recipe, for the proportions of the ingredients are different. (See recipe, page 435.) The oven for baking a cake should be lighted and set at correct temperature before you start. Keep in mind that eggs and fat should be at room temperature. Follow your recipe exactly and use the exact size of pan called for in the recipe. A pan that is too small causes uneven browning, breaking in the middle, uneven top, overcooking at the sides, and undercooking in the middle. Too large a pan causes the cake to cook too quickly, with possible burning and less attractive shape. Most cake recipes are made for two standard-size cake pans.

Sponge cakes contain no fat and are leavened with egg white to hold air plus the steam formed in baking. Sponge cakes

Quick Cake Method: (1) Have all ingredients at room temperature. Place fat in mixing bowl. (2) Sift in dry ingredients and add three-fourths of milk and flavoring. Beat 2 minutes by electric mixer (slow speed) or 300 strokes by hand, scraping bowl and spoon frequently. (3) Add eggs and remaining milk and beat in the same way for 1 minute or 150 strokes. (4) Fill oiled pans 1/2 full and bake in moderate oven (375°F) until done (25 minutes for layers, 35 minutes for oblong). (5) Loosen cake with spatula (or if pan is lined with wax paper, remove it) and cool. (6) Frost between layers, then the sides, and finally the top. Use a knife to make swirls.

are made with eggs, sugar, flour, and flavoring. This gives a beautiful light, fluffy-textured cake that keeps well and has a delicate flavor. The angel food cake, which contains a cup of egg whites without the yolks, is excellent in protein, and is a good dessert for adults who can't eat egg yolks. The yellow sponge contains the white plus the yolks, and adds more nutrients than the angel food. Sponge cakes, delicious unfrosted, are excellent for weight watchers, or those who would keep down the fat in a diet. They are fine also for a children's party. One piece of this cake (2x3x3 inches is ideal) gives only 100 calories. Butter cake of the same size would give you as much as 300 to 450 calories, depending on the amount and kind of frosting.

Naturally the method of mixing is different from that of a butter cake. (See pages 436 and 437 for recipes.) But it is easy once you get the eggs properly beaten and use the easy light touch to fold in the other ingredients.

Angel cakes are usually baked in a tube pan. The pan is ungreased. This helps the egg white to take hold and rise.

Cream of tartar helps give firmness in the beating and holding of the egg white, resulting in a more tender, lighter cake.

Sponge cakes are placed upside down on a rack to cool. When completely cool, loosen sides with a spatula and remove.

Chiffon cakes are made by the quick method, using vegetable oil and five or six eggs. This gives the cake the tenderness of the butter cake and the lightness of the sponge cake. A chiffon cake keeps well. (See recipe in Cookbook, pages 435–6.)

Other cakes include the ready-prepared mixes, ready-baked cakes, and frozen

Steps in Making Angel Food Cake: (1) Have all ingredients at room temperature. Sift measured sifted flour with 1/3 of sugar three times.

(2) Beat egg whites, salt, and cream of tartar until foamy. Add remaining sugar 2 tablespoons at a time, beating for 10 seconds at medium speed after each addition. Beat until all sugar is added and meringue stands in moist peaks. Sift flour mixture over meringue (3 tablespoons at a time) and fold gently until smooth. Spoon and level batter into an ungreased tube pan. Bake in moderate oven (375°F) until top springs back when lightly touched (30 to 35 minutes).

(3) Loosen sides of cake from pan with a spatula and invert on a cake rack to cool.

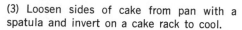

273

Steps in Making Jelly Roll (Sponge Cake): (1) Oil a 15 x 10 inch pan and line bottom with aluminum foil. Sift dry ingredients together in mixing bowl and set aside. Beat eggs until light in color and add sugar gradually, beating after each addition. Add vanilla and fold in dry ingredients gently.

(2) Spread batter evenly over all the pan and bake in hot oven (400°F) for 10 to 12 minutes. (3) Sprinkle a smooth clean towel with confectioner's sugar. Invert pan on towel and gently remove cake with spatula. Remove foil and cut crisp edges from cake. Turn up end of cake with towel and roll, allowing towel to roll up with cake. When cool, unroll and spread with jelly; then roll again and cover with towel.

cakes. Though the ready-made mixes and prepared cakes do not necessarily save money or equal the flavor of home-made cake, they do save time. Mixes may have chemicals added to prevent their getting rancid and lumpy. For best enjoyment, they should be eaten on the day baked. It is sometimes less expensive to buy a ready-made cake such as angel food (with a dozen egg whites in it) than to make one.

Cakes are served on a five- or seven-inch pie plate, and are eaten with a fork.

Cookies are really tiny cakes. They are preferred by children because they are easy to handle, crisp, and tasty. The cookie is associated with childhood and the love of family and home. With so many new desserts today, it is not as important as formerly. But there are still times when the cookie is just the right dessert.

Cookies contain less liquid and more flour and fat than cakes, and are of quite a different texture, size and taste.

Types of cookies include the following:

(1) Rolled cookies contain more flour than other types, and are rolled thin on wax paper that is lightly floured or oiled. They are cut and cooked on a cookie sheet. This was the cookie of your great-grandmother and the legendary cookie jar.

(2) The drop cookie is a favorite modern cookie. It has a softer dough than the rolled, gives a richer flavor, and is easy to mix, easy to drop from a spoon, and quick to bake. This dough may be stored in the refrigerator and baked as desired.

(3) Bar cookies are cooked in sheets spread over a pan, and cut into bars when done. The brownie is an example. They

Top, left: Drop cookies. Middle: Roll cookies. Bottom: Quick roll cookies. Place small balls of dough 2 inches apart on a cookie sheet and press with a covered glass. Top, right: Refrigerator cookies. Shape dough into a roll and wrap in wax paper. Seal, store in refrigerator, and bake fresh cookies as desired.

have a softer dough than other cookies. Many rich fruit cookies are cooked in sheets and cut into bars.

(4) Refrigerator cookies are popular because they can be kept rolled in wax paper, uncooked, and refrigerated for several weeks. They supply fresh warm cookies as you need them. This saves fuel and energy, for the cookies can be baked when the oven is in use for other reasons.

(5) The filled cookie is a variation on the refrigerator, rolled, or bar cookie. A layer of cookie dough is covered with a fruit and nut mixture, chocolate or jam, and another layer of dough is placed on top. Wet fingers and press edges of dough together. This prevents the filling from running out. Then bake the cookies. This is a tasty cookie that remains fresh for a

long time if stored in the refrigerator in a tight container. (For recipes for these cookies, see the Cookbook, pages 442-445.)

Cookies are usually served to accompany fruit or ice cream, and are eaten as a snack.

How to Store Cakes and Cookies

Cakes that will be used quickly can be stored in a regular cake container. But if the cake is to last several days, wrap it carefully in wax paper or foil and store in the refrigerator. To save time on the day of a big party, bake your cake ahead, wrap securely, and store in the deep freeze. If it is frosted on the day of the party, it will taste and look like a fresh-baked cake. In freezing a cake, be sure it is wrapped in moisture-proof paper. Fruit cakes are made more mellow by standing in storage in a cool place.

Store cookies that will be eaten quickly in an ordinary cookie jar—one kind to a container, as the flavors mix. Store crisp cookies in a tight metal container, such as a fruit cake tin. Cookies that have stood as much as a week should be heated in the oven for a few minutes to regain crisp texture and fresh flavor.

Decorate cookies with fruit, nuts, or frosting.

Frostings

The frosting on the cake helps keep it moist, makes it more attractive, and adds the sweet taste we enjoy. Many cakes are left unfrosted, such as the pound cake, angel food, sponge, and chiffon. Those who watch calories may prefer molasses cake or gingerbread. These cakes are high in nourishment and low in calories, because they have the iron and B vitamins from molasses, and the full rich flavor needs no frosting. The simplest frosting for these cakes is apple sauce. A light sifting of confectioner's sugar over a warm cake is appropriate for any kind.

There are two types of moist frosting:

(1) *Uncooked frosting* is easy to make, inexpensive, takes little time, and gives good results if directions are accurately followed.

Uncooked frosting is made with confectioner's sugar and butter or cream or both. Flavoring of your choice can give wide variety. Egg is sometimes called for

TEMPERATURES AND TESTS
FOR SYRUPS AND CANDIES*

Product	Temperature at Sea Level (Degrees F)	Test	Description of Test
SYRUP	230 to 234	THREAD	Syrup spins a 2″ thread when dropped from fork or spoon.
FONDANT FUDGE PENOCHI	234 to 240	SOFT BALL	Syrup forms soft ball when dropped into cold water, and flattens on removal from water.
CARAMELS	244 to 248	FIRM BALL	Syrup forms firm ball when dropped into cold water, and does not flatten upon removal.
DIVINITY MARSHMALLOWS POPCORN BALLS	250 to 266	HARD BALL	Syrup forms a hard ball that holds its shape, yet is plastic when dropped into cold water.
BUTTERSCOTCH TAFFIES	270 to 290	SOFT CRACK	Syrup separates into threads which are hard but not brittle when it is dropped into cold water.
BRITTLE	300 to 310	HARD CRACK	Syrup separates into threads which are hard and brittle when dropped into cold water.

Handbook of Food Preparation. American Home Economics Association, Washington, D.C., 1964.

in this type of frosting, but use of raw egg white in a frosting is discouraged (see page 75). If you wish a colored frosting, fruit juice gives both color and flavor. For yellow frosting, add one or two tablespoons of grated orange peel soaked in orange juice. Strawberry or raspberry juice gives a soft pink color and a good flavor. Grape juice gives a lavender color.

Another type of uncooked frosting is apricot, peach, or pineapple preserves, conserve, or apple sauce. These are excellent in flavor between layers, and more desirable than pure sugar frostings. The top may have a light dusting of confectioner's sugar, or a dip of ice cream.

(2) *Cooked frostings* are the same as candy and are made with the same precautions. The problem is to prevent crystals from forming; a candy thermometer helps you get best results.

Varieties of cooked frostings include: chocolate or fudge, penuche, divinity, and variations of these.

This quick strawberry shortcake is made with cookies.

Here are some hints for making good frostings:

(a) A cake frosts better when the crumbs are removed and it is cool.

(b) Cooked frostings do not soak in as much if they have cooled.

(c) With a layer cake the bottom layer is turned upside down for frosting, and it is frosted first. Then the second layer is placed right side up on top of the first layer, and the sides are frosted. The top is frosted last.

(d) Use a spatula for swirling the frosting. It gives a decorative effect.

(e) If cooked frosting is used, work quickly before it gets too stiff.

Frostings pile up the calories. As you look through recipe books to find frostings, keep in mind what you have learned about sugar. The standard recipe for fudge frosting calls for two cups of sugar. That alone gives you 1746 calories. When you add that to the sugar and fat in the cake, you may well run your calories to between 3000 and 4000 for the cake! If you use the new quick method of mixing, the total is even higher.

Use your knowledge of nutrition by choosing frostings with little sugar; not making the frosting so thick on the cake; learning to use fruit with plain cake; or making fresh cake and eating it unfrosted while it is fresh, or with a scoop of ice cream. Angel food and sponge cakes are the lowest in calories and fat content. Use them often.

How to Judge a Good Cake

A good cake is level or slightly rounded on top. Before it is frosted, the color is golden brown. It has a velvety crumb, with even grain of fine texture. It is tender to touch and taste. The flavor is well blended, moist, delicate, and sweet. In addition, a sponge cake should spring and break easily with the fingers.

A frosted cake should be well covered and attractive, with a firm but not hard surface. The flavor of the frosting should blend with and bring out that of the cake.

THINKING IT OVER

1. Why is sugar a "quick energy" food? When is there need for quick energy?

2. What are the contributions sugar makes to your life?

3. In what ways may too much sugar be harmful to your teeth? Your figure? Your general health?

4. What is the place of sweet foods in the diet?

5. If you need to gain weight, do you look upon sugar as the best food to help you? Explain your answer.

6. If you need to lose weight, how can you control the amount of sugar you eat at breakfast? At lunch? At dinner? In snacks?

7. Why should you have a glass of milk with cookies or a sweet dessert?

8. How can eating enough meat, milk, vegetable, and fruits help you cut down on sugar in your meals and snacks? How will this help you?

9. What are the types of cakes? How do they differ? What makes a good cake?

10. In what ways do cookies differ from cakes? What are the main types of cookies?

11. How should cakes and cookies be used in meals?

PROBLEMS TO SOLVE

1. Learning to evaluate advertising.
   (1) Study magazine, newspaper, radio, and television advertisements of food, and bring examples of different types of advertisements to class. In what other ways is food advertised?
   (2) Have a panel of class members discuss food advertising.
   (3) Invite a person in the community connected with food advertising to speak to you or enter into the panel discussion.
   (4) Invite a qualified person from the community to speak on health as influenced by food.
   (5) Discuss the ways advertising can assist you in making good use of your money, time, and energy in buying food.
   (6) Discuss ways in which some advertising concerning the use of food money may mislead.
   (7) Allow time for a general class discussion and evaluation of food advertising. This should include a period for questions from the class.

APPLYING WHAT YOU KNOW

1. *Baking cakes:* Make one or more of the following. (Individual families might try different types of cakes. See Cookbook for recipes.)
   (1) Butter cake by the standard method; bake as cup cakes or layers.
   (2) Butter cake by the quick method; bake as cup cakes, oblong, or layers.
   (3) Sponge, angel food, or chiffon cake.
   (4) Fruit frosting.
   (5) Uncooked frosting.
   (6) Cooked frosting.

2. *Cookies:* Make one of the following.
   (1) Rolled cookies.
   (2) Drop cookies.
   (3) Refrigerator cookies.

3. Planning menus using cakes and cookies as dessert.
   (1) Plan two balanced dinner menus using unfrosted cake or cookies.
   (2) Plan two balanced dinner menus using a frosted cake as the dessert.
   (3) Plan a light Sunday night supper with the dessert giving a big part of the nourishment. What will guide you in making this plan?

EVALUATING

1. Compare the quality of your cake, cookies, or frosting with the standard for that food. Does your work measure up on all scores? How can you improve it?

2. Compare the cost in time, money, energy, and calories in making the cakes by the standard and the quick method. Compare the flavor and the number of servings.

3. When would you think it good judgment to buy a ready-made cake? A mix?

4. Compare the butter cake and sponge cake in time, money, energy, flavor, calories, and nourishment. Which cake is higher in protein? in fat?

5. In which do you get most needed nutrients for the money? Why?

HOME EXPERIENCE

Prepare and serve a cake as the dessert for a meal that is properly planned and prepared at home.

FURTHER READING

Betty Crocker's New Picture Cookbook. McGraw-Hill Book Company, New York, N.Y., 1961.

Cake-Mix Cakes, Shortening Type. First Report, 1961. American Home Economics Association, Washington, D.C.

Eat Well and Stay Well, rev. ed., Ancel and Margaret Keys. Doubleday & Company, Inc., New York, N.Y., 1963.

Fatty Acids in Food Fats. U.S.D.A., Washington, D.C., 1959.

Honey . . . Some Ways to Use It. Home and Garden Bulletin 37. U.S.D.A., Washington, D.C., 1953.

Low Fat Cookery, rev. ed., Evelyn S. Stead and Gloria K. Warren. McGraw-Hill Book Company, New York, N.Y., 1959.

Nutrition . . . Up to Date, Up to You. U.S.D.A., Washington, D.C., 1960.

Pie Crusts—from Recipe and Mix. Third Report, 1962. American Home Economics Association, Washington, D.C.

Using Maple Sirup. Cornell Extension Bulletin E 985. Cornell University, Ithaca, N.Y.

A World of Baking, Dolores Casella. David White Company, New York, N.Y., 1968.

"Youth Learns About Food," S. F. Adelson *et al. Yearbook of Agriculture,* U.S.D.A., Washington, D.C., 1959.

unit **11**

Dinner Is Served

25

Meal Service and Manners

Dinner Time Is Family Time

In modern America, members of the family often rush off in different directions in the morning. This means that some families do not eat breakfast together. At lunch the family is scattered. But at dinner many families return to the family table to enjoy a good meal and share with those they love the experiences of the day.

Eating together as a family and with friends is a mark of civilized man. It is to strengthen not only the body, but the spirit. For there is a wide social value in companionship at mealtime.

Dinner time can be the best time of the day. What are the various ways in which a wisely selected, well—prepared dinner contributes to the happiness and contentment of family life?

The Atmosphere of a Meal Is Important

In many respects, where we eat, how we eat, and with whom we eat is as important as what we eat.

The scientist Pavlov proved that anger, fear, anxiety, and worry cause the digestive juices to halt their flow and the digestive tract to become tight and rigid. On the other hand, relaxation and happiness help the digestive juices to flow naturally, and the digestive tract to relax and do its work.

The place where we eat can give us a feeling of delight or depression. The appearance of the table and the food, and the conversation of those present, can make eating dinner a pleasant climax to a day. And this should be our goal for the evening meal. By thinking and planning and practicing what we know, we can make dinner a very happy family time. What makes this desirable atmosphere?

The Dining Area Contributes to a Good Atmosphere

Today many families use a part of the living room as a dining area. Whether your family eats in the living room, dining room, breakfast nook, or a nook in the kitchen, the dining area can be attractive. No matter how modest, it can be neat and orderly, with good lighting and ventilation. Place the table so that you have a good view, if possible.

The kind of *table* you have and its location influence the number sitting together and the way you will serve the meal. A small, narrow table for a big family would make it necessary for the plates to be served

This table setting is elegant yet simple and inexpensive, using a plastic table cloth, and a cover of stainless steelware and plastic dishes. The centerpiece is from the garden, using flowers in season.

in the kitchen. There would be no room for service at the table. Tables vary in size, shape, and type of materials from which they are made. Tables in breakfast nooks and kitchen nooks are often made with a hard formica top that doubles for a work table. Tables in the dining room or living room are larger and also may serve a double purpose—many young people study around the dining table after dinner. Living room and dining room tables are usually of some sturdy but beautifully grained wood such as cherry, mahogany, maple, pine, or walnut.

Once the type of *table cover* used was a white linen cloth. Now linen and lace are used only for formal meals and party occasions. The place mat replaces the

Fruit is a suitable centerpiece for any occasion and can serve also as a dessert.

flowers, leaves, berries, pine cones, and evergreens are just a few examples of simple materials that can be used to enliven the beauty of the table and add pleasure to the meal.

Candlelight is the most flattering to ladies. Many homes do not use candles except for "company meals" and parties. Other families regularly use candles in the evening for dinner. If you use candles, choose a candle holder that fits in with your table and service. The candle flame should be below eye level, as it is unpleasant to look into the flickering flame.

Setting the Table

Setting the table for a family meal is very simple. The rules are based on comfort, common sense, and consideration for all present. The place setting is called a "cover." This includes all of the silver and dishes for one person. At least 22 to 24

(Above) Dinner cover: bread and butter plate doubles for salad plate. (Below) Luncheon cover when only butter knife is used.

table cloth for many family meals. This is because it saves so much expense, energy, and time in laundry. But place mats of plastic, cork, spun glass, straw, and other materials are so attractive in color and design and so inexpensive that we have gained by this change. It is more pleasing to see a table with clean place mats that fit the color scheme and season and type of meal than to see the finest white linen showing soil marks from use. Plastic tablecloths are preferred by some.

The *centerpiece* can be a point of beauty and give color and atmosphere to the whole table. Yet it need not be expensive or elaborate. A bowl of fresh fruit makes a good centerpiece and may be used for dessert. A tray of attractively arranged raw vegetables may serve as the salad and the centerpiece, or a fresh-made cake, pie, or gelatin dessert may be used.

Potted geraniums, African violets, and ivy can be set in an attractive bowl for a centerpiece. Cut flowers in season, wild

inches of space is allowed for each cover. Covers should be far enough apart to give plenty of room to eat without touching a neighbor on the left or right.

The simplest place setting or cover, is arranged as shown in the diagram.

The entire cover is lined up one inch from the edge of the table, with the plate set in the exact center of the cover. *Place the dinner knife on the right of the plate*, with cutting edge in. Then to the right of the knife place the spoons. The first spoon to be used goes on the outside. The last spoon to be used is next to the knife. Lay spoons with bowls up.

Place the fork or forks to the left of the plate. It is acceptable today to use the dinner fork for the salad too, and thus save one fork. If salad forks or pie forks are used, follow the same rule and lay them in order of use.

The *napkin* is laid to left of the forks, with hemmed and opened edge at the lower right hand corner on a straight line with the silver. Paper napkins are acceptable today because they save time and labor for the busy homemaker, and do

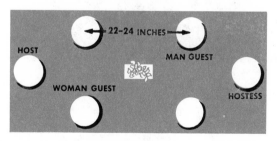

Seating arrangement.

not detract from the beauty of the meal. A large dinner napkin (18 inches or more wide) is opened halfway on the lap and

it is pressed to the lips to keep the mouth neat during the meal. Linen napkins are usually used for formal occasions.

Chairs are placed before the meal is called, and should stand a few inches from the edge of the table so that a person can be comfortably *seated from the left*. The gentleman (young or old) stands behind the chair of the lady to his right and seats her. The mother or the hostess first takes her seat, then the others follow. The father or the host sits at the head of the table, and the mother or the hostess at the opposite end. The woman guest of honor is seated to the right of the host; the man guest of honor to the right of the hostess.

Serving a Family Dinner

The place setting and dining area need the same simple treatment for any meal, but the serving of dinner is usually the most time-consuming and attractive. Dinner usually has at least two courses, even just for the family. If there is an appetizer, there are three courses. The appetizer may be served in the living room a few minutes before the meal is served; this cuts down on service and gives the hostess more time for the many last-minute jobs. The appetizer may also be served at the table. If it is a fruit juice or tomato juice, place the glass on a five-inch plate and set it inside the dinner plate, if the dinner plate is on the table. A younger child can remove this service while the father carves the meat.

As indicated above, there are different types of simple family service. If the space is crowded, it may be easier to serve the meal on warm plates in the kitchen

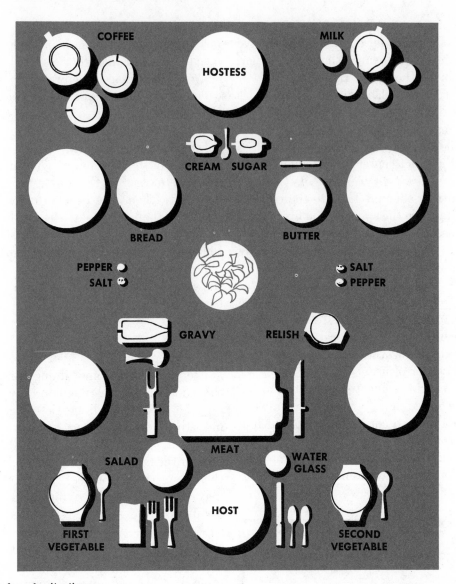

COFFEE

HOSTESS

MILK

CREAM SUGAR

BREAD

BUTTER

PEPPER
SALT

SALT
PEPPER

GRAVY

RELISH

MEAT

SALAD

WATER
GLASS

HOST

FIRST
VEGETABLE

SECOND
VEGETABLE

Service for a family dinner

and bring them to each person. They are placed on the table before the family is seated, if there is no first course.

The type of service many families use is to have the meat and vegetables placed on a hot platter in front of the father. Warm plates are placed to the front or side, according to the space. The father carves the meat, and serves it and vegetables. The mother usually serves the salad, dessert, and beverages. A daughter sitting to the right or left of the father may serve the vegetables. This speeds up the meal service and gives a feeling of sharing. It is not considered good taste for the mother to jump up and wait on the

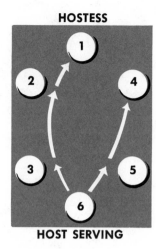

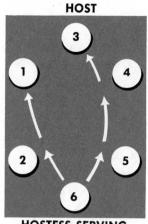

Order of service.

table. This responsibility is assigned to the young people, letting each take his turn.

The mother or hostess is served first, and after the hostess, the lady guest of honor is served. For family meals it is good taste to serve all on one side of the table first and then those on the other side. But it is a nicety to serve all the ladies first. The hostess takes the first bite, giving the signal for the others to begin eating.

Plates are served either to the left or right, and food may be passed either way. But whichever direction is started, keep that direction. (See diagrams above).

Another type of family service is to place all the food on the table and pass it, letting each help himself.

If the table is crowded, set a tray on a small table or use a cart to hold the bread, butter, salt, pepper, gravy, and jelly, and such extras as might crowd the table.

The electrically heated serving trays and carts are a fine invention to help the busy homemaker who does all of her own work. They enable the homemaker to enjoy the first course in the living room with guests. Hot trays are excellent for buffet meals.

Carving the Meat

To carve meat or see it carved is a social experience that adds grace and charm to a meal. The father or the host is the one who usually carves at the table, though this honor is often shared with sons.

The carving and serving equipment is placed beside or in front of the meat platter. The carver needs a tender, well-cooked bird or roast or steak. A large roast of meat carves better if it is removed from the oven 15 to 30 minutes before the meal is served. It is more difficult to carve if overcooked. A sharp carving knife and a carving fork are essential. (See that the knife is sharp before the meal is served.)

The fork should be large enough to go deep into the bird or roast up to the guard prongs. This holds the meat firmly. Today

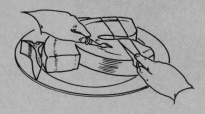

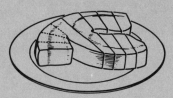

Carving a Porterhouse Steak: (1) Place the steak with the flank end to the left. Holding the steak with the fork inserted at the left, cut around the bone and lift it to one side. (2) Cut across the steak, making wedge-shaped portions that are widest at the far side. Each serving will include a piece of tenderloin and a piece of large muscle. (3) Serve the flank end if additional servings are needed.

Carving a Standing Rib Roast: (1) Have the butcher remove the short ribs and separate the backbone from the ribs. Place the roast on a platter with the small cut surface up and the rib side to the left. Insert the fork between the two top ribs and slice across the grain from the outside edge toward the ribs, making the slices ⅛ to ⅜ inch thick. (2) Release each slice by cutting close along the rib with the tip of the knife. (3) Lift each slice on the blade of the knife to the side of the platter. Slice enough to serve all guests before transferring to individual plates.

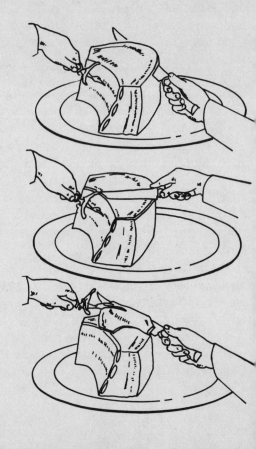

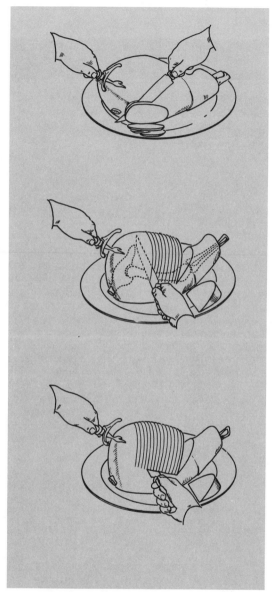

Carving a Ham or Leg of Lamb: (1) Place with the shank end to the right. Insert the fork and cut several slices parallel to the length. (2) Turn so that the meat rests on the surface just cut, hold with the fork at the left, and cut a small wedge from the shank end. (3) Cut thin slices down to the leg bone, and release them by cutting along the bone at right angles to the slices.

wooden serving trays contain steel spikes to hold meat and prevent slipping. The fork can do this job too.

The one who carves needs to learn the anatomy of a bird, leg of lamb, or any meat with bone. Study the diagrams to see how to carve different types of meat.

In general, meat is sliced in thin slices across the grain. Even a tough roast seems more tender when sliced thin. An exception is broiled steak. It is sliced in larger pieces straight across, and then divided into small enough pieces so that everyone has a piece of the most tender part and some of the less tender.

The host carves enough meat to serve all places before he stops. It is a great help to him if the hostess does not crowd

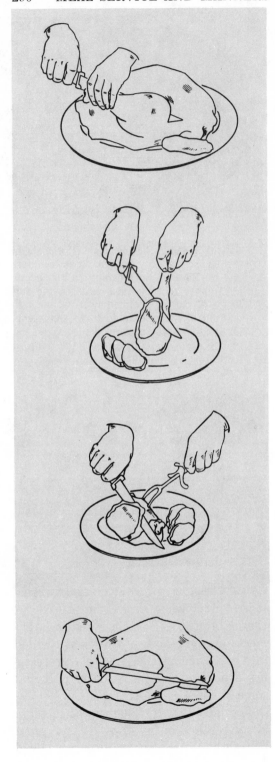

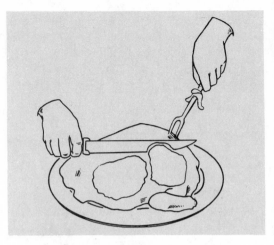

Carving Poultry: (1) Place the bird with the legs to the right. Hold the leg in the left hand and cut through the skin and joint joining the leg to the backbone. Cut the drumstick from the thigh on a service plate. (2) Holding drumstick at a convenient angle, cut down while turning drumstick to get uniform slices. Chicken drumsticks and thighs are usually served without slicing. (3) Holding the thigh with a fork, cut slices parallel to the bone. (4) Make a deep cut into the breast parallel to and as close to the wing as possible. (5) Beginning at the front and starting halfway up the breast, cut thin slices down to the cut made parallel to the wing. Slices will fall away as they are cut.

the platter with vegetables, which can make him seem untidy in doing his job. If the platter is crowded with meat, use bowls for all vegetables.

The platter, serving bowls, and plates should all be warmed before the meal is served. This can be done in space adjoining the oven, as most stoves have a shelf or drawer there which is quite warm when the oven is being used. Plates may also be warmed above the oven ventilator, or in the oven.

When enough meat is carved for all, the host serves each plate, taking care to place the food neatly and attractively. By careless serving, a host can spoil the artistic effect the hostess wishes. It is well for the hostess to talk over plans for plate arrangement with the host before guests arrive, if this is not understood.

Garnishes for meat add to the beauty of the meal, if not overdone. Watercress or parsley is attractive for poultry or beef. Fresh mint leaves are first-rate for lamb. Ham or pork needs spiced crab apples, apricots, pineapple, or orange slices. Fish needs lemon or lime and any green such as watercress or parsley. One sprig of garnish may be placed on each plate.

The host watches to see when seconds are needed, and then carves more meat.

Clearing the Table for Dessert

Clearing the table is a task that a younger member of the family can be trained to do. Some families let the children alternate in helping with serving the dinner. One child sets the table, waits on it, and clears it after the meal. Another helps with the meal preparation.

In clearing the table, first remove the food and dishes in the center, such as meat platter, vegetables, bread, butter, jelly, and salt and pepper. The small articles may be removed at one time with a tray. Then remove covers, beginning with the mother or the hostess. The person doing the clearing stands sideways at the left of each person and removes the plate first with the left hand, places this in the right hand, and removes the remainder of the cover, except the water glass. When these things have been taken to the kitchen, continue around the table to the left until all has been cleared.

Food is also served from the left, with the exception of beverages. This rule is

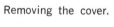

Removing the cover.

not as rigid today as formerly, but it is still a good rule, and saves confusion. You think, "Serve and remove from the left except beverages."

When the table is clear, it is crumbed by using a brush or soft napkin and a plate. Then the dessert and beverage are placed in front of the hostess, with necessary serving dishes and silver. In the meantime, the person whose job it is to fill the water glasses has done that. The hostess may serve the dessert and beverage at the table, or they may be brought directly from the kitchen. Social pleasure is shared if you serve an attractive dessert at the table.

Table Manners

Whether we like it or not, people form opinions of us by the way we eat. Table manners mark you quickly when you are not known.

Young people are often handicapped by feeling ill at ease when eating away from home. This need not be. If you know how to use your silver and what to do while eating, you have a feeling of security and poise. If good manners become a habit, your mind is free to take part in interesting conversation. While certain families and communities may accept behavior

Holding the knife and fork for cutting.

that others do not accept, it is best to know what the standard is. What, then, is the best approach to good table manners?

Good manners are not something to put on and take off like gloves; they should spring from within. They reflect your care and consideration for others. This attitude holds true for good table manners too. If you keep this as the basic guide, it will help you. But there are details to fill in which also help. Manners of different national groups differ in detail; but in all groups neatness of mouth and hands and consideration of others are basic.

In our country we think first of posture at the table. The correct posture is to sit with back erect, shoulders back, feet flat on the floor and the hand that is not in use held in the lap. The arms are kept close to the sides when cutting, so that you do not touch your neighbor. It also looks better. The body is leaned forward when eating, but we never stoop the head close to the plate, nor do we lift a plate or dish, except beverages, closer to the mouth. It is the hand which goes back and forth to the mouth.

The proper use of silver adds to your pleasure and comfort in dining. When cutting, *the knife* is held lightly by the handle in the right palm, and the forefinger rests along the back at the end of the handle near the blade. *The fork* is held in a similar position in the left hand. The forefinger rests on the back of the fork, just above the tines. (See figure to the left for correct position.)

Cut one or two bites of food at a time. Transfer the fork to the right hand. Lay the used knife across the outer edge of the plate, with the handle to the right and

Holding the fork for eating.

cutting edge of knife toward you. Eat by lifting the food to the mouth with the fork. The fork goes under the food to lift it. A small piece of bread may be used to assist getting the food on the fork if it is difficult. (In Europe the knife is used to push the food on the back side of the tines of the fork, and the food is brought to the mouth with the left hand.)

Bites should be small enough not to fall off the fork or cause you to open the mouth abnormally wide to receive them. Food is chewed with the mouth closed. It is better to chew and swallow one bite at a time than to fill the mouth too full. People who chew with their mouth open or talk with a mouth full of food are not pleasant dinner companions.

Spoons are used for stirring, testing the temperature of a beverage, and eating

Holding and dipping soup spoon.

thin foods. It is not good manners to stir and stir a food. Take two or three turns of the cup. Then remove the spoon and lay it in the saucer. When eating hot soup, take very small amounts in the spoon. It will cool quickly in small amounts. Use the soup spoon by dipping away from you. When finished, lay the spoon on the plate beneath the soup bowl. A flat bowl is better for serving soup because the soup cools more quickly.

If a *bread and butter plate* is part of your cover, you will have a *butter knife*. On the bread and butter plate, place your bread, butter, and jam; and it may double

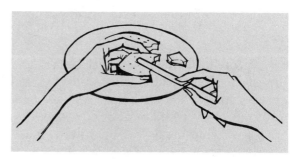

Holding and breaking bread for buttering.

for foods such as celery, radishes, and carrot strips. A small amount of bread is buttered at one time, breaking the slice or roll in half. Small hot biscuits, muffins, or tiny rolls may be pulled apart and butter placed in the middle. In this case, depending on the size, you may or may not break the half from which you eat.

After the butter knife is used, place it on the bread and butter plate in a position similar to that of the dinner knife. (See diagram on next page.)

When the fork is not in use, it is placed with tines up beside the knife. Silver that has been used is never placed on the table-cloth or mat, or left hanging from the side of the plate. It is placed completely on the plate. Be sure it is securely placed so that it will not fall when your place cover is removed.

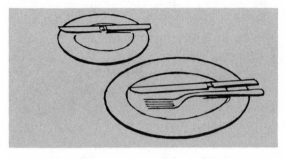

Placing silver when meal is finished.

Some foods are eaten with fingers and called "finger foods." These include bread and crackers of all kinds, cookies, cupcakes, raw vegetable sticks, olives, pickles, potato chips and similar tidbits, nuts, candy, fruit, corn on the cob, hamburgers, hot dogs, and, in some parts of the country, fried chicken.

The napkin is opened halfway if it is an 18-inch dinner napkin, and fully if it is a 12-inch luncheon napkin. It is laid across the lap except in the case of small children and elderly people, when it may be tucked beneath the chin. If you use heavy lipstick, you may wish to blot your lips before using a fine linen napkin.

Table conversation reflects our consideration for others, and helps or hurts the atmosphere of the meal more than almost anything. A show of temper at the beginning of a meal can spoil the enjoyment of food for all. On the other hand, good meal conversation is a delightful and stim-

ulating art that can be learned. And what better place to practice this than in your own home at dinner! Good conversation at mealtime is a mark of social cultivation, and one of the deep joys in living.

By thinking ahead you can make a genuine contribution to your family's happiness and your own development. Plan ahead as to what you can bring to your family at dinner time. Avoid topics that you know will anger or worry a member of your family. What constructive thought can you offer? What progress have you made in your own growth that you can report? What good thing has come to a member of your family or friends that you can relate? What plans do you have which you would like to share with the family? What time or service can you offer to help another member of your family? About what important event in

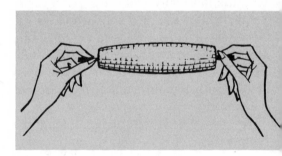

Holding corn on the cob.

the community do you wish to find out your family's feelings? It is a fortunate young person who learns to take part in lively conversation with her own family at the relaxed hour of dinner! She is preparing herself to live with poise, confidence, and dignity throughout her whole life.

THINKING IT OVER

1. Is dinner time family time in your home? If not, what can you do about it?
2. What did Pavlov discover that can help us at mealtime?
3. Why is the place where the family eats so important?
4. In what ways can the dining area, table, centerpiece, and table setting affect the atmosphere of a meal?
5. Describe three ways to serve a family dinner simply but attractively.
6. What do you need in order to do a good job of carving meat?
7. Suggest garnishes that make different meats attractive and that blend with them in flavor.
8. Explain how silver is laid at the table, how it is held and used while eating, and how it is placed after eating.
9. Who in the family should wait on and clear the table? How is this done?
10. What is the basis of good table manners? What details do you think that you need to practice in order to have acceptable manners?
11. How can good table manners help your life now and in the future?

PROBLEMS TO SOLVE

1. With your school family or your mother, or alone, make a trip to a big department store to see:
   (1) Different types of dining tables and their prices.
   (2) Different types of china, pottery, and glassware, and their prices.
   (3) Different types of linen, place mats, silver, stainless steel, and their prices.
2. Make a plan for table service at low cost, moderate cost, and higher cost. Consider selection of table china, silver, glassware, and linen or mats that you would use together.

APPLYING WHAT YOU KNOW

1. With your family group and the equipment you have, plan a family dinner for four. Work through all the steps, including the table service, conversation, and manners and the organization of time and tasks to be done. This preliminary practice will help you have more confidence when you serve your family dinner at the end of the next lesson.
2. Study the work and time schedule you have made and plan the most economical ways to do your various tasks.
3. Discuss a person whose manner of conversation puts people at ease. How is this done? Try to keep your table conversation on a high level when you serve your dinner, and practice this at home.

HOME EXPERIENCE

With your mother, decide in what ways you can improve the atmosphere, service and good fun of your family dinner hour. Help her with any changes that your family would like to make.

26

Planning, Preparing, and Serving Dinner

Choosing the Dinner Menu
Requires Background Knowledge

One of the finest compliments that can be paid to a hostess is that her excellent dinner seemed so effortless to those present. Such a result shows thorough knowledge of how to plan a well-balanced menu —foods that meet health needs and that look good and taste good together. Such a dinner also shows the ability to plan ahead in marketing and in timing of the work of preparing dinner. This is good management of food, on the highest level. The hostess is unhurried at meal time. Because she has things under control, she is relaxed and her family and guests enjoy the meal all the more. They are not

Sweet potatoes and apples in any form combine well with pork.

aware, by any sign of strain on her face, of the planning, skill, and work that went into the meal.

Good dinners are no accident. They represent a scope of knowledge and a plan as definite as a builder needs when he sets out to construct a house. What should we think of as we sit down to plan our dinner menu?

Just as the builder looks over all the details before he breaks ground for the new house, you should look over the whole day's meals before you select your dinner menu. Begin with today. What did the family have for breakfast? And what will they eat for lunch? If you started the family off with a hearty break-

fast and everyone had a hearty lunch, then you may need only a supper meal in the evening. But if the family ate a medium breakfast, and a medium lunch, such as most of us need, then you should have a moderate but balanced dinner. Dinner enables you to make up for the weaknesses of the other two meals and bring the day to a perfect ending.

Also look ahead to the menus for the whole week. This is especially important for the meat and vegetables. At least this much of the menu should be planned in terms of a week. For instance, on a low-cost plan for a week it might run something like this for the meat or protein food: Sunday, tenderized chuck roast;

This well-planned kitchen-dining area uses space and equipment that save time and energy. Note that the table is correctly set.

Monday, left-over chuck in hash; Tuesday, liver smothered with onions; Wednesday, macaroni and cheese casserole; Thursday, pork chops baked in milk; Friday, fried ocean perch; Saturday, baked beans.

The money you have to spend sets limits for your menu. The less you have to spend, the more you need to know in order to feed your family well. On low food budgets it is too easy to let meat and sweet foods take the lion's share. This is a mistake, as you learned in your study of meat and sugars in the diet. See to it that these foods fit into a balanced whole on the price level you can afford. Poor judgment is sometimes shown in buying vegetables, too. For instance, if your food budget is low and you see corn at ten cents an ear and potatoes at two or three cents per serving, it is sound judgment to pass up the corn. Buy it as a treat for an occasion, and, until the price goes down, use the nourishing potato that fits into your budget for the standby. Similarly, if watercress is 25 cents for a five-ounce bunch and escarole lettuce is 25 cents a pound, the price and the nourishment-

What other protein foods besides spareribs can be combined with sauerkraut for a quick dinner?

value of the escarole plainly dictate which you should buy.

Putting the Dinner Menu Together

With the above discussion in mind, let us make the dinner menu. How shall we go about it? Here is one pattern.

Teen-ager preparing an oven dinner.

Pattern for a Balanced Dinner	
	Appetizer*
Meat	Meat juice or gravy
Potato or other vegetable	Green or yellow vegetable
	Salad
Bread	Butter (or margarine)
	Dessert
	Beverage
*Optional	

The first principle is that the dinner shall meet the health needs of every member of the family, from the youngest to the oldest, with the foods your family enjoys, and within the food budget. Bal-

anced meals may have many different combinations to fit your individual taste, if you understand the values in various foods. Here are some guides for selecting the ingredients:

(1) In choosing the dinner menu, first select the *protein* dish. This can be meat, fish, poultry, organ meat, or the meat substitutes—cheese, beans, peas or lentils.

(2) Next choose the vegetables that are in season or within your budget and that go well with the meat or protein

Sliced tomatoes are good with fish.

dish. Choose one starchy vegetable, such as white potato, sweet potato, winter squash, corn, parsnips, or occasionally rice or macaroni as a cereal alternate.

Choose a green leafy or yellow vegetable to cook. (See list on page 125.) This vegetable should also combine well with your meat. Any green vegetable, such as green peas or green beans, may be used as an alternate to the leafy ones when the

latter are scarce. These vegetables provide vitamins, minerals, roughage, and contrast in flavor and texture for the meal.

(3) The salad should be either raw vegetable or fruit or a mixture. It gives the meal contrast in texture, flavor, and color. But the primary purpose is to bring a good source of vitamin C into the meal, as this vitamin is so easily destroyed by cooking. The best vitamin C foods for salad are tomatoes in any form; oranges, grapefruit, tangerines in any form; raw cabbage; raw green lettuce; raw green and red bell peppers; melons; strawberries; and other raw vegetables and fruits. The salad brings a healthy roughage to the meal, as well as vitamins and minerals. It enlivens dinner with a sour or nippy flavor in contrast to the more bland foods. It can also add a fresh, colorful note to your table and crisp texture to your meals.

(4) The appetizer is not used as a rule in a family dinner if there is a salad. It may be alternated with a salad.

Formerly soup was often used as an appetizer. This has about disappeared from the family dinner menu. There are two reasons. Most moderns do not need or want the extra calories in soup. We ride instead of walk. We sit and watch television instead of playing tennis or doing outdoor chores. We think of the 120 calories from a half-cup of cream of tomato soup in addition to a big dinner, and would rather save those calories for a dessert and take a half-cup of tomato juice, with only 25 calories.

In most homes when soup is served, it is used not as the appetizer but as the main dish of the meal, with meat and vegetables in it to make a hearty dish.

This is good judgment and sound nutrition, when the soup is properly balanced with other foods that are needed.

A good appetizer is low in calories, stimulates your appetite instead of satisfying it, and either substitutes for the vitamin C salad or builds up a richer reserve in this nutrient. If your budget permits, you may wish to serve both an appetizer and a salad. First-rate choices include tomato juice; tomato and sauerkraut juice mixed in equal parts; any citrus juice mixed with apricot juice, pineapple juice, cranberry juice, or prune juice. Mix juices in any blend you wish to create. Try to keep one high-vitamin-C fruit in your appetizer juice and use natural foods instead of imitation fruit drinks containing empty calories.

Fresh fruit cup, or a fruit salad, is also used as an appetizer. Melon is an excellent appetizer, salad, or dessert.

Juice as an appetizer may be served by a younger member of the family in the living room. This gives the mother or

For a quick dessert for a baked bean dinner serve grated cheese on a pre-baked pie—heat until cheese melts.

hostess a little extra time for the many last-minute tasks of getting the meal served.

If you are interested in controlling weight, it is better to serve the appetizer with only simple low-calorie foods, such as the small cheese crackers. Rich spreads and such delicious tidbits as hot sausages and "pigs in a blanket" are high in fat and not for those who have a weight-control problem. They are for the occasion when the appetizer is the main meal!

(5) Dinner should include milk, cheese, or both. It is difficult to meet either your calcium or riboflavin need without milk or cheese at dinner. Young people need an 8- to 10-ounce glass of milk, or more. Adults need 4 to 6 ounces of milk or some cheese.

(6) Dessert is the luxury food that brings a good meal to a perfect climax. Choose the dessert to blend with and balance the whole menu. If the meal is a hearty one, choose a light dessert such as fruit. But if you have kept down the starch, sugar, and fat content of the meal, you can choose a pie or cake, with its higher calories from sugar and fat. If your meal has two or more foods high in starch or sugar, you need a light dessert.

(7) The primary purpose of bread and butter in the dinner is to add energy foods. Each contributes certain additional nutrients, you will recall. How much of these foods you need will depend on your activity, rate of growth, food budget, and menu. Hot bread and butter with a good homemade jam is sufficient dessert in itself. Tiny hot biscuits or rolls give a fine touch to a dinner.

Now let us turn our menu into a real meal.

Whipped non-fat dry milk, sour cream, custard sauce, fruit sauce, or ice cream enhance an ordinary pudding or left-over cake.

Good Management in Preparing the Dinner

All that has gone before is a part of the good management required to prepare a well-balanced, tasty, and unhurried dinner. In addition, there are some other activities that must go on behind the scene before you reach your goal.

After the dinner menu has been selected, the shopping list must be made. When you shop for dinner keep in mind the same things we discussed in Chapter 11 in connection with preparing a shopping list for breakfast.

Then you should make a work plan. Every good homemaker has a work plan for her dinner, though some carry the plan in their heads instead of on paper. Until you become skilled in management, it is better to write down your plan and then follow it. If it does not work out as you planned, make notes of changes; this will guide you to do a better job next time. The principles for this work plan are the same as for the breakfast plan, but the timing is different. (See pages 116–117.)

Here is a work plan used by Carol, a high school girl, who prepared and served dinner for the family when her mother had to stay late at a meeting.

Carol had planned the menu with her mother a week ahead. All of the supplies needed were in the house. She had prepared each separate dish in her menu both at school and as part of the family dinner at home on different occasions. She knew how each food should look and taste and about how much time was required for each. She had noted her mistakes and now avoided them.

Carol chose an oven meal, because she had to do all of the work. She divided her work plan into three parts: (1) work immediately after school; (2) free time; (3) finishing and serving the meal. She made a list of all jobs to be done in each part, with approximate time. This is how it looked:

Menu (moderate cost)

Tomato juice cocktail

Pork chops   Baked sweet
(baked in milk)   potatoes

Frozen green beans and frozen okra

Tossed green salad

Bread   Margarine

Baked apple and whole milk

Milk   Coffee

PLAN OF WORK

4:30 Personal preparation (arrange hair neatly, put on clean apron, wash hands).

4:35 Arrange dining area, set table, place glasses and cheese crackers on tray for tomato juice, place glasses for milk on another tray, place cups and saucers on side table in dining room, measure coffee and water and set aside, assemble serving dishes and place on top of oven to warm.

4:45 Light oven, set at 350° F. Wipe off pork chops with clean damp cloth, season, place in pan, add ¼ inch

Mixing Area: Mixing jobs are easier when the homemaker can sit comfortably and have utensils and ingredients at her fingertips. Notice the storage bins at the back of the counter and the revolving shelves at the right.

Cooking Area: A wall oven at the correct height (32 inches from the floor) saves bending and lifting. Utensils needed for cooking are stored in the cabinet above the oven or they are hung on the peg board.

evaporated or dried milk mixture and place in oven. Scrub potatoes and place in pressure saucepan. Cook 5 minutes. Scrub apples, core, fill hole with raisins and brown sugar, sprinkle top with nutmeg; place in pan to bake; add ½ cup water to pan.

5:00 Set potatoes and apples on lower shelf of oven. Set timer for 5:30. Clean up table tops and sink.

5:15 to 5:30 Free time to use as needed or to relax.

5:30 As soon as apples are done, remove and set aside to cool. (Time required depends on variety and size.)

5:40 Prepare ingredients for salad; do not add dressing. Cover bowl and place in refrigerator. Place salad dressing on table.

5:50 Place bread, butter, cream, and sugar on table. Give first warning for dinner. Pour tomato juice, take to living room with cheese crackers. Pour milk and place.

5:55 Call family for appetizer. Cook green frozen beans and okra in pressure saucepan. Test meat and potatoes to

see if they are done. Take up meat and vegetables and place on table. Place hot plates and cold salad on table.

6:00 Dinner is served.

One and a half hours of work. Result: a delicious, well-balanced meal. Carol's dinner was attractive, and was served in a happy atmosphere. The aroma of the good food brought smiles and pleasant comments as the family came to dinner. The contrasting color of green beans and yellow sweet potato was good with the pork chop. The soft texture of the potato with the firm texture of the meat and salad and the medium texture of the beans was pleasing. Furthermore, the flavor of meat and vegetables and salad gave a blended whole. The baked spicy apple for dessert rounded out this dinner to a good climax. This was an autumn dinner, and Carol took advantage of the lower prices of pork, apples, and sweet potatoes to provide a meal that looked good and blended in flavor.

The parents were proud of Carol's ability to plan, prepare, and serve such a

All food is easily seen and reached in this wall refrigerator. The base cabinet is useful for resting a tray of glasses while pouring milk. The cart, which is stored under the base cabinet, is used for transferring heavy food and dishes.

Dining Area: The pull-out shelf brings appliances within easy reach of the homemaker when she is seated at the table. Dishes are conveniently arranged for setting the table and for putting away after washing.

delicious, attractive, and nourishing meal. Her younger sister and brother looked up to her with admiration. She felt this approval and knew deep within that the respect of a family you love is something well worthwhile to achieve.

Carol moved up the ladder one step closer to mature womanhood.

PROBLEMS TO SOLVE

1. Planning menus for the day within a definite food budget.

   (1) Plan menus for the whole day *using meat as a protein*, on low, moderate, and higher cost levels. Evaluate each by the standard of good nutrition, good flavor, and good appearance.

   (2) Follow the same plan *using cheese as the protein* food for dinner.

   (3) Follow the same plan *using fish as the protein* food for dinner.

   (4) Plan a moderate-cost dinner that you could help prepare and serve to guests in three courses.

      (a) Make a work plan for this dinner, showing the part you will do and the part your mother will do.

      (b) Prepare the market list and, if possible, assist with the marketing. Decide on your budget and stay within it.

APPLYING WHAT YOU KNOW

1. If possible, considering the time at hand, prepare and serve a simple, well-balanced dinner with your family group at school.

EVALUATING

1. Did you stay within the budget for each type of daily menu planned?

2. In each meal did you adequately meet the needs for the following: protein? calcium? vitamin C? B vitamins? vitamin A?

3. Check your menus for the day against the chart on page 13, to see if you included

all of the foods you need in suitable amounts.

4. Did your dinner menus balance in color? Texture? And did the flavors blend as a whole?

5. If the time to prepare dinner is short, how would you solve this problem and give the family a balanced meal? Put your plan on paper and compare it with those of other members of the class.

HOME EXPERIENCE

Talk over with your mother what you learned at school about planning and preparing the family dinner. With her, plan the dinner menus for a week. Fit them into the whole pattern for each day's meals. Prepare and serve one dinner for the family, assigning others to help you if you wish. Report results to your teacher.

FURTHER READING

Betty Crocker's Dinner for Two Cook Book. Golden Press, New York, N.Y., 1958.

Family Food Plans and Food Costs. U.S.D.A., Washington, D.C., 1962.

Family Meals and Hospitality, Dora S. Lewis, Gladys C. Peckham, Helen S. Hovey. The Macmillan Company, New York, N.Y., 1960.

Home Care of Purchased Frozen Foods. U.S.D.A., Washington, D.C., 1960.

Manners Made Easy, 3rd ed., Mary Berry. McGraw-Hill Book Company, New York, N.Y., 1966.

Modern Encyclopedia of Cooking, Meta Given. J. C. Ferguson Publishing Co., Chicago, Ill., 1955.

New Fannie Farmer Boston Cooking-School Cook-Book, 10th rev. ed. Little, Brown and Company, Boston, Mass., 1959.

New Good Housekeeping Cookbook, ed. by Dorothy B. Marsh. Harcourt, Brace & World, Inc., New York, N.Y., 1963.

Our Family Meals. HE-13 Extension Bulletin. Iowa State University, Ames, Iowa, 1953.

Quick Cook Book, Lois S. Kellogg. Pocket Books, Inc., New York, N.Y., 1961.

Southern Cook Book, Marion Brown. Pocket Books, Inc., New York, N.Y., 1951.

Spice Cookbook, Avanelle Day and Lillie Stuckey. David White Company, New York, N.Y., 1964.

Stay Slim for Life, Ida Jean Kain and Mildred B. Gibson. Doubleday & Company, Inc., New York, N.Y., 1958.

VISUAL AIDS

Proof of the Pudding. (10 min. film, color, one reel). Shows how physical fitness comes through good nutrition. Scenes selected from a zoo, a nutrition laboratory, and a family. Produced by Metropolitan Life Insurance Co., in cooperation with U.S. Public Health Service. Metropolitan Life Insurance Co., 50 East 25th Street, New York, N.Y.

Foods for
Special Needs

27

You and Your Weight

Research continues to provide nutritional information to improve the diet.

What Causes Overweight?

Despite the many reasons given for overweight, in most instances it is caused by one thing—eating more food than you need or can use. Of course, you may not weigh the same as a friend who is your age and height, since the size and shape of your body frame influence what is normal in weight for you. You inherited the tendency to have small bones or large bones. To this extent, heredity does influence your weight. But you did not inherit the fat that goes on the frame. Fat in unwanted places is the result of eating more food than you need in your meals and snacks.

In the preceding part of this book you learned how each food relates to weight control. You learned which foods offer generous amounts of vitamins, minerals,

HOW CALORIES SNEAK INTO THE DIET THROUGH SNACKS AND EXTRAS.

Food	Size of Portion	Calories*
Malted milk shake	fountain size	500
Milk shake, chocolate	fountain size	400
Soda	fountain size	260
Carbonated drink	8 ounces	110
Fudge candy	1 piece (1" square)	100
Mint (fondant pattie)	1 piece	40
Peanut brittle	1 piece (2½x2½x¼")	120
Peanuts	1 ounce (30)	150
Peanut butter	2 tablespoons (1 ounce)	185
Brownies	1 piece (2x2x¾")	140
Cookies	1 large (or 2 small)	100-115
Cake, not frosted	medium piece (2x3x1½")	175-300
Cake, plain frosting	medium piece layer (1" of 6" cake)	250-400
Angel or sponge cake	2" sector	115
Doughnut	1 medium	135
Chocolate éclair	1 medium	250
Chocolate sauce	2 tablespoons	90
Butterscotch sauce	2 tablespoons	200
Sweet roll	1 medium	180
Waffle	1 medium (4½x5½x½")	215
Syrup, sugar, jam	1 tablespoon	55
Butter or margarine	1 teaspoon (or small pat)	35
French dressing	1 tablespoon	60
Mayonnaise dressing	1 tablespoon	90
Cooked-type dressing	1 tablespoon	30
Hollandaise sauce	1 tablespoon	90
Pie, two-crust fruit	1/7 (medium-size piece)	300-350
Pie, custard type, 1 crust	1/7 (medium-size piece)	250-300
Pizza, quick type	1 medium (4" diameter)	185
Potato chips	7 large, 10 medium	110

* Calories are rounded, that is, 39 is counted 40.

and high-quality protein as well as calories. You also learned which foods have "empty" calories and should be used sparingly if you have an overweight problem. If you have to "watch" your calories to control your weight, every calorie must count for health too. (Of course, there is also the danger that you will choose a well-balanced diet, and simply eat too much of it.)

Since over a fourth of the adult population is overweight, and many of these people say that their problem started in childhood, it may be well to see what you can do to control your weight while you are young. This is especially desirable because overweight tends to cause emotional distress and to affect one's health and activity in many undesirable and unattractive ways.

What You Can Do to Control Your Weight

Probably one of the most important things you can do is to examine your attitude. Does it really make any difference in your happiness if you are overweight? Do you really wish to have normal weight? If you are determined to attain it, you can.

If you have a weight problem (either overweight or underweight) and you have made up your mind to do something about it, the next step is to see your physician. By a thorough examination he can tell you whether by proper control of your diet you can attain normal weight. This rules out all possibilities that something besides food may be causing your weight problem. Under the guidance of a physician, even severely overweight people are able to attain normal weight, and remain in perfect health.

However, physicians will tell you that they see many women and teen-age girls who have undermined their health by going on a fad diet to reduce weight.

You may have read the story of a 19-year-old girl who was about 100 pounds overweight. Upon examination by a physician it came to light that this young woman had produced these pounds by poor choice of food and by overeating. She loved bread, butter, cakes, pies, and gingerbread with whipped cream, ate peanut butter and hot chocolate frequently between meals, and took second helpings of these and other fattening foods. The fatter she got, the lonelier and unhappier she became.

Under the guidance of a physician, this girl reached normal weight within one year. How did she do this? She did it be-cause she wanted to be normal in weight more than she wanted to eat fattening foods. If such an extremely overweight girl can correct her problem of weight through developing better food habits, you can too. Crash diets fail because the key to weight control is not "magic" but better eating habits that you can follow every day.

Exercise is a fine help in controlling weight. Studies show that girls who exercise little and spend much time sitting and watching sports, TV, and the like tend more to be obese. Inactive people are more inclined to nibble sweets and fatty foods, and to drink soda water—which add undesired calories. When you are grown, you need about 15 calories per pound to maintain your weight. If your normal weight is 125 pounds, you need 15 x 125 = 1875 calories daily.

Wise Use of Food Is the Key to Weight-Control

If you will read again the unit on fats and sugars in your diet (pages 256-278) and rethink the place of the other foods in the diet, you will have your basic information on how to control your weight.

The chief difference between a good weight-control diet and the normal diet is in the amount of food you eat. This is the reason fad diets always fail. They are not patterned on healthy, well-balanced meals. But if you can cut down your weight by following the recommended daily diet on page 12, you can hold this weight throughout your life. Isn't this your goal—to reach the desired weight on a diet that you can keep eating? The variety of food should remain the same, but you should eat a little less of the high-calorie foods. You need the same amount of milk, and an egg every day. You can eat more fruit and more green leafy and juicy vegetables, and more lean meat, fish, and poultry. But you should eat less of the fat foods in any form, and less starch and sugar foods, especially the concentrated sweets. Although it is wise to cut down on fats and sugars, you should not cut them completely out of your diet.

The idea is to drop off about 500 calories from your daily diet and force your body to burn your excess body fat for these calories. In one week you will have dropped from your normal diet 3500 calories and lost about one pound. This is considered about right for a girl in her teens. An adult might lose as much as two pounds a week.

Thus, in a well-planned weight-control diet, you maintain your normal balance of essential nutrients, but drop calories by eating less of the least-needed foods.

A Daily Food Plan to Control Overweight

Eat a good breakfast. This is most important to hold up your strength and keep you from nibbling foods that give calories but not health.

Eat a well-balanced lunch and dinner too, at a regular time each day. Eating at mealtime the foods you need helps you to depend on meals instead of snacks for your calories. This is sound for your health now, builds good habits for the future, and in addition will help you meet your goal of losing weight. Studies of dietary habits bear out this point.

Make your snacks count for health and for your total daily need of food. Cheating just a little on snacks can defeat your purpose. One big sundae or pie a la mode can add 450 calories! Only one sundae a week can add 6½ pounds of weight in a year if it is in addition to your real calorie need. In Chapter 23 you noted how a baked potato of 100 calories became 393 when French fried and 544 calories as potato chips. Weight watchers can have snacks, but select foods such as those suggested on page 310. Stop eating when you feel as if you could eat a little more, and at no time gorge yourself. Small meals and little snacks can meet your health needs if you select them wisely. Remember that weight for weight, fat has 2¼ times more calories than protein and carbohydrates. Starch foods such as vegetables, cereal-breads, and sugars in natural fruits provide minerals, vitamins and protein, along with a good source of energy. And these should form the backbone of your calories instead of concentrated fats, or sweets.

You do not have to "give up" any one food. It is better to eat a little of your choice foods. But learn to eat just a little, and accept that amount without cheating! Have a small piece of pie, or a small piece of cake. Make pies with only one crust, and use pie fillings in individual custard cups without any crusts, but topped with meringue. You have the flavor and emotional satisfaction of eating a favorite food, without the extra calories usually found in pies.

The real secret of weight-control is self-control at meals and between meals. You can exercise the self-discipline required, if the goal—normal weight—is worth the price you have to pay in self-control. Your family and friends can be sympathetic and help you, but in the end you must take the responsibility.

A BALANCED
DIETARY GUIDE
FOR TEEN-AGE REDUCING

BREAKFAST   **Calories**

Fruit: 1 medium orange, ½ grapefruit,
  ½ cup citrus fruit juice, or
  1 cup tomato juice......................... 45
1 egg, cooked without fat 80
1 serving whole grain or enriched bread..... 55
1 teaspoon butter or other fat 35
1 glass whole milk (8 ounces or ½ pint)... 160
                                         ─────
                                         375

LUNCH

Meat, 2 ounces; or cheese, 2 ounces;
  or 2 eggs; or 2 tablespoons
  peanut butter 175
Vegetable, generous serving, raw or
  cooked; or fruit, fresh or frozen
  or cooked............................20-40
1 serving whole grain or enriched
  bread.................................. 55
1 teaspoon butter or other fat 35
1 glass milk (8 ounces or ½ pint)..... 160
                                         ─────
                                         465

DINNER

Lean meat, fish, poultry, or
  glandular organs (3 oz) (120- 250)
  (cooked without added fat).......... 215
Vegetables, green or yellow,
  ½-¾ cup 40
1 small potato cooked in skin,
  or other vegetable................40-95
1 teaspoon butter or other fat....... 35
Fruit or raw salad 25-60
1 glass milk (8 ounces) 160
                                         ─────
                                         605

SNACK

1 glass milk; or 1½ ounces
  Cheddar-type cheese; or
½ glass skim milk plus
  ¼ pint ice cream................160
If second snack desired:
  1 medium orange or juice.........70

Total calories from meals for day   1675

* If snacks are omitted, the day's calories total about 1445.
This is the type of diet you need for good health as you attain the
desired weight.

FAMILY MENUS FOR A DAY: SHOWING VARIATIONS
FOR THE OVERWEIGHT AND UNDERWEIGHT

Overweight	Normal	Underweight
BREAKFAST		
1 orange or ½ grapefruit	Same	Same
1 poached or boiled egg	Egg of choice	Egg of choice
1 thin slice whole wheat or enriched bread	Same	2 slices
	Bacon, if desired	Bacon or meat, if desired
1 teaspoon butter or other fat	Same	2 teaspoons
1 glass whole milk	Same	Same
		Cereal, whole grain or enriched, with cream
LUNCH		
2-ounce hamburger and bun	Same	Same with cheese
1 vegetable, cooked, or salad	Same	Same
Salad dressing of lemon juice	Choice	Choice
1 teaspoon butter or other fat	Same	Same
1 glass whole milk	Same	Same
	Fruit or milk dessert	Same, plus cake or cookie, if desired; and cream on fruit, if desired
DINNER		
1 lean pork chop	Same	Chop with fat
1 small potato baked or boiled in skin	1 medium potato	1 medium to large potato
1 serving green or yellow vegetable	Same	1-2 servings
¾ cup raw salad	Same	½ cup
Lemon juice dressing	Choice	Choice
1 glass whole milk	Same	Same
1 teaspoon butter or other fat	Same	2 teaspoons
	Enriched or whole grain bread, if desired	Same
Plain raw fruit if no salad	Ginger bread and apple sauce	Same, plus whipped cream on gingerbread
SNACK		
1 glass milk	Same	Same, with bread and butter or fruit

Keep a record of your weight only once a week. Do not be discouraged by the loss of only one pound per week. Remember that with steadfast determination you can lose 12 pounds in three months.

If you will study page 311, which shows family menus for a day, you can see how the overweight or underweight person can adjust daily diet to meet individual needs. You will observe that though the variation from the normal diet is very slight, if you can hold to this, you can adjust your weight. The habit of eating the recommended daily diet, not crash diets, is the key to your success.

Page 310 shows a day's menu for a girl who might normally need 2200 calories a day. The calories in this menu may be further cut under the guidance of a physician. For instance, your doctor might give you a vitamin A supplement and allow you to drink skim milk instead of whole milk; or leave out the bread in a meal where you have potato, or cut out one snack. Once you have attained the desired weight, practice the same good habits of meal planning and cooking of food, and you may be able to allow yourself slightly larger portions of some of your favorite foods. If you keep your eye on your mirror and your scales, they can help guide you before you go too far.

Underweight Can Be Helped with Proper Food

Severe underweight brings health and figure problems too. Among the causes for underweight are: infections and disease; poor appetite; irregularity of meals; missing meals; food dislikes; poor choice of foods in meals and snacks; over-activity; and emotional problems.

To gain weight, follow the basic pattern for a well-balanced diet given on page 12. Keep the variety the same as in the normal diet. You will observe on page 311 a pattern to increase your calories and nutrients in the normal family meal. A bedtime snack is a good opportunity to add 300 to 500 calories. Avoid overeating of sweets and fats. These may dull your appetite. Take second helpings of concentrated but nourishing foods, such as cheese, meat, whole grain or enriched bread, and butter. Milk is not concentrated, but is a good food for extras. Use cream on your cereal and over fruit instead of milk. Remember that your greatest help in either gaining or losing weight is to really want to reach your goal.

When you have reached your normal weight, adjust your food intake to help you hold this weight. You will have to experiment and add or leave off foods as fits your need.

 THINKING IT OVER

1. What is the main cause of overweight?
2. Why is it important that you learn to control your weight when you are young?
3. Why is your own attitude a key to your success in either losing or gaining weight?
4. If you plan to lose or gain weight, why is it important first to have a good physical examination by a competent physician?

5. What is the real difference between the normal diet and a good weight-control diet? Can you explain from this why most fad diets for reducing fail?

6. About how much weight should a teen-ager lose per week, and why should you not lose as fast as an adult?

7. Do you think most people think too much about calories, and too little about the health value in the foods they eat when they are losing weight? On the basis of what you have learned in other units of this book, explain how this might undermine your health.

8. Why is a good breakfast so important if you wish to lose weight?

9. Explain how snacks can cause you to fail in controlling your weight, if thought and planning is not given to them. What are some good snacks for those who wish to lose weight?

10. Why is it important to control yourself every day, and eat a small amount of the foods you enjoy, instead of attempting complete self-denial of your favorite foods?

11. What are the causes of underweight, and how can you gain to a normal weight?

12. Discuss the foods you should avoid and the ones which must be included in your diet if you are overweight. Underweight.

APPLYING WHAT YOU KNOW

1. Finding out where you are.
   (1) Check your weight by the chart on page 16. Make a chart for your own weight record, and weigh yourself once each week. Are you within the normal range for your height, body structure (i.e., large or small bones), and age?
   (2) Check your food habits at mealtime and for snacks. Will your habits pro-

duce overweight through your meals as you get older? Through your snacks? How can you change or control this?

2. Planning menus.
   (1) Make a plan for your daily meals which will help you reach and hold the proper weight and meet your health needs.
   (2) Decide how many snacks you can have during the day and what foods you can eat as snacks and still hold your normal weight. Keep in mind that snacks must contribute towards your total need of food.
   (3) Plan a week's menus for a family that needs to control overweight.
   (4) Plan a week's menus for an underweight teen-age girl whom you know.

3. If time permits, prepare and serve with your family group one or more of the following:
   (1) A balanced breakfast for an overweight or underweight teen-age girl or boy.
   (2) A balanced lunch that you might select in the school cafeteria or bring from home, for an overweight or underweight teen-age girl or boy.
   (3) A balanced dinner for an overweight or underweight teen-age girl or boy.
   (4) A snack that would nourish but add few calories, for an overweight young person.

HOME EXPERIENCE

Discuss with your family what you have learned about controlling weight and if they are willing, check the weight of each member. If any members are over- or underweight and they are willing to cooperate, make a plan for family meals which will help your family control their individual weight problems. Help in making the menus and in doing the cooking.

Parties—
The Art of Entertaining

The Art of Entertaining
Can Be Learned

Entertaining in your home is one of the most creative experiences you can have. It makes use of your imagination and your total knowledge and skills in home-making. Some hostesses are so famous for their hospitality that people eagerly await invitations to their homes. Others fear to entertain lest they fail; but this need not be, for entertaining is an art that can be learned.

Food sparks the party! Mugs of thick, hot soup, fried chicken and biscuits, finger relishes, crackers and cheeses, glasses of milk, iced cupcakes and fresh fruit—delicious! Add a planned activity, a dash of concern for others' enjoyment, and blend in good companionship and any party is off to a very good start.

The Things That Make a Party "Click"

It is a combination of many things little and big that makes a party "click." Careful planning of every detail, so that each separate part is ready before the hour of the party, is an important duty of the host and hostess. But the guests have a big responsibility too.

The Good Host and Hostess. The greatest responsibility for the success of the party is that of the host and hostess. You need not fear taking this responsibility if you understand a few fundamental things about entertaining and simply put them into practice.

A successful host and hostess consider the happiness of the guests in making plans for the party. This attitude is far more important than the money you have to spend on food, the elaborateness of your decorations, or the spaciousness of your home. It is the key to your success, and if you have this trait, you can learn the other things.

Good Management

Good management on the part of the hostess is essential for success in entertaining at home. It begins with the invitations, and covers every detail of the party.

(1) The successful host and hostess *make* and *follow* a careful *plan* for any type of party. You think of the people who are congenial with each other; you think of newcomers who should be brought into this group. You invite those who seem to fit together. This does not mean a sameness. There should be a contrast of the witty, outgoing person with the more shy but equally fine person.

(2) The invitation to a party is important, and it can be given correctly in many different ways. The invitation should suit the occasion, either formal or informal. The *formal invitation* is engraved or printed for weddings or receptions. A formal invitation should be sent two or three weeks in advance of the date.

The informal invitation is given by phone or in person, or written. It can be on the spur of the moment or a week or two ahead of time. Many of the parties which are the most fun are the ones that are quickly arranged. For instance, "Come over to my house after the game" is sufficient.

(3) *How much money you can spend* for the whole party is decided before you give the invitations. This may limit the number you can invite, and it will certainly affect your choice of refreshments. But money need not limit your entertaining. Young people have just as much fun from popping corn and eating it together as from sharing more elaborate food, if other opportunities for fun are present. You can make 24 glasses of lemonade for about 2½ cents apiece. On a warm day that, plus a few simple cookies, is all you need. A homemade milk shake can be produced for 7 to 12 cents apiece, whereas one at the drug store might cost 35 cents or more. Home is the least expensive place in which to entertain, and there you are free to be completely relaxed.

(4) Make a *time plan* of work for your party, just as you did in planning and preparing breakfast and dinner. (See pages 116 and 301.) You have learned how to plan meals that are nourishing, attractive, and tasty. Apply this knowledge to your party. You have learned how to market

wisely and prepare food to save the nourishment. Make use of this knowledge. Make a work plan for all the things that have to be done, from the invitations and menu planning to arranging the house, preparing the table centerpiece, and other details.

(5) *Plan possible menus ahead.* This enables you to have friends in on the spur of the moment as well as inviting them well beforehand. If you keep such things as refrigerator or drop cookies mixed up and ready to cook in 12 minutes they can make quick refreshments seem special. Keep canned and frozen fruit juices on reserve. Always have cans of popcorn on hand. Cheese and crackers are good foods to fall back on for a quick-toasted hot treat. Dried and evaporated milk with cocoa can produce an excellent hot drink in a few minutes without using up milk meant for the family meals. Remember, you can make a quart of cocoa from dried milk for around one-third the price of fresh milk, and from evaporated milk at about one-half the price of fresh milk. The evaporated milk is just as nourishing as the whole. In the autumn, a big bowl of apples can be the only refreshment, or to this add fresh popcorn.

Choose a menu that can be prepared for the most part ahead of time, and get everything ready as soon as you can. Check this list as you work. This saves the frustrated, panicky feeling of too much to do and not enough time at the last, and helps you to be rested and relaxed and able to enjoy your own party.

At the hour for the party, everything must be ready. Allow free time at the last to groom yourself. Everyone enjoys the party that seems effortless. Such a party is the result of good planning and work ahead of time. Remember the key is to do everything that is possible the day before or sooner.

The food itself is important for the success of the party. It can be simple, plain, and inexpensive. It should fit the occasion, the season, and your budget. It should be attractive, tasty, easy to serve, and easy to eat without silver or with only one piece of silver. In addition, it should contribute to good health and good looks, without adding high calories. What is more appetizing as a beverage than natural fruit drinks like those pictured on page 87! Use a dash of green fruit coloring with fresh, frozen, or canned lime juice, garnish with a slice of lime—and you have a drink that is different and delicious. Or add a little red coloring to make pink lemonade, and watch your friends come for seconds. When you make beverages that show imagination, taste good, and are beautiful, and which provide foods needed in the daily diet, you will soon find yourself a popular hostess. Good food does not make a party, but it goes a long way towards making a good party better or lifting a sagging one. Whatever the food, there should be plenty of it. We do not expect a second helping of a homemade milk shake or soda, or ice cream and cake. But we do expect a second helping of cookies and punch or a cold drink such as lemonade.

(6) In case something is spilled or an accident occurs, the host and hostess must first make the guest feel comfortable. If a guest's clothes become soiled, and also your carpet or chair, take care of his difficulty first. Make him feel the damage to your possessions is of slight importance.

(7) The host and hostess should move among all the guests. If there is a guest of honor, special attention is paid to him. But equal attention is paid to all others. It is bad taste for either a host or a hostess to disappear from his or her own party with one guest. If it is necessary to leave on an errand, let this be known. It is the responsibility of host and hostess to spot the shy boy or girl and bring that one into a group without seeming to do so. A shy young person may need special attention. It is often surprising what a fine contribution this shy person can make when "brought out" by a considerate host or guest.

The Good Guest. *The guest has a big responsibility in helping make a party "click."* The ideal guest thinks beforehand of what he can contribute to the party. Here are some of the important things a guest can do:

(1) Accept the invitation promptly and with enthusiasm. Let your hostess know that you feel honored to be included. Then prove this by your spirit of cooperation throughout the party. You will be wanted as a guest at other parties.

In replying to a formal invitation, write your acceptance (or regret) in ink on a good grade of plain white paper, and use the language of the invitation. For instance, suppose you have been invited to a wedding and the reception afterwards. Your reply might be something like this:

Mary Jones is delighted to accept the kind invitation of Mr. and Mrs. Robert Brown to the marriage of their daughter Ann to Mr. Milton Dodd, on Saturday, October 20 at four in the afternoon, at the White Stone Church, and to the reception afterwards in the church parlors.

If you receive a less formal but written invitation to a party, reply in writing at once in a friendly, informal style.

If you cannot go, be prompt in replying. State your reason for declining and let the hostess feel that it is your loss. When you receive an invitation and cannot go, it is then your responsibility to entertain that person. If you are close friends, she may offer to give you a "rain check" or you may ask for one. This makes the relation easy and without strain. But it does not excuse you from your social responsibility to entertain that person.

(2) A guest has a responsibility first to the host and hostess. Arrive on time and depart at the hour set in the invitation. If you sense strain on the part of your host and hostess, try to put them at ease. Be quick to fall in with the plans for the party and help make those plans succeed. One phrase from a guest can make a host or hostess feel terrible—for example, "No, I don't want to play that" or "You know I hate dancing." If you don't want to play or dance, don't accept the invitation. If you accept, go along wholeheartedly with the plan for the party.

(3) When you leave a party, bid the hostess and host and the parents good-bye, and express your sincere appreciation for the occasion. Try to think of some specific thing that pleased you, and mention that. Make the hostess feel your happiness in having been there.

Easy Ways to Entertain at Home

Some young people become discouraged with having parties in their home, because they begin with the hardest type before they are ready. Let us see how you can begin with something in which

you may feel certain to succeed. With skill and experience you can then advance to more difficult ways of entertaining.

Snack or Dessert Party. The *snack or dessert party* is one of the easiest and least expensive ways to entertain, requiring only one to three types of foods. They can be prepared ahead, or quickly prepared after the gang arrives. And the menus can vary to fit your purse.

When you choose your menu, whatever the occasion, you will wish to keep in mind the points we have discussed, concerning costs, menu planning, and work and time management.

The Tea Party. *The tea party* is one of the most frequently used types of entertaining, and is a broad term used for simple or elaborate entertaining taking place between lunch and dinner, usually from 3 to 5 or 4 to 6. You can entertain one or two friends or many people. The tea party is used at school after the club meeting, at a student council reception for a noted speaker, or at open house of any kind. It is used for the formal or informal reception after a wedding, or for a shower for a friend going on a trip, or for any occasion to honor a person. The refreshments for a tea are simple, and for a larger party include a choice of tea, coffee, or other beverages. Sandwiches, cakes or cookies, candies, and nuts may be served. Tea sandwiches are often open, that is, made with just one piece of bread. This fits in with the modern idea of weight control. However, tiny ribbon, rolled, and

Simple foods may be served for special events, such as this Easter dinner, if you use imagination to make them attractive.

pinwheel sandwiches are also used. Fillings are made of cheese, fish, chicken, liver pâté, and all kinds of meat.

The dip is becoming more popular for teas today than sandwiches. There are many different types of dips made with cheese, various meats, shell fish, and fruit such as avocado. (See recipes in cookbook, pages 410–411.) Place the dip in a bowl, and dip crackers or potato chips into the mixture. It should be soft enough to dip onto the cracker, but not so soft that it runs. The advantages of the dip are that it takes less time to prepare than making sandwiches, and the mixture can be prepared the day ahead and placed on the tea table in time to reach room temperature before the party. There is no soaking or drying out of bread, as so often happens with party sandwiches when not properly prepared ahead of time, and no waste in leftovers. The dip is also appreciated today because the value of protein is better known. People prefer more meat or cheese and less bread, even at teas!

A variety of breads are used at tea parties. If you make dips, place small slices of whole wheat and rye bread beside the dips with a knife for spreading. Have loaves of quick breads such as orange, banana, and nut bread on a tray with a sharp knife for guests to use in doing their own cutting. Butter is an appropriate spread for a quick sweet bread, or, even better, serve the bread plain.

Because we are so conscious of the value of vitamin C in meals today, it is fashionable to have a tray of raw vegetable strips and curls, as nibbles,

Fruit bits on toothpicks disappear fast at tea parties. One beautiful way to serve bite sizes of fruit is to cut a large pineapple in half, leaving the stem on. Hollow out and then refill with bite sizes of the fresh pineapple on colored picks, along with other fresh fruits. In the summer, melon balls can be placed in the hollowed half of watermelon—very attractive and delicious. These bits of fruit are more popular on the modern tea table than the sweet cakes and cookies which were formerly preferred. However, there is still a place for the cookie and cake on the tea menu. Tea cakes should be dainty and tasty. A good slice of fruit cake and a cup of tea for each guest is sufficient for a small party.

The Buffet Meal. *The buffet* (boŏ fā) is used for breakfast, brunch (which is halfway between breakfast and lunch in time and menu), lunch, and supper. It is a completely balanced meal served on a central table from which guests help themselves. It is acceptable form to let the guests stand and eat, sit where they choose, use trays on which to put serving dishes, or hold the tray on the lap. The advantages of the buffet meal in modern living are many:

(1) The planning and much of the preparation can be done ahead of time.

(2) You can entertain a large stand-up group easily with a finger buffet.

(3) It requires a smaller amount of space, less work, and less equipment than a meal where all are seated.

(4) It is less expensive, if properly planned.

The principle of the buffet meal is to keep your menu simple, but let each item on the menu blend with the others in flavor and balance with them in color, texture, and nutrition. Each separate dish must be delicious, and remain hot if it is supposed to be hot, or cold if it is supposed to be cold. It should be easy to eat and require no cutting more difficult than can be done with a fork.

As with other meals, the buffet can be excellently done on a high or low budget.

Informal tea service for a group of friends.

Steps in Making a Party Sandwich Loaf: (1) Select loaf of day-old enriched bread that is unsliced. Prepare fillings day before and refrigerate. (2) Trim crusts from bread. (3) Slice bread lengthwise into four even slices about ½ inch thick. (4) Spread both sides of two slices with butter or margarine; spread one side of the other two slices. Stack slices with alternate layers of cheese, chicken salad and ham salad. (5) Frost top and sides of loaf with cream cheese softened with milk and garnish with nutmeats. Wrap loosely in wax paper and chill in refrigerator 3 to 4 hours. (6) Cut into ½-inch slices and serve with tomatoes, olives, or other relishes as the main dish for a buffet lunch or supper.

A buffet supper for after the football game. A buffet meal enables you to entertain a large number in a small space at low to moderate cost.

A variety of conserves accents a meal with color, flavors, and texture. Conserves and hot breads make an excellent dessert.

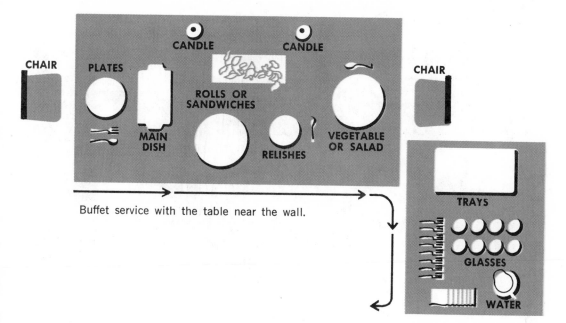

Buffet service with the table near the wall.

A *potluck supper* is one where each person brings a dish from home already prepared. It is the least expensive type of entertaining, and one that is light in work for the hostess. But the menu should be planned and followed for a well-balanced meal. Any kind of potluck entertainment enables those who can't entertain at their own home to take their share of responsibility, in the home of those who can entertain. This was a favorite way for our pioneer forefathers to have parties. At a quilting bee, corn huskings, and other types of social get-togethers, every woman brought a favorite dish.

To avoid a sameness of menu, it is best to have an able committee plan the meal when the refreshments are to be potluck. Then tell each person what to bring. The hostess usually furnishes the beverages, and bread and butter, and gets the table and service ready. There should be a committee for cleaning up the dishes and kitchen after the party. A potluck is a fine

type of party, from snacks after the game, beach parties and cook-outs, to the more formal tea or buffet meal.

Community suppers (given by church, PTA, Grange, social club, or other organization) are not usually sponsored by teen-agers, but often teen-agers are asked to help in the service of them. In the past, community suppers have often been poorly planned from the standpoint of good nutrition. This situation is improving. You can help in further improvement if you are on a community supper committee. Do not leave to chance the food that will be donated. Make a balanced menu for the meal and set up committees to see that the right amounts of meat, vegetables, salads, bread, and dessert are donated. Community meals should represent the best we know in good meal planning,

You see from this discussion that entertaining is an art that can be learned. It is more than mastering mechanical de-

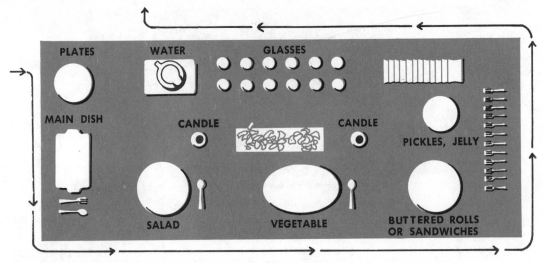

Buffet service, table in center of room, dessert and hot beverage to be served later from trays.

tails; good planning and work ahead of time are needed for success. Early experiences in entertaining can be fun if you keep your plans simple, and make each occasion a success. To be an able host or hostess is one of the most creative and satisfying social experiences. It is almost equally gratifying to be a welcome guest.

 WORDS TO WORK WITH

> **Buffet** (boŏ fā′): a meal at which guests serve themselves from a sideboard or table.

 THINKING IT OVER

1. Explain what is meant by the art of hospitality.

2. In what way do the hostess and host set the atmosphere for a party?

3. Explain how different types of invitations should be given and answered.

4. Why does the able hostess plan her party well ahead? What things should be done a week or more ahead? Which the day before the party? Which should be done last?

5. Why do you have a better time at a party when everything seems easy? How can this effect be produced?

6. Suppose you were hostess and a guest spilled a cup of chocolate on her dress and on the rug; what would you do?

7. As a guest, what responsibilities toward your hostess should you take? Toward the other guests?

8. How can a girl contribute to the success of a party if she has to dance with a boy much shorter than she is?

9. Give examples of easy and inexpensive ways in which you can entertain at home with a snack, dessert, or tea party.

10. When would you entertain with a buffet meal? How would you plan it?

11. What are the advantages of a "potluck" buffet supper?

12. Is a theme important for your party? In what different ways could you work out a theme for different seasons and occasions?

APPLYING WHAT YOU KNOW

1. Plan and prepare one or more of the following:
   (1) A snack for friends in your home, after a summer swim.
   (2) The same after school in the autumn.
   (3) The same after an evening event at the school or church.
   (4) A dessert party in the spring, before some event.

2. Plan a formal tea and invite your mothers or some other group.
   (1) *Plan* the tea first as a class, writing invitations. See that each girl has an opportunity to be both hostess and guest. Make your work plan complete and see that every detail is carried out. Study your plan for wasted motion and improve it.
   (2) *Give* a real tea for which you prepare all of the food. Write your invitations two weeks in advance. Select a theme for your party and carry this through in the centerpiece, in the invitations, and in other ways.

3. Serve a buffet meal for 10 to 12 people. (1) Limit yourself to spending a definite amount of money per person. (2) Arrange menus for a low-cost buffet meal and show how you would vary this if you could spend more money. (3) Check your plans with local prices. (4) Plan the order of work and timing for the meal. (5) Assign duties to different members of the class and check your plans as you proceed, from the things that can be done first to the last-minute work.

EVALUATING

1. Did your menu meet the standards set for a good party menu?
   (1) Did you stay within your budget?
   (2) Did you take advantage of the seasonal foods?
   (3) Was the menu balanced in color, texture, and nutrition?
   (4) Was your table attractive, the food tasty, and the service smooth and easy?
   (5) Was your meal ready when the guests arrived? Were you? Were you relaxed and rested?
   (6) Did the guests have a good time? Did you?

2. As a hostess, do you feel that your good planning and work ahead of time helped make your party a success?

3. As a guest, did you measure up to your full responsibility?

4. Recount the places where you did not do well, and make a plan to improve. Do you think you undertook too difficult a type of entertainment for your party?

HOME EXPERIENCE

With your family, plan a party which the family would like to give; help in this planning, using what you have learned. Help in the preparation and service of the menu and in inviting the guests. This might be a holiday dinner to which you would invite another family. Report your results to your teacher.

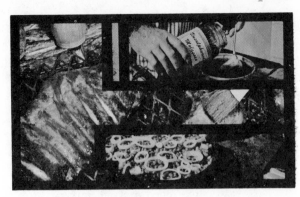

29

The Man in the Family Entertains

The modern family is discovering that the man of the house deserves a high place as host and cook. Some of the best times families enjoy with friends are when the father and son, together or separately, entertain. A man can handle any type of entertainment we have discussed. Often the man prefers to entertain with a cookout, or to take the family or friends to a restaurant. Men share in the preparation and cooking of many types of meals. When married women work, the family

A quick, low-cost cookout meal that features canned baked beans with frankfurters as the main dish.

must share more of the responsibility that once was considered "woman's work."

The change in family living today encourages this. More emphasis is placed on outdoor living. Grills are built as a part of a patio or yard. The portable charcoal grill goes to the beach, park, lake, or river. The family can enjoy a swim, a skating party, or a hike, and cook a good meal wherever they choose. The place and meal to suit the season and occasion can take a variety of forms.

Planning Outdoor Meals

A barbecue, picnic, or outdoor meal should be well planned, for it presents some special problems. Make a check list for everything from buying food planned in the menus to packing it in the car. Check every item off as you pack it. It is an unhappy moment when you have invited friends for a cookout dinner at the lake 15 miles away and discover after you get there that you forgot to take the

Planning ahead is the basis of a successful family picnic.

steaks out of the refrigerator! Select equipment that will keep your food in first-class condition and produce a tasty, nourishing meal.

The food is a high point in an outdoor party. Today many people are not content with a picnic of potato chips, hot dogs, rolls, pickles, cake, and soda water. We know that such foods, with the exception of hot dogs, give very little nourishment for health. They pile up the fat, starch, and sugar. What, then, makes a good cookout menu? Here are a few suggestions.

BARBECUED STEAK DINNER
Fresh fruit (appetizer or dessert)
Barbecued steaks
Buns   Butter or margarine
Baked potatoes (wrapped in foil)
Salad: raw onions, sliced tomatoes, green lettuce, pickles
Fresh fruit   Sharp cheese   Cookies
Milk   Coffee

This menu can range from moderate to high cost, depending on your choice of steak. If you choose prime, choice, or good sirloin, the menu will cost more than if you choose a prime or choice grade boneless chuck roast and cut it in steaks. Hamburgers and hot dogs give a low-cost menu. One pound of hamburger gives five medium-size or four thick hamburgers. In a low-cost meal, omit the pickles. Fruit is a good picnic dessert for all ages, and usually a fruit may be selected which will fit into the low-cost meal as well as the moderate- and higher-cost ones.

If the meal is served at home in the dining room, add a green cooked vegetable. If you bake potatoes in foil, put them on to cook about 40 minutes before the meat, depending on size. They should be within 10 to 15 minutes of being done when you start the meat. Meat should be broiled to the liking of each guest—rare, medium, or well done. (A favorite cookout plan is to let each guest cook his meat

When barbecuing pork, test for doneness before serving. No pink or rare pork should be served. Do you know why?

to his own liking.) Remember that if you broil *pork chops*, they *must be well done.*

Poultry, spare ribs, and lamb chops are also excellent when broiled outside. Choose your menu to fit the season, your taste, and your budget. Barbecue sauce adds variety to meats on a cookout meal. The food can be as well chosen for a picnic as for any other occasion, for you plan it by the pattern for a well-balanced meal.

Dining Out

Another way in which men entertain their family and friends is to take them out to dinner. Dining out has an etiquette (ĕt′ĭ kĕt)—a system of good manners— all its own. The earlier we learn to dine out with ease, the greater our enjoyment in being a citizen of the world. There are a few simple things to observe that help put you at ease whether you go to the most elegant hotel or restaurant, the diner on a train, or a cafeteria.

(1) The host has certain responsibilities when he takes a girl or a group out to eat. He may simply arrange the party and have it on the plan of a "Dutch" treat, where each pays his own. This should be clearly understood by all who go. The one who makes arrangements finds out what the total cost of food, tips, transportation, and any other expenses will be. It is embarrassing for the bill to be presented when the purse does not measure up, and this can be avoided by careful planning.

If the man is paying for the party, he selects a place to go which is within his means. He finds out if there will be dancing or other entertainment and tells

his guests the place, the time, how to get there if they do not know, and the type of party. In some public places you may reserve tables ahead of time for a small party; in others you have to take your turn for service. It is well to know such things, as well as the cost of food and its quality, before choosing the place to dine.

In large places, men check their coats and hats. A girl may keep her wrap, if she wishes, and lay it back on her chair while dining. She lays her purse in her lap and places the napkin over it. If it is a large dinner party, the host will have place cards. At a small one he simply designates where people will sit. The girl sits to the right of her date. The man seats the girl on his right before he is seated, unless this is done by the head waiter.

(2) Ordering the meal takes place next. The girl chooses first. She looks the whole menu over rather quickly. One way to order is a la carte, which is selecting each dish separately. This is the least expensive way if you wish only a sandwich and a beverage or a dessert. But it is often most expensive if you wish a complete meal. Your host may suggest something. If it is the most expensive, he may be trying to indicate his generosity and you will have to judge whether you should take this or something less expensive.

A complete meal listed in the menu is called "table d'hôte" (tä′blĕ dōt′). In this case the price of the entrée (än′trā)—the main dish—includes the price of the complete dinner, unless otherwise stated. That is, you would have three or four courses as follows: (a) choice of fruit juice, melon, fruit cup, or seafood such as shrimp, oysters, or crab; (b) soup or jellied madrilene; (c) meat, choice of two vegetables, and a salad; (d) dessert— choice of ice cream, sherbet, parfait (pär fä′), Jell-O, pie, cake, fresh fruit in season, or cheese such as Gruyère, Roquefort, or Camembert with Saltines. The beverage is served with the dinner if you wish; otherwise it comes with dessert. Read the menu carefully to find exceptions to the above pattern.

The girl states her choice from the first course right through, except that in most places dessert is ordered after the dinner has been eaten.

(3) The guests have the same responsibilities in a public eating place as in a home, with this addition: in a public place you show more restraint. That is, you keep your voice lower. Laughter is natural but lower in tone. As a guest, your conduct should be above reproach. Anything less reflects on your host as well as yourself and your family. Guests do not ask special favors from the waiter. If you have not been served, tell your host and he will take care of the matter. Keep up with the group in your eating, and do not cause others to wait unnecessarily for you. But do not eat so fast that you are the first one finished. Observe the progress of others and try to stay with them. If you are in doubt about which silver to use, watch your host or your hostess if you have one. These two should know the correct form for each service. Keep your conversation gay, light, and away from any subject which might cause anger or embarrassment to anyone present. Be careful not to talk too much; give others a chance. Don't try to be witty at the risk of hurting people.

When a dinner at a public place is over, the host indicates the time to leave. He pays the bill and leaves a suitable tip. If the hour is such that a guest must leave the party, he should excuse himself quietly, thanking the host and trying not to interfere with the fun of others. The girl enters and leaves a public dining room ahead of her escort. Her escort assists her into her wraps, and sees her to her door.

Whether the party is at home, a cookout, or in the finest restaurant, good manners make you a delightful host or hostess and a sought-after guest.

 ## WORDS TO WORK WITH

A la carte (ä lä kärt′): order[ed] dish by dish from the menu, with a stated price for each.

Entrée (än′trä): In England, a dish (usually fish) served before the roast; in our country, the main meat dish, the listed price of which usually is the price of the whole dinner.

Etiquette (ĕt′ĭ kĕt): a system of good manners observed by cultivated people in social relations or business.

Parfait (pär fä′): a dessert made of alternate layers of different kinds of ice cream or sherbet with fruits and nuts, and served in a special tall, slender glass.

Table d' hôte (tȧ′blĕ dōt′): a type of meal service in a public eating place, in which you pay a fixed price for the whole meal.

THINKING IT OVER

1. Why do men share more in the preparation of meals today than they did formerly?
2. Why does a well-planned menu and a plan of work make entertaining more fun?
3. What does a man need to keep in mind when he plans his party?
4. Should teen-age boys take responsibility for parties in their homes? Explain your answer.
5. In what ways has the portable grill made cookouts more fun?
6. What are the responsibilities of the host when he takes a girl or a group out to dine in a public restaurant?
7. What are the responsibilities of the girl or guests when going out with a young man to dine?
8. Explain what is meant by: a la carte; table d' hôte, entrée.
9. Which is the most economical way to order if you wish only a snack? If you wish a full meal? How can you tell the price of a full meal?
10. Describe the choices in a four-course dinner.
11. Describe what makes good manners in dining out.

APPLYING WHAT YOU KNOW

1. Planning menus.
   (1) Plan a menu for an outdoor spring breakfast.
   (2) Plan a menu for a balanced dinner cookout after a summer swim.
   (3) Plan a menu for a cookout corn roast after an early autumn hike.
   (4) Plan a menu for a winter kitchen meal after a November football game.

   (5) Plan a party with your family or group, to be held at a restaurant or hotel.
2. Choose a menu for a broiled meat cookout, and plan and carry out all of the steps, such as:
   (1) Marketing.
   (2) Time and work schedule written out for the whole plan.
   (3) Assignment of work for preparing, serving, and cleaning up after the meal.

EVALUATING

1. Was your menu well balanced for health? Did you stay within your budget? Did the food taste good? Did it blend together?
2. Was your work well organized? Did you have it properly thought out as to which step should be done first? Did a few people do most of the work or was it well divided? Were the foods all ready at the proper time?
3. How could you plan a good menu and spend less money? If you had more to spend, how would you change your menu?
4. Make a plan that would be an improvement over that for the meal you prepared.

HOME EXPERIENCE

With your family, plan a picnic either at home or away from home. You be chairman of the planning committee, if your family agrees. Organize the work after the menu is planned, and practice what you have learned. Let others help you, and you assign the part they are to do and the time to do it. Report the results to your teacher.

30

Food Preserving:
Food for the Future

Surplus fruits may be frozen in small or large amounts according to your space.

Why Preserve Food at Home?

Before the modern industry of canning and freezing food, there was good reason to preserve food at home. It enabled families to have far more interesting meals during the periods when some foods were not in season, and also meant improved health. Thus it was the part of wisdom and good management to grow surplus food to can for winter use. Many who could not grow food bought it in season and canned it at home.

Some may ask, Why preserve food at home today? In the large modern supermarket you can find a wide range of all kinds of canned, frozen, fresh, dried, and pickled foods, and a variety of jams, jellies, and preserves. For many people there is no reason to can or preserve food. The commercial canners and freezers of food are doing an excellent job at a reasonable price. They are serving us well.

However, there is reason to preserve food at home if you grow a surplus and have the equipment, time, and energy to preserve it. There is double reason to do this if it saves you money and gives you better meals and more individualized flavors in foods than you would have otherwise.

Foods are preserved at home by freezing, canning, pickling with vinegar, spices, or brines, and preserving with sugar.

Freezing

Quick freezing is a modern method of preserving food. The food is subjected to temperatures of from 0° to 40° F below zero, and quickly frozen. Then it is stored at 0° F or lower.

Freezing food to preserve it is quick and easy to do, and leaves a product quite close to the fresh food in taste, color, nutritive value, and general appearance. Freezing food does not stop spoilage, but delays it until the food thaws. Freezing does stop the action of enzymes (ĕn′zīm), which are substances that can be both helpful and harmful. Enzymes are found in both animal and plant tissue and help carry on the life processes within cells. After a food is harvested, enzymes hasten over-ripening and loss of vitamins, especially vitamin C.

Freezing also stops the growth of bacteria, yeasts, and molds that are found in the air, soil, and water. These tiny growing substances cause food to spoil. (That is, all food except cheese, which is made by the growth of molds.)

The fruits best suited to freezing are all types of berries, peaches, fruit juices, and sour cherries. Many vegetables and combinations of vegetables are excellent frozen. These include green peas, black-eyed peas, green beans, yellow beans, lima beans, broccoli, collards, turnip greens, mustard greens, spinach, okra, kale, Brussels sprouts, asparagus, kernel corn, corn-on-the-cob, and squash.

If you do not own a freezer, it might be well to investigate all costs of freezing food at home before you decide to buy one. One study made by the U. S. Department of Agriculture indicated that it costs between 13 and 26 cents per pound of frozen food to own and operate your own freezer. This figure would vary according to the rate you have to pay for electricity, packaging materials, and the cost of food. The more you freeze and use, the lower the rate. This cost does not include the time and energy required to prepare and freeze the food. If you wish to freeze food at home, see the references at the end of this unit, and send for the latest government bulletins on the subject.

One good use to make of a freezer is to cook surplus food, such as soup, bread, casseroles, meat balls, prepared sandwiches, and the like, and freeze it at once

Surplus meat, either raw or freshly cooked, may be stored in the refrigerator freezer. Be sure to wrap food so that no air enters package.

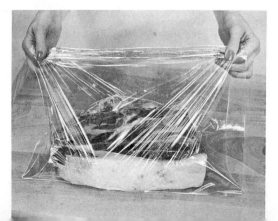

in quantities needed for your family. Thaw and heat such food just before serving to retain maximum flavor and nutrients. This saves time, energy, and fuel in cooking. You can quickly and easily serve nourishing and attractive meals that taste good. This is good management.

Canning Food

Canning is the most popular method of preserving perishable food. The colors, flavor, and appearance of some food is not as good when it is canned as when it is fresh or frozen. But aside from some loss of vitamin C and thiamine in canning, the food value is high when all the juice is used.

In canning, food is preserved by heat. Unlike freezing, when a food is canned, the enzymes, bacteria, molds, and yeast plants are destroyed. We call this "sterilization" (stĕr'ĭ lĭ zā'shŭn). The food, if properly canned, is pure and free from all substances that cause decay. That is why it will keep indefinitely.

All foods except fruits, tomatoes, and pickles should be canned in a pressure canner for best results. With your pressure canner comes a book of directions and recipes. Follow these directions exactly for recipes and time given for each food. The people who made your pressure canner are most able to tell you how to use it. Keep these directions in a safe, clean place and use them.

Jellies, Jams, Preserves, and Conserves

Many people who do not preserve food in any other way make jellies, jams, pre-

Why should you label food canned at home? What should the label include besides the name of the product?

serves, and conserves at home. These colorful and tasty foods add accent to a meal in flavor and texture. They are high in calories and give little return in health values, but they greatly enliven a meal. They may be used as a simple, quick, and excellent dessert with hot breads.

Before modern knowledge of food chemistry, good results in jelly-making were uncertain. The kind and ripeness of fruit had a lot to do with success. To make good jelly one needed exactly the right proportions of acid and pectin in fruit to sugar. Today you can buy natural pectin from fruit in either liquid or dry form. Food experiments have been done to indicate the amount of pectin and sugar to use for jelly or jams with the common fruits. If you follow the recipes given on these commercial pectins, you will get good results in making jellies or jams.

Some fruits that contain abundant acid and pectin, when slightly underripe, are crabapples, apples, currants, blackberries, raspberries, Concord grapes, wild grapes, cranberries, and some plums. Most other fruits must have acid, pectin, or both added. Adding lemon juice and rind to sweet fruits increases the acid, and often improves the flavor.

Jellies are made from the clear strained juice of fruit, which gives a firm, clear, attractive product. *Jams* are made by crushing the fruit, adding sugar, and cooking with or without added pectin and acid. *Preserves* are made by adding sugar while cooking to a firm fruit such as the peach, apricot, or pineapple. These fruits are also used for conserves. A *conserve* is made by cooking two or more fruits together to the preserve stage of thickness. Often nuts and raisins are added to conserves. All of these are easy to make, with either fresh or frozen fruit. It is best to make small amounts at a time and serve them fresh. (See the Cookbook, page 447, for recipes for the above.)

Pickles

Salt, sugar, vinegar, and spices are used to pickle fruits and vegetables. Among fruits there is the pickled peach, pear, apricot, apple, and melon rind. These fruits are served with meats or as a relish. They help give a meal contrast in flavor and texture and make it something special.

Many vegetables are pickled, producing dishes that are interesting in flavor, color, and texture, and thus make a meal more stimulating. English chutney is a special relish preferred by many homemakers. The most common vegetables for pickling are cabbage, onion, green and red tomato, peppers, cauliflower, green beans, and beets.

Only top-quality food should be used for pickling. (See Chapters 10 and 12 for quality.) Because of the way most pickles and relishes are made, they have lost most of the water-soluble vitamins. They are no substitute for a raw salad, but they do add a nippy taste to a meal of bland foods.

Owing to the acid used, you should cook pickles in enamel cooking utensils or porcelain-lined glass.

How Your Government Can Help You Preserve Food at Home

Your government is interested in improving the meals and health of its citizens. Except in the field of infant and child welfare, there is scarcely a field in which you can get more help from the government, than in preserving food at home. Millions of dollars have been spent to help us make the best use of the land to grow nourishing food; but the government has not stopped there. Much money is spent in finding out what people are eating, how their health is, and how it can be improved through better use of food. This information is free to you in the form of bulletins and pamphlets that may be secured through your county extension office, through your State Agricultural Extension and Experiment Service, and through the United States Department of Agriculture.

Looking Ahead in Food Preservation

Scientific work is now being done which may greatly alter our methods of food preservation. As indicated in a preceding

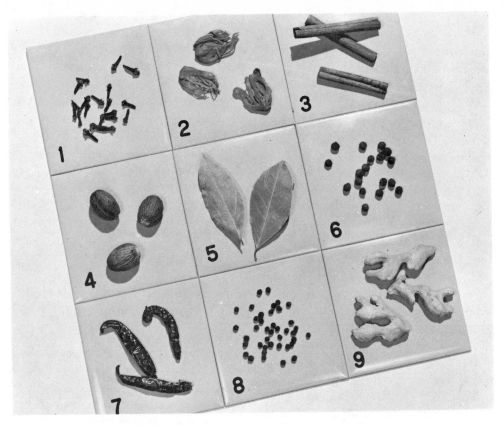

Common spices used in preserving, pickling, and general cooking: (1) cloves; (2) mace; (3) cinnamon; (4) nutmeg; (5) bay leaves; (6) allspice; (7) red pepper; (8) black pepper; (9) ginger.

unit, the method of freeze-drying food is being extensively studied. The addition of certain substances (antibiotics) to meat, fish, and poultry to preserve the fresh quality and delay spoiling is also under study. Another possible method of food preservation is by radiation. For example, experiments have been made to show that spoilage of meat can be greatly delayed by radiation, and that mold on bread, and the sprouting of potatoes, can also be prevented.

WORDS TO WORK WITH

Enzyme (ĕn′zīm): a substance present in plant and animal tissue that increases chemical changes, such as causing fruit to ripen and over-ripen, and aiding in the digestion of food within the intestinal tract.

Sterilization (stĕr′ ĭ lĭ zā′shŭn): the process of destroying the bacteria, enzymes, yeasts, molds, and other substances that might cause food to spoil.

THINKING IT OVER

1. When is it a good use of time and energy to preserve food at home?

2. Under what circumstances is it poor judgment to do this?

3. What are the common methods of preserving food at home, and what foods are best suited to each?

4. What is the value of jellies and preserves, pickles, and relishes in a meal?

PROBLEMS TO SOLVE

1. Planning to get further information on home preservation methods.
   (1) Write to your State Agricultural Extension Service and to the U.S.D.A. for any free information on the subject in which you are interested.
   (2) If any type of food-processing plant is located near you, see if you can plan a trip through it as a class. If this is not possible, try to plan a trip through it with your family or some of your friends.

APPLYING WHAT YOU KNOW

1. Discuss the value of preserving food at home, and decide which type of food preservation is best suited to your family and why.
   (1) Compare the cost of home-frozen or home-canned fruits, vegetables, and meats with the cost of those at the market. Keep in mind possible savings on sales when the food is at the height of its season. Also keep in mind the fact that home-grown food will go to waste if not used promptly.

2. Prepare at school one or more of the following:
   (1) Make jelly, jam, preserves, or conserve.
   (2) Can tomatoes or some fruit by the hot-water-bath method.
   (3) Prepare and pack a fruit for home freezing.
   (4) Prepare and pack a vegetable for home freezing.

3. Plan balanced dinner menus for three days, using home-canned food as a part of each meal.

4. Do the same with home-frozen foods.

EVALUATING

1. On the basis of your studies, is it economical for you to freeze or can food at home if you do not have a garden with surplus food?

2. When might these circumstances change so that it would pay you to do this?

3. What did you learn from your trip to a food-processing plant, or from the government bulletin, that can help you manage family food better?

4. In your canning experience, what mistakes did you make that you can correct? How will you avoid these mistakes next time?

HOME EXPERIENCE

Discuss with your mother what you have learned at school about food preservation, and see if you can make use of any of this knowledge at home. If she agrees, make a jam, a conserve, or some other preserved food which you learned to make at school and could well use at home. Report results to your teacher.

31

Meals for Children and Older Persons

Meals for the young and for older persons need special attention.

The Nutrition of the Child Affects His Later Life

The Federal government believes so strongly that the nutrition of the child is important to his later life that it spends a great deal of money to help children have better diets. Many states, counties, and cities spend additional money so that the expectant mother may be well nourished, and so that the baby may have the right food. Bulletins on how to feed the expectant mother, baby, and small child are written and given to parents. Trained nutritionists are placed in free clinics at hospitals so that personal help may be given to those who need it. Why do we spend so much money to see that babies and small children eat the food they need?

The Food of the Mother Affects the Baby

The baby's proper development before birth is related to the food of the mother. The mother's state of health and nutrition can influence the quality not only of the baby's first teeth but even of his permanent teeth. It can influence his health and development in other ways that are not so easily seen by the eye. The expectant mother needs a diet rich in protein of good quality, vitamins, and minerals. But the diet should contain only a very few more calories than usual.

Studies show that one out of every four mothers bearing a first child is still in her teens. The expectant teen-age mother has to provide food not only for the unborn baby but for her own growth. Girls who eat the foods they need daily are preparing themselves physically for this responsibility. Insofar as the physical well-being helps the way they feel about themselves and their relation to others, good nutrition aids them also to prepare themselves psychologically for motherhood. The expectant mother who uses her daily calories for the foods she needs instead of ill-chosen snacks is more likely to maintain her weight and health at the desired level. She is building up a reserve of good nutrition which will pay further dividends as she takes her place as a mature woman. Sound nutrition on the part of the mother greatly influences proper formation of the baby and its future health as well.

Baby's Food Starts with Milk

The infant's first food is mother's milk or a formula, but no formula has yet been worked out which is as good for the baby as mother's milk. This is the food nature meant for the young child to have. It is not necessary that the mother provide all of the baby's milk, even at the beginning. On the other hand, there is some evidence that it is best for the baby if the mother can provide at least a part of his milk for the first few months of life. Mother's milk helps give the infant temporary immunity to or ability to resist certain diseases. This is a great advantage in early life.

The baby naturally likes milk. All other foods he must learn to like—one by one— as they are introduced into his diet. Learning to like the foods his body needs makes a big difference to his future resistance to disease, his feeling of vitality, and his appearance. The mother and others who help feed the baby have a very large responsibility. If he learns to like the foods he needs when he is small, it is far more likely that the child will have good food habits as he grows older.

The food of the baby and the young child determines how fast he will grow, and his general health and vitality. It influences his disposition—that is, whether he is happy or irritable. Babies that have too little vitamin C in the diet, for instance, are irritable and cry a great deal. A baby that does not have enough vitamin D to assist in the formation of bones does not walk as soon as he should; and if the deficiency is severe, when he does walk, his legs will be crooked. Before modern knowledge of how to control disease, children by the thousands died before they reached two years of age. While this was partly due to disease and poor sanitation, poor food was also a basic factor.

Good food habits and good manners, taught early, are an asset throughout life.

What Food Does the Pre-School Child Need?

As indicated above, the baby begins on a completely fluid diet. Very quickly orange juice is given and then soft thin cereals, egg yolk, and other foods. By the end of the first year, a child is eating a variety of the foods you eat. His food, however, is mashed or finely chopped or sieved. By the end of the second year, he is eating at the family table and from the family menu.

The variety of food which the pre-school child needs is that given in the recommended diet on page 12. The chief difference from your diet is in smaller portions of food, more mildly seasoned and more simply prepared. By the time the child enters school, he usually likes and eats what his family likes and eats. This is why the family example in eating and enjoying a variety of food is so important for the good food habits of children.

A child who learns to enjoy eating nutritionally-balanced meals is establishing good food habits that will help him throughout life.

Unless a child shows a need for a mid-morning or afternoon snack, do not start this habit. Children differ in their needs because they grow differently and vary in activity. A pre-school child who is growing fast and is very active might need the snack. A less active child might not. If the child nibbles, it is better that you give him a well-balanced snack. Nibbling the wrong foods can start tendencies that lead to poor food habits and over-weight. If he likes candy, teach him to save it for dessert, by serving candy as dessert now and then.

Small children should not be given coffee, tea, or stimulating carbonated drinks. These are not foods, but stimulants. Fried foods and heavily sweetened foods should be avoided. Fried foods may take the edge off the appetite for the next meal because they are more slowly digested. The diet of the small child has this in common with the diet of those who wish to control weight—every bite should count for good health. Unless the food gives something the child needs for health, don't serve it. The health of a small child is dependent on his family's providing the food he needs and preparing this food in meals that he enjoys eating.

How Children Can Begin Good Food Habits

A child is not born with feeding problems. Yet feeding is one of the most serious problems for many young mothers.

How can you prepare yourself to prevent or meet such a problem?

A very tasty, nourishing meal for a child does him no good if he will not eat it. Small children like what they are used to having and often resist change. They must be taught to accept and enjoy the foods they need.

Introducing new foods in the diet of the baby is often where some food problems start. *Introduce only one new food to the baby at a time.* When he accepts it and enjoys it thoroughly, then introduce another food. This same plan works with the older child who needs help in learning to like new foods.

Serve a child *small servings.* Small servings help him to eat all of the food served, which gives him a feeling of success. He can ask for more if he wants it.

A *regular time for meals* is important for a young child. He should not wait an hour for some member of the family. Hunger causes irritability in a small child. Here is an example of how one mother prevented a problem from developing. She noticed that her 2½-year-old went into a temper tantrum every morning at about 11:30. The child was usually a very happy one, and the mother reasoned that the child was not naughty, but hungry. The next day she had the child's lunch ready at 11:20 and there was no tantrum.

Prepare a child for leaving his interests before mealtime. To do this happily helps him enjoy his meals more and make an important adjustment to all of life.

Feeding problems may start with snacks and parties. Much of the food given to children at parties is not what they need, and often it takes the "edge off" the following meal.

The habit of running for crackers, cookies, cakes, candies, or soda water to "fill up" between meals spoils the child's appetite for the next meal and starts a feeding problem. Prevent such a habit by letting him have between meals a choice of milk and bread, fresh fruit, or fruit juice. He will learn how good these foods are by eating them.

Make your remarks about food in front of a child *constructive.* Some families contribute feeding problems by talking about the child's poor eating habits in front of him. Talk about your *food likes* instead of dislikes. With your own spoon, taste his food and show him you like it. Let your face reflect relaxation and the happiness of your words. A small child soon "catches on" and follows the example of those he loves.

If a child refuses to eat, take his food away and excuse him from the table. Never allow him to play with his food. Loss of appetite in a young child is a first symptom of illness. But if he seems well, do not let him have any food until he eats the meal he missed. If you let him satisfy his hunger with a snack of sweets, he may miss the next meal in the same way. This can start a food problem. Serve him the meal he missed when he is hungry enough to eat it.

Feeding problems are often started by forcing the child into good table manners too soon. Remember *your first aim is to teach the child to like all of the foods he needs to eat.* He will soon pick up the correct manners by your good example, and you can help him by showing the same politeness you would like to receive.

Learn to cook food so that it tastes good. If the food is not well cooked, children will not eat it. Highly seasoned, burned, or unattractively served foods may cause the child to refuse to eat. In such a case, respect his wish and give him properly cooked and attractively served food. It is easier to prevent poor eating habits than to change bad ones.

Food for the Older Person

It may seem strange to put food for the older person in a chapter with meals for young children. But young children and older persons have a great deal in common as far as food is concerned. Both need the same variety of well-balanced food in each meal, but fewer calories than people in their working years. Both need small servings at regular meals, and the food they eat should count for health (that is, it should be rich in vitamins, minerals, and a high-grade protein, and low in fat).

Many families have one or more grandparents living in their homes. Their food needs are important, for often older persons have minor ailments that good food can improve.

It is not easy to change the food habits of a lifetime as we become less active when we are older. Many older people have an excellent appetite, and wish to eat as heartily as ever. Naturally, this adds a few pounds every year. Weight increases steadily as they get older, and by age 65 they may find themselves decidedly overweight. This is a disadvantage for health. The weight which is normal for an individual at 22 years of age is the weight which should be maintained throughout the remainder of life.

There are many things we do not know about the human body, but one thing that is agreed upon is that an older person needs about 20 percent fewer calories than people who are under 55. It is desirable to eat less and change food habits gradually in relation to activity, from age 18 on. This accomplishes the goal of holding the weight to what is normal for each one of us at 22 years, and helps maintain vitality as the years go by.

Good Food Helps Older Persons Enjoy Better Health and Greater Independence

One of the most undernourished groups in our population is the elderly. You can see the reason for this. A lifetime of poor food habits catches up with some people in their youth, and with others in their middle years, but it always adds up in the later years to troubles. Many older people show one or more food deficiencies. What, then, is a good diet for the average normal person advanced in years? It is exactly the same well-balanced diet we all need (milk, meat, eggs, fruits, vegetables), with 20 percent fewer calories. The need for protein is now greater than ever before. An older person has a rapid rate of cell breakdown. Many older persons are weak and trembling, exhausted from eating too many starches, sweets, and fats and not getting enough good protein, vitamins, and minerals. They need calcium in their meals to maintain their bones, and this is often far too low. Milk or cheese in meals is good for them. They also need citrus fruit, tomato, or some other good source of vitamin C in meals. Some older people refrain from eating eggs, but unless the doctor forbids it, an aging person needs the variety of excellent nutrients that eggs supply. Look at the pattern for balanced meals on page 13, and follow this, keeping in mind where to cut calories. Better food can help older people retain their memory and enjoy more physical vigor and greater activity in their later years. This gives them more independence, and brings them deeper happiness.

THINKING IT OVER

1. In what way can planning and serving meals to your little sisters or brothers, or baby sitting, help you when you have a family of your own?

2. Why is it important to start a young child liking each new food he tastes?

3. What are some indications of good nutrition in a child?

4. How does a well-balanced diet for an expectant mother help her baby? What foods does she need more than usual? Which foods less than usual?

5. What is the pattern for a well-balanced diet for the pre-school child? How would you decide whether a child needs a snack or not?

6. Describe how you would try to help a young child learn good food habits.

7. What are the benefits from learning good food habits when you are young, rather than breaking bad ones after you are older?

8. In what ways are the food needs of small children and the elderly alike? How do their needs differ from yours?

9. Why do elderly people need 20 percent fewer calories than when they were more active? How can families help them meet their health needs.

APPLYING WHAT YOU KNOW

1. If there is a nursery school in your school or community, get a list of the menus for a week and check them according to the standard for a well-balanced diet for a child. How would these vary from the elderly?

2. Planning menus.
   (1) Plan menus for three days for a family of four with children of one and four years of age.
   (2) Plan complete menus for three days for a family of six including an overweight 75-year-old grandmother, a three-year-old, a 10-year-old boy, a 16-year-old girl, and the parents.

3. Preparing a meal.
   (1) Prepare one or more of the following for a pre-school child, an elderly person, or both.
      (a) Starting with one egg, prepare a balanced breakfast.
      (b) Starting with Welsh rarebit, prepare a balanced lunch.
      (c) Starting with broiled ground beef, prepare a balanced dinner.
   (2) What would you serve for a mid-morning snack for the child and the elderly person in the daily diets you have planned? Mid-afternoon?

HOME EXPERIENCE

1. If there are children in your home, discuss with your mother the possibility of your planning and preparing at least one meal for the youngest child each week. Try to apply what you have learned in preparing the meal, and in helping the child enjoy eating it.

2. Help plan and give a party for a pre-school child. Report your results to your teacher.

32

The Convalescent Needs Good Meals

Who Is a Convalescent?

A convalescent (kŏn'vȧ lĕs'ĕnt) is a person recovering from an illness. The convalescence may be of short duration, as in recovering from a childhood disease such as chicken pox or measles, or from a broken bone, or of longer duration from such an illness as rheumatic fever. Whatever the cause of illness, the patient must have rest, good care, and a nourishing diet that contains a variety of nutrients needed by the body.

A convalescent will get well faster if you give intelligent thought to foods in his diet which build cell tissue. From your study of the preceding units in this

Milk with fruit is a good dish for a convalescent. How can the milk be further enriched to give the patient extra nourishment?

book, you can see that more protein of high quality is needed for a convalescent than is normally needed—for building new tissue and repairing worn tissue. This is because the rate of building new cells is greater. More vitamins and minerals are also needed to bring back the strength faster.

A patient who has had a high fever for a long period of time may have lost weight, because calories are burned faster during a fever. The patient needs the same variety of nutrients as required in a well-balanced diet when he is well. However, the convalescent sometimes has a poor appetite and may not wish to eat the food needed. When this is the case, try to give first the foods which the patient does enjoy eating, provided they are on the diet that has been prescribed by the physician.

Often you need to have patience with the convalescent concerning food. Do not try to force him to eat the food he needs. Rather make as nourishing as possible the foods which he will eat. As he can eat more, his appetite will return, and your task will be easier. An adequate intake of B vitamins is closely related to appetite, and it is well to give thought to increasing these in his diet.

Your physician will tell you the type of diet that your patient needs, and when you can change this.

Types of Diets for a Convalescent

There are three types of diets for the convalescent which the doctor may prescribe.

(1) The *liquid diet* is given to patients who are too sick to eat a soft or solid diet. This diet is easy to eat and quick to digest. It includes:

MILK: Whole and homogenized milk, buttermilk, eggnog, milk shakes, malted milk, cocoa, and skim milk.

EGGS: Soft poached, and soft boiled.

FRUIT AND VEGETABLE JUICES: Citrus, tomato, apricot, prune, and others, strained.

MEAT BROTHS AND SIEVED CREAM SOUPS: Meat, chicken, fish, vegetable.

WHOLE GRAIN OR ENRICHED COOKED CEREALS

DESSERTS: Ice cream, floating island, plain gelatin.

(2) The *soft diet* is more nourishing, and the patient goes on it as soon as possible. It contains meat instead of meat broth, thus giving more protein and other needed nutrients, along with the greater fruit and vegetable content. It will improve the patient's strength faster than the liquid diet. In it you can use all of the foods of the liquid diet plus these:

MILK: In any form, plus cottage cheese.

EGGS: Soft boiled, poached, or scrambled.

FRUITS: Sieved fruits plus juices.

VEGETABLES: Sieved vegetables, boiled or baked rather than fried.

CEREAL-BREAD: Cooked whole grain or enriched.

MEAT: Ground, broiled, baked, or roasted meat of choice, but no fat added.

DESSERTS: Sieved fruit, milk desserts—custards, junket, ice cream, sherbet.

(3) The *light diet* is close to the standard balanced diet pattern given on page 13. It requires a variety of the foods you need in every meal. Nothing has to be sieved or ground. The difference between a light diet and the regular one is in the way the food is cooked and seasoned, and

the amount served. No highly seasoned food is used, nor fried food, nor dishes containing excess fat or sugar. Vegetables should be cooked quickly and simply. Meat should be broiled or roasted or braised, and excess fat should be cut off. Food should be prepared in a way that will save all of the nourishment possible. Since the convalescent is not active, *portions need to be smaller*.

How You Can Help the Patient with Better Food

The doctor tells you which type of diet your patient needs. However, with your scientific knowledge of food you can make this diet far more nourishing. You know that the convalescent needs more high-quality protein, more B vitamins, more of vitamins C and A, and more iron and calcium, and that he may need more calories to help him regain lost weight.

Fortify the diet your patient needs with added high-quality foods. For instance, suppose your patient is on the liquid diet at first. How can you make this more nourishing? Often the doctor prescribes a high intake of liquids. This can be milk drinks, eggs, fruit and vegetable juices, meat broths, and ice cream or soft custard desserts.

Fortify the milk with an egg and dry milk solids. Make the eggnog by the recipe on page 369, but add to one cup of whole milk a half-cup of dry milk solids. This is tripling his riboflavin, thiamine, protein, and calcium and adding a variety of all the other nutrients in milk except fat and vitamin A. You might give him three to five of these a day. Make up a basic recipe at one time for all five

eggnogs, then vary the flavoring with chocolate, vanilla, sieved frozen strawberries, butterscotch, or his other favorite flavors, and include a mashed banana. You can add up to 500 calories in one such drink, and have the important body-building nutrients your patient needs.

To repeat: begin with what your patient likes and build strength and nourishment into those foods. You will soon see his normal appetite returning, and his taste for food enlarging. The sooner he can return to a normal well-balanced diet, the better.

Other Care That Helps the Convalescent

A convalescent in the home requires attention and care, which falls for the most part to the mother. Young people can share this added work. This can be done in helping with the food shopping, cleaning the room, arranging flowers, and bringing books, magazines and other things of interest to the patient. A young person can make many trips back and forth when the patient is upstairs. This greatly cuts fatigue for the mother.

Preparing and serving the patient's meal is an important part of the work for a convalescent. Try to serve his meal before the family eats. Cook his food as part of the family meal if he is on a light diet. A liquid or soft diet requires special preparation.

Alert the patient before the meal is ready, if he is not sleeping. If he is sleeping, let him sleep, and serve the meal when he awakes. When he is ready to eat, help him to the bathroom to refresh himself for eating. If he is well enough

Why is liver an excellent meat for the convalescent? Which type of grapefruit would you serve to a small child? Why?

to sit up in the room, arrange a table or tray near a view at the window. A patient should get out of bed to eat as soon as he can. Arrange the food attractively on a tray. Have contrast in color, texture, and flavor of food, if possible. Place a small bouquet or a flower on the tray. Fresh fruit is attractive and may also serve as dessert.

The convalescent on a liquid diet may need straws. Do not fill the cup or glass so full that he cannot suck the food through the straw without spilling. Straws that can be discarded are more sanitary if the patient has an infection or a contagious disease. The doctor will advise you if the dishes need to be boiled.

After a patient has finished eating, always give him a glass of water so that he may refresh his mouth. This will make him feel better, and it is helpful for mouth hygiene.

Encourage the patient to feed himself as soon as he is able. A convalescent should not be allowed to depend on others when he is well enough to feed himself.

If the patient wishes you to stay while he eats, do so if you can. Keep your conversation light and happy. Bring him news of his friends. Love and kindness are great medicines to heal the sick! Young people are often surprised, when ill, to learn how many people really care.

Let the convalescent see by the expression of your face and the tone of your voice how happy you are to help him. Remember that it is a humbling experience for a person who has been well and strong to find himself sick and dependent on others. If you can put yourself in his place, it will help you know how to make him happy. Let him see that what you do for him you do freely because you love him and want him to be well. He may forget the flowers sent and the food served, but he does not forget what you give of your own mind and spirit to make him happy.

When You Are the Convalescent

Few people live out their lives without finding out what it is like to be a convalescent. If you are the convalescent, turn the above picture around.

Cooperate with those who take care of you. Try to eat some of every food served. Even a little food brings you strength and helps you eat more next time. In the end it is up to each convalescent to bring himself back to health. You can have the finest doctor and loving care from your family, but you can do more for yourself than anyone else can. Let your worries fall away and think how lucky you are to be as well off as you are. Obey the doctor's directions exactly, and cooperate in eating and resting.

Try to be considerate and not ask for help you do not need. Express your appreciation to those who help you. This fine attitude helps heal your body just as does the food which nourishes and rebuilds your tissue. When you do all that you can for yourself, it lightens the burden of illness in the home and helps you get well faster.

Keeping the Record

If the doctor asks that a record be kept of the patient's temperature, the liquid he takes, the food he eats and his symptoms, do this accurately. If the patient is old enough and not too ill, he may do this for himself. The person who keeps the record is acting in the capacity of nurse. The doctor depends on a good record from the nurse to guide him in what to prescribe next for the patient. If you do not understand what type of diet the doctor wishes the patient to have, write it down. Follow the diet just as he prescribes it. Little things such as these add up to speed the recovery of the convalescent.

 WORDS TO WORK WITH

Convalescent (kŏn′vȧ lĕs′ĕnt): One who is recovering from an illness.

 THINKING IT OVER

1. When is a person a convalescent?
2. What role does food play in bringing health to a convalescent?
3. Explain what you would give for each meal to a patient who needs a liquid diet. A soft diet. A light diet.

4. How can you speed recovery by fortifying the nourishment in the diet prescribed for the patient?
5. The diet of the convalescent needs to be high in what nutrients?
6. How does the light diet differ from the normal diet?

7. Why is it important for the convalescent to feel that those who help him do so because they love him?

8. How could you be the "ideal" convalescent?

9. How can keeping a record help the recovery of the convalescent?

PROBLEMS TO SOLVE

1. Ask a parent who is a doctor or nurse to speak to your class on the role of food in the convalescent's recovery.

2. Look into the possibility of showing a film that explains how to care for a convalescent.

3. Discuss:
   (1) The kind of care you desire when you are the convalescent.
   (2) How you can help yourself get well.

APPLYING WHAT YOU KNOW

1. Planning menus for a convalescent.
   (1) Plan menus for three days for a boy of 14 on a liquid diet.
   (2) Plan menus for two days for a child of five on a soft diet.
   (3) Plan menus for yourself on light, soft, and liquid diets for three days each.

   (4) Plan what you would give between meals to a convalescent on each type of diet you have studied.

2. Plan an emergency shelf of food that might be used for a convalescent for one day on each type of diet.

3. If time permits, prepare and serve a day's menu for one or more of the following: a liquid diet; a soft diet; a light diet.

EVALUATING

1. Did each meal meet the standard given on page 13 for the ideal pattern?

2. Where did it fail to measure up to standard? What can you do about this?

3. Did the tray look attractive? Was the food well prepared?

4. If you were the patient, would you enjoy the meals you prepared?

HOME EXPERIENCE

With your mother's cooperation, plan and shop for an emergency food shelf for the convalescent. Prepare some of the foods which you learned to cook at school, and serve as a part of a balanced meal. Should someone be ill in your home, make a plan to use for his benefit what you have learned.

FURTHER READING

"Aging and its Social Aspects," Breen. *Journal of Home Economics*, Oct., 1962.

Chicken in the Freezer. U.S.D.A., Washington, D.C., 1957.

Complete Book of Home Preserving, Anne Seranne. Doubleday & Company, Inc., Garden City, N.Y., 1955.

"Filial Responsibility and the Aging," Schorr. *Journal of Home Economics*, April, 1962.

Food and Your Weight. Home and Garden Bulletin 74. U.S.D.A., Washington, D.C., 1967.

Food for the Family with Young Children. Home and Garden Bulletin 5. U.S.D.A., Washington, D.C., 1960.

Food for Young Children in Group Care. Publication 295. U.S. Dept. of Health, Education, and Welfare, Washington, D.C.

Food Guide for Older Folks. Home and Garden Bulletin 17. U.S.D.A., Washington, D.C., 1954.

Foods Your Children Need. Leaflet 14, prepared by Children's Bureau in cooperation with Institute of Home Economics. U.S.D.A., Washington, D.C., 1958.

Freezing Combination Main Dishes. Home and Garden Bulletin 40. U.S.D.A., Washington, D.C., 1954.

Home Canning of Fruits and Vegetables. Home and Garden Bulletin 8. U.S.D.A., Washington, D.C., 1957.

"Home Economics Philosophy on Aging," *Journal of Home Economics*, Oct., 1962.

Home Freezers . . . Their Selection and Use. Home and Garden Bulletin 48, U.S.D.A., Washington, D.C., 1961.

Home Freezing of Fruits and Vegetables. Home and Garden Bulletin 10. U.S.D.A., Washington, D.C., 1957.

Home Freezing of Poultry. Home and Garden Bulletin 70. U.S.D.A., Washington, D.C., 1960.

How to Control Your Weight. Booklet. Metropolitan Life Insurance Company, New York, N.Y.

How to Make Jellies, Jams and Preserves at Home. Home and Garden Bulletin 56. U.S.D.A., Washington, D.C., 1957.

How to Reduce Surely and Safely, Herbert Pollack, M.D., and A. D. Morse, McGraw-Hill Book Company, New York, N.Y., 1955.

Making Pickles and Relishes at Home. Home and Garden Bulletin 92. U.S.D.A., Washington, D.C., 1964.

"Nutritional Status and Dietary Habits of Older People," E. Batchelder, *American Dietetic Association Journal* 33(5):471–476 (May, 1957).

Reduce and Stay Reduced, rev. ed., Norman Joliffe. Simon & Schuster, Inc., New York, N.Y., 1957.

Reduce with Low Calorie Diet, Marvin Small. Pocket Books, Inc., New York, N.Y., 1959.

Stay Slim for Life, Ida Jean Kain and Mildred B. Gibson. Doubleday & Company, Inc., Garden City, N.Y., 1958.

"The White House Conference on Aging," Hawkins. *Journal of Home Economics*, March, 1961.

Your Child from One to Six. Publication 30. U.S. Dept. of Health, Education, and Welfare, Washington, D.C., 1956.

Cookbook

INCLUDING LOW-CALORIE, HIGH-NUTRIENT RECIPES

Table of Contents

Consult index for individual recipes.

Before You Begin

Good cooking is an art which applies the science of nutrition in preparing balanced meals. You can learn this art. It is through accurate, dependable recipes that we bring what we know about food to the place where it can help us—the family table. You should use accurately proportioned recipes, applying modern knowledge of nutrition, to prepare food that is appetizing in appearance and tasty in flavor. This is important for your appearance and your health now and affects you in many ways throughout life.

Basic recipes have been selected for this cookbook to help you achieve these goals. Through practice in using them, you acquire the skill of a good cook—one further step in becoming a manager of family food on the highest level. The recipes are arranged in units to supplement the subject matter in the text. They are simply written, and the steps are easy to follow. The steps in the recipes will help you establish good work habits in the use of your time and energy (such as measuring dry ingredients before liquid ones so that the same utensil may be used without washing, or sifting dry ingredients into the bowl where they will be used, or browning onion in the pan where the recipe will be cooked). The recipes aim to help you apply the newer knowledge of nutrition in the selection and preparation of food—for example, less use of high fat content items and a greater use of vegetable oil instead of firm fat wherever possible. Using dry skim milk is an example of saving money while retaining high nourishment.

The recipes have been tested by homemakers feeding their own families, and by teachers and pupils in the schools. However, this is not to suggest that they cannot be improved. On the contrary, the author suggests variations for basic recipes, with the hope that you will adapt a basic recipe to fit the particular taste and income of your

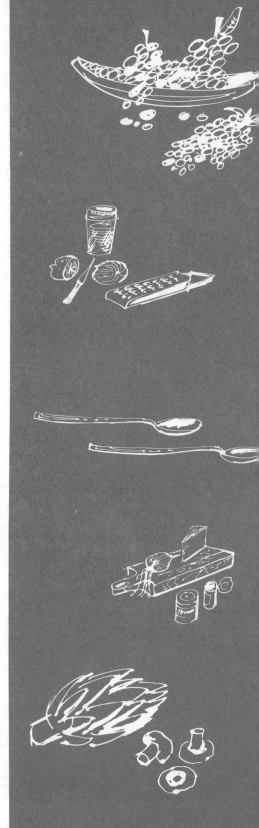

352

own family. This is to further encourage you to look upon cooking with an experimental attitude and to try to reach new heights in preparing attractive, tasty, healthy meals that you and your family will enjoy. When you can do this, cooking becomes a creative experience that brings deep satisfaction now, and will help you when you have your own home.

1 · HOW TO USE RECIPES FOR SUCCESS IN COOKING

1. In selecting the recipe, check it to see *if*: (1) it fits your needs for the meal planned; (2) it is within your food budget; (3) it suits the tastes of your family; (4) it can be made in the amount of time available; (5) the ingredients it contains, and the steps in making it, follow good nutritional principles; (6) you have the ingredients and utensils needed, or suitable substitutions; and (7) you are making the best use of seasonal foods, and spending your food money wisely.

2. Read the entire recipe carefully and critically before you start to cook. Be sure that you understand what is meant by each word, and how to follow each step.

3. Assemble ingredients and utensils in one working center before you start.

4. Keep in mind that it is usually not wise to alter the amount of flour, sugar, fat, or liquid in recipes for baked foods, but that you may change flavoring and seasoning to suit your taste. In other foods, alter fat to suit your taste.

5. Follow the directions for mixing just as they are given.

6. Be accurate with time to save flavor and food values. Preheat an oven to correct temperature before baking, and time a baked food exactly with a timer or an alarm clock. A thermometer is most accurate for timing the cooking of meats and some other foods.*

7. Plan ahead and learn to prepare recipes that require more than one work period, such as yeast bread and baked beans.

8. Study variations given with recipes, and experiment with flavorings and seasonings to suit the tastes of your family.

2 · ABBREVIATIONS FOR MEASUREMENTS

(All measurements in this book are level.)

teaspoon = t.	ounce = oz.	minutes = min.
tablespoon = T.	pound = lb.	inch = in.
cup = c.	gram = gm.	degree Fahrenheit = ° F
pint = pt.	milligram = mg.	square = sq.
quart = qt.	hour = hr.	package = pkg.
gallon = gal.		

3 · EQUAL MEASURES

dash / pinch } = less than ⅛ t.	¾ c. = 12 T.	1 lb. = 16 oz.
1 T. = 3 t.	½ c. = 8 T.	1 pt. = 2 c.
1 c. = 16 T.	⅓ c. = 5 T. plus 1 t.	1 qt. = 2 pt.
	¼ c. = 4 T.	1 gal. = 4 qt.

* Cooking temperatures in the following recipes are given in degrees Fahrenheit (F).

4 · EQUAL MEASURES IN FOOD

4 c. all-purpose flour = 1 lb.
4¾ c. cake flour = 1 lb.
2¼ c. granulated sugar = 1 lb.
2¼ c. brown sugar = 1 lb.
4 c. grated cheese = 1 lb.
2 c. fat = 1 lb.
2½ c. solid hydrogenated
    shortenings = 1 lb.
2 c. milk or water = 1 lb.
1 stick butter = ¼ lb. or ½ c.
5-7 whole eggs = 1 c.
8-9 egg whites = 1 c.
1 c. uncooked rice = 2½ c. cooked
1 c. uncooked macaroni = 2 c. cooked
1 large lemon = ¼ c. juice
1 medium orange = ⅓ c. juice
3 large bananas = 1 lb.

1 whole egg = ½ t. baking powder
1 c. nutmeats = ⅓ c. fat
1 c. honey = 1¼ c. sugar plus ¼ c.
    liquid
1 sq. chocolate (1 oz.) = 3 T. cocoa
    plus ½ T. fat
1 c. sour milk = 1 c. sweet milk plus
    2 T. lemon juice
1 c. sifted all-purpose flour less 2 T.
    = 1 c. cake flour
1 T. cornstarch = 2 T. flour
1⅓ c. dry milk plus 1 c. water = 1 c.
    skim milk (follow directions on
    package)
½ c. evaporated milk plus ½ cup of
    water = 1 c. whole milk

5 · CAKE PAN SIZES

Layer: 8 x 1¼ or 9 x 1½
Square: 8 x 8 x 2 or 9 x 9 x 2
Loaf or oblong: 9 x 5 x 3 or 10 x 5 x 3
Jelly roll: 15½ x 10½ x 1

6 · MEANING OF OVEN TEMPERATURES (FAHRENHEIT)

Very slow: 250°-275°
Slow: 300°-325°
Moderate: 350°-375°
Hot: 400°-425°
Very hot: 450°-475°

7 · TEMPERATURE DEFINITIONS (FAHRENHEIT)

Boiling point of water: 212°
Simmering point of water: 180°-185°
Soft ball stage for syrups: 234°-240°
Hard crack stage for syrups: 255°
Caramel stage for syrups: 320°
Jellying point for jams and jellies: 220°

8 · TEST FOR DONENESS IN BAKED FOODS

Since ovens are not always accurately regulated, time stated in a recipe has to be checked with some practical tests for doneness.

1. A baked product is done if a metal cake tester or toothpick comes out clean when inserted in the center. If it is wet or sticky, cook a few minutes longer until it tests clean.

2. A baked product is done if the center is firm, and springs back when touched lightly with the finger; or if it shrinks slightly from the sides of the pan.

9 · KINDS AND USE OF BAKING POWDERS*

Tartrate: use 1½ t. per cup of flour
Phosphate: use 1½ t. per cup of flour
Double-acting baking powder (also called S.A.S.): use 1 t. per cup of flour
(Unless otherwise specified, the baking powder used for these recipes is double acting.)

* *Foods and Principles of Cookery.* N. K. Finch and C. A. Francis, (Prentice-Hall, Inc.. Englewood Cliffs, N.J., 1948) page 87.

10 · COOKING TERMS AND DEFINITIONS

Add alternately: to add a part of one ingredient and then part of another, as flour and milk are added in making a cake.

Bake: to cook in a heated oven. This is called roasting when applied to meat.

Beat: to mix until smooth with a spoon, an egg beater, an electric mixer, or an electric blender.

Blanche: to submerge first in boiling water for a few seconds or minutes, and then in cold water, as for tomatoes, peaches, or almonds.

Blend: to combine two or more ingredients until thoroughly mixed.

Boil: to cook at boiling temperature in liquid. (When bubbles form in a liquid, the mixture is boiling. This can take place on low heat.)

Braise: to cook meat or vegetables in a small amount of liquid by covering and simmering until tender.

Broil: to cook under direct heat, as in a broiler or on live coals.

Chop: to cut into small pieces.

Cream: to soften and blend fat and sugar until smooth and light by mixing with a spoon or an electric mixer.

Cube: to cut into small even pieces.

Cut in: to mix evenly a solid mixture, such as fat, into a dry mixture, such as flour, by using knives, a pastry blender, finger tips, an electric mixer, or an electric blender.

Dash: a shake of a shaker for a small amount of salt, or pepper, or spice.

Dice: to cut into small pieces.

Dissolve: to mix a dry ingredient with a liquid until in solution, as sugar and water.

Dredge: to coat lightly with a dry substance, such as flour, meal, bread crumbs, or sugar.

Fold in: to blend by use of a wide spoon, spatula, or wire whip by cutting down through a mixture such as beaten egg whites, bringing a portion up, and folding it over into mixture gently.

Fry: to cook in fat.

Garnish: to add color or to decorate.

Grate: to cut by rubbing against a grater, as lemon or orange peel, or an onion.

Grind: to cut by putting through a food chopper or blender.

Ingredient: one of the separate items that make up a recipe.

Mince: to cut into fine pieces.

Pan-broil: to cook on a hot ungreased or lightly greased skillet or griddle, pouring off fat as it accumulates.

Pare: to remove outer covering, as in peeling potatoes, with a knife or peeler.

Peel: to remove outer covering.

Preheat: to heat to desired temperature before starting cooking.

Purée: cooked food pressed through a food mill or a sieve to form a smooth product.

Sauté: to cook in skillet or saucepan in small amount of hot fat until tender.

Scald: to heat milk or other liquid hot (until bubbles form on sides) but not boiling.

Scallop: to bake in layers with a sauce.

Sieve: to press through a strainer.

Simmer: to cook in a liquid just below the boiling point.

Steam: to cook in a covered pan over boiling water.

Thicken: to make liquid more dense, as a hot meat or vegetable broth with flour, cornstarch, or other thickening agent.

Toast: to brown in a toaster, broiler, oven, or on live coals.

Toss: to mix lightly with two forks or spoons.

Whip: to lighten a mixture by incorporating air into it to increase the volume with an egg-beater or electric beater, as in beating whipped cream or egg whites.

Appetizers

CHEESE KABOBS

Cut assorted cheeses in ½-in. cubes and arrange alternately on picks; or arrange alternately with fresh fruit, such as grapes, cherries, berries, or cubes of apple, pineapple, orange, or grapefruit.

CREAM CHEESE-STUFFED FRUIT

1. Mix one 8-oz. package of cream cheese with ¼ lb. blue cheese, ½ c. broken nutmeats, 2 T. lime juice, and enough sour cream to make a paste.
2. Stuff cheese mixture between halves of dried dates, prunes, figs, or apricots, and serve instead of cookies for refreshment or dessert, or as part of a salad.

TOASTED CHEESE DREAMS

1. Prepare a spread of ½ lb. grated sharp cheese, 1 t. Worcestershire sauce, 1 T. grated onion, and a dash of cayenne pepper.
2. Spread on crisp crackers and quickly toast under broiler until cheese is melted (leave broiler door open while toasting).
3. Serve hot at once as an appetizer or with a salad, or for party refreshments.

RUTH WHITE'S COTTAGE CHEESE SHRIMP DIP

1 c. cottage cheese
⅔ c. shrimp (4½ oz. can)
1 T. lemon juice
1-2 t. prepared horseradish
1 t. paprika
   dash Tabasco sauce
⅛ t. pepper
¼ c. chili sauce
½ c. sour cream
2 t. grated onion

Yield: 2½ cups

1. Place all ingredients except sour cream in mixing bowl or blender and blend till smooth.
2. Fold in sour cream. Cover and chill till ready to use.
3. Bring to room temperature and use as dip or spread. Freeze leftovers for future use.

Milk in Beverages

RUTH WHITE'S LOW-CALORIE, LOW-FAT COCOA

¼ c. cocoa
¼ c. sugar
½ c. water
2 c. nonfat dry milk
1 c. evaporated milk
1 t. vanilla   dash salt
4 c. water

(High in nutrients. Each 8-oz. serving contains about 18 grams protein.)

4-6 servings

1. In 2-qt. saucepan blend first 3 ingredients until smooth. Heat to boiling and boil 1 minute.
2. Mix dry milk with 1 cup water until smooth; add this and remaining ingredients except vanilla. Heat scalding hot. Add vanilla. Serve at once.
3. Garnish with marshmallow, if desired.

Variations

COLD CHOCOLATE MILK: Place ice cubes in glass; and when cocoa is cool, pour over the ice. If desired, add scoop of ice cream.

HOT SPICED COCOA: To step 1, add ¼ t. cinnamon, ¼ t. allspice, ⅛ t. nutmeg, 1 T. grated orange peel.

QUICK COCOA: To hot milk mixture, as given, add 6 T. instant chocolate-flavor mix.

ORANGE CHOCOLATE MILK: Chill cocoa and add one 6-oz. can frozen orange juice blended with 1 pt. vanilla ice cream and pour into glasses. Top with slice of fresh orange or scoop of orange sherbet.

MALTED MILK: To cocoa recipe add malted-mix powder according to directions on package. Serve hot or cold, as in preceding recipes.

STRAWBERRY MILK SHAKE

1 pkg. frozen strawberries
2 c. nonfat dry milk
1 c. water (cold)
dash salt
1 t. vanilla
1 T. lemon juice
1 pt. ice cream

4-6 servings

1. Blend dry milk and water until smooth.
2. Add remaining ingredients, and blend.
3. Pour into tall glasses over ice cubes.
4. Garnish top with a piece of fresh fruit, if desired.

Variations

For other fruit-flavored milk shakes, use instead of strawberries: 1, 6-oz. can frozen *orange juice;* 1 c. *crushed pineapple, peaches, bananas,* or other fruit of choice.

Cereal Cooked in Milk

OATMEAL COOKED IN MILK

4 servings

1½ c. quick or rolled oats
1⅓ c. nonfat dry milk
3 c. boiling water
½ t. salt
2 T. brown sugar

1. Mix water, salt, sugar, and milk and bring to boil.
2. Gradually stir oats into boiling milk.
3. Reduce heat as low as possible, or place pan over boiling water (double boiler).
4. Cover and cook until it suits your taste (5 min. for quick oats, to 30 min. for rolled oats).
5. Serve hot as main dish for breakfast, with brown sugar and milk.

Variations

1. Add 1 c. of raisins, dates, or figs at Step 1.
2. Mix equal parts of other whole grain or enriched cereals with oats, following directions on package for amount of liquid.

MILK CINNAMON TOAST*

4 servings

8 slices of whole wheat or enriched bread
1⅓ c. nonfat dry milk
4 c. water
1-2 T. fat of choice
4 T. honey or brown sugar
2 t. cinnamon
dash salt

1. Mix milk with water, and heat over low heat in covered pan until scalding hot.
2. Toast bread in broiler until brown on one side.
3. Turn bread, and spread with the mixture of fat, honey, and cinnamon.
4. Toast with broiler door open until golden brown.
5. Place toast in large soup bowls, pour hot milk over it, and serve at once.

* This is a quick, nourishing, and tasty hot cereal that is also inexpensive.

Variations

CHEESE BISCUITS: Add ½ cup shredded cheddar cheese at step 3. Sprinkle tops with ½ cup shredded cheese.

CINNAMON BISCUITS: Pat dough ¼ inch thick. Spread with topping (page 406). Roll as for jelly roll. Slice ¾ inch thick. Bake on lightly oiled cooky sheet at 450°F. for 12-15 minutes. Serve as dessert, for breakfast, for a party with a salad as main dish, or with cocoa or other beverage.

> ## Cheese Dishes as a Meat Alternate for Lunch or Supper

WELSH RAREBIT*

4 servings

1 T. vegetable oil
3 T. flour
1⅓ c. nonfat dry milk
3 c. water
½ t. salt
¼ t. celery salt
½ t. dry mustard
1 T. grated onion
2 c. grated sharp cheddar cheese (½ lb.)
6 slices toast, or English muffins

1. Place oil in saucepan, add onion, and cook over moderate heat 1 min.
2. Mix milk with water, salt,. celery salt, and mustard, and blend.
3. Add flour and ½ c. of milk mixture and blend. Then add remaining milk mixture.
4. Turn heat low, cover pan, and cook until thickened, stirring to keep smooth.
5. Add grated cheese, and stir until melted.
6. Serve on hot toast as the protein dish for lunch or supper. (Garnish with tomato sections, paprika, or parsley.)

Variations

1. Add 1 t. of Worcestershire sauce, or 1 t. curry powder, or 1 t. chili powder at Step 4.
2. Add 1½ c. chopped hard-cooked eggs at Step 4.
3. Add 1 c. diced poultry, fish, or ham at Step 4.
4. Add 1½ c. of cooked vegetable of choice at Step 4.

* Welsh Rarebit originated in Wales, and as a joke was called "rabbit," a substitute for meat. The dish became popular in other parts of Europe and the name eventually became "Welsh rarebit."

QUICK CURRIED WELSH RAREBIT

4 servings

1 can cream of mushroom
    soup
1 c. whole or evaporated milk
½ lb. diced sharp cheddar
    cheese
½ t. dry mustard
½ t. curry powder
1 t. Worcestershire sauce
4 slices toast

1. Heat soup and milk (in covered pan) over low heat until scalding hot.
2. Add cheese and remaining ingredients, and stir until smooth.
3. Serve hot at once on toast.
4. Garnish with tomato wedges, parsley, or watercress.

Variations

1. Use cream of tomato soup instead of mushroom.
2. Add 1 c. diced poultry, tuna fish, or other meat or vegetable of choice at Step 2.

CHEESE SALADS

For a variety of cheese salads see page: 99, an example of how cottage cheese may be used with any combination of fruits in a salad; 381, stuffed fruit with cheese; 413, chef's salad bowl.

CHEESE FONDUE

4 servings

1½ c. water
⅔ c. nonfat dry milk
1½ c. bread crumbs
2 c. (½ lb.) grated sharp
    cheddar cheese
¼ t. celery salt
½ t. salt
1 T. grated onion
½ t. dry mustard
    dash Tabasco
3 slightly beaten egg yolks
3 egg whites

1. Preheat oven to 375°.
2. Mix milk with water and heat in covered pan over low direct heat.
3. Add bread crumbs, grated cheese, and all seasonings to hot milk.
4. Add egg yolks and mix.
5. Beat egg whites until they stand in moist peaks and fold hot mixture into egg whites, using a broad spatula with an over and under movement.
6. Pour into a 1½ qt. oiled baking dish.
7. Set dish in pan of hot water and bake until knife comes clean when inserted in middle (about 40 min.).
8. Serve hot at once as meat alternate for lunch or supper.

MACARONI AND CHEESE

4 servings

1¼ c. dry macaroni (broken)
2½ c. water
1 t. salt
3 T. flour
2 T. grated onion
¼ c. diced celery
½ lb. grated sharp cheddar cheese
1 t. vegetable oil
¾ c. nonfat dry milk*
½-¾ c. water*

*If richer sauce is desired, omit dry milk and water and use ½ to ¾ c. evaporated milk.

1. Bring 2½ c. water to boil. Add macaroni.
2. Cover pan, reduce heat, and simmer 10 min. Add diced celery and onion and simmer 5 min. more.
3. Preheat oven to 375°.
4. Add flour to dry milk, blend with ½-¾ c. water until smooth, and pour over macaroni and remaining water.
5. Stir lightly until sauce is thick and smooth.
6. Add one-half cheese and remaining ingredients, and mix lightly.
7. Pour into oiled baking dish (1½ qt.), top with remaining cheese, and bake about 15 min., or until brown.
8. Serve hot as a meat alternate for a balanced lunch or supper.

Variations

1. Substitute 1 c. canned tomatoes for milk and water in Step 4.
2. Add 1 pkg. frozen peas at Step 5.
3. Add 1 c. of diced left-over chicken or ham at Step 5.

QUICK PIZZA PIE**

6 servings

1 recipe biscuit dough (see page 360)
1 c. cottage cheese (or ricotta)
½ lb. grated sharp cheddar or mozzarella cheese
1 T. vegetable oil
¼ t. garlic salt (or crushed clove garlic)
¼ t. oregano
1½ c. tomato paste or tomato sauce (see page 428)
grated parmesan cheese

1. Preheat oven to 425°. Oil pans.
2. Pat or roll biscuit dough into two 9"-10" pie pans, or make 6 individual pies, shaping them on cookie sheet.
3. Mix tomato sauce with seasoning and heat.
4. Spread half of cheese on dough evenly, and cover with tomato sauce.
5. Spread remaining cheese, using cottage cheese first, then sharp cheddar; top with grated parmesan.
6. Bake in hot oven about 20 min. or until done.
7. Serve hot at once with a salad, a green vegetable, milk, and a fruit dessert.

** A generous use of cheese makes this a nourishing dish.

Variations

1. Add ½ lb. mushrooms that have been sautéed in fat at Step 5.
2. Add ½ lb. diced and cooked sausage links at Step 5.
3. Add ½ c. sliced olives at Step 5.
4. Substitute yeast dough (see page 407) for biscuit dough and take two class periods to make.

RUTH WHITE'S LOW-FAT CHEESE SOUFFLÉ

4 servings

6 T. flour
⅛ t. celery salt
1 t. paprika
½ t. salt
1 T. grated onion
dash Tabasco sauce
1 t. Worcestershire sauce
2 c. water
⅔ c. nonfat dry milk
5 egg yolks
5 egg whites
½ lb. (2 c.) grated sharp
  cheddar cheese

1. Preheat oven to 375°.
2. Blend flour and seasonings with ½ c. water until smooth. Add nonfat dry milk and remaining water, blend, and cook until thickened.
3. Stir grated cheese into hot white sauce, and cook until smooth, stirring constantly.
4. Beat egg whites until they stand in moist peaks.
5. Beat egg yolks slightly and add to hot mixture.
6. Fold hot mixture into egg whites, and pour into an ungreased baking dish (1½ qt.) and bake until done and golden brown (about 40-45 min.).
7. Serve hot at once as a meat alternate in a balanced lunch or dinner.

Variations

1. Add 1 c. ground or diced ham at Step 4.
2. Add 1 c. leftover ham to 2 c. Ruth White's Tomato Sauce (see page 428) and serve over soufflé.
3. Substitute tomato juice for milk.

Milk in Desserts

VANILLA FLUFF PUDDING

1 c. evaporated milk
1 c. water
4 T. flour
½ c. sugar
½ t. salt
⅛ t. nutmeg
1 t. vanilla
2 egg yolks
2 egg whites
½ c. milk

6 servings

1. Mix evaporated milk with water in top of double boiler, cover, and heat until scalding hot.
2. Mix sugar, flour, and ½ c. cold milk until smooth. Add egg yolks and blend.
3. Gradually add hot milk to egg-yolk mixture, stirring constantly until smooth and thickened.
4. Add salt to egg whites and beat until they stand in moist peaks.
5. Add vanilla to egg-yolk mixture, blend, and fold hot mixture into the beaten egg whites. Cover and let stand for 10 min.
6. Pour into individual sauce or sherbet dishes, and chill.
7. To serve, garnish with fresh, frozen, or canned fruit, toasted nuts, or shaved chocolate.

Variations

1. Pour into a prepared pie shell, spread meringue on top, and bake at 425° for 10-12 min. or until brown.
2. For Caramel Pudding, substitute brown sugar for white sugar and add ½ t. mapelene flavoring.
3. For Chocolate Pudding, add ¼ c. cocoa and ¼ c. more sugar at Step 2.
4. For Coconut Pudding, add ½ c. moist coconut at Step 5.
5. For Banana Pudding, line a casserole with vanilla wafers, a layer of sliced bananas, and a layer of pudding. Repeat. Chill and spread a thin layer of whipped cream over top when ready to serve. Garnish with fresh banana slices or sliced almonds.
6. For Pineapple Pudding, add 1 c. drained crushed pineapple at Step 5.

RICE OR BREAD PUDDING

4 servings

2 c. milk
1 c. cooked rice or 1½ c. bread
   crumbs
1 t. fat
⅓ c. brown sugar
¼ t. salt
¼ t. nutmeg
½ c. raisins
2 eggs, beaten

1. Heat milk. Gradually add all remaining ingredients, stirring as added.
2. Pour into greased baking dish (1 qt. size). Sprinkle top with coconut, if desired.
3. Bake at 350° (moderate oven) about 1 hour, or until set.

FLOATING ISLAND

4-5 servings

PART ONE   1½ c. milk (fresh)   2 T. sugar
             1 T. flour   1 t. vanilla
             3 egg yolks

1. Heat milk until scalding hot in a covered wide pan or skillet.
2. Beat egg yolks lightly, and add sugar, flour, vanilla, and ¼ c. hot milk.
3. Stir egg-yolk mixture gradually into hot milk and heat over very low heat until mixture coats spoon, being careful not to boil.
4. Cover, turn off heat at once, and prepare Part Two.

PART TWO   3 egg whites   ½ c. granulated sugar
             ¼ t. salt   ½ t. almond extract
             ½ t. cream of tartar

1. Beat egg whites with salt and cream of tartar until foamy.
2. Add sugar, 1 T. at a time, beating after each addition until all sugar is dissolved and meringue stands in moist peaks.
3. Add almond extract with last addition of sugar.
4. Drop meringue by tablespoons onto hot custard.
5. Cover pan tightly and let stand for 10 min. or until meringues are firm and set.
6. Remove meringues carefully with a slotted spoon or pancake turner and set aside on a cookie sheet or waxed paper.
7. Pour custard from Part One into a large glass bowl or individual sherbet dishes, and top with meringue. Chill in refrigerator.
8. Garnish with fresh or frozen fruit, toasted almonds, or semi-sweet chocolate slivers and serve cold as dessert or party refreshments.

ORANGE REFRIGERATOR ICE CREAM

4-5 servings

1 c. evaporated milk
1 c. nonfat dry milk
1 6-oz. can frozen orange
    juice concentrate
3 T. lemon juice
½ t. vanilla
    dash salt
½ c. sugar

1. Blend evaporated and dry milk until smooth and chill in refrigerator tray until crystals form around edge of tray.
2. Whip cold milk in cold bowl until stiff (at high speed with electric beater, or dover beater by hand).
3. Combine remaining ingredients, and add a small amount at a time to whipped milk, blending after each addition.
4. Turn into refrigerator tray, and chill in freezing compartment until firm (about 3 hr. if set at coldest point, or overnight at regular temperature).

Variations

Substitute any of the following fruit juices for orange juice—lemon, lime, apricot, pineapple, grape.

QUICK FUDGE SQUARES

3 dozen squares

1 can (14 oz.) sweetened con-
    densed milk
14 finely crushed graham
    crackers
1 pkg. semi-sweet chocolate
    chips
1 t. baking powder
1 t. vanilla
    dash salt
½ c. broken nutmeats

1. Preheat oven to 325°. Oil a 10 x 6 pan.
2. Place graham crackers between wax paper and crush with rolling pin to a fine meal.
3. Place all ingredients in mixing bowl in order given, and mix thoroughly.
4. Pour into oiled pan, and bake until done (about 25 min.).
5. Remove from oven, cut in 1½-in. squares, and when cool remove from pan with a spatula.
6. Serve plain as dessert, or cut in large squares and top with ice cream.

STRAWBERRY BAVARIAN *(See photo of dessert, page 318.)*   *8-10 servings*

2 T. gelatin	3 egg whites	¼ t. almond extract
2 c. water	½ t. salt	½ c. ground toasted
1 c. nonfat dry milk	½ t. cream of tartar	almonds, if desired
2 T. flour	½ c. sugar	1 qt. fresh strawberries or
3 slightly beaten egg yolks	1 t. vanilla	1 pkg. frozen
		1 c. whipping cream

1. Soften gelatin in ¼ c. of the water.
2. Blend milk and remainder of water in top of double boiler; cover and heat scalding hot.
3. Blend flour with equal amount of sugar and add slightly beaten egg yolks and gelatin mixture.
4. Stir egg-yolk mixture gradually into hot milk and cook until slightly thickened. Then turn off heat and add vanilla and almond extract.
5. Add salt and cream of tartar to egg whites and beat until foamy.
6. Add sugar 1 T. at a time and beat after each addition until dissolved.
7. Fold hot custard into beaten egg whites, cover, and let stand until cool.
8. Whip cream, add almonds, and fold into cool custard.
9. Pour into a 1½-qt. circle-mold and chill in the refrigerator overnight.
10. To serve, set mold in pan of hot water to loosen, and turn upside down on a serving plate. Fill hole with fresh or frozen strawberries (or other fresh fruit in season). Slice and top with strawberries and nonfat dry milk topping, or whipped cream, if desired.

Variations

1. Line mold with lady fingers or sponge cake before pouring in the custard.
2. Fold 2 c. cake crumbs into custard at Step 8.

WHIPPED NONFAT DRY MILK TOPPING

2½ cups

½ c. nonfat dry milk	1. Mix cold water with dry milk in a cold bowl.
½ c. cold water	
2 T. lemon juice	2. Pour into freezing tray and chill until crystals form around edge of pan.
1 t. vanilla	
¼ c. sugar	3. Empty into a cold bowl, add lemon juice and vanilla, and beat at high speed until stiff (or by rotary beater for 10 min.).
	4. Add sugar gradually as for meringue.
	5. Serve as topping on fresh, frozen, or canned fruit, cake, pie, or pudding.

Beverages

EGG-NOG (hot or cold)*

4 servings

1 qt. milk
4 eggs
⅓ c. brown sugar (packed)
dash salt
1 t. vanilla
dash nutmeg

1. Heat milk covered over low direct heat or in top of double boiler until scalding hot.
2. Beat eggs, add remaining ingredients, and mix.
3. Blend ½ c. hot milk into egg mixture.
4. Add egg mixture to hot milk gradually, beating with dover egg beater.
5. Serve hot, or chill and serve cold with scoop of ice cream.
6. Add dash of nutmeg to each glass and serve either as a snack or, without ice cream, for breakfast.

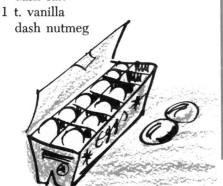

Variations

1. To make more nourishing for a convalescent add 1 c. dry milk at Step 1.
2. To increase vitamin C, add 1 c. fresh or frozen strawberries or frozen orange juice concentrate to chilled egg-nog at end of Step 5.
3. Omit nutmeg and add chocolate or malted milk powder to taste.

* See reason on page 75 for not serving raw egg in beverages.

Eggs for Breakfast or Lunch

POACHED EGGS ON TOAST

4 servings

4 eggs (grade AA or A)
boiling water
salt, pepper, fat
4 slices toast

1. Pour boiling water into skillet about ½ in. deep.
2. Break eggs and slip into water from a saucer.
3. Cover pan, turn off heat, and let stand until white is firm (about 2-3 min. for soft yolk; 5 min. for hard).
4. Lift from water with slotted pancake turner.
5. Serve on a hot plate on hot toast, and season to taste.

Variations

1. Use egg poacher and follow directions that come with it.
2. Serve poached eggs in any of the following ways: on toasted English muffin, split corn bread, ham slice, mashed potatoes, creamed vegetable, cooked greens, hash, or Welsh rarebit on toast.

FRIED EGGS BLINDFOLDED*

4 servings

4 eggs
1 t. fat of choice
1 T. water
salt, pepper

1. If bacon is fried, pour off fat (if not, lightly oil skillet).
2. Break eggs in saucer and slip into hot slightly-oiled skillet.
3. Add water, and cover tightly.
4. Reduce heat as low as possible and cook until white is firm and yolk is blindfolded with white (about 2 min. for soft yolk, and 5 min. for hard).
5. Serve at once on a hot plate and season to taste.

Variations

1. Place a thin slice of cheese in skillet for each egg and break egg on top of cheese.
2. Set covered skillet in oven and bake at 325° for about 15 min.

* Frying eggs by this method is tasty, saves riboflavin, and keeps fat content low.

SCRAMBLED EGGS WITH COTTAGE CHEESE

1. For 1 scrambled egg place 1 teaspoon of vegetable oil in fry pan and heat to spread over the bottom.
2. Add ¼ cup of cottage cheese, 1 large egg, dash of salt and pepper; stir until whites are congealed and egg mixture is soft-firm done. (If several eggs are cooked at once, cover pan and cook slowly until firm.) Serve hot at once as a good protein dish. (1 serving contains 13½ grams protein.)

EGGS COOKED IN THE SHELL*

4 servings

METHOD ONE

1. Place 4 cold eggs in 1-qt. tap water in a 2-qt. sauce pan.
2. Bring water to boil, cover, and turn off heat. Let stand 5 min. for soft-cooked eggs and until water is cold for hard-cooked eggs (about 30 min.).

METHOD TWO

1. Have eggs at room temperature, and slip from a spoon into boiling water as above.
2. Reduce heat to simmer. Cook 3 min. for soft-cooked eggs and 7-10 min. for hard-cooked eggs.
3. Season and serve from shell, or peel and stuff with favorite seasonings, or chop hard-cooked eggs and add to creamed vegetables, meat, cheese sauce, white sauce, or salads.

SHIRRED EGGS AND BACON

4 servings

4 eggs
dash salt
dash pepper
4 T. milk
4 slices bacon

1. Preheat oven to 350°.
2. Line each individual baking dish with a ring of bacon. Cook half-done in oven and pour off fat.
3. Break each egg in saucer and slip into hot bacon ring.
4. Add seasoning and 1 T. milk to each egg, and bake until white is firm (5-8 min.).
5. Serve at once in the dish in which it was cooked.

Variation

Add 1 T. grated sharp cheese to top of each egg instead of milk.

* Eggs cooked in the shell lose no nutrients in cooking.

EGGS AND HAM CREOLE

4 servings

6 hard-cooked eggs
¼ c. diced onion
¼ c. diced celery
1 t. vegetable oil
4 T. flour
2 c. canned tomatoes
1 t. salt
1 t. chili pepper
1½ c. ground ham
¼ lb. grated sharp cheddar
cheese

1. Preheat oven to 375°. Peel hard-cooked eggs and cut in halves lengthwise.
2. Sauté onion and celery in fat until soft (about 3 min.). Pour off surplus fat.
3. Add flour and blend; add tomatoes and seasonings; cook over moderate heat until thickened and smooth.
4. Place eggs in baking dish with yolk sides up; sprinkle ground ham over eggs, and pour tomato sauce over this.
5. Sprinkle grated cheese over top and brown in moderate oven (375°) until cheese is melted and golden brown.
6. Serve hot as a main protein dish.

Variations

1. Add one or more of the following at Step 3: ½ c. diced green pepper, ½ c. cooked or canned mushrooms, more chili pepper if hotter flavor is desired.
2. For Curried Eggs, substitute 1 t. curry powder for chili pepper.
3. Omit chili pepper, and at Step 3 add ham and blend. Serve as egg sauce over cooked broccoli or cauliflower.

TOASTED EGG SANDWICHES OR EGG SALAD

6 servings

4 chopped hard-cooked eggs
½ c. grated carrot
½ c. finely diced celery
1 T. grated onion
2 diced sweet pickles
½ t. salt
2-3 T. mayonnaise
6 large rolls
green lettuce
butter
pepper to taste

1. Prepare sandwich filling by mixing all ingredients except butter, rolls, and lettuce.
2. Slit rolls, butter, and toast in broiler.
3. Add sandwich filling, and serve as part of a lunch, adding green lettuce leaves.

Variations

1. Serve on untoasted roll or with rye or whole wheat bread.
2. Place on cracker rounds, toast, and serve for party refreshment.
3. For Egg Salad, serve on a bed of green lettuce with tomato sections.
4. For Egg and Bean Salad, add 1½ c. cooked red beans and serve on a bed of green lettuce, garnishing with green pepper rings.

FRENCH OR PLAIN OMELET

(See page 62 for illustration.)

4 servings

5-6 eggs
¼ c. milk
¾ t. salt
1 T. vegetable oil
    dash pepper

1. Beat eggs until foamy and add remaining ingredients.
2. Heat fat in skillet, lightly oiling sides of pan. Pour off surplus.
3. Pour egg mixture into skillet and reduce heat.
4. Cover pan, but occasionally lift omelet with fork at sides, allowing egg to run under.
5. When center is firm and bottom is brown, crease in middle with spatula, and fold over to form a half circle.
6. Remove with pancake turner to a hot platter.
7. Garnish with parsley or crisp bacon, and serve at once as part of a balanced meal.

Variations

1. Add ½ c. grated cheese over top of omelet before folding.
2. Make mushroom sauce by adding ½ lb. mushrooms sautéed in fat to 1 can cream of celery soup and serve for lunch as meat alternate.
3. Sprinkle top with 1 c. ground ham at Step 5.
4. For Fluffy Omelet, separate eggs, beat whites separately and fold whites into yoke mixture at end of Step 1.

FRENCH TOAST (using 1 egg per slice of bread)

4 servings

4 eggs
1 t. cinnamon
½ t. salt
1 T. vegetable oil
4 slices enriched bread

1. Beat eggs and add cinnamon and salt. Dip each slice of bread into egg mixture until thoroughly soaked on one side.
2. Turn bread and soak on other side.
3. Fry in lightly-oiled, moderately hot skillet until golden brown on one side; turn and brown on other side.
4. Serve on hot plate with honey, syrup, or jam of choice as part of a balanced breakfast or lunch.

Variations

1. Omit cinnamon.
2. Serve with crisp bacon, ham, or sausage.

Eggs in Bread

POPOVERS

    2 large or 3 medium eggs
    1 c. sifted all-purpose flour
    ½ t. salt
    1 T. brown sugar
    1 c. milk less 2 T.

10-12 popovers

1. Preheat oven to 450°.
2. Oil large muffin tins or custard cups.
3. Beat eggs. Add milk, sugar, salt, and flour. Mix thoroughly with electric or rotary egg beater.
4. Fill heated muffin tins half full.
5. Bake for 15 min.
6. Reduce heat to 350° and bake until golden brown and dry (about 20 min.).
7. Pierce each popover with tooth pick to test for doneness and let steam escape.
8. Serve hot at once as part of a balanced breakfast, lunch, or supper.

RUTH WHITE'S SPOON BREAD

    4 c. water
    2 c. nonfat dry milk
    1 t. salt
    2 T. brown sugar
    1 c. yellow cornmeal
    6 egg yolks
    6 egg whites
    1 T. vegetable oil

(When done, this is soft and similar to a soufflé. It is served with a spoon.)

4-6 servings

1. Preheat oven to 375°.
2. Oil 1½-qt. baking dish (oblong preferred).
3. Mix dry milk and water until smooth and bring to boil.
4. Add all dry ingredients gradually, stirring constantly to prevent lumping (if lumps form beat them out with dover egg beater). Add oil and mix.
5. Cook until thickened (about 2-3 min.).
6. Beat egg whites until they stand in peaks.
7. With same beater, beat egg yolks, and add to hot cornmeal mixture, blending in smoothly.
8. Fold cornmeal mixture into beaten egg whites, pour into hot oiled baking dish, and bake until golden brown (about 30 min.).
9. Serve hot at once with crisp bacon, Canadian bacon, ham, or sausage and syrup or honey as main dish for a balanced breakfast, lunch, or supper.

Variation

Add ½ lb. grated sharp cheese and 1 t. curry powder at Step 4. Serve with a tomato sauce, mushroom sauce, or ham sauce to which has been added 1 t. curry powder (see pages 427-428).

DROP BISCUITS

1. Use recipe for biscuits (see page 360). Add 2-4 T. milk, mix, and drop from spoon on lightly oiled cookie sheet. Bake as for biscuits.
2. Drop into chicken broth and cook as dumplings.
3. Spread over fruit for cobbler and cook as top crust; spread over top of creamed meat or poultry for meat pie.

Eggs in Desserts

RUTH WHITE'S APRICOT SOUFFLE

6 servings

5 eggs separated
2 c. thick apricot pulp
½ c. sugar
½ t. almond extract
dash salt
3 T. lemon juice
1 t. grated lemon rind
½ c. nutmeats (optional)
½ t. cream of tartar

1. Preheat oven to 350°.
2. Prepare thick apricot pulp by cooking dried fruit or using canned fruit. Push through a sieve or food mill, or blend in an electric blender.
3. Mix fruit, almond extract, lemon juice, rind, and nutmeats.
4. Beat egg whites, salt, and cream of tartar until foamy. Then add sugar, 1 T. at a time, beating after each addition until all is used and meringue stands in moist peaks.
5. Fold fruit mixture into egg whites, and bake in an ungreased 1½-qt. baking dish until firm and golden brown (about 45-55 min.).
6. Serve warm or cold with a topping of nonfat dry milk (see page 368), whipped cream, or custard sauce (see page 376).

Variations

1. Ruth White's Quick Apricot Fluff: heat apricot mixture (end of point 3) boiling hot and add egg yolks. Fold hot mixture into beaten egg whites, cover, and let stand for 10 min. Spoon into sherbet dishes and top with sour cream and toasted almonds. Serve warm or chilled.
2. Ruth White's Prune Soufflé: substitute prunes for apricots.

QUICK "BOILED" EGG CUSTARD (sauce)

3 cups

4 eggs
2½ c. low-fat milk
¼ c. sugar
½ t. salt
1 t. vanilla
1 T. flour

1. Heat 2 c. milk scalding hot in covered pan over direct low heat, or in top of double boiler.
2. Beat eggs lightly and add sugar, flour, salt, flavoring, and ¼ c. cold milk; gradually add ¼ c. hot milk, stirring constantly.
3. Add egg mixture to hot milk gradually, stirring until custard coats spoon (the mixture should remain below the boiling point for a smooth texture).
4. Chill and serve as a thin sauce over fruit, pudding, or cake, or in sherbet dishes as dessert (can be made in 10-15 min.).

Variations

1. For Lemon Sauce, use 1 t. grated lemon peel and 1 T. lemon juice.
2. Place fruit of choice in bottom of sherbet dish before pouring in the hot custard mixture. Use such fruits as: half peach, apricot, pineapple chunks, pitted prunes, orange sections with coconut, pitted cherries, fresh peaches, pears, blueberries, bananas, or other fruit of choice.

BAKED CUP CUSTARDS

1. Preheat oven to 350°. Substitute brown sugar for white sugar in egg custard sauce recipe.
2. Pour hot custard mixture into custard cups at Step 3 and set in pan of scalding hot water. Bake until a silver knife comes out clean when inserted in center of custard (about 25-30 min.).
3. Chill and serve in custard cup, or remove and serve with a chocolate sauce or fruit sauce; or top with nutmeats, grated semi-sweet chocolate, or nutmeg.

RUTH WHITE'S FLUFFY CUSTARD

1. Separate eggs in basic egg custard sauce recipe. Beat egg yolks and follow Steps 1, 2, and 3.
2. Beat egg whites until they stand in peaks and are firm, but not dry. Add ½ t. almond extract.
3. Fold hot custard sauce over egg whites, cover, and let stand until cool.
4. Serve chilled in sherbet dishes and top with fresh or frozen fruit.

Variation

Freeze mixture in tray and serve as frozen custard.

RUTH WHITE'S BANANA MERINGUE

4 servings

2 large bananas
2 T. lemon or lime juice
½ c. sieved apricots (stewed or canned)
½ c. cookie or cake crumbs
2 egg whites
5 T. sugar
¼ t. almond extract
dash salt
½ t. cream of tartar
¼ c. coconut

1. Preheat oven to 400°. Split bananas lengthwise, dip thoroughly in lemon juice, and arrange equal distance apart on cookie sheet.
2. Mix remaining lemon juice with apricots and crumbs.
3. Cut each banana slice in halves and stuff apricot mixture between halves, pushing halves together.
4. Add salt, cream of tartar, and almond extract to egg whites and beat until foamy.
5. Add 1 T. of sugar at a time to egg whites, beating after each addition until dissolved.
6. Spoon meringue that stands in firm peaks onto stuffed banana, covering top completely.
7. Sprinkle top with coconut and bake in hot oven (400°) until golden brown (about 8-10 min.).
8. Serve at once or later as dessert or party refreshment.

RUTH WHITE'S CHOCOLATE FLUFF

4-6 servings

½ c. nonfat dry milk
½ c. water
12 marshmallows
½ c. semi-sweet chocolate chips
2 eggs separated
dash salt
½ t. vanilla
7 crushed graham crackers
⅓ c. whipped heavy cream
12 toasted almonds (optional)

1. Place dry milk mixed with water, marshmallows, and chocolate in top of double boiler, mix, and heat until smooth and blended.
2. Add 1 egg yolk at a time and mix until smooth.
3. Beat egg whites with salt until stiff.
4. Add vanilla and fold hot egg-yolk mixture into egg whites.
5. Cover and let stand 10 min.
6. Fold in graham cracker mixture, pile into individual sherbet dishes, and chill overnight.
7. Top with whipped cream and slivered toasted almonds, and serve as dessert or party refreshment.

Fruit Beverages

PINK LEMONADE *(See picture on page 87.)*

6-8 servings

¾ c. lemon juice (4-6 lemons)
½-¾ c. sugar *
6 c. cold water
ice cubes
mint, cherries or lemon rind curls
pink coloring

1. Wash lemons and squeeze juice.
2. Mix juice, cold water, sugar, and syrup, then add coloring, being careful not to make ade too pink.
3. Pour into tall glasses over ice cubes.
4. Garnish with mint, cherry, or a curl of lemon rind, and serve.

LIMEADE

Follow above directions for lemonade, substituting lime juice for lemon juice and green coloring for red. Serve over crushed ice and garnish with slice of fresh lime.

PARTY PUNCH *(See picture on page 87.)*

15-20 servings

Make 2 quarts tea, add sugar to taste, and cool. Add: 1 medium can of pineapple juice, 1 can grapefruit juice, 1 can frozen orange juice, 1 can frozen lemonade, and mix. Pour over large chunk of ice in punch bowl. Add lime, lemon or orange slices, and broken bits of cherry to garnish.

GRAPE JUICE-GINGER ALE FIZZ

6 servings

1 qt. grape juice
1 qt. ginger ale
ice cubes
mint, or lime peel curl

1. Mix juice and ginger ale just before serving and pour over ice cubes.
2. Garnish with twist of lime peel or fresh mint.

TOMATO-SAUERKRAUT JUICE COCKTAIL

Mix equal parts of canned tomato juice with canned sauerkraut juice. Pour over ice cubes and serve as an appetizer before a buffet supper.

* Make a sugar syrup if desired by boiling sugar with equal amounts of water for 5 minutes and use instead of granulated sugar.

HOT MULLED CIDER

10-12 servings

½ gallon cider
6 whole cloves
1 t. cinnamon sticks
1 sliced orange
1 sliced lemon
½ c. sugar
2 c. water

1. Mix water, sugar, spices, and fruit and simmer 15 min.
2. Add cider, heat, and keep at simmering temperature until served.
3. Serve in punch cups with gingerbread, molasses cookies, hot cinnamon rolls, or pumpkin pie for party refreshments, or serve instead of tea at a tea party.

Raw Fruits

PARTY MELON

12-15 servings

½ ripe red watermelon
1 ripe cantaloupe or other yellow melon
1 ripe honeydew or other white-green melon
½ c. lime juice
2 T. honey

1. Scoop out red from one-half watermelon, leaving ½ in. thickness of red.
2. Cut melons into balls with melon spoon.
3. Mix lime juice and honey, and lightly toss with melon balls.
4. Pile melon balls with juice into watermelon half, chill, and serve as the salad, appetizer, or dessert for a buffet meal. This is a colorful, crisp, appetizer-salad for a special summer party such as a bridal party or a buffet meal.

Variation

Add white seedless grapes, red bing cherries, or avocado balls.

ORANGE SLICE RING

4 servings

1. Peel 4 oranges around fruit, and slice circling the fruit.
2. Serve on 7-in. plate, forming a circle around the plate, as first course for breakfast or any meal. Garnish with berries or cherries in season.

Variation

For a salad, arrange orange circles on a bed of lettuce and top with cottage cheese, sweet onion slices or berries in season and your favorite salad dressing.

ORANGE OR GRAPEFRUIT HALF

4 servings

1. Wash and dry 2 grapefruit or 4 oranges and cut in halves.
2. With grapefruit knife or sharp paring knife carefully cut around the fruit next to the white inner lining.
3. If desired, run knife around each section to separate in bite sizes, and cut center from grapefruit (but this step is not necessary for ease in eating, if the outer rim is loosened).
4. Serve at once on 5- or 7-in. plate as first course for any meal, or as dessert or salad for lunch or dinner.

GRAPEFRUIT OR ORANGE SECTIONS

4 servings

1. Peel 2 grapefruit or oranges, removing white tissue around fruit, and separate sections with sharp knife.
2. Arrange in wheel-spoke shape on 5- or 7-in. plate and serve on a bed of green lettuce as a first-course salad.

Variations

1. Prepare grapefruit and oranges in sections and arrange alternately on bed of green lettuce or watercress.
2. Arrange grapefruit, orange, and apple sections (with red skins left on) alternately on bed of green lettuce and top with dressing (see page 430).
3. Arrange sections of grapefruit, oranges, and pears alternately on a bed of green lettuce, and top with a blue cheese dressing. Use avocado pears for variety.

FRUIT KABOBS

On an attractive plate, arrange bite sizes of different fresh fruits on picks, and let guests help themselves.

WALDORF SALAD

4 servings

2 c. diced unpeeled apples
1 c. finely diced celery
¼ c. broken nutmeats
1 T. lemon juice
2-3 T. mayonnaise
green lettuce

1. Prepare fruit and toss lightly with remaining ingredients (except lettuce).
2. Place on bed of green lettuce on 5- or 7-in. salad plates, and serve cold as part of a balanced meal.

Variations

Instead of apples use pears, grapes, oranges, or tangerines.

RAW CRANBERRY-ORANGE RELISH

1 quart

1 lb. fresh cranberries
1 orange
1 apple
2 c. sugar

1. Wash fruit thoroughly and dry.
2. Quarter orange and apple in skins and remove seeds.
3. Run all fruit (with peels) through food chopper.
4. Add sugar, mix thoroughly, and store in covered jar in the refrigerator.
5. Serve as relish with meat, or use to top salad.

Variation

Place halves of orchard fruit on bed of lettuce and stuff with cranberry relish.

RAW FRUIT AND CHEESE

Arrange raw fruits of choice on a tray with a variety of cheese. Use for center piece on table, and then for dessert.

RUTH WHITE'S
FRESH PEAR SALAD-DESSERT

8 servings

1. Peel 4 fresh ripe pears, cut in halves, and remove seeds. Brush with lemon or lime juice (allow one-half pear per serving).
2. Cut and mix 1 c. dates, ¼ lb. blue cheese, 1 3-oz. pkg. cream cheese, and ¼ c. nutmeats with the juice of 2 limes and stuff cavity of pears with this mixture.
3. Serve on bed of lettuce or watercress as salad-dessert; or with hot homemade cinnamon rolls as party refreshments. This is a tangy salad-dessert.

FRESH FRUIT CUP

1. In sherbet dishes, arrange layers of fresh fruit in season—oranges, grapefruits, apples, pears, berries, melons, grapes, and other fruits.
2. Garnish with a sprig of mint or a cherry, and serve cold as a first course, a salad alternate, or a dessert.

Cooked Fruits

COOKING FRESH FRUIT

1. Wash orchard fruits such as apples, pears, plums, peaches, and apricots thoroughly and wipe skins dry.
2. Cook in skins, or peel as thin as possible with sharp knife or peeler.
3. Place fruit in saucepan or pressure saucepan, and add boiling water according to amount and kind of fruit. For 6 apples allow ⅓-⅔ c. boiling water, depending on variety. Berries, cherries, rhubarb, peaches, and apricots need no added water.
4. Cover saucepan and cook fruit until it is just tender when pierced with a fork.
5. If a pressure saucepan is used for orchard fruit, let the pressure rise to 15 lbs., and turn off heat at once.
6. If a smooth sauce is desired from apples, push cooked apples through a sieve or food mill, or use a blender.

BAKED APPLES*

    4 tart apples
    ¼ c. brown sugar (packed)
    ¼ t. nutmeg
    ½ t. cinnamon
    ¼ c. raisins
    1 t. grated lemon rind

7. If sugar is needed, add it when fruit is cool.
8. Store cooked fruit in a covered container in the refrigerator and use as a part of any meal.

COOKING DRIED FRUITS

1. Wash in boiling hot water sulfur-dried fruit, such as apricots and peaches.
2. Cover dried fruit with boiling water in the saucepan in which it is to be cooked.
3. Cook dried apricots, prunes, or other dried fruit in pressure saucepan for 2 min. at 15 lbs. pressure. Turn off heat and let fruit stand in juice until pressure returns to normal. Store fruit in juice in a covered jar in refrigerator overnight for a delicious flavor.
4. If regular saucepan is used for dried fruit, prepare as above, and cook until soft. Serve as a part of any meal.

4 servings

1. Preheat oven to 400°.
2. Wash, dry, and core apples, leaving about ¼ in. at blossom end to hold stuffing. Cut a thin line around the center of each apple (to prevent splitting).
3. Mix ingredients, stuff center of each apple, and place in baking dish.
4. Add ½ c. boiling water to baking dish, cover, and bake 25 min. Uncover and continue baking until apples are tender when pierced with a toothpick.
5. Serve warm with milk or cool with a scoop of ice cream for dessert.

° Apples may be baked at any temperature with good results. Bake them when you have an oven meal, and let the apples fit into the temperature you need for other food. Other apple recipes may be found on pp. 440 and 441.

Variations

1. Stuff hole with mincemeat mix, and add a twist of orange peel.
2. Stuff hole with cranberry relish (see page 381).

BAKED APPLESAUCE

1. Quarter and core tart apples that have been thoroughly washed, but do not peel. Place a layer in a covered baking dish. Sprinkle with brown sugar, and repeat until dish is full.
2. Add ⅓-⅔ c. of boiling water and dash of cinnamon and nutmeg.
3. Cover and bake with an oven meal until apples are tender.

CRANBERRY SAUCE

3½ cups

1 lb. fresh cranberries
2 c. sugar
2 c. water

1. Wash cranberries and place in saucepan with boiling water.
2. Cover and cook until all berries pop.
3. Add sugar and cook until thick sauce is formed.
4. Pour into dish from which it is to be served and chill.
5. Serve with poultry or other meat.

Variations

1. Add ½ orange peel while cooking and remove when sauce is done.
2. For Cranberry Jelly, push through sieve or food mill when sauce sheets from spoon, or blend in blender.

RUTH WHITE'S QUICK CRANBERRY PIE*

6-7 servings

12 graham crackers crushed
   into meal
1 t. fat
½ can whole cranberry sauce
1 14-oz. can sweetened condensed milk
⅓ c. lemon juice (fresh)
⅓ c. orange juice (fresh)
1 t. grated lemon rind
1 t. grated orange rind
½ t. almond extract
3 eggs separated
¼ t. salt
1 t. cream of tartar
10 toasted almonds (optional)

1. Preheat oven to 375°F.; butter an 8- or 9-in. pie plate.
2. Place graham cracker meal in pie plate and press into shape of crust.
3. Mix cranberry sauce, sweetened condensed milk, lemon, orange juice, rinds, almond extract, and egg yolks in mixing bowl.
4. Beat egg whites with salt and cream of tartar until they stand in moist, but firm peaks.
5. Fold cranberry mixture into egg whites.
6. Pile gently into pie crust, and sprinkle slivered almonds on top.
7. Bake 25 min. Turn off heat. Open oven door. Leave in oven 30 min.
8. Chill and serve, garnishing with sour or whipped cream and an almond. (Make pie the day before you intend to serve it and store it covered in the refrigerator.)

RUTH WHITE'S QUICK FRUIT PUDDING

4 servings

1 No. 2 can of fruit (applesauce, cherries, apricots,
   or rhubarb sauce)
   brown sugar** (¼ c. for
   apple sauce; ¾ c. for
   cherries)
¼ t. nutmeg
½ t. cinnamon
1 T. table fat
5 crushed graham crackers

1. Preheat oven to 400°.
2. Butter a pyrex or heat-proof pie plate.
3. Pour fruit into plate.
4. Crush graham crackers to a fine meal and sprinkle over fruit.
5. Mix sugar and spices, and spoon evenly over fruit.
6. Dot with fat, and bake for 20 min.
7. Serve warm or cool with milk, cream, or scoop of ice cream.

* The ingredients in this dessert are high in needed nutrients, and low in fat. (Greasing the pan helps the graham crackers to cling, thus eliminating the high fat content of the usual pie crust.)

** Amount of sugar depends on tartness of fruit.

**RUTH WHITE'S QUICK
BERRY DESSERT**

4 servings

1 10-oz. pkg. of frozen berries
(or 1 qt. fresh berries
and ⅓ c. sugar)
1 c. sour cream
⅛ t. freshly ground nutmeg
1½ c. sponge or angel cake
cubes or 1 c. crushed
vanilla wafers

1. Mix thawed berries with remaining ingredients.
2. Spoon into sherbet dishes.
3. Top with a spoonful of sour cream, or fresh or frozen berries, and serve at once.

QUICK FRUIT SHORTCAKE

4 servings

1½ c. fresh, frozen, or canned
fruit
4 slices of sponge or angel
cake
ice cream or whipped
cream

1. Place sliced cake on 7-in. plate.
2. Spoon fruit on cake and top with a scoop of ice cream or whipped cream; then add more fruit and serve at once.

Vegetables

SEASONING TO POINT UP FLAVOR

The following seasonings when properly used improve flavor in cooking vegetables:

chives
onions and tops
celery and leaves
parsley
green and red
peppers
mint
hot pepper
paprika
vegetable oil
butter
margarine

bacon drippings
ham drippings
pork chop drippings
sour cream
sweet cream
vinegar
lemon juice
mustard
horseradish
celery seeds
dill
rosemary

METHODS OF COOKING

3 c. of cooked vegetable yields 4 servings.

By Steam: This is the way vegetables are cooked by either waterless cooking, pressure cooking, or other saucepan-casserole types of cooking. Fresh or frozen vegetables should be cooked in the smallest amount of water possible in a covered pan until just tender and no longer. Remaining vegetable water should be used.

Creamed: Use 1 c. hot white sauce to 3 c. cooked vegetables to yield 6 servings. Among the vegetables suited to creaming are: peas, asparagus, cauliflower, celery, green beans, carrots, potatoes, cabbage, and onions.

Au gratin: Add cheese or cheese sauce to any of the vegetables that will cream, top with buttered bread crumbs, and brown in moderate oven.

Scalloped: Lay alternate layers of vegetables and cream, cheese sauce, or milk, and bake until tender.

Dolma or Stuffed Vegetables: Use left-over bread or cereal, vegetables, and meat for stuffing. Some vegetables suited for stuffing are: egg plant, green and red peppers, tomatoes, squash, cabbage leaf, and grape leaf. For recipe for vegetable stuffing see page 432

Frying: is cooking by steam produced from hot fat. See page 127 for description of pan frying; and pages 259-260 for description of deep-fat frying.

Broiling: is cooking by steam produced within the vegetable under direct heat. See page 127 for description of method.

Baking in skins: is cooking by steam produced within vegetable from dry heat, usually in the oven. Some vegetables suited to baking in skins are: white and yellow potatoes, squash, and onions.

SERVING VEGETABLES

Use a large hot chop plate or platter. Place meat in center, and circle meat with vegetables; or arrange vegetables in center and arrange chops, fish, or poultry around vegetables; or serve vegetables in hot covered or uncovered bowls.

Arrange vegetables on a plate for color and texture contrast and for flavors and nutrients that blend and balance. Here are some examples:

1. Meat roast in center of platter: Franconia potatoes at outside circle; mashed carrots piled at one end of platter next to meat, and peas or green beans at the other end.

2. Whole carrots at one end of platter; meat roast in center; whole asparagus or broccoli at the other end.

3. Meat in center of platter; mashed or cubed rutabaga at one end, and whole green okra at the other.

4. Broccoli or Brussels sprouts in center, circled by lamb chops; rim of baked squash.

5. Kernel corn in center of hot chop plate, circled by whole green beans; rim of whole baked onions and sausage.

6. Red cabbage in a bowl in center, circled with baked potatoes and ham slices.

7. Cauliflower head in center topped with cheese sauce; whole carrots arranged as spokes from cauliflower with rim of green peas or spinach.

8. Mashed potatoes center, circled by green beans and mushrooms; rim of fried chicken.

9. Bowl of turnip greens or kale in center, circled with baked sweet potatoes and baked pork chops.

10. Bowl of stewed tomatoes, pepper, okra, and onion in center, circled with brown rice and fried fish.

11. Meat loaf center, circled with stuffed tomatoes; rim of corn on cob.

12. Large hamburgers center, circled with baked potatoes; rim of sliced tomatoes, green peppers, and large sweet onions.

MAKE YOUR OWN QUICK VEGETABLE COMBINATION

Cooking vegetables together gives variety and saves time in preparation, meal service, and dishwashing. Here are some examples of vegetables that taste good together.

1. Green peas, green beans, and onions

2. Green peas, carrots, onion, and celery

3. Green peas, green beans, and mushrooms
4. Green beans, baby lima beans, and onions
5. Kernel corn, zucchini squash, onion, celery, and garlic
6. Kernel corn, green or lima beans, onion
7. Brussels sprouts or broccoli with onions and celery
8. Whole carrots, whole white turnips, onion, and celery
9. Mixed greens of any variety, such as kale and spinach or turnip greens and mustard
10. Any green leafy vegetable, onion, celery, and celery leaves.
11. Green beans, potatoes, onions, and okra

Vegetable Soups

BEAN, PEA, OR LENTIL SOUP*

1 c. dry beans, peas, or lentils
6 c. water for boiling or 4 c. for pressure saucepan
½ c. diced onion
½ c. diced celery with leaves
1 meaty ham hock, or 1 T. fat
1 t. salt
⅛ t. each of pepper and celery salt
½ t. dry mustard

4 servings

1. Wash beans, place in saucepan with all remaining ingredients, and cover.
2. For boil method: Bring to boil, and boil 2 min.
3. Turn off heat and soak 1 hr.
4. Bring to boil, and cook slowly for 2 hr. or until soft. Remove meat and bone, and set aside.
5. Push beans through food mill or sieve, or blend in electric blender.
6. Cut ham in bite sizes, return to soup, heat soup, and serve hot as a meat alternate for lunch or dinner.
7. Pressure saucepan method: Pre-boil and soak as for boiling; then bring beans and seasoning to boil and let steam escape for 1 min. Put on pressure vent, and let pressure slowly rise to 15 lbs. Cook navy beans and pinto beans at 15 lbs. for 10 min., but other beans, peas, or lentils for 5 min. Turn off heat and let pressure slowly return to normal. Then proceed at Step 5 above.

Variations

Add garlic, chili pepper, Worcestershire sauce, green pepper, or other seasoning to taste.

* For boiled beans use 3 c. water per cup dry beans for boiling; or 2 c. water for cooking in pressure saucepan.

VEGETABLE CHOWDER

4 servings

3 slices diced bacon
1 diced onion
2 diced carrots
1 diced turnip
1 diced potato
1 diced green pepper
2 diced sticks of celery and
    leaves
2 c. boiling water
1 No. 2 can tomatoes
1 t. salt
  dash pepper
2 T. minced parsley

1. Prepare vegetables.
2. Sauté onion and bacon until soft.
3. Add boiling water, seasonings, and all vegetables except canned tomatoes, and bring to boil.
4. Cover and reduce heat to simmer, and cook until vegetables are tender (7-10 min.).
5. Add canned tomatoes and heat to boiling.
6. Serve hot. Garnish with parsley and serve with toasted cheese sandwiches as main dish for lunch.

Variations

1. At Step 2, sauté ½ lb. ground beef instead of bacon.
2. Omit bacon and use 3 chicken or beef bouillon cubes when adding tomatoes. Add 1 c. sour cream or evaporated milk and 1 can clams if desired.

CREAM OF TOMATO SOUP

4 servings

2½ c. fresh or canned tomatoes
¼ c. diced onion
1 T. vegetable oil
2 T. flour
1 t. salt
¼ t. celery salt
  dash pepper
2 T. minced parsley
1 c. evaporated milk

1. Bring tomatoes, onions, and seasoning to a boil.
2. Cover and simmer over low heat 7 min.
3. Push through sieve or food mill, or blend in blender.
4. Blend fat and flour, and then add milk gradually.
5. Cook over low heat until smooth and thickened.
6. Add hot tomato mixture gradually to hot white sauce, stirring constantly.
7. Garnish with parsley and serve hot as part of a balanced meal.

Variations

Use other vegetable of choice instead of tomatoes, and vary seasonings to suit taste.

Vegetable Salads

COLESLAW

4 servings

1 qt. shredded cabbage
½ c. diced celery
1 diced green pepper
1 T. grated onion
4 sliced radishes (in season)
½ t. salt
dash pepper
1 T. sugar
2-3 T. lemon juice or vinegar
¼ c. sour cream or 1 T. oil

1. Chill a firm cabbage head. Quarter and shred fine with sharp knife.
2. Place at once into mixing bowl, and add remaining prepared ingredients.
3. Toss and serve cold immediately, or cover firmly with foil and store in refrigerator until ready to serve.

Variations

1. Plain cabbage with seasonings only and dressing of choice.
2. To cabbage add tomatoes, carrots, or any desired vegetable in season.
3. Cabbage with fruit combinations for salads:

cabbage, tangerine, apple
cabbage, banana, pineapple
cabbage, pineapple, pear
cabbage, orange, apple

cabbage, orange, banana, pineapple
cabbage, grapes, apples, nuts
cabbage, carrot, nuts, raisins
cabbage, celery, orange, pineapple

TOMATO SALAD COMBINATIONS

1. Bed of green lettuce circled with sliced tomatoes, cucumbers, and onion rings; seasoned with salt, sugar, pepper, lemon juice, and vinegar sprinkled over it.
2. Same as above with slices of hard-cooked eggs and radishes.
3. Add three or more of following: cottage cheese, green pepper rings, cabbage salad, sliced avocado, grapefruit sections.

BEAN-STUFFED TOMATO SALAD

4 servings

2 c. cooked dry beans
½ c. diced luncheon meat
¼ c. diced green pepper
2 diced hard-cooked eggs
⅓ c. tart salad dressing
4 tomatoes
green lettuce
1 onion, cut in thin rings
½ c. diced celery
dash salt, dash pepper

1. Mix beans, meat, celery, pepper, salt, and hard-cooked eggs with the dressing.
2. Split tomatoes in 6 sections, cut ⅔ of the way through, and spread open. Fill center with bean mixture.
3. Serve on greens and garnish with onion rings or cottage cheese.

TOSSED GREEN SALAD

4 servings

1 qt. green lettuce (use more
  than one variety)
½ crushed clove garlic
2 tomatoes cut in wedges
1 sliced cucumber
2 diced sticks of celery and
  leaves
1 T. grated onion
4 sliced radishes
2 diced hard-cooked eggs
  (optional)
 French dressing
¼ t. salt
 dash pepper

1. Place in salad bowl clean, cold, dry, crisp ingredients cut or broken into bite sizes.
2. Add dressing and seasoning and toss just before serving.
3. Serve immediately on 7-in. salad plate; or serve from bowl on plates at the table.

Variations

1. Add any of the following: blue cheese, green pepper, fresh green peas, raw cauliflower sections, new green onions with stems, or grated raw beets.
2. For Chef's Salad, add 2 c. diced poultry, meat, fish, or cheddar cheese.

POTATO SALAD

4-6 servings

3 c. diced potatoes (cooked in
  skins and peeled)
1 c. diced celery and leaves
¼ c. diced onion and stems
1 grated carrot
2 T. minced parsley
2 T. vinegar or lemon juice
½ t. dry mustard
1 t. salt
⅛ t. pepper
⅛ t. celery salt
3 hard-cooked eggs sliced in
  rings
 mayonnaise or cooked
  salad dressing to moisten

1. Place potatoes in mixing bowl.
2. Add all remaining ingredients and toss lightly.
3. Cover and chill.
4. Garnish with egg slices.

Variations

1. Add 2 diced pickles, or 6 sliced olives.
2. Garnish with tomato, green pepper, or pickled beets.
3. Use one-half French dressing with mayonnaise.

Cooked Vegetables

Cook greens such as kale, collards, savoy cabbage, turnip greens, Brussels sprouts, broccoli, and mustard by the method given below. But to the following greens—spinach, beet tops, dandelion, swiss chard, and all wild greens—add a clean egg-shell while cooking (the calcium in eggshells combines with oxalic acid in these greens, making them more healthful and flavorful).

GREEN LEAFY VEGETABLE

4 servings

2 lb. fresh or 2 pkgs. frozen greens
¼ c. onion, chopped fine
4 slices of bacon, chopped fine
½-¾ t. salt
⅛ t. pepper
2-4 T. water (for pressure saucepan)

1. Wash fresh greens until clean and drain well.
2. Sauté onion and bacon in pan where greens will be cooked until onion is soft (about 3 min.). Add greens and water.
3. Cover and cook until tender (see time table page 125 for waterless cooking and pressure saucepan).
4. Serve hot at once as part of a balanced meal.

Variations

1. When ready to serve, add chopped hard-cooked eggs in 3 T. hot vinegar.
2. Add 1 T. horseradish in 2 T. hot vinegar.

WILTED GREENS (hot salad)

4 servings

1½ qts. chopped green lettuce*
2 diced fresh onions with greentops or 2 T. grated onion
3 strips bacon
¼ c. hot vinegar
¼ t. salt
⅛ T. pepper and celery salt

1. Brown bacon in large skillet; pour off fat and crumble bacon.
2. Add greens, and 2 T. bacon fat and stir so that greens are coated with fat.
3. Cover and heat 1 min. or until greens wilt.
4. Add seasoning to hot vinegar and pour over greens just before serving. (If added before, it will turn greens olive color.)
5. Mix and serve *at once*.

Variation

Add diced radishes and green pepper.

* Wilted greens reduce greatly in bulk; use enough to make ½-¾ c. serving for each person.

CRISP 5-MINUTE CABBAGE

4 servings

1 c. milk
1 qt. shredded cabbage
1½ T. flour
1 T. fat
½ t. salt
⅛ t. celery salt
1 t. sugar

1. Heat ¾ c. milk scalding hot. Add cabbage, bring to boil, and simmer for 2 min. Add seasonings and sugar.
2. Mix flour, melted fat, and ¼ c. milk.
3. Stir this mixture into the cabbage, and cook 3 min., or until thickened, stirring constantly.
4. Serve hot at once as part of a balanced meal.

Variation

Add 1 c. grated cheese at Step 3.

VIENNESE CABBAGE

4-6 servings

1 head of red cabbage
   (1½-2 lbs.)
¼ c. cider vinegar
¼ c. brown sugar (packed)
1 t. salt
¼ t. celery salt
1 T. fat of choice

1. Shred cabbage.
2. Bring vinegar to boil.
3. Add cabbage and other ingredients.
4. Cover pan and bring to boil quickly.
5. Reduce heat and simmer until tender (about 7-10 min. or 1 min. in pressure saucepan at 15 lbs. pressure).
6. Serve hot immediately as part of a balanced meal.

Variations

1. Add ½ c. sour cream to top of cabbage when ready to serve.
2. Before cooking, add 3 diced tart apples in skins and substitute ¼ c. water for vinegar.

STEWED OKRA, TOMATOES, GREEN PEPPER

4 servings

3 slices bacon
1 chopped onion
2 c. sliced okra
1 No. 2 can tomatoes (grade C)
½ t. salt
1 diced green pepper

1. Slice bacon in saucepan.
2. Add onion and okra and brown slightly.
3. Add tomatoes, green pepper, and salt.
4. Cook covered over low heat until okra is tender and mixture is thick (about 5-8 min.).
5. Stir occasionally to prevent sticking.
6. Serve with rice in a meal of fish, salad, milk, and dessert.

**PANNED FRENCH FROZEN (or fresh)
GREEN BEANS OR GREEN PEAS**

3 servings

1 pkg. (10 oz.) of frozen
    beans or peas (or 1 lb.
    fresh beans or peas)
½ c. thinly sliced mushrooms
1 T. grated onion
1 T. vegetable oil
½ t. salt
    pepper to taste

1. Place oil in skillet and add all other ingredients, stirring until all vegetables are coated with fat.
2. Cover and cook over low heat until tender stirring or shaking occasionally to prevent sticking (about 3 minutes).
3. Serve hot immediately. They should be firm, crisp, and green in color.

BAKED ONIONS

4 servings

1. Preheat oven to 375°.
2. Peel 6 medium-sized onions and cut them crosswise. Place them in a baking dish, sprinkle with salt and pepper, and dot with table fat.
3. Add enough water to cover bottom of dish.
4. Cover and bake about 30 min.
5. Top with crumbs and grated cheese and bake uncovered 15-20 min. longer, until crumbs are brown and onions tender.

Variation

Season and cook onions whole in covered baking dish. Test with a fork or toothpick for doneness, sprinkle with cheese when tender, and melt under broiler.

BUTTERED MINT CARROTS

4 servings

1 bunch carrots
2 sprigs fresh mint or ½ t.
    dried mint
½ t. salt
1 T. fat
1 t. honey
¼ c. water

1. Prepare carrots (if young and tender, cook in skins; if not, scrape skins).
2. Place carrots in saucepan with boiling water, add all seasoning, and cover with tight-fitting lid. Bring to boil quickly; then turn fire low, and simmer until tender (about 15-25 min. for whole carrots; in pressure saucepan, about 3-5 min. for whole carrots).
3. When tender, remove and serve hot as part of a balanced meal.

Variations

1. Add 2 T. sour cream or sweet cream, and mash.
2. Omit mint and add 1 T. grated onion.
3. Add dash of nutmeg and cook with slice of orange peel.
4. Omit mint and add ¼ c. minced parsley, or green celery leaves.

BROCCOLI-CHEESE CASSEROLE

4-6 servings

2 pkg. frozen broccoli (or 1 bunch fresh)
¾ c. nonfat dry milk
1 c. water
2 slightly beaten eggs
1 c. grated sharp cheddar cheese (¼ lb.)
2 T. lemon juice
1 T. vegetable oil
1 t. salt
⅛ t. pepper
⅛ t. celery salt

1. Preheat oven to 375°.
2. Cook frozen broccoli according to package directions and place in baking dish.
3. Mix nonfat dry milk with water until smooth.
4. Add eggs, cheese, oil, salt, celery salt, and pepper. Mix and pour over broccoli.
5. Bake about 25 min. or until firm.
6. Pour lemon juice over top, and serve hot at once.

QUICK BOSTON BAKED BEANS

4 servings

3 c. cooked or canned pea beans
2 T. grated onion
¼ c. dark molasses
½ t. mustard
4 slices bacon

1. Preheat oven to 375°.
2. Mix all ingredients except bacon and pour into 1½-qt. baking dish.
3. Place bacon across top and bake 25-30 min.
4. Serve hot with brown bread or corn sticks as part of a balanced meal.

BOILED BEANS AND HAM HOCK

See pages 165-166 for method. Use 2 c. water and 2 T. fat per cup dry beans when using pressure saucepan, or 3 c. water per cup dry beans for boiling.

SUCCOTASH

6 servings

1 No. 2 can whole kernel corn or 1½ c. cooked corn
1 No. 2 can green or lima beans or 1½ c. cooked beans
1 T. fat
1 t. salt
⅛ t. pepper
1 T. grated onion
¼ t. celery salt

1. Combine all ingredients and heat but do not boil.
2. Serve hot at once as part of a balanced meal.

PAN-FRIED EGGPLANT

4 servings

1 eggplant
1 egg
  salt
  celery salt
2-4 T. vegetable oil
  paprika
⅓ c. bread crumbs or flour

1. Wash and dry eggplant and slice in circles ½ in. thick (leaving skin).
2. Dip each slice in egg to which all seasonings have been added and roll in crumbs, or flour.
3. Place slices in hot oil and brown.
4. Turn and brown on other side.
5. Remove, drain on absorbent paper, and serve hot at once.

CORN PUDDING

4 servings

1 No. 2 can cream corn or
  1½ c. fresh corn
1 c. milk
2 eggs
2 T. flour
½ t. salt
1 T. fat
2 T. grated onion
¼ t. celery salt
  dash garlic salt
  paprika

1. Preheat oven to 375°.
2. Oil a 1½-qt. baking dish.
3. Heat milk to scalding hot in covered pan over low heat.
4. Beat eggs lightly in mixing bowl, add corn, flour, salt, fat, onion, and celery and garlic salt, and mix.
5. Add scalding milk to corn, gradually, and mix.
6. Pour into oiled baking dish and sprinkle top with paprika.
7. Bake for 30-40 min. or until knife comes clean when inserted in center.
8. Serve hot as alternate for potato.

Variation

1. At Step 4, add 1 c. of zucchini squash sautéed in the fat with 1 clove garlic.
2. Sprinkle top with sharp cheese before last 15 min. of cooking.

HARVARD BEETS

4 servings

1 t. cornstarch
3 T. sugar
½ t. salt
¼ c. vinegar
¼ c. water
1 T. fat
2 c. sliced cooked or canned beets

1. Mix cornstarch, sugar, salt, vinegar, and water. Boil gently until slightly thickened, stirring constantly.
2. Add fat and beets, and reheat.
3. Serve hot.

BAKED WINTER OR ACORN SQUASH

1. Preheat oven to 400°.
2. Wash, dry, cut squash in halves, and remove seeds.
3. Salt and rub inside with table fat and brown sugar.
4. Place on cookie sheet. Cover with foil, and bake until tender when pierced with fork. Serve hot as an alternate for potato.

BAKED POTATOES—WHITE OR SWEET

4 servings

METHOD ONE

1. Preheat oven to 425°.
2. Scrub 4 medium potatoes until clean. Cut away defects. Dry and rub with fat.
3. Bake 40-45 min. or until tender when pierced with a fork (yams cook in less time than sweet and white potatoes).

METHOD TWO

Precook in pressure cooker 5 min. and complete cooking in oven (cuts time in half or more).

BAKED WHITE POTATOES ON HALF SHELL*

8 servings

1. Preheat oven to 425°.
2. Bake 4 smooth, large, oblong potatoes until done (do not grease skins).
3. Cut in halves lengthwise and scoop out baked potato, reserving shells.
4. Add ½ t. salt, 1 T. fat, ¼ c. evaporated milk, dash pepper, and ½ mashed clove of garlic or 1 T. grated onion, and mash thoroughly.
5. Spoon into shells, sprinkle with grated sharp cheese (if desired); then add paprika and bake for 15 min. at 375°.
6. Serve hot, mixed with sour cream, chopped chives or grated onion.

POTATOES "BOILED" IN SKINS

1. Scrub potatoes clean, and place on rack of saucepan or pressure saucepan.
2. Add boiling water to cover bottom of pan, but not to touch rack.
3. Cover saucepan with tight-fitting lid, and bring to a vigorous boil.
4. Reduce heat to a simmer, and cook until potatoes are tender when pierced with a fork (about 25-45 min. for whole potatoes; 15-25 for quartered).
5. For pressure saucepan bring pressure to 15 lbs. and cook 8-11 min. for whole potatoes, and 4-8 min. for quartered potatoes.

* Use *sweet potato* in same way. Omit garlic or onion, add pineapple or orange cubes, and top with marshallow. Brown in moderate oven (375°) and serve at once.

Serve potatoes cooked in skins in one of the following ways:

1. *Plain:* Serve with salt, pepper, and butter.
2. *Mash:* Peel and mash with potato masher, or beat with electric beater; season with evaporated milk, salt, pepper, and table fat.
3. *Broil:* Peel, and slice around the potato. Place on cookie sheet. Brush with fat, season with salt and paprika, and broil at 400° until golden brown.
4. *Cream:* Peel, dice, and add 1 c. of medium white sauce to 3 c. of potatoes.
5. *Au gratin:* Place the potatoes prepared for creaming in a casserole. Cover with white sauce, top with grated sharp cheese, and then top with bread crumbs. Heat in oven (375°) until golden brown (about 15-20 min.).
6. *Scallop:* Alternate layers of peeled and sliced potatoes with thin white sauce and brown under the broiler or bake in the oven until brown.
7. *Franconia or Pan Baked Potatoes:* Peel potatoes, and place whole around a beef, lamb, or pork roast. Season and turn to brown on all sides in the last 20 min. of roasting.
8. *Rice:* Peel and force through ricer into serving bowl. Add butter, season, and serve hot at once.

FLUFFY MASHED POTATOES*

4 servings

5-6 medium potatoes
½ c. evaporated milk
1 T. fat
salt, pepper

1. Cook potatoes in skins as above, or pare thinly, quarter, and cook by waterless cooking or pressure saucepan.
2. If water remains when done, drain and save for gravy, soup, or vegetable gelatin salad.
3. Dry out potatoes over low heat, shaking pan to keep from scorching.
4. Mash or beat thoroughly. Add hot milk, seasoning, and beat until light and fluffy.
5. Serve hot at once in a hot bowl, or spoon potatoes around the meat.

Variation

For parsley potatoes, add ½ c. of finely minced parsley at end of Step 4.

* Mashing and whipping potatoes causes increased loss of vitamin C. When this method of preparation is used, also serve a vitamin C-rich food.

Vegetables in Dessert	

RUTH WHITE'S PUMPKIN FLUFF PIE*

2 8-inch pies

1½ c. fresh-cooked or canned
    pumpkin
⅔ c. brown sugar (packed)
3 separated eggs
1 T. flour
1 t. cinnamon
½ t. allspice
½ t. nutmeg
½ t. vanilla
½ c. nonfat dry milk
¾ c. water
1 c. evaporated milk
½ t. salt
½ t. cream of tartar
¼ c. pecans
    sour cream
    honey
    pastry for 2 pie shells
    (See page 439.)

1. Preheat oven to 425°.
2. Prepare pastry. Line two 8-in. pans and chill in refrigerator.
3. Separate egg whites into one mixing bowl.
4. Place yolks, pumpkin, sugar, milk, water, spices, and flour in another mixing bowl and blend thoroughly.
5. Add cream of tartar and salt to egg whites and beat until they stand in moist peaks.
6. Fold pumpkin mixture into egg whites and pour into pie shells.
7. Bake at 425° for 15 min.; reduce heat to 375° and bake until custard is set (about 30 min.).
8. Cool, cut, and top each wedge of pie with a thin layer of sour cream, a teaspoon of honey, and a pecan half—a beautiful, tasty, and nourishing dessert.

Variations

Substitute thick mashed winter squash or sweet potatoes for the pumpkin and proceed as above.

PEANUT BUTTER COOKIES

4 dozen

1 c. sifted all-purpose flour
1½ t. baking powder
½ t. salt
⅓ c. vegetable oil
1 c. brown sugar (packed)
2 eggs
½ c. peanut butter
¼ c. nonfat dry milk
1 t. vanilla

1. Preheat oven to 375°.
2. Cream oil and sugar in mixing bowl until light and fluffy.
3. Add eggs and mix; blend in peanut butter and vanilla.
4. Sift measured dry ingredients into mixing bowl and blend.
5. Drop from spoon on cookie sheet 2 in. apart.
6. Bake 10-12 min.

* If you wish to reduce baking time, heat milk before adding.

PECAN PIE

1 9-inch pie

3 separated eggs
½ c. brown sugar (packed)
1 c. light brown corn syrup
1 t. vanilla
¼ t. salt
1 c. broken pecans
½ t. cream of tartar

1. Preheat oven to 450°.
2. Prepare pastry shell, and chill in refrigerator.
3. Mix egg yolks, brown sugar, syrup, vanilla, and nutmeats.
4. Beat egg whites with salt and cream of tartar until they stand in firm, moist peaks.
5. Fold nut mixture into egg whites, and pour into prepared pastry shell.
6. Bake at 450° for 10 min.; then reduce heat to 350° and bake for 35 min.
7. Chill. Serve in small pieces. Garnish with whipped cream and a pecan half if desired.

NUT CONFECTION

1. Grind 1 c. each of raisins, dates, apricots, and nuts in food chopper or blender.
2. Moisten with lemon juice (1-2 T.).
3. Roll in confectioner's sugar and serve as dessert.

Cereal-Bread

METHODS OF COOKING CEREALS

1. Cook cereals by low direct heat to save time, energy, fuel, and thiamine. Select a fairly heavy utensil with tight-fitting lid.
2. Bring water and salt to boil. Add cereal slowly enough to maintain boiling, stirring constantly. (If nonfat dry milk is used, it may be mixed with water or dry cereal.)
3. Reduce heat to a simmer (as low as possible) when cereal is boiling. Cover and cook to desired time to suit your taste. (Time of cooking for taste varies greatly with individual families. A cereal is done in a few minutes but may not suit your taste.)

4. Do not stir rice or macaroni products after they are covered. All water will be absorbed and each grain of rice will stand perfect and whole if properly measured and cooked according to directions. (The washing of macaroni or rice after cooking causes loss of valuable B vitamins.)

5. When using a double boiler, follow directions for direct method through Step 2, and then place double boiler over boiling hot water and cook until done.

6. If pressure saucepan is used, follow directions for cereal appearing in recipe book that came with pressure cooker.

7. Cereals cooked by the above method are usually served hot with milk or cream, sugar, and fruit as a main dish for breakfast.

GUIDE FOR COOKING COMMON CEREALS

DRY CEREAL (cups)	WATER (cups)	SALT (teaspoons)	DIRECT HEAT (minutes)	DOUBLE BOILER (minutes)	SERVINGS
Quick oats—1½	3	1	5	10	4
Rolled oats—1½	3	1	10	20	4
Whole wheat—1	3	1	10	20-30	4
White rice—1	2	1	25	35	4
Brown rice—1	2	1	35-45	45-60	4
Macaroni products—1¼	2	1	15-20		4
Corn meal—1	4	1	5-30	45	4

Cereal Products in Main Dishes

BROWN FLUFFY RICE *

1 c. brown rice
2 c. water
1 t. salt

* See reasons for using brown rice, pages 180–181.

4-6 servings

1. Bring water to boil in saucepan with tight-fitting lid.
2. Add brown rice gradually, maintaining water at a boil. Add salt and cover.
3. Reduce heat to simmer (185°).
4. Cook until all water is absorbed (over direct heat, about 45 min.).
5. Pour into hot bowl and serve at once as an alternate for potatoes or with milk as a cereal for breakfast.

Variations

1. When serving rice with poultry, add 2 chicken bouillon cubes at step 1.
2. When rice is done, stir in 2 T. minced chives or grated onion.

RUTH WHITE'S SPANISH RICE*

4-6 servings

3 c. cooked brown rice
   (1 c. uncooked)
1 lb. hamburger
2 medium onions
1 clove garlic
3 celery sticks with leaves
1 No. 2 can tomatoes (grade
   C)
1 can tomato paste (6 oz.)
⅓ lb. grated sharp cheddar
   cheese
1 t. salt
  pepper

1. Preheat oven to 375°.
2. Use left-over rice or cook rice according to directions on page 400.
3. Crumble hamburger into skillet and brown on one side. Pour off surplus fat, and turn.
4. Add finely diced garlic, onion, and celery to meat, and cook until slightly soft. Pour off excess fat.
5. Add tomatoes, tomato paste, salt, and pepper, and bring to boil.
6. Spread half of rice in the bottom of a 2½-qt. baking dish, and cover with half the sauce, then half the cheese.
7. Repeat, sprinkling remaining cheese over top.
8. Bake about 20 min. or until cheese is melted and browned.
9. Serve hot with coleslaw or green salad, French garlic bread, milk, and fruit dessert.

Variations

1. Add ½ c. of green or red diced pepper at Step 5.
2. Substitute 2 c. of ground ham for hamburger.
3. Substitute 2 c. left-over diced turkey for hamburger.
4. Add 1 c. diced zucchini squash at Step 4.
5. Substitute spaghetti for rice.

   * A low-cost main dish for dinner or a buffet that may be prepared ahead, taking Step 8 just before serving.

RUTH WHITE'S QUICK NOODLE-CHICKEN CASSEROLE

4-6 servings

1 whole canned chicken or cooked chicken
4 oz. noodles (1¼ c. uncooked)
2 T. grated onion
1 c. diced celery with leaves
1 pkg. frozen green peas
1 t. salt
dash pepper
1 diced green pepper (optional)
½ lb. (2 c.) grated sharp cheddar cheese
3 T. flour
¼ c. nonfat dry milk
broth from chicken and water to make 3 cups

1. Boil noodles with salt and pepper in chicken broth (8-10 min.).
2. Remove chicken from bones, and cut in large pieces.
3. Preheat oven to 350°.
4. Add all vegetables and 1 c. cheese, stirring in gently.
5. Pour into oiled casserole, sprinkle top with remaining cheese, and bake for 20-25 min. (vegetables in casserole should be crisp).
6. Serve hot with a tossed salad, corn sticks, milk, and a fruit dessert.

Variations

1. Substitute spaghetti or brown rice for noodles.
2. Substitute left-over poultry, beef, or ham for canned chicken.

Quick Breads

BASIC MUFFINS (drop batter)

12 muffins

2 c. sifted all-purpose flour
⅓ c. nonfat dry milk
4 t. baking powder
1 t. salt
3 T. sugar
2 T. vegetable oil
1 egg
1 c. water (or milk)

1. Preheat oven to 400° and lightly oil muffin pans. Sift dry ingredients together in mixing bowl and blend thoroughly.
2. Make a hole in center of dry ingredients and add liquid ingredients.
3. Mix until dry ingredients are just moistened. Do not overmix.
4. Fill muffin pans two-thirds full of batter and bake until done (about 20-25 min.).
5. Remove from pan and serve hot as part of any meal.

Variations

1. For Corn Muffins, substitute 1½ c. yellow corn meal for 1½ c. of flour.
2. For Whole Wheat Muffins, substitute 1 c. whole wheat (graham) flour for 1 c. of white flour.
3. For Blueberry Muffins, add 1 c. of fresh or frozen blueberries, ¼ c. sugar, and 2 T. oil.
4. For Dried Fruit Muffins, add 1 c. of finely diced raisins, dates, figs, or prunes at Step 3.
5. For Jelly Muffins, place 1 t. of jelly or marmalade in center of each muffin at Step 4.

GOLDEN LIGHT WAFFLES

4 servings

1½ c. sifted all-purpose enriched flour
½ c. nonfat dry milk
2 t. baking powder
½ t. salt
1 T. sugar
2-3 T. vegetable oil
3 separated eggs
1¼ c. water (or milk)

1. Heat waffle iron according to manufac-turer's directions.
2. Sift flour and all dry ingredients into mixing bowl and make a hole in center.
3. Add egg yolks, water, and oil, and mix with dry ingredients until smooth.
4. Beat egg whites until they stand in firm peaks.
5. Fold waffle mixture into beaten egg whites and bake in hot waffle iron.
6. Remove from waffle iron when golden brown, and serve hot at once as main dish for breakfast with melted butter or margarine, syrup, honey, or conserve; or serve as shortcake with fresh peaches, strawberries, or other fresh fruit in season. Serve as main dish for lunch or supper with creamed chicken, dried beef, or Canadian bacon.

Variations

1. Substitute ¼ c. yellow corn meal and ¼ c. wheat germ for equal amount flour.
2. For Blueberry Waffles, fold in 1 c. fresh blueberries at end of Step 3.
3. For Nut Waffles, fold in ½ c. finely cut nutmeats at end of Step 3.
4. For Cheese Waffles, fold in 1 c. of grated processed cheese at end of Step 3.
5. For Bacon Waffles, fold in 4 slices of crisp bacon crumbles at end of Step 3.

HOMEMADE READY-MIX QUICK BREAD

8 c. sifted all-purpose flour
4 T. baking powder
2 t. salt
1 T. sugar
1½ c. nonfat dry milk

1. Sift together measured dry ingredients until thoroughly blended (3 times).
2. Store dry ready-mix in covered jar on pantry shelf.
3. To use:

   Biscuits: 2 c. mix to ¾ c. water and 3 T. vegetable oil

   Muffins: 2 c. mix to 1 c. water, 3 T. vegetable oil, and 1 egg

   Pancakes or waffles: 1 c. mix to about 1 c. water, 2 T. vegetable oil, and 2-3 eggs.

Variations

1. For Corn Muffin Ready-Mix, substitute 6 c. cornmeal for 6 c. flour. When ready to use, add 1 egg to 2 c. of mix.
2. For Bran Muffin Ready-Mix, substitute 4 c. bran for 4 c. flour.

PANCAKES (pour batter)

10-12 pancakes

2 eggs
1½ c. sifted all-purpose flour
⅓ c. nonfat dry milk
1¼ c. water
2 t. baking powder
½ t. salt
1 T. sugar
2 T. vegetable oil

1. Set griddle over low heat (griddle is ready to cook pancakes when a drop of water "dances" on it).
2. Beat eggs, add water and oil, and mix.
3. Sift flour and all dry ingredients into mixing bowl with egg mixture and blend.
4. Pour batter from pitcher or large spoon onto properly heated griddle to a 3-in. diameter.
5. Cook until pancake is full of bubbles and rim is golden brown.
6. Turn with pancake turner and brown on other side.
7. Remove browned pancakes to hot plate, 3 in a stack, and serve at once as part of a balanced breakfast with melted butter or margarine, and syrup, honey, molasses, or jam of choice.

Variations

1. For Blueberry Pancakes, add ¾ c. fresh or well-drained frozen blueberries at end of Step 3.
2. For Corn Pancakes, substitute ½ c. yellow corn meal for ½ c. flour.
3. For Buckwheat Pancakes, substitute ¾ c. buckwheat flour for ¾ c. all-purpose flour.

BANANA-NUT BREAD

*1 oblong pan 13 x 9 or
1 loaf pan 9 x 5 x 3*

1¾ c. sifted all-purpose flour
3 t. baking powder
½ t. salt
2 eggs
¾ c. milk
½ c. fat of choice
1 c. brown sugar
1 c. mashed ripe bananas (about 3)
½ c. nutmeats
1 t. vanilla

1. Preheat oven to 350°; oil pan.
2. Cream fat and sugar until fluffy.
3. Add eggs, and beat thoroughly.
4. Sift measured dry ingredients together, and add alternately with milk and mashed bananas to creamed mixture, blending after each addition. Add nutmeats and vanilla and mix.
5. Spoon into oiled bread pan and bake until bread is done (about 1 hr. and 10 min.).
6. Let set 5-10 min. before removing from pan.
7. Remove from pan, cool, and serve as tea bread for breakfast, or dessert at lunch or dinner.

RUTH WHITE'S GINGERBREAD

1 loaf 8 x 11 x 2

½ c. fat
½ c. brown sugar
1 c. molasses
½ c. warm milk
2 eggs
2 c. all purpose flour
½ t. soda
1 t. baking powder
¼ t. ginger
1½ t. cinnamon
¼ t. nutmeg
½ t. salt

1. Preheat oven to 350°.
2. Cream sugar and fat.
3. Add molasses, eggs, and mix thoroughly.
4. Sift together all measured dry ingredients and add alternately with milk, and mix until blended.
5. Pour into a greased and floured 8 x 11 in. pan and bake at 350° (moderate oven) about 40 min. or until done.
6. Serve warm, or cool with applesauce topping; or with sour cream topped with 1 t. of honey.

QUICK COFFEE CAKE

6-8 servings

1 c. sifted all-purpose enriched flour
2 t. baking powder
½ t. salt
½ c. firmly packed brown
  sugar
1 egg
½ c. milk (or ⅓ c. nonfat dry
  milk and ½ c. water)
3 T. vegetable oil
1 t. each of grated lemon and
  orange rind

1. Preheat oven to 375°. Sift dry ingredients into mixing bowl and blend thoroughly.
2. Add other ingredients and mix until smooth.
3. Spread dough evenly into 9-in. oiled pie pan, using a spatula.
4. Spread dough with topping of choice (see recipes below), and bake 25 min. or until done.
5. Cut coffee cake and serve warm or cool for breakfast or dessert.

Toppings for Coffee Cakes

CINNAMON

½ c. brown sugar, 1½ t. cinnamon, 2 T. melted table fat.

HONEY

½ c. honey, 1½ t. cinnamon, 2 T. fat (1 t. grated lemon rind optional).

CRUMB

½ c. brown sugar, ¼ c. table fat, 1½ t. cinnamon, ½ c. quick oats.

ORANGE-LEMON

Mix together ½ c. brown sugar (packed), ¼ c. melted fat, grated rind of 1 lemon and 1 orange, ½ c. nutmeats, and 1½ t. cinnamon.

UPSIDE-DOWN TOPPING

Mix ¼ c. honey, ¼ c. brown sugar, ¼ t. nutmeg, 1 t. cinnamon, ½ c. broken nutmeats, ½ c. raisins. Spread over bottom of pan, and add coffee cake batter before baking.

Yeast Bread

RUTH WHITE'S QUICK YEAST BREAD

(refrigerator)

2 pkg. granular or com-
  pressed yeast
1 c. nonfat dry milk °
2 c. warm water (110°)
2 eggs
1 T. vegetable oil
½ c. brown sugar
2½ t. salt
5-6 c. sifted enriched all-purpose flour

2 one-pound loaves 9 x 5 x 3 or 3 dozen rolls

1. Place warm water (slightly warmer than body temperature—110°) in mixing bowl and add yeast, sugar, salt, oil, eggs, dry milk, and mix thoroughly.

2. Add half the flour; beat 2 min. Work in remaining flour 1 c. at a time until soft dough forms.

3. Turn onto floured board and knead until soft and smooth. (See pp. 186-7.)

4. Oil mixing bowl and dough, and place dough in bowl. Cover, and set in warm place until it rises to double in bulk (about 1 hr.).

5. If time permits, a second proofing improves texture and flavor but is not necessary. Knead gently until smooth. Shape into loaves or rolls and brush top with oil. Place in oiled pan and let rise in warm place until double in bulk (about 1 hr.).

6. Preheat oven at 400°. When bread is double in bulk, bake for 15 min. at 400°. Reduce heat to 350° and bake until golden brown. (The time required depends on the size of loaf. Rolls are baked at 425° for about 12-15 min., depending on size.)

7. Remove bread from pan by loosening with spatula and cool on rack. Brush crust with melted fat and cover with clean towel for a few minutes to soften crust. Serve warm; or cool, wrap, and store.

8. Store remaining dough in lightly oiled bowl, oiling top of dough, and covering with wax paper. Place in refrigerator, and bake fresh bread as desired.

° Any type of milk may be used such as buttermilk, whole, or evaporated.

Variations

1. For Whole Wheat Bread, substitute 3 c. whole wheat flour for 3 c. white flour and ⅓ c. dark molasses for sugar.
2. For Rye Bread, substitute 3 c. rye flour for 3 c. white flour and add 1 T. caraway seeds and ⅓ c. dark molasses for sugar.
3. For Raisin Bread, add 1 c. seeded raisins in Step 2.
4. For Cheese Bread, add 1 c. grated sharp cheese at Step 4.
5. For Bran Bread, substitute 1 c. all-bran for 1 c. flour at Step 1 and soak in warm milk mixture until bran is soft. Add ⅓ c. dark molasses.
6. For Oatmeal Bread, substitute 3 c. quick dry oats for 3 c. flour in Step 4. Oatmeal and rye make a sticky dough and are harder to work with.
7. For Honey Bread, substitute ½ c. honey for sugar at Step 2.

PARKER HOUSE ROLLS

3 dozen small

1. Preheat oven to 425°.
2. Roll yeast dough at end of Step 5 in basic recipe to ¼ in. thickness, and brush top with melted fat.
3. Cut rolls with biscuit cutter, fold over, and place closely in pan; brush top with melted fat, let rise until double in bulk, and bake for 12 min. Serve hot.

CLOVER LEAF ROLLS

3 dozen

1. Preheat oven to 425°.
2. Form yeast dough at end of Step 5 in basic recipe into yeast balls of equal size about 1 in. in diameter.
3. Place 3 balls in each oiled muffin tin, and let them rise until double in bulk.
4. Bake until golden brown (about 12 min.) and serve hot.

CRESCENT ROLLS

3 dozen

1. Preheat oven to 425°. Divide basic yeast dough into small portions.
2. Roll dough into circle about ¼ in. thick and brush with melted fat.
3. Cut dough into wedges and roll each wedge from outer edge toward center, fastening securely by pressing. Place with center points down on oiled cookie sheet and let rise until double in bulk (about 30 min.). Bake for about 12 min. until golden brown.

YEAST COFFEE CAKE DOUGH
(basic recipe) *

2 *coffee cakes (13 x 9½ x 2)*

2 pkg. granular yeast or
    compressed yeast
2 c. warm water (110°)
    (or milk)
1 c. nonfat dry milk
½ c. brown sugar
2 t. salt
⅓ c. vegetable oil
2 eggs
5-5½ c. flour
2 T. grated lemon rind
2 T. lemon juice

1. Pour warm water in mixing bowl.
2. Add yeast, sugar, dry milk, salt, eggs, oil, juice, and rind, and beat.
3. Add half the flour, and beat 2 min.
4. Add remaining flour, mix, and turn onto slightly floured board; knead lightly to a smooth, soft dough.
5. Place in oiled bowl, cover with warm, damp towel, and let rise in warm place until double in bulk (about 1 hr.).
6. Fold under and let rise again until double in bulk (45 min.).
7. Shape one-half of dough in desired shape in an oiled baking pan.
8. Preheat oven to 375°.
9. Top with favorite topping (see page 406), let rise in warm place until double, and bake until brown (20-30 min.).
10. Serve warm or cold (store remaining dough in covered bowl in refrigerator until ready to use).

CHRISTMAS APPLE STOLLEN

1. Use one-third of basic coffee cake dough and roll ¼ in. thick.
2. Brush top with melted fat and sprinkle with cinnamon and brown sugar.
3. Place thinly sliced apples ** over this and add ½ c. each of broken nutmeats and raisins (soften raisins in juice of 1 lemon with grated rind).
4. Sprinkle top of fruit with cinnamon and brown sugar.
5. Fold dough over fruit loosely, and press edges firmly together.
6. Place on oiled cookie sheet, and brush top with melted fat.
7. Let rise in warm place until double in bulk.
8. Preheat oven to 400°, bake for 10 min., and then reduce heat to 375° until done (about 30-35 min.).
9. Cool, sift confectioner's sugar over top, and slice into servings. Delicious for breakfast or dessert.

    * Use half basic recipe until you are at ease with yeast coffee cake dough. This dough should be softer than bread dough.

    ** Use apples that cook quickly, and slice very thin.

Appetizers and Spreads

CHICKEN SPREAD

2 cups

1½ c. ground, cooked, or can-
    ned lean poultry
2 ground hard-cooked eggs
1 c. finely diced celery
1 T. grated onion
½ t. salt
    dash pepper
⅛ t. celery salt
2 T. water
2 chicken bouillon cubes
    mayonnaise to moisten
    bread for sandwiches

1. Dissolve bouillon cubes in 2 T. boiling water and pour into mixing bowl.
2. Prepare all remaining ingredients and mix thoroughly in mixing bowl.
3. Spread butter or other fat on bread which has had crusts trimmed, and spread chicken mixture on one slice.
4. Press second slice of bread on filling, and cut sandwiches in desired shapes.
5. Wrap securely in suitable paper, and freeze until ready to use; or cover with damp cloth and store in the refrigerator until ready to serve.
6. Serve on a dainty plate for a party and garnish with sprigs of parsley, watercress, or radish roses.

Variations

1. Substitute cooked or canned fish, ham, or other meat for chicken.
2. Mix 1 c. sour cream and 1 pkg. dry onion soup at Step 2 and use as a dip with crackers or potato chips.

CLAM-CREAM CHEESE DIP

2 cups

1 8-oz. pkg. cream cheese
3 cans of drained minced clams
2 T. lemon juice
1 T. clam juice
1 t. horseradish
1 t. grated onion
    dash celery salt
    dash Tabasco sauce
1 t. Worcestershire sauce

1. Mix in order given, and add sufficient clam juice to make a dip.
2. Place in bowl and surround with potato chips and crackers when ready to serve.
3. Prepare the day before a party. Cover securely and store in refrigerator. Remove in time to reach room temperature before serving. If desired for sandwiches, use less clam juice, and spread on bread.

QUICK LIVER DIP

2 cups

½ lb. liverwurst
4 slices crisply fried minced
   bacon
½ t. prepared mustard
1 t. horseradish
1 c. sour cream
1 pkg. dry onion soup

1. Mash liverwurst and add remaining ingredients, blending thoroughly.
2. Serve as a dip in a bowl surrounded with a variety of crackers and potato chips.

RUTH WHITE'S HAM SPREAD WITH HOT ROLLS

3½ cups

2 c. ground baked ham
½ c. finely diced celery
½ c. ground carrots
1 T. grated onion
½ c. diced stuffed olives or
   diced pickle
   mayonnaise to moisten
   hot rolls or bread

1. Mix ingredients in the order given until well blended.
2. Serve between tiny hot rolls as a party refreshment, or with sliced bread for party or lunch sandwiches.

Meat, Fish, and Poultry Soups

BASIC FISH CHOWDER*

6-8 servings

3 slices of bacon or salt pork
   diced
½ c. diced onion
1 lb. boned fish cut in
   1-in. cubes
2 c. diced potatoes
1 c. diced celery and leaves
3½ c. (No. 2½ can) tomatoes
1½ t. salt
   pepper to taste
4 c. water
2 T. minced parsley
3 T. flour
2 c. nonfat dry milk

1. In saucepan in which soup will be made, sauté bacon and onions until soft but not brown.
2. Add fish, water, seasonings, and all vegetables except tomatoes.
3. Simmer covered until vegetables are almost tender. Add tomatoes mixed with flour and nonfat dry milk.
4. Bring to boil, add parsley, and serve hot as main dish for lunch or supper. Serve with a salad, bread, milk, and dessert of choice.

* This is a highly nourishing and tasty main dish.

RUTH WHITE'S
BEEF-VEGETABLE SOUP

8 servings

1 split marrow bone
1 lb. of chuck beef cut in cubes
1 lb. beef heart cut in cubes
1 c. diced onion
2 c. diced potato
1 c. diced celery and leaves
1 c. diced carrot
3½ c. (No. 2½ can) tomatoes
1 c. minced parsley
1½ t. salt
¼ t. black pepper
dash cayenne pepper
1½ qt. water

1. Place bones, salt, pepper, and all meat in 1 pt. water in pressure saucepan. Cook at 15 lbs. pressure for 20 min., or simmer in kettle with all the water for 3 hr. Skim off fat.
2. Remove meat, gristle, and marrow from bones, and add to stock.
3. Add vegetables and remaining ingredients, (except water if cooked in pressure pan). Bring pressure to 15 lbs.; then turn off heat and allow pressure to return to normal. If cooked in kettle, cover and cook until vegetables are tender (10-15 min.). Add enough water for a good soup.
4. Season to taste, and serve hot as main dish for lunch or dinner.
5. Store remaining soup in tight containers; freeze to be used later for a quick meal, or store for a few days in the refrigerator.

Variations

1. Substitute turkey or other poultry and bones for the beef. Add 4 chicken bouillon cubes when vegetables are added.
2. Substitute ½ c. rice or macaroni for potato.
3. Add 1 c. diced okra.
4. Add 1 bay leaf and 1 green pepper.
5. Add 1 c. kernel corn.

Salads with Meat, Fish, and Poultry

CHEF MEAT SALAD BOWL

4-6 servings

2 c. diced meat (ham, beef, lamb, tongue, beef heart)
2 diced hard-cooked eggs
1 c. diced sharp cheddar cheese
4 c. mixed greens in bite size
2 T. grated onion
1 c. finely diced celery
2 tomatoes cut in wedges
salad dressing of choice
½ t. salt
¼ crushed clove of garlic
pepper to taste

1. Place ingredients in mixing bowl in order given.
2. Toss lightly with dressing just before serving; serve cold.
3. Garnish with watercress or parsley.

Variations

1. Substitute chicken or turkey for meat.
2. Substitute fish for meat: tuna, salmon, halibut, or swordfish for moderate cost; shrimp, crab, or lobster for higher cost.

Broiling Meat

BROILING (see pages 227-228)

1. Select grade of beef to broil such as: prime, choice, and good grades 1 in. to 2 in. thick. (*Lower grades* may be used with tenderizer.)
2. Select cuts such as: porterhouse, filet mignon, club or rib steak, boneless loin or strip steak, or the full cut of sirloin, which is a good family buy. (*Less tender cuts* may be used with tenderizer.) Other kinds of meat such as chicken, turkey, lamb, cured ham, and fish also may be broiled.
3. Preheat oven to 350°.
4. Place steak on broiler rack so that the top of a 1-in. steak is 2 in. from the heat, and a 2-in. steak is 3 in. from the heat.
5. Time according to desired doneness by table on page 414.
6. Serve at once on hot platter or plate as part of a balanced meal.

PAN-BROILING (see page 228)

1. Select any cut that can be broiled for pan-broiling. Have it cut ½ in. to ¾ in. thick.
2. Heat heavy skillet or griddle, grease lightly, and place steak on it.
3. Cook on each side as for broiling, turning frequently and pouring off fat. Season after steak is browned.
4. Serve on hot plate or platter at once as part of a balanced meal.

TIME TABLE FOR BROILING MEAT [1]

Cut	Thickness	Minutes to Broil Each Side	
		(Rare)	(Medium)
BEEF [2]			
Porterhouse steak	1 in.	10	12
	2 in.	20	22
Sirloin steak	1 in.	10	12
	2 in.	20	22
Rib steak	1 in.	7	10
	2 in.	17	22
Chuck steak	1 in.	12	15
	1½ in.	20	22
Ground beef patties	1 in.	7	12
LAMB [3]			
Loin chops	1 in.		6
	2 in.		11
Rib chops	1 in.		6
	2 in.		11
Shoulder	1 in.		6
	2 in.		11
Ground patties	1 in.		9
SMOKED PORK [4]			
Ham slice, tenderized	½ in.		5-6
	1 in.		8-10
Bacon			2-3

[1] National Livestock and Meat Board, page 34, 1957-58. Figures based on broiling at moderate temperature (350°). Rare steaks are broiled to an internal temperature of 140°; medium to 160°; lamb chops are broiled to 170°; smoked ham is broiled to 170°. The time for broiling bacon is based on personal preference for crispness.

[2] Less tender cuts of beef may be broiled when commercial tenderizer is properly used.

[3] Lamb is not served rare.

[4] Pork is always cooked well done.

SHISH-KABOB

8 servings

2 lbs. boned leg of lamb
1 T. lemon juice
1 T. vegetable oil
1 round sliced medium onion
3 whole tomatoes
3 round sliced green peppers
  sliced egg plant
3 bay leaves
  dash salt
⅛ t. pepper

1. Cut meat in 1-in. cubes.
2. Mix oil, lemon juice, salt, and pepper, and rub on meat thoroughly.
3. Cover with sliced onion, pepper, and bay leaves and refrigerate for 4-5 hr. in covered bowl or overnight.
4. Arrange meat on skewers alternately with vegetables dipped in the seasoning.
5. Broil over charcoal or wood fire or in stove broiler, turning as needed.
6. Serve hot as part of a balanced meal.

Roasting Meat

DIRECTIONS FOR ROASTING MEAT AT LOW TEMPERATURE (see pages 226-227)

1. Wipe ready-to-cook meat with a clean damp cloth. Wash and dry freshly prepared fowl or fish. Thaw frozen meat. Season to taste.

2. Preheat oven to desired temperature (300° for beef, lamb, veal, or smoked pork; 350° for fresh pork; 325° for poultry).*

3. Use a meat thermometer. Cut a gash in meat with a paring knife, and place thermometer in center of cut, not touching bone or fat.

4. Place roast in shallow pan on a rack with fat side up, and set in a preheated oven, maintaining a constant temperature throughout roasting.

5. Consult time table for doneness desired. If you do not have a thermometer, test meat for doneness by inserting a skewer. For rare meat, the juice is red; for medium meat, the juice is pink. When meat is well done, there will be no pinkness. Well-done meat is desirable for pork, fowl, and lamb.

6. Basting, wrapping in foil, or the addition of water is not desirable by the low-heat method of roasting.

7. Remove roast from oven at once when desired temperature is reached as meat continues to cook for a few minutes by its own heat outside the oven.

8. Remove fat. Use brown drippings and measured fat to make gravy. See page 431.

9. Serve roast surrounded by vegetables on a hot platter, or garnish to suit the meat and occasion.

* Some recent research indicates that, particularly in the case of beef, more servings per pound are obtained by roasting at 200°, for a longer period of time.

TEMPERATURE AND TIME
FOR ROASTING MEATS[1]

Cut	Weight in Pounds	Oven Temperature	Interior Temperature When Done	Minutes per Pound
BEEF ROASTS[2]				
Standing rib roast	6-8	300°	140° rare	18-20
			160° med.	22-25
Rolled rib roast	5-7	300°	140° rare	32
			160° med.	38
Standing rump (high quality)	5-7	300°	150°-170°	25-30
Rolled rump (high quality)	4-6	300°	150°-170°	25-30
LAMB ROASTS				
Leg	5-8	300°	175°-180°	30-35
Shoulder (bone in)	4-6	300°	175°-180°	30-35
Rolled	3-5	300°	175°-180°	30-35
VEAL ROASTS				
Leg	5-8	300°	170°	25-35
Loin	4-6	300°	170°	30-35
Shoulder (bone in)	5-8	300°	170°	30-35
Rolled	4-6	300°	170°	40-45
FRESH PORK				
Loin—center	3-5	350°	185°	35-45
Whole	10-12	350°	185°	30-35
Half	5-7	350°	185°	22-25
SMOKED PORK				
Whole ham[3]	10-14	300°	160°	18-20
Half ham	5-7	300°	160°	22-25
Picnic shoulder	5-7	300°	170°	35

[1] National Livestock and Meat Board, page 33, 1957-58.

[2] Less tender cuts of beef may be roasted if commercial tenderizer is applied according to directions and meat is cooked at a low temperature.

[3] Hams are on the market which require shorter periods of cooking due to method of processing. Fresh pork and poultry should be roasted well done—until no pink shows in the meat or juice. Poultry is done when the joints are loose and the meat is tender when squeezed between the fingers.

Braising Meat

BASIC POT ROAST

4 lbs. beef pot roast
   (rump, chuck, or
   round)
3 T. vegetable oil
2 t. salt
¼ t. pepper
½ c. water
6 medium whole carrots
4-5 medium potatoes
8-10 small onions
2 sticks diced celery and
   leaves

4-5 servings

1. Brown meat on both sides in hot oil in a Dutch oven or pressure saucepan. Then pour off surplus fat.
2. Season with salt, pepper, and other seasoning of choice.
3. Add water; cover pan tightly and simmer over low heat 2½-3 hr., or until very tender when pierced with a fork (or 20 min. at 15 lbs. pressure in pressure saucepan).
4. About 30 min. before end of cooking time, add vegetables if meat is being simmered. In pressure saucepan, when meat is tender, add vegetables and bring pressure to 15 lbs. Cook whole vegetables 5 min., and diced vegetables 1 min.
5. To make gravy, skim off all fat; mix 3 T. flour to a smooth paste with ½ c. water and stir into 1½ c. of water; add to drippings. Cook until thickened, stirring constantly. Season to taste with salt, pepper, and crushed clove of garlic or grated onion.

Variation

Use lamb shoulder or lamb shanks instead of beef and serve with mint in sauce.

SWISS STEAK

2-3 lbs chuck or round beef 1½
   in. thick
2 T. vegetable oil
½ c. flour
½ c. diced onion
1 No. 2 can tomatoes
   (grade C)
¼ t. celery salt
1 t. salt
⅛ t. pepper
2 T. parsley
2 sticks of diced celery

4-6 servings

1. Wipe steak with clean damp cloth.
2. Mix seasoning and flour, and pound into steak with meat pounder or hammer.
3. Heat oil and brown steak on each side.
4. Pour off surplus fat.
5. Add tomatoes, onions, celery; cover and bring to boil; turn heat low and simmer until steak is tender when pierced with fork (about 20-30 min.).
6. Garnish with parsley and serve on a hot deep platter as part of a balanced meal.

TIME TABLE FOR COOKING MEAT IN LIQUID*

Cut	Average Weight in Pounds	Minutes Per Pound	Hours of Total Cooking Time
Smoked ham (old style and country cured)			
Large	12-14	20	
Small	10-12	25	
Half	6-8	30	
Smoked ham (tendered)			
Shank or butt half	5-8	20-25	
Smoked picnic shoulder	4-8	45	
Fresh or corned beef	4-6	40-50	
Beef for stew			2½-3½
Veal for stew			2-3
Lamb for stew			1½-2

* National Livestock and Meat Board

TIME TABLE FOR BRAISING MEAT*

Cut	Average Weight or Thickness	Total Cooking Time
BEEF		
Pot-roast	3-5 lbs.	3-4 hours
Swiss steak	1½-2½ in.	2-3 hours
Fricassee	2 in. cubes	1½-2½ hours
Short ribs	Pieces (2 x 2 x 4 in.)	1½-2½ hours
Round steak	¾ in.	45-60 minutes
Stuffed steak	½-¾ in.	1½ hours
PORK		
Chops	¾-1½ in.	45-60 minutes
Spareribs	2-3 lbs.	1½ hours
Tenderloin		
Whole	¾-1 lb.	45-60 minutes
Fillets	½ in.	30 minutes
Shoulder steaks	¾ in.	45-60 minutes
LAMB		
Breast—stuffed	2-3 lbs.	1½-2 hours
Breast—rolled	1½-2 lbs.	1½-2 hours
Neck slices	¾ in.	1 hour
Shanks	½ lb. each	1-1½ hours
Shoulder chops	1 in.	45-60 minutes
VEAL		
Breast—stuffed	3-4 lbs.	1½-2½ hours
Breast—rolled	2-3 lbs.	1½-2½ hours
Chops	½-¾ in.	45-60 minutes
Steak or cutlets	½-¾ in.	45-60 minutes
Shoulder chops	½-¾ in.	45-60 minutes

PORK CHOPS BAKED IN MILK

1. Preheat oven to 350°.
2. Select pork chops 1 in. thick and wipe with clean damp cloth.
3. Season with salt, pepper, and celery salt.
4. Place in flat baking dish and add milk to ¼ in. depth.
5. Bake until chops reach 170° or until all pink disappears (about 1 hr.).
6. Serve hot at once.

Variation

Place pork chops on top of scalloped potatoes and bake.

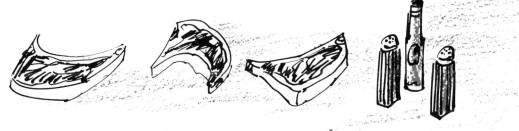

SWEET-SOUR SPARERIBS, CHINESE STYLE

4-6 servings

2 lbs. spareribs
½ c. water
¼ c. pineapple chunks
½ t. salt
2 long sliced green peppers
1 T. cornstarch
¼ c. sugar
¼ c. vinegar
    soy sauce

Pork chops or shoulder steaks may be substituted for spareribs.

1. Cut spareribs into serving portions and brown in hot fat on each side. Drain fat.
2. Add water and salt to spareribs.
3. Cover pan tightly and simmer for 20 min.
4. Blend cornstarch, sugar, vinegar, and add.
5. Cover and continue cooking over low heat for 20 min. Stir occasionally and add more water as needed to prevent drying.
6. Before serving add pineapple, soy sauce to taste, and green peppers. Mix and serve hot at once with rice, hominy grits, or sweet potatoes. Green beans or other green vegetables, a green salad, and milk, provide a balanced meal.

Variation

Bake spareribs at 350° (moderate oven) until the meat is tender (about 1½ hr.); serve plain or with a barbecue sauce if desired, as part of a balanced dinner.

SWEDISH MEATBALLS

8 2-in meat balls
(2 doz. party-size appetizers)

1 lb. ground beef
½ lb. ground cooked lean pork
1 c. bread crumbs
½ c. milk
1 egg
½ t. salt
⅛ t. pepper
⅛ t. allspice
⅛ t. of each: oregano, dry mustard, marjoram
¼ c. diced onion
2 T. flour
1½ c. beef broth
    (or bouillon cubes with vegetable juice)
2 T. vegetable oil

1. Soak crumbs in milk until soft (2-3 min.).
2. Sauté onion in oil (about 3 min.) but do not brown.
3. To bread crumbs add meat, egg, and all seasoning including drained onion.
4. Shape into balls using about 2 level tablespoons for each ball.
5. Fry over moderate heat in skillet where onions were sautéed, browning on all sides.
6. Remove meat from skillet, and drain fat.
7. Add flour, beef broth, salt, and pepper, and cook until thickened.
8. Return meat balls to sauce and serve hot.

Variations

1. Make meat balls smaller and serve on picks as a first course for a party.
2. Make larger and broil as for hamburgers after Step 3.
3. Shape and cook; then freeze and serve as needed by heating in a slow oven.
4. Use as meat for spaghetti and meat balls.
5. Shape into a loaf after Step 3 and bake at 300° until done (about 1 hr.).

HUNGARIAN GOULASH

4-6 servings

¼ lb. mild salt pork
¾ lb. lean raw beef or veal
¾ lb. lean raw pork
    dash salt
    dash pepper
    flour
1 sliced onion
1 sliced green pepper
1 bay leaf
3 whole cloves
3 diced potatoes
3 diced carrots
2 diced sticks celery

1. Dice the salt pork and fry until crisp.
2. Cut the lean raw meat in 1-in. cubes, sprinkle with salt, pepper, and flour, and brown in salt pork drippings. Drain surplus fat.
3. Add cloves, salt, pepper, and bay leaf.
4. Add water to cover, and cook until meat is tender (about 2½-3 hr. by simmering, 20 min. by pressure at 15 lbs).
5. Add vegetables, cover, and cook until tender (about 10 min. for boiling; or 1 min. in pressure saucepan at 15 lbs. pressure).
6. Thicken sauce and serve hot at once.

Poultry

BROILED CHICKEN

breasts, legs, and thighs of
tender poultry, or half of
young broiler
vegetable oil °
salt
paprika
thyme
clove of garlic
chicken bouillon cubes

Allow ¾ pound per person

1. Preheat oven to 325°. Wash fresh poultry thoroughly, and dry. Cut into suitable size for serving.
2. Rub both sides with oil, salt, and paprika.
3. Place a pinch of thyme and 1 thin sliver of fresh clove of garlic beneath each piece of chicken. Place chicken with skin side down in a flat pan.
4. Broil at 325° for 15 min. on one side (or until brown). Turn and broil until brown on other side.
5. Add ½ c. boiling water in which 2 chicken bouillon cubes have been dissolved, and cover.
6. Place in oven at 275° and bake 20 to 30 min., or until tender. (Young broilers require no oven baking and may be served at end of Step 4.)
7. Serve on hot platter with brown rice or potato as part of a balanced meal.

ROAST CHICKEN (or other poultry)

1 4-5 lb. roaster
2 T. flour
2 T. vegetable oil
2 T. lemon juice
1½ t. salt
⅛ t. pepper
¼ t. celery salt
1 recipe for stuffing
(see page 432)

5-6 servings

1. Preheat oven to 325°.
2. Mix salt, pepper, and celery salt and rub bird inside and out.
3. Stuff crop and tail end of bird and pin opening with skewer (do not pack stuffing tightly).
4. Mix flour, fat, and lemon juice and rub outside of bird.
5. Set bird on rack in shallow pan.
6. Roast 35 min. per pound (2½-3½ hr. for a 4-6 lb. bird) or until done (when leg joint is tender to pressure).
7. Remove bird to hot platter, make gravy (see page 431), and serve hot.

° Omit oil if chicken is baked in broth after broiling.

QUICK CHICKEN PIE

6 servings

1 whole canned chicken
2 c. biscuit mix
2 T. grated onion
3 c. medium white sauce *
2 T. diced pimento
2 T. diced green pepper
½ c. diced celery
1 pkg. frozen peas
1½ t. salt
2 T. parsley

* Or 2 c. undiluted cream of mushroom soup.

1. Preheat oven to 425°.
2. Cut chicken from bone in bite sizes.
3. Make medium white sauce using chicken broth (see page 427).
4. Mix hot white sauce, chicken, all vegetables, and seasoning, and pour into 2-qt. oblong baking dish. Add parsley and pimento.
5. Make biscuits according to directions (see page 360) and set ¼ in. apart over pie and bake 18-20 min., or until biscuits are done.
6. Serve hot as main dish with salad, milk, and fruit dessert.

Variations

1. For Curried Chicken, add 1 t. curry powder at Step 3 and serve with hot brown rice instead of biscuits.
2. For Chicken à la King, serve as creamed chicken on toast or hot biscuits.
3. At Step 4 add 1 c. sliced almonds and serve with hot brown rice.

FRIED CHICKEN WITH MILK GRAVY

4 servings

½ c. evaporated milk
3 lbs. cut up broiler-fryer
½ c. flour
1 t. salt
½ t. paprika
⅛ t. pepper
vegetable oil

1. Put the evaporated milk into a bowl; dip chicken pieces into milk (reserve milk for gravy).
2. Combine flour, salt, paprika, and pepper; roll chicken pieces in mixture (or shake in a paper bag).
3. Brown chicken on both sides in hot oil ½ in. deep in skillet, and cook until tender (about 30 min.).
4. Remove chicken; place in covered pan and keep hot in low oven (250°) until ready to serve.
5. To make milk gravy, drain off all fat. For each cup gravy use 1 T. fat, 2 T. flour, 1 c. water, ⅓ c. nonfat dry milk, ¼ t. salt, and 1 bouillon cube.
6. Cook, stirring until mixture thickens.
7. Serve hot at once.

... chicken fat
3-6 T. flour
   dash salt
⅛ t. pepper

2. Remove pieces of chicken from the broth and keep hot; skim fat from broth.
3. Blend fat and flour, mix with ⅓ c. of broth, and pour into hot broth, stirring until thickened.
4. Turn off heat until ready to add dumplings.

PART TWO

¾ c. sifted flour
2 t. baking powder
½ t. salt
1 egg
½ c. nonfat dry milk
2 T. chicken fat
⅓ c. water

1. Sift flour, baking powder, dry milk, and salt together in mixing bowl.
2. Add egg, water, and fat, and mix with the dry ingredients.
3. Drop by spoonfuls on boiling chicken gravy.
4. Reduce heat, cover tightly, and simmer 15 min. without lifting lid.
5. Serve hot with green cooked vegetables, vegetable salad, milk, and dessert.

Variations

1. Use cold stewed chicken for chicken salad (see page 413).
2. Use cold stewed chicken in croquettes by grinding through food chopper, and mixing with thick gravy, bread crumbs or potatoes, grated onion, and seasoning. Shape into croquettes and fry in hot fat until golden brown.

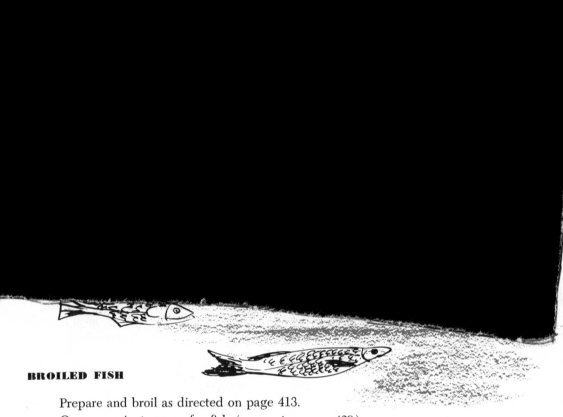

BROILED FISH

Prepare and broil as directed on page 413.

Or use marinate sauce for fish (see recipe page 429).

BAKED FISH

1. Prepare as for pork chops (see page 419). Season to taste and bake in ⅛ in. milk until fish is tender (about 20-25 min. at 325°).

2. Serve hot with lemon or lime wedge or favorite fish sauce.

SALMON LOAF

4 servings

1 1-lb. can pink or chinook
    salmon
2 T. grated onion
½ c. milk
    dash salt
    dash celery salt
⅛ t. pepper
2 T. catsup
1 T. lemon juice
1 c. soft bread crumbs
    lemon or lime wedge

1. Preheat oven to 350°. Mash canned salmon, bones, and juice.

2. Blend all ingredients and shape in an oiled loaf pan (9 x 5 x 3).

3. Bake 35-40 min. or until brown.

4. Garnish with lemon or lime. Serve hot with baked potatoes, a cooked green vegetable, a vegetable salad, a fruit whip or stewed canned fruit, and milk.

STUFFED BAKED HEART

4 servings

1 beef heart or 2 veal hearts
2 c. beef stock, or 2 bouillon
    cubes and 2 c. tomato
    juice
1 clove garlic
1 medium onion
1 t. salt
    dash pepper
⅛ t. basil
⅛ t. celery seeds
1½ c. stuffing (page 432)
3 T. flour

1. Remove all veins and arteries, and wash heart.
2. Place heart with ½ c. beef stock and seasoning in pressure saucepan; cook for 20 min. at 15 lbs. pressure, or simmer until tender (about 2½ hr.).
3. Remove heart, stuff cavity with prepared stuffing, and fasten with skewers or sew. Then rub with fat and paprika.
4. Heat in a hot oven (400°) for about 15-20 min. or until thoroughly hot.
5. Serve at once as part of a balanced meal with a gravy made from juices, liquid, and flour.

Variations

1. At Step 2 add vegetables of choice and cook until tender for a beef heart stew.
2. Slice heart and fry.

RUTH WHITE'S RECIPE FOR BRAINS AND CHEESE

4 servings

1 set brains (beef or veal)
3 eggs
¼ lb. grated sharp cheddar
    cheese
2 T. grated onion
1 diced green pepper
¼ c. diced celery and leaves
3 slices bacon
⅛ t. each of: oregano, thyme,
    celery salt
    dash pepper
½ t. salt

1. Wash brains in cold water, and remove membrane and fine bones.
2. Fry bacon crisp in a large skillet and remove from pan.
3. Slice brains in about ½ in. cubes, drop into hot bacon fat, and brown on one side.
4. Turn and add grated onion, celery, green pepper, and all seasoning except cheese; cover and simmer until vegetables are tender but not soft (about 5 min.).
5. Beat eggs and add cheese. Add to brains, stirring gently until cheese is melted and eggs firm.
6. Serve in a hot bowl or on a hot platter, garnishing with crumbled bacon as part of a balanced luncheon or dinner.

Variation

Sweetbreads may be substituted for or combined with brains in this dish.

FRIED CHICKEN LIVERS

4 servings

1 lb. fresh or frozen chicken
   livers
½ t. salt
⅛ t. pepper
2 T. vegetable oil

1. Wash livers and dry in absorbent paper.
2. Season livers with salt and pepper and drop in skillet with hot vegetable oil.
3. Reduce heat, and brown on one side; turn and brown on other side.
4. Remove to absorbent paper. Place in pan and keep warm in oven (250°) until ready to serve.
5. To prepare a sauce, blend 3 T. flour with fat in skillet and add 2 chicken bouillon cubes and 1½ c. milk. Cook until thickened and smooth.

Variations

1. Dip chicken livers in flour before frying, and add mushrooms (½ lb. fresh, or 1 3-oz. can) when livers are brown.
2. Use beef or lamb liver instead of chicken and add ½ c. diced onion at Step 3.

LIVER LOAF

8 servings

1 lb. beef, lamb, or pork liver
½ lb. pork sausage
½ lb. ground beef
1 t. salt
½ t. thyme
2 T. grated onion
¼ c. diced celery
1 egg
½ c. quick-cooking oats
   or bread crumbs
½ c. milk
⅛ t. pepper

1. Wash liver and remove membrane.
2. Sauté liver with sausage, onions, and celery over low heat until slightly brown. Cool and grind through food chopper.
3. Mix with all remaining ingredients in mixing bowl, and shape into an oiled loaf pan (9 x 5 x 3).
4. Bake in a moderate oven (350°) until done (about 40 min.).
5. Serve as meat for main meal, or as spread for sandwiches.

Variations

1. Mix all ingredients, shape into patties, and broil or fry.
2. Blend in blender with mayonnaise, sour cream, and a package of dried onion soup and serve as a liver dip for a party.

Sauces, Syrups, Salad Dressings, Stuffings, and Gravy

RUTH WHITE'S WHITE SAUCE*
TYPES AND USES

Type	Tablespoons of Fat	Tablespoons of Flour	Teaspoons of Salt	Cups of Milk	Uses
Thin	1	1	¼	1	cream soups, welsh rarebit
Medium	1	2	¼	1	creamed meat and vegetables, welsh rarebit, scalloped meat and vegetables
Thick	1½	3	¼	1	soufflés, croquettes

METHOD I

1. Melt fat in sauce pan or top of double boiler.
2. Add flour and seasonings and blend.
3. Add milk gradually, stirring constantly to make a smooth thickened mixture.

METHOD II

1. Heat milk scalding hot.
2. Blend flour, seasoning, and fat with twice the amount of liquid as flour used (such as ¼ c. flour to ½ c. liquid) until smooth.
3. Stir gradually into hot milk and cook until thickened and smooth.

Variations

1. For Cheese Sauce, add 1 c. grated sharp cheese (¼ lb.) per cup of thin or medium white sauce.
2. For Egg Sauce, add 2 chopped hard-cooked eggs and seasoning of choice per cup of medium white sauce.
3. For Mock Hollandaise Sauce, add 2 beaten egg yolks, 2 T. lemon juice and a dash of Tabasco or cayenne pepper per cup of medium white sauce at end of Step 3. (This sauce is lower in calories than standard hollandaise sauce.)

* This white sauce uses less fat than the conventional recipe.

427

RUTH WHITE'S TOMATO SAUCE

3 cups

2 T. vegetable oil
3 T. flour
1 t. salt
   dash pepper
½ c. diced celery with leaves
½ c. diced onion
1 bay leaf
4 cloves
2½ c. canned tomatoes or tomato juice
½ c. water
   dash cayenne pepper

1. Sauté onion and celery in oil until soft but not brown (2 min.).
2. Add water, salt, pepper, cloves, and bay leaf; cover and simmer over low heat 5 min.
3. Remove bay leaf and cloves.
4. Mix flour with ¼ c. tomatoes. Add flour paste and canned tomatoes or juice to mixture, cooking until it thickens.
5. Push mixture through sieve if desired, or serve hot and unstrained over omelet, cheese soufflé, curried spoonbread, fried fish, meat loaf, or liver.

Variations

1. Add 1 diced raw green pepper before serving.
2. Add ½ c. sliced, cooked, or canned mushrooms at Step 4.
3. Add 1 c. ground cooked ham and 1 t. curry powder before serving and heat to boiling.

TARTAR SAUCE (for fish)

1¼ cups

1 c. mayonnaise or cooked
   salad dressing
2 T. chopped sour pickle
1 t. grated onion or juice
1 T. minced parsley

1. Combine all ingredients, chill, and serve with fish.

Variations

Add 2 T. chopped olives, 1 t. horseradish, 1 T. chopped capers, or 2 T. lemon juice.

MINT SAUCE (for lamb)

¾ cup

½ c. water
¼ c. lemon juice
1 T. sugar
¼ t. mint extract
1 t. dried mint or 1 T. minced
   fresh mint
¼ t. salt

1. Heat water, salt, and dried mint to boiling.
2. Add remaining ingredients, mix, and serve hot with lamb.

LEMON-BUTTER SAUCE
(for vegetables)

½ cup

½ c. creamed butter or margarine (or vegetable oil if preferred)
2 T. lemon juice
1 t. salt
2 T. minced parsley
   dash cayenne pepper or Tabasco sauce
1 T. grated onion

1. Melt fat, and add remaining ingredients.
2. Serve hot on asparagus, broccoli, or any green vegetable.
3. May also be used on fish.

MARINATE SAUCE (for fish)

½ cup

Blend in small mixing bowl: 2 T. oil, 1 crushed clove garlic, 2 T. grated onion, 1 t. salt, 1 t. paprika, 1 t. bouquet sauce, black ground pepper, ¼ t. celery salt, ¼ t. thyme, and 3 T. lemon juice or wine vinegar. Brush large fish, inside and out with marinate sauce. Bake or broil.

Sauces for Desserts

HARD SAUCE

1 cup

½ c. butter or margarine
1 c. confectioner's sugar
1 t. vanilla
¼ t. almond extract

1. Cream fat, vanilla, almond extract, and sugar until light and fluffy.
2. Serve with fruit cake, plain cake, bread puddings, or as icing for cake.
3. Store in covered jar in refrigerator.

HOT FUDGE SAUCE

1½ cups

2 c. brown sugar (packed)
¼ c. light corn syrup
⅔ c. evaporated milk
2 sqs. unsweetened chocolate (2 oz.)
   dash salt
1 t. vanilla

1. Melt chocolate in top of double boiler. Add remaining ingredients except vanilla; beat.
2. Boil until smooth and thick, stirring. Add vanilla and beat.

RUTH WHITE'S "MAPLE" SYRUP

2 cups

2 c. brown sugar (packed)
1¼ c. water
½ c. honey
¾ t. mapelene flavoring

1. Mix first three ingredients, bring to boil, and boil slowly until smooth (about 2 min.).
2. Add mapelene; mix and serve hot over pancakes, waffles, French toast, or spoon bread.

Variations

1. Add ¼ c. chopped nutmeats at Step 2.
2. Add ½ c. orange marmalade at end of Step 1.

Salad Dressings

RUTH WHITE'S LOW-CALORIE BASIC FRENCH DRESSING

2-3 cups

1 c. vegetable oil
1 c. vinegar, lemon juice, or lime juice (or mixture)
1 t. salt
1 t. sugar
1 t. dry mustard
¼ t. celery seeds
¼ t. basil
1 crushed clove garlic
1 T. grated onion
3 pieces cinnamon bark
¼ lb. minced blue cheese

1. Mix oil with all ingredients except vinegar, lemon juice, or lime juice.
2. Pour into a clean jar, cover, and store in the refrigerator.
3. When you are ready to use, add lemon juice, lime juice, or vinegar in equal parts.

Variations

Add any herb or seasoning of choice. Use tarragon or wine vinegar.

MAYONNAISE WITH VARIATIONS (quick)

1 cup

½ c. mayonnaise
½ c. sour cream
1 T. grated onion
1 T. horseradish
1 T. honey

1. Mix and store in covered jar in refrigerator.
2. Use within a week, with vegetable or fruit salad or on hot cooked vegetables.

THOUSAND ISLAND DRESSING

Add diced hard-cooked eggs, diced green pepper, minced parsley, and grated onion to 1 c. mayonnaise.

RUSSIAN DRESSING

1½ cups

1. Blend ½ c. mayonnaise, ½ c. French dressing, ½ c. chili sauce, 1 T. grated onion, and 1 T. diced green pepper.
2. Store in covered jar in refrigerator and use on vegetable salads as needed.

QUICK FRUIT SALAD DRESSING

1 cup

⅓ c. nonfat dry milk
⅓ c. mayonnaise
⅓ c. frozen concentrate orange juice
2 T. lemon juice
1 T. honey
1 t. grated onion
½ t. salt
dash cayenne

1. Place dry milk and juice in bowl and beat with rotary egg beater.
2. Add remaining ingredients and beat until smooth.
3. Serve with fruit salad.

Variation

Add ¼ lb. crumbled blue cheese.

Gravy and Stuffings

MEAT OR POULTRY GRAVY

METHOD ONE

1. Remove fat from dripping pan but leave all of brown watery drippings (for flavor, vitamins, and minerals).
2. For each cup of gravy, add 1 T. fat and 2 T. flour to pan with drippings and blend. Add 1 c. water, 2 T. grated onion, and/or 1 clove of crushed garlic and cook until smooth and thickened, stirring to prevent lumping.

METHOD TWO

1. Proceed through Step 1 above, but for each 1 c. liquid blend 2 T. flour with ¼ c. of the liquid.
2. Bring remaining liquid to boiling point and then gradually add flour paste to hot liquid, stirring constantly until thickened and smooth.

BREAD STUFFING

4-5 servings

5 c. bread crumbs
2 T. vegetable oil
¼ c. diced onion
¼ c. diced celery
2 chicken bouillon cubes
½ t. salt
   dash pepper
½ c. minced parsley
½ t. thyme or poultry seasoning
2 eggs
½ c. hot poultry broth (or hot
   water with dissolved
   bouillon cubes)

1. Sauté onion and celery in oil.
2. Place all ingredients in mixing bowl, and thoroughly blend.
3. Stuff crop of bird lightly and then tail end. Fasten with picks or skewers.
4. Cook remaining dressing in pan.
5. Serve hot with giblet gravy.

Variations

1. For Rice Stuffing, substitute 5 c. cooked brown rice for bread crumbs.
2. For Corn Bread Stuffing, substitute one-half to two-thirds corn bread for bread crumbs.
3. For Mushroom Stuffing, add ½ lb. cooked mushrooms at Step 2.
4. For Sausage Stuffing, omit fat, and sauté vegetables with diced sausage. Pour off all surplus fat, and proceed to Step 2.
5. For Chestnut Stuffing, add 1 c. cooked mashed chestnuts (½ lb.) at Step 2.
6. For Apple-Raisin Stuffing, add 3 c. finely diced tart apples and 1 c. seeded raisins at Step 2.

STUFFING FOR VEGETABLES ("DOLMAS")

4-6 servings

1 c. cooked ground beef, lamb,
   pork, or poultry
2 T. grated onion
2 T. minced parsley
2 T. finely diced celery and
   leaves
1 t. salt
   dash pepper
2 T. catsup (optional)
1 egg
1 c. bread crumbs, or cooked
   rice
2 T. vegetable oil
   finely diced vegetables

1. Preheat oven to 375°.
2. Cut out center from pepper, egg plant, crooked neck squash, zucchini squash, or firm tomatoes.
3. Dice vegetables removed, and mix with other vegetables and seasoning, and sauté in oil 3-5 min.
4. Mix in all remaining ingredients, stuff vegetable, and bake about 25 min.
5. Top with sharp grated cheese last 10 min. of cooking if desired.
6. Serve hot as main dish for meal.

Cakes, Cookies, and Pastries

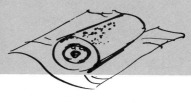

Cakes

PLAIN CAKE (standard mixing) *

2 9-in. layers or 1 loaf 13 x 9 x 2

2½ c. sifted cake flour	1½ c. sugar	3 separated eggs
3 t. baking powder	½ c. fat	1 t. vanilla
½ t. salt	1 c. milk	

1. Preheat oven to 375°. Oil cake pans.
2. Cream fat and sugar in mixing bowl until light and fluffy and sugar is thoroughly dissolved.
3. Add vanilla and egg yolks and mix.
4. Measure sifted flour and other dry ingredients and sift together three times, blending thoroughly.
5. Add one-third of flour mixture to creamed mixture and blend with a circular motion; then add one-third of milk and blend.
6. Repeat, adding flour and milk alternately until all is added.
7. Beat egg whites until they stand in moist peaks and fold batter into egg whites.
8. Spoon batter into pans, and bake until firm when touched in center or until a toothpick inserted in center comes out clean (about 25-30 min. for layers; 50-60 min. for loaf; test at 25 min.).
9. Cool in pan on rack for 10 min.; then loosen edges with spatula. Place rack over cake and invert (turn pan upside down).
10. When thoroughly cool, ice with favorite icing.

Variations

1. For white cake, omit egg yolks.
2. For spice cake, add 1 t. cinnamon, ¼ t. nutmeg, ¼ t. ginger, and ¼ t. allspice. to dry ingredients at Step 4.

° If you use the electric mixer be careful not to over-mix. By hand, blend until just mixed but do not beat.

UPSIDE-DOWN CAKE

1. Use any of above recipes and an oblong pan (13 x 9 x 3). Preheat oven to 350°.

2. Oil pan with table fat, and press 1 c. of brown sugar evenly over the bottom.

3. Dot sugar with broken nutmeats.

4. Place on this any of the following fruits: pineapple rings, peach halves, apricot halves, fresh blueberries, or fresh peaches.

5. Spoon cake batter evenly over this topping, and bake until done (when toothpick inserted in center comes out clean; about 40 min.).

6. Cut in square servings, and top with whipped cream. Garnish with cherry or broken nutmeats if desired.

RUTH WHITE'S APPLESAUCE CAKE*

½ c. vegetable oil
1 c. brown sugar (packed)
2 eggs
1¾ c. sifted cake flour
3 t. baking powder
½ t. salt
1 t. grated lemon rind
1 t. grated orange rind
1 t. cinnamon
¼ t. nutmeg
¼ t. allspice
1 t. vanilla
1 c. thick applesauce
1 c. raisins
½ c. currants (optional)
½ c. broken nutmeats
¼ c. milk

8- or 9-in. tube pan or 1 loaf 9 x 5 x 3

1. Preheat oven to 350°.

2. Oil and flour pan; if tube is used, line pan and tube with wax paper and then oil.

3. Cream oil and sugar until fluffy in mixing bowl; then add eggs, spices, and vanilla, and mix thoroughly.

4. Add dried fruits and applesauce, and mix.

5. Sift flour before measuring; then measure, add baking powder and salt, and sift together, blending thoroughly.

6. Add one-half of dry ingredients to applesauce mixture and blend; then add milk and blend; then remaining flour and blend.

7. Add nutmeats, mix, and spoon into prepared pan.

8. Bake until done (about 45 min.).

9. Remove cake from pan by loosening sides with a spatula. Let stand for 10 min., before turning upside down on cake rack.

10. Sprinkle with confectioner's sugar, or frost with your favorite frosting.

* This is a moist cake and may be baked several days before you wish to use it.

CHOCOLATE CAKE
(quick method using vegetable oil)

2 9-in. layers or 1 loaf 13 x 9 x 2

2 c. sifted cake flour	¾ c. milk	3 t. baking powder
2 c. sugar	2 oz. melted chocolate	3 eggs
½ c. vegetable oil	1 t. salt	1½ t. vanilla

1. Preheat oven to 350°. Oil pan and flour lightly.
2. Sift all measured dry ingredients into mixing bowl. Blend thoroughly.
3. Melt chocolate in top of double boiler.
4. Make a well in dry ingredients and add chocolate, oil, half of milk, and vanilla; mix at medium speed on electric mixer 2 min., or 300 strokes by hand.
5. Add remaining milk and eggs and beat 2 more min., or 300 strokes by hand, scraping sides of bowl constantly and blending all of the mixture evenly.
6. Spoon batter into prepared pans, dividing evenly, and place pans in oven, staggering them so that they do not touch each other or walls of oven.
7. Bake until done or about 30-35 min. for oblong cake. (If glass pan is used, bake at 325°.)
8. Remove from oven when done and let stand in pans 10 min. Then loosen sides with spatula. If underbaked, cake will fall in center.
9. Place rack over cake and turn cake upside down to remove from pan.
10. Frost when cool, by first spreading frosting between layers, then on sides, and then on top.

Variations

1. Add ½ c. broken nutmeats at Step 5.
2. For Cupcakes, fill muffin tins half full and bake 18 to 20 min.
3. For Yellow Cake, omit chocolate.

ORANGE CHIFFON CAKE

PART ONE

10 x 4 tube or 13 x 9 oblong pan

2½ c. sifted cake flour
1 c. sugar
3 t. baking powder
½ c. vegetable oil
6 egg yolks
¾ c. frozen orange juice concentrate
2 T. grated orange rind
½ t. almond extract
½ t. vanilla

1. Preheat oven to 325° for tube and 350° for oblong pan.
2. Set out pan but *do not grease*.
3. Sift together in mixing bowl all of the measured dry ingredients in Part One, blending thoroughly.
4. Make a well in dry ingredients and add: oil, egg yolks, orange juice, and all flavorings. Mix until smooth.

PART TWO

1 c. egg whites (7-8)
½ t. cream of tartar
1 t. salt
½ c. sugar

1. Beat egg whites with salt and cream of tartar until foamy. Then start beating in ½ c. sugar 1 T. at a time until it is dissolved, and all sugar is used. (Meringue should stand in firm, moist peaks.)

2. Fold egg-yolk mixture gently into egg whites with a broad spoon or spatula. Use an over-and-under movement until blended.

3. Spoon into ungreased pan and bake at 325° for 55 min. (in a tube); then increase heat to 350° and bake 10-15 min. longer or until top springs back when lightly touched.

4. Remove from oven. Turn pan upside down on funnel, and cool. Remove from pan, using a spatula to loosen.

5. Serve plain with fruit, or frost if desired.

Variations

1. Bake as cupcakes. Fill pans ⅞ in. full.

2. Add ½ c. diced almonds at Step 2, Part Two, and sprinkle almonds over top before baking.

ANGEL FOOD CAKE

10 x 4 tube

1 c. sifted cake flour   ¼ t. salt   1 t. vanilla
1½ c. sugar   1¼ t. cream of tartar   ½ t. almond extract
1¼ c. egg whites (11-12)

1. Preheat oven to 375°, and set out tube pan, but do not grease.

2. Sift measured sifted flour with ½ c. sugar three times.

3. Beat egg whites (room temperature), salt, and cream of tartar together in large mixing bowl until foamy.

4. Add granulated sugar 2 T. at a time, and beat 10 sec. after each addition (at medium speed in an electric mixer), or until sugar is dissolved. When all sugar is added and meringue stands in moist peaks, add flavoring.

5. Sift 3 T. of flour mixture over meringue and fold in. Repeat until all is used.

6. Spoon batter into ungreased tube pan and cut through batter with a knife until it is smooth and level.

7. Bake for 30-35 min., or until cake top springs when lightly touched.

8. Loosen sides of cake with spatula and invert pan over rack to cool. Gently ease cake out of pan. Serve plain or frosted as desired.

Variations

1. For Chocolate Angel Cake, substitute ⅓ c. cocoa for ⅓ c. flour.
2. For Layer Angel Cake, make 2 or 3 days ahead of use and bake in layers or in 2 or 3 circles. Put lemon or vanilla filling (see page 446) between layers and frost top with whipped cream and toasted almonds.

JELLY ROLL (sponge cake)

15 x 10 jelly roll

1 c. sifted cake flour	4 eggs (⅔ c.)	1 t. vanilla
1 t. baking powder	1 c. sugar	1 c. tart jelly
¼ t. salt		

1. Preheat oven to 400°. Oil pan, line bottom with aluminum foil, and oil.
2. Sift flour, baking powder, and salt together in large mixing bowl.
3. Beat eggs in another mixing bowl until lemon-colored and thick, adding sugar gradually and vanilla with last addition.
4. Gradually fold flour mixture into egg mixture, or mix in electric mixer at low speed, until batter is smooth.
5. Spread batter evenly over pan until it fills all corners and bake for 10-12 min., or until top springs when touched with finger.
6. Remove, loosen edges with spatula, and turn onto a clean smooth towel that has a thick sifting of confectioner's sugar over it.
7. Remove paper, and trim edges while cake is hot.
8. Turn up end of cake with towel and roll cake with towel. Leave to cool on wire rack.
9. Unroll cake when cool. Spread with jelly or other filling and roll again.
10. When ready to serve, sprinkle with confectioner's sugar and cut in slices.

Variations

1. Cook in layers and frost or serve with fresh fruit.
2. Cook in oblong pan and frost. Cut in squares to serve.
3. Add ½ c. ground toasted almonds at Step 4.

RUTH WHITE'S CHEESE PIE

8 servings

CRUST

14 graham crackers
¼ t. each of cinnamon and nutmeg
1 t. each of grated lemon and orange rind
1 T. soft table fat

1. Preheat oven to 350°.
2. Grease a 9-in. pie plate with table fat.
3. Roll graham crackers into a fine meal and blend with spices and lemon rind. Then press into shape of plate. Chill.

FILLING

3 oz. pkg. cream cheese
6 oz. cottage cheese
4 separated eggs
⅓ c. sour cream
1 T. grated orange rind
2 t. grated lemon rind
2 T. lemon juice
1 c. sugar
½ t. cream of tartar
½ t. salt
1 t. vanilla
12 toasted almonds sliced in halves

1. Push cheese through sieve or food mill, or blend in blender. Mix thoroughly with well-beaten egg yolks, ½ c. sugar, vanilla, lemon and orange rind, and juice.
2. Beat egg whites with salt and cream of tartar until foamy.
3. Add remaining sugar 1 T. at a time, beating after each addition until sugar is dissolved, and meringue stands in moist firm peaks.
4. Fold cheese mixture into meringue, and turn into prepared graham cracker crust.
5. Bake until cake is done (about 1 hr.).
6. Cool and cut in 8 pieces. Top each piece with whipped or sour cream and toasted almonds.

Cream Pie

COCONUT CREAM PIE

9-in. pie

1½ c. evaporated milk	5 T. flour	1 t. vanilla
1½ c. water	½ t. salt	½ c. coconut
½ c. sugar	3 eggs, separated	½ t. cream of tartar

1. Preheat oven to 450° and prepare pastry shell by recipe for one-crust pie (see page 439).
2. Heat milk in top of double boiler covered.
3. Beat egg yolks lightly in mixing bowl. Blend ½ c. sugar, flour, coconut, and ½ c. hot milk. Mix with beaten egg yolks.
4. Add egg-yolk mixture to scalding hot milk gradually, stirring constantly until thick and smooth (2-3 min.).
5. Add vanilla, mix, pour hot mixture into baked pastry shell and top with prepared meringue.
6. Prepare meringue by beating egg whites with cream of tartar and salt until foamy. Add sugar 1 T. at a time, beating after each addition until sugar is dissolved and all is used.
7. Spread meringue over warm pie, touching crust at the edge, and top with coconut.
8. Bake until golden brown (about 5-10 min.).
9. Cool and serve as dessert with light meal.

Pie Crust

PASTRY FOR TWO-CRUST PIE
(standard recipe)

2 9-in pie crusts or 1 2-crust pie

2 c. sifted all-purpose flour
1 t. salt

4-5 T. cold milk
⅔ c. fat

1. Sift flour and salt in mixing bowl.
2. Add fat and cut into flour with pastry blender, knives, forks, or fingers.
3. Sprinkle liquid (3 T.) over flour mixture and form into ball of dough that is neither sticky nor dry. Add remaining liquid as needed to use all flour.
4. Divide dough in halves, and if time permits, chill for 30 min. in refrigerator before making crust.
5. Place one ball of dough between pieces of wax paper and roll with rolling pin from center out to ⅛-in. thickness. (Roll dough 1 in. larger than pan.)
6. Remove top piece of wax paper, invert dough over pie pan, and remove remaining wax paper.
7. Fit dough firmly into pan without stretching it.
8. For fruit pie, fill bottom crust with prepared fruit and lay top crust over fruit, making a pattern of holes in top crust to let steam escape.
9. Press top and bottom crust together to seal with a fork or make a fluted edge. Trim off remaining dough. (A fluted edge increases calorie content of pie.)
10. Cover outer edge of two-crust pie with foil and bake at 450° for 15 min. Remove foil, reduce heat to 375°, and bake for 20 min. (Apple pie may require 30 min.)
11. Cool fruit pie and serve with sharp cheese or garnish with sour cream.
12. For one-crust pie: bake crust before adding filling by placing dough on outside of pie pan. Prick holes at intervals in dough with fork. Secure dough firmly around edge of pan by pressing with damp fingers. To keep from slipping, place another pie pan over dough. Trim surplus dough and bake at 450° for 5 min. Remove pan which is holding dough in place and bake 5 min. more at 450°. Remove and cool. (This is an easy way to succeed in making a single crust for a pie.)

FLUTED CRUST RIM

1. Trim pastry 1 in. larger than pie pan.
2. Turn edge under, and raise this double fold so that it stands up with the top side against rim of pie pan.
3. Dampen fingers, and place tip of right index finger against inner edge of fold of pastry. Then place tips of thumb and index finger of the left hand on either side and against the outer edge of fold.
4. Pinch and press until all of rim is fluted.

WOVEN LATTICE PIE CRUST FOR TOP

1. Leave ½ in. overhang of dough on lower crust.
2. Roll dough for top crust ⅛ in. thick and cut in ½-in. wide strips.
3. Lay strips in one direction over fruit, about ½ in. apart.
4. Weave cross strips, starting at center and laying ½ in. apart.
5. Press outer edge with damp fork to seal pie, or flute edge.
6. Trim off surplus dough, and bake as directed for fruit pie.

GRAHAM CRACKER PIE CRUST*

8- or 9-inch crust

1. Place 12-14 graham crackers between two sheets of wax paper and roll into a fine meal.
2. Oil pan.
3. Press graham cracker meal to line pan completely.

Variations

Substitute 1 c. vanilla, chocolate, or ginger snap wafers for graham crackers.

Fruit Pie

APPLE PIE

9-inch pie

6 medium-size sliced tart cooking apples or enough to fill pie crust
¾-1 c. brown sugar
½ t. cinnamon
¼ t. nutmeg
1 T. lemon juice and grated rind of lemon
1 T. soft margarine
pastry for two-crust pie

1. Preheat oven to 450°.
2. Wash, pare, and cut apples into thin slices.
3. Mix apples, sugar, spices, and lemon juice and rind, and place in pastry-lined pie plate.
4. Dot with butter and cover with pastry.
5. Bake at 450° for 15 min.; reduce heat to 375° and bake 20-30 min., or until apples are tender and the crust brown.

DEEP DISH APPLE PIE

1. Using above recipe, place apples in oiled baking dish 13 x 9 x 2.
2. Mix sugar and seasonings and press over top; dot with butter and add ¼ c. hot water.
3. Add top crust of pastry or biscuit dough and bake as for fruit pie.

° Fat may be omitted entirely except for greasing pan. (Graham cracker meal stays in place pressing against oiled sides of pan.)

APPLE CRISP

1. Prepare apples as for deep-dish pie and place in 13 x 9 x 2 in. dish. Add ½ c. boiling water.

2. For crumb top blend ¾ c. packed brown sugar, ¼ c. soft margarine, ¾ c. dry quick oatmeal, 1 t. cinnamon, ¼ t. nutmeg, 1 T. lemon juice, grated rind of 1 lemon. Press as cover over apples.

3. Bake in preheated oven at 450°F. for 15 min. Reduce heat to 400° and bake until apples are tender and crust is golden crisp.

Variations

Use cherries, berries, peaches, or other fruit and vary sugar to taste.

Chiffon Pie

RUTH WHITE'S ORANGE-LEMON CHIFFON PIE

9-inch pie

2 T. unflavored gelatin	1½ t. grated orange rind	½ t. salt
½ c. lemon juice	½ c. nonfat dry milk	½ t. cream of tartar
½ c. orange juice	1 c. water	½ c. sugar
1½ t. grated lemon rind	3 separated eggs	1 graham cracker crust

1. Prepare graham cracker crust (see page 440).
2. Soak gelatin in fruit juice.
3. Mix water, dry milk, and grated lemon and orange rind, and heat to scalding hot in top of double boiler.
4. Beat egg yolks lightly and add ¼ c. sugar and ¼ c. hot milk; cook until slightly thickened.
5. Add gelatin-fruit juice mixture and cook until gelatin is dissolved (mixture may be slightly flecked).
6. Add salt and cream of tartar to egg whites which are at room temperature and beat until foamy.
7. Add ½ c. sugar 1 T. at a time, beating after each addition until all is dissolved. When all sugar is added, whites should stand in moist peaks.
8. Fold hot fruit mixture into meringue. Cover and let stand 5 min.
9. Spoon into graham cracker crust and chill in refrigerator 3-4 hr., or overnight.
10. For topping, whip ½ c. heavy ceam, add 1 T. sugar and ¼ t. vanilla, and spread over top. If it is desirable to keep calories low, omit topping or use nonfat dry milk topping (see page 368). Garnish with a circle of fresh strawberries or other fruit and serve.

Cookies

OATMEAL COOKIES (drop)

2 eggs
1 c. vegetable oil, less 2 T.
2 c. dark brown sugar
   (packed)
2 T. milk (warm)
2 c. sifted whole wheat flour
   (or enriched white flour)
3 t. baking powder
½ t. salt
2 c. quick dry oats
½ c. coconut
½ c. broken nutmeats
1 t. vanilla

90-100 cookies

1. Preheat oven to 375° and set out un-greased cookie sheets.
2. Beat eggs in large mixing bowl, add oil, sugar, vanilla, milk, coconut, nut-meats, and quick oats, and blend to-gether.
3. Measure sifted flour, baking powder, and salt and sift together into mixing bowl, blending thoroughly.
4. Drop from spoon in equal portions 2 in. apart onto a cookie sheet.
5. Bake 10-12 min. until done.
6. Remove at once with a pancake turner, and cool on wax paper.
7. Store in tightly-covered cookie jar, or tin container, and use for dessert or refresh-ment with fruit or milk.

Variations

1. Add 1 c. of raisins or other dried fruit of choice.
2. Roll cookies over the handle of a wooden spoon just as you take them from the hot cookie sheet. This gives a spiral, party cookie.

TOLL HOUSE COOKIES (drop)

1 egg
½ c. vegetable oil
1 c. brown sugar (packed)
½ t. vanilla
1 c. sifted all-purpose flour
   plus 2 T.
½ t. salt
1 t. baking powder
1 6-oz. pkg. chocolate chips
½ c. broken nutmeats

45-50 cookies

1. Preheat oven to 375°, and lightly grease cookie sheets.
2. Beat egg in mixing bowl; add sugar, fat, and vanilla, and blend thoroughly.
3. Measure sifted flour, baking powder, and salt, and sift into mixing bowl, blending thoroughly.
4. Add chocolate and nuts, and blend. Drop onto cookie sheet about 2 in. apart.
5. Bake 10-12 min. or until done. Remove and store as for oatmeal cookies.

MOLASSES COOKIES (drop)

45-50 cookies

1 egg
¾ c. vegetable oil, less 1 T.
¼ c. dark brown sugar
   (packed)
⅓ c. dark molasses
¾ c. quick oats
1½ c. sifted all-purpose flour
2 t. baking powder
½ t. cinnamon
½ t. ginger
¼ t. cloves
½ t. salt

1. Preheat oven to 375°; lightly grease cookie sheets.
2. Beat egg in large mixing bowl, and add all ingredients in the order given (except flour and baking powder), and mix until thoroughly blended.
3. Measure sifted flour with baking powder and sift into mixing bowl, blending thoroughly.
4. Measure 1 level T. of dough for each cookie, and drop onto cookie sheet, placing cookies 2 in. apart.
5. Bake about 10 min. or until done.
6. Remove at once with a pancake turner, and cool on wax paper.
7. Store in tightly-covered cookie jar, or tin container, and use for dessert or refreshment with fruit juice, milk, or apple cider.

Variation

Add 1 c. of dried fruit of choice.

REFRIGERATOR COOKIES

45-50 cookies

1 egg
½ c. vegetable oil
1 c. brown sugar (packed)
1 T. milk
1 t. vanilla
2 c. sifted all-purpose flour
1½ t. baking powder
½ t. salt
½ c. broken nutmeats

1. Beat egg in mixing bowl. Add sugar, oil, milk, and vanilla, and mix thoroughly.
2. Measure sifted flour with baking powder and salt, and sift together into mixing bowl, blending thoroughly.
3. Add nutmeats, and blend.
4. Shape dough on wax paper into rolls 1½ in. in diameter and fasten roll firmly.
5. Chill overnight in refrigerator, and cook fresh cookies as desired by slicing dough ⅛ in. thick.
6. Bake at 375° until done (about 10 min.).

ROLLED SUGAR COOKIES

70-75 cookies

½ c. soft margarine or ⅜ c.
  vegetable oil
1 c. brown sugar
1 egg
¼ c. milk (approx.)
2 c. sifted all-purpose flour
2 t. baking powder
½ t. vanilla
1 t. each grated lemon and
  orange peel
¼ t. salt

1. Preheat oven to 375°.
2. Cream fat and sugar until fluffy.
3. Add eggs, vanilla, and fruit rinds and mix.
4. Add sifted dry ingredients alterately with milk to form a firm, but not dry, dough.
5. Form dough in a ball and chill ½-1 hr. or overnight.
6. Divide into small portions, and roll ⅛ in. thick between slightly oiled or floured wax paper.
7. Cut with floured cookie cutter, and place on oiled cookie sheet.
8. Sprinkle top with granulated sugar, and bake at 375° for about 10 min. or until lightly browned.
9. Store in clean, tightly-covered cookie jar, and, to freshen before serving, warm in a low oven (300°) for 4-5 min.

Variations:

1. For Vanilla Cookies, omit fruit rinds.
2. For Lemon Cookies, add 1 t. lemon extract and omit orange rind.
3. Refrigerate in rolls and slice for refrigerator cookies.
4. Substitute 1 t. almond extract for fruit rind for almond cookies.

FRUIT BARS

DOUGH

36 bars

1 c. brown sugar (packed)
⅓ c. vegetable oil
1 egg
1½ c. sifted all-purpose flour
1½ t. baking powder
1 t. salt
1 t. vanilla
2-3 T. milk
½ c. broken nutmeats

1. Preheat oven to 350°, and oil pan.
2. Beat egg, add oil, sugar, milk, and vanilla, and mix.
3. Measure sifted flour and other dry ingredients and sift into mixing bowl. Add nutmeats and blend thoroughly.
4. Spread half of mixture in bottom of a 12 x 6 x 2 pan. Then spread a layer of filling. Cover filling with remainder of dough, pressing into place.
5. Bake for about 25 min. or until brown.
6. Remove, cool, cut in bars, and store in tightly-covered container.

FILLING

1 7½-oz. pkg. pitted dates
1 7½-oz. pkg. figs
1 T. grated lemon peel

1. Chop dates and figs. Mix all ingredients and simmer until thick and smooth (stir to prevent burning).
2. Spread a layer of mixture on cookie dough, and store remainder in covered jar in refrigerator for future use.

Frostings and Fillings *

VANILLA CREAM FROSTING

Frosts 2 9-inch layers

½ c. soft margarine
2 c. sifted confectioner's sugar
2 T. evaporated milk or cream
1 t. vanilla
dash salt

1. Cream fat, and add sugar and milk gradually, blending after each addition until right consistency to spread.
2. Add vanilla and salt and spread on cake. (To remove "raw" flavor, let stand over hot water for 15 min., stirring at intervals.)

Variations

1. Chocolate: add 2 sqs. unsweetened melted chocolate at Step 2.
2. Orange: add 1 T. grated orange rind and 2 T. orange juice instead of milk.
3. Lemon: add 1 T. grated lemon rind and 2 T. lemon juice instead of milk.

PENUCHE FROSTING

Frosts 2 9-inch layers

2 c. brown sugar (packed)
½ c. undiluted evaporated milk
½ T. table fat
1 t. vanilla
½ c. nutmeats
1 c. diced dates
2 T. light corn syrup

1. Boil sugar, syrup, salt, and milk slowly, stirring until sugar is dissolved.
2. Boil briskly until mixture forms soft ball when dropped in saucer of cold water (240°).
3. Add fat, dates, nuts, and vanilla, and beat until thick enough to spread.

* The cooked frostings in this section can be made into candy by cooking to the required temperature (see the table on page 277).

SEVEN-MINUTE FROSTING

2 egg whites (¼ c.)
1½ c. sugar
2 T. cold water
2 T. lemon juice
1 T. light corn syrup
1 t. vanilla extract
½ t. cream of tartar
    dash of salt

Frosts 2 9-inch layers

1. Place all ingredients except vanilla in top of double boiler over rapidly boiling water and beat constantly with rotary egg beater or electric mixer until frosting stands in peaks (about 7-10 min.).
2. Remove from heat, add vanilla, and beat until thick enough to spread.

Variations

1. Chocolate: Fold 3 squares of melted chocolate into frosting after it is removed from heat.
2. Coconut: Add 1 c. fresh or canned shredded coconut after removing from heat. Spread on cake. Sprinkle more coconut over top.
3. Nut: Add ½ c. nutmeats after removing from heat.
4. Fruit: Add 1 c. candied diced fruit after removing from heat.
5. Lemon: Omit vanilla and add 1 T. grated lemon rind and 5 T. lemon juice instead of water.
6. Orange: Substitute orange for lemon.

FUDGE FROSTING

2 c. sugar
2 T. light corn syrup
½ c. undiluted evaporated
    milk
2 sq. chocolate or 5 T. cocoa
1 T. table fat
1 t. vanilla
    dash salt

Frosts 2 9-inch layers

1. Melt chocolate in top of double boiler.
2. Add sugar, milk, syrup, and salt, and cook over low direct heat, stirring gently until all sugar dissolves.
3. Cover and cook 2 min. Then uncover and cook until it forms a soft ball when dropped from edge of spoon into cold water (240°).
4. Add vanilla, mix, and cool.
5. Beat until it starts to thicken. Quickly spread on cake.

Variation

Add ½ c. nutmeats.

Fruit Conserves, Jellies, Jams, and Relish

Fruit Conserves

RUTH WHITE'S
PLUM-PEACH-APPLE CONSERVES

About 4 pints

2 c. diced peeled peaches
2 c. diced tart apples in skins
2 c. cooked and seeded damson
   plums
4 c. sugar
1 sliced lime (optional)

1. Wash fruit thoroughly. Prepare peaches and apples as indicated.
2. Cook plums in small amount of water until soft. Push through sieve or food mill to remove seeds and skins.
3. Place all ingredients in a large-bottomed kettle, and bring to rapid boil.
4. Boil vigorously (stirring to prevent scorching) until mixture thickens and 2 drops pull together to sheet from edge of spoon when tested.
5. Pour into hot sterilized jars or glasses, and seal with melted paraffin, rotating glass to make perfect seal.
6. Cool, cover, and store in cool place. Serve with hot bread for dessert or as frosting for cake. Use within a year.

Variations

1. Add 1 c. of seedless raisins or ½ c. nutmeats at Step 2.
2. Substitute pears, apricots, or pineapple for peaches.

Jellies and Jams

Recipes for making jellies and jams are in the leaflet that comes with pectin, which is needed for jelly and jam. Follow the directions given on the pectin leaflet. In general, the method for jelly and jam is the same except that jelly is made from the juice and jam is made from the crushed whole fruit.

447

Relish

UNCOOKED RIPE TOMATO RELISH*

2 qts. (about 12 to 14 med-
    ium-sized finely chopped,
    peeled tomatoes
1 c. finely chopped celery
¾ c. finely chopped onion
½ c. finely chopped green
    pepper
2 t. salt
3 T. sugar
1 T. mustard seed
¼ t. ground nutmeg
¼ t. ground cinnamon
⅛ t. ground cloves
½ c. vinegar

4 pints

1. Combine all ingredients and stir until well blended.
2. Pour into clean jars, cover, and store in refrigerator. Relish will keep 2 to 3 weeks.

Sandwiches for Teas and Parties

GUIDE TO MAKING PARTY SANDWICHES

1. Use unsliced day-old bread of several varieties.
2. Slice bread thin.
3. Cut crusts from outer edges for fancy sandwiches.
4. Have butter for bread at room temperature and cream it.

5. Butter bread to outer edges to prevent soaking of bread from filling.
6. Use enough filling, but not so much that it falls off sandwich.
7. Prepare sandwiches well ahead. Wrap in wax paper, foil, or Saran, and store in refrigerator; or prepare ahead by sealing and freezing. Defrost on day of party.
8. Nut breads should be served plain in thin slices like fruit cake.

   * The usual method of making pickles permits the loss of minerals and vitamins. Such pickles may be a relish, but they are not a substitute for a salad. This recipe prevents the destruction of vitamins and minerals by eliminating the soaking, draining, and cooking of the ingredients.

RIBBON SANDWICHES

1. Stack by alternating 3 slices of whole wheat and white bread; hold firmly and cut crusts away.
2. Butter each slice and spread cream cheese on first slice. On second slice spread crab meat, tuna, sardine, ham, or chicken filling.
3. Top with third slice of bread, and press firmly together. Wrap securely in wax paper, cover with damp cloth, and store in refrigerator, for several hours until ready to serve.
4. Slice fresh as needed in ½-in. ribbon slices.

PINWHEEL SANDWICH

1. Use unsliced day-old bread.
2. Slice off top and side crusts.
3. Cut loaf into lengthwise slices ¼ in. thick, and roll with rolling pin for easier handling.
4. Butter each slice to edge, and spread with filling of choice.
5. Roll bread tightly lengthwise and wrap roll securely in foil.
6. Refrigerate overnight and cut in ¼-in. slices just before serving, lifting with spatula to serving plate.

Sandwich Fillings

CREAM CHEESE SANDWICH SPREAD

1 8-oz. pkg. cream cheese
¾ c. finely ground chicken, turkey, or ham
¼ c. ground olives
2 t. grated onion
1 t. Worcestershire sauce
mayonnaise to moisten

2 cups

1. Mix in order given and spread on bread for party sandwiches. This spread is creamy and will hold to bread. It is also tasty.

Variations

1. Substitute dates, figs, raisins, or pineapple (drained and crushed) for meat.
2. Substitute ¼ c. mashed blue cheese and ¼ c. sour cream for meat.
3. Substitute ½ c. ground canned ham and 2 hard-cooked finely diced eggs for meat.

Recommended Daily Dietary

Designed for the maintenance of good nutrition of practically all healthy people in the U.S.A.

	Age[2] Years From Up to	Weight Kg (lbs)		Height cm (in)		K calories	Protein gm	Fat-Soluble Vitamins		
								Vitamin A Activity I.U.	Vitamin D I.U.	Vitamin E Activity I.U.
Infants	0 - 1/6	4	9	55	22	kg x 120	kg x 2.2[3]	1500	400	5
	1/6 - 1/2	7	15	63	25	kg x 110	kg x 2.0[3]	1500	400	5
	1/2 - 1	9	20	72	28	kg x 100	kg x 1.8[3]	1500	400	5
Children	1 - 2	12	26	81	32	1100	25	2000	400	10
	2 - 3	14	31	91	36	1250	25	2000	400	10
	3 - 4	16	35	100	39	1400	30	2500	400	10
	4 - 6	19	42	110	43	1600	30	2500	400	10
	6 - 8	23	51	121	48	2000	35	3500	400	15
	8 - 10	28	62	131	52	2200	40	3500	400	15
Males	10 - 12	35	77	140	55	2500	45	4500	400	20
	12 - 14	43	95	151	59	2700	50	5000	400	20
	14 - 18	59	130	170	67	3000	60	5000	400	25
	18 - 22	67	147	175	69	2800	60	5000	400	30
	22 - 35	70	154	175	69	2800	65	5000	—	30
	35 - 55	70	154	173	68	2600	65	5000	—	30
	55 - 75+	70	154	171	67	2400	65	5000	—	30
Females	10 - 12	35	77	142	56	2250	50	4500	400	20
	12 - 14	44	97	154	61	2300	50	5000	400	20
	14 - 16	52	114	157	62	2400	55	5000	400	25
	16 - 18	54	119	160	63	2300	55	5000	400	25
	18 - 22	58	128	163	64	2000	55	5000	400	25
	22 - 35	58	128	163	64	2000	55	5000	—	25
	35 - 55	58	128	160	63	1850	55	5000	—	25
	55 - 75+	58	128	157	62	1700	55	5000	—	25
Pregnancy						+200	65	6000	400	30
Lactation						+1000	75	8000	400	30

1. The allowance levels are intended to cover individual variations among most normal persons as they live in the United States under usual environmental stresses. The recommended allowances can be attained with a variety of common foods, providing other nutrients for which human requirements have been less well defined. See text for more detailed discussion of allowances and of nutrients not tabulated.

2. Entries on lines for age range 22-35 years represent the reference man and woman at age 22. All other entries represent allowances for the midpoint of the specified age range.

Allowances, Revised 1968

Food and Nutrition Board, National Academy of Sciences, National Research Council

Water-Soluble Vitamins							Minerals				
Ascorbic Acid mg	Folacin[4] mg	Niacin mg equiv.[5]	Riboflavin mg	Thiamine mg	Vitamin B_6 mg	Vitamin B_{12} µg	Calcium gm	Phosphorus gm	Iodine µg	Iron mg	Magnesium mg
35	0.05	5	0.4	0.2	0.2	1.0	0.4	0.2	25	6	40
35	0.05	7	0.5	0.4	0.3	1.5	0.5	0.4	40	10	60
35	0.1	8	0.6	0.5	0.4	2.0	0.6	0.5	45	15	70
40	0.1	8	0.6	0.6	0.5	2.0	0.7	0.7	55	15	100
40	0.2	8	0.7	0.6	0.6	2.5	0.8	0.8	60	15	150
40	0.2	9	0.8	0.7	0.7	3	0.8	0.8	70	10	200
40	0.2	11	0.9	0.8	0.9	4	0.8	0.8	80	10	200
40	0.2	13	1.1	1.0	1.0	4	0.9	0.9	100	10	250
40	0.3	15	1.2	1.1	1.2	5	1.0	1.0	110	10	250
40	0.4	17	1.3	1.3	1.4	5	1.2	1.2	125	10	300
45	0.4	18	1.4	1.4	1.6	5	1.4	1.4	135	18	350
55	0.4	20	1.5	1.5	1.8	5	1.4	1.4	150	18	400
60	0.4	18	1.6	1.4	2.0	5	0.8	0.8	140	10	400
60	0.4	18	1.7	1.4	2.0	5	0.8	0.8	140	10	350
60	0.4	17	1.7	1.3	2.0	5	0.8	0.8	125	10	350
60	0.4	14	1.7	1.2	2.0	6	0.8	0.8	110	10	350
40	0.4	15	1.3	1.1	1.4	5	1.2	1.2	110	18	300
45	0.4	15	1.4	1.2	1.6	5	1.3	1.3	115	18	350
50	0.4	16	1.4	1.2	1.8	5	1.3	1.3	120	18	350
50	0.4	15	1.5	1.2	2.0	5	1.3	1.3	115	18	350
55	0.4	13	1.5	1.0	2.0	5	0.8	0.8	100	18	350
55	0.4	13	1.5	1.0	2.0	5	0.8	0.8	100	18	300
55	0.4	13	1.5	1.0	2.0	5	0.8	0.8	90	18	300
55	0.4	13	1.5	1.0	2.0	6	0.8	0.8	80	10	300
60	0.8	15	1.8	+0.1	2.5	8	+0.4	+0.4	125	18	450
60	0.5	20	2.0	+0.5	2.5	6	+0.5	+0.5	150	18	450

3. Assumes protein equivalent to human milk. For proteins not 100 percent utilized factors should be increased proportionately.

4. The folacin allowances refer to dietary sources as determined by *Lactobacillus casei* assay. Pure forms of folacin may be effective in doses less than ¼ of the RDA.

5. Niacin equivalents include dietary sources of the vitamin itself plus 1 mg equivalent for each 60 mg of dietary tryptophan.

Nutritive Values in Common Portions of Food*

Pct. = Percent
Cal. = Calorie
Gm. = Gram
Mg. = Milligram
I.U. = International Unit
Tr. = Trace, or an insignificant quantity
— = No value imputed, but possibly present

* From *Nutritive Value of Foods*, Home and Garden Bulletin 72, Revised Sept. 1964. Adapted from the more comprehensive tables in "*Composition of Foods —Raw, Processed, Prepared*," *Agriculture Handbook No. 8*, Revised Dec. 1963. Both are for sale by the Superintendent of Documents, Washington 25, D.C.

FOOD AND APPROXIMATE MEASURE OR COMMON WEIGHT	WATER	FOOD ENERGY	PROTEIN	FAT	TOTAL CARBOHYDRATE	CALCIUM	IRON	VITAMIN A VALUE	THIAMINE	RIBOFLAVIN	NIACIN VALUE	ASCORBIC ACID
	Pct.	Cal.	Gm.	Gm.	Gm.	Mg.	Mg.	I.U.	Mg.	Mg.	Mg.	Mg.
MILK AND MILK PRODUCTS:												
Buttermilk, from skim milk, 1 cup	90	90	9	Tr.	13	298	0.1	10	0.09	0.44	0.2	2
Milk, cow:												
Fluid, whole, 1 cup	87	160	9	9	12	288	.1	350	.08	.42	.1	2
Fluid, nonfat (skim), 1 cup	90	90	9	Tr.	13	298	.1	10	.10	.44	.2	2
Evaporated (undiluted), 1 cup	74	345	18	20	24	635	.3	820	.10	.84	.5	3
Condensed (undiluted), 1 cup	27	980	25	27	166	802	.3	1,090	.23	1.17	.5	3
Cheese, 1 ounce:												
Cheddar (1 in. cube)	37	70	4	5	Tr.	128	.2	220	Tr.	.08	Tr.	0
Cheddar, processed	40	105	7	9	1	219	.3	350	Tr.	.12	Tr.	0
Cottage, from skim milk, uncreamed	79	25	5	Tr.	1	26	.1	Tr.	.01	.08	Tr.	0
Cream	51	105	2	11	1	18	.1	440	Tr.	.07	Tr.	0
Swiss	39	105	8	8	1	262	.3	320	Tr.	.11	Tr.	0
Cream, 1 tablespoon:												
Light	72	30	Tr.	3	1	15	Tr.	130	Tr.	.02	Tr.	Tr.
Heavy	57	55	Tr.	6	Tr.	11	Tr.	230	Tr.	.02	Tr.	Tr.
Beverages, 1 cup:												
Cocoa (all milk)	79	235	9	11	26	286	.9	390	.09	.45	.4	2
Malted milk	78	280	13	12	32	364	.8	670	.17	.56	.2	2
Desserts:												
Custard, baked, 1 cup	77	285	13	14	28	278	1.0	870	.10	.47	.2	1

Food												
Ice cream, plain:												
⅛ of quart brick	62	145	3	9	15	87	.1	370	.03	.13	.1	1
8 fluid ounces	62	295	6	18	29	175	.1	740	.06	.27	.1	1
EGGS:												
Eggs, raw, large:												
1 whole	74	80	6	6	Tr.	27	1.1	590	.05	.15	Tr.	0
1 white	88	15	4	Tr.	Tr.	3	Tr.	0	Tr.	.09	Tr.	0
1 yolk	51	60	3	5	Tr.	24	.9	580	.04	.07	Tr.	0
FRUITS:												
Apples, raw, 1 medium (2½ in. diam., about 3 per lb.)	85	70	Tr.	Tr.	18	8	.4	50	.04	.02	.1	3
Apple juice, fresh or canned, 1 cup	88	120	Tr.	Tr.	30	15	1.5	—	.01	.04	.2	2
Applesauce, canned, sweetened, 1 cup	76	230	1	Tr.	60	10	1.3	100	.05	.03	.1	3
Apricots:												
Dried, cooked, unsweetened, fruit and liquid, 1 cup	76	240	5	1	62	63	5.1	8,550	.01	.13	2.8	8
Avocados, raw, ½ peeled fruit	74	185	2	18	6	11	.6	310	.12	.21	1.7	15
Bananas, raw, 1 medium (6 by 1½ in., about 3 per lb.)	76	85	1	Tr.	23	8	.7	190	.05	.06	.7	10
Blackberries, raw, 1 cup	84	85	2	1	19	46	1.3	290	.05	.06	.5	30
Blueberries, raw, 1 cup	83	85	1	1	21	21	1.4	140	.04	.08	.6	20
Cantaloupes, raw, ½ melon (5 in. diam.)	91	60	1	Tr.	14	27	.8	6,540	.08	.06	1.2	63
Cherries, 1 cup pitted:												
Canned, red sour	76	230	2	1	59	36	.8	1,680	.07	.06	.4	13
Cranberry sauce, sweetened, 1 cup	62	405	Tr.	1	104	17	.6	40	.03	.03	.1	5
Dates, "fresh" and dried, pitted and cut, 1 cup	22	490	4	1	130	105	5.3	90	.16	.17	3.9	0
Fruit cocktail, canned, solids and liquid, 1 cup	80	195	1	1	50	23	1.0	360	.04	.03	1.1	5
Grapefruit, raw, sections, 1 cup	89	75	1	Tr.	20	31	.8	20	.07	.03	.3	72
Grapefruit juice:												
Canned, unsweetened, 1 cup	89	100	1	Tr.	24	20	1.0	20	.07	.04	.4	84
Frozen concentrate, 6-ounce can	62	300	4	1	72	70	.8	60	.29	.12	1.4	286

FRUITS—Continued

FOOD AND APPROXIMATE MEASURE OR COMMON WEIGHT	WATER	FOOD ENERGY	PROTEIN	FAT	TOTAL CARBOHYDRATE	CALCIUM	IRON	VITAMIN A VALUE	THIAMINE	RIBOFLAVIN	NIACIN VALUE	ASCORBIC ACID
	Pct.	Cal.	Gm.	Gm.	Gm.	Mg.	Mg.	I.U.	Mg.	Mg.	Mg.	Mg.
Grapes, 1 cup:												
American type (slip skin)	82	65	1	1	15	15	.4	100	.05	.03	.2	3
Grape juice, bottled, 1 cup	83	165	1	Tr.	42	28	.8	—	.10	.05	.6	Tr.
Lemon juice, fresh, 1 cup	91	60	1	Tr.	20	17	.5	40	.08	.03	.2	113
Lime juice, fresh, 1 cup	90	65	1	Tr.	22	22	.5	30	.05	.03	.3	80
Oranges, 1 medium (3 in. diam.)	86	75	1	Tr.	19	67	.3	310	.16	.06	.6	70
Orange juice:												
Fresh, Florida, 1 cup	90	100	1	Tr.	23	25	.5	490	.22	.06	.9	127
Canned, unsweetened, 1 cup	87	120	2	Tr.	28	25	1.0	500	.17	.05	.6	100
Frozen concentrate, 6-ounce can	58	330	5	Tr.	80	69	.8	1,490	.63	.10	2.4	332
Peaches:												
Raw, 1 medium (2 in. diam., about 4 per lb.)	89	35	1	Tr.	10	9	.5	1,320	.02	.05	1.0	7
Canned in syrup, 1 cup	79	200	1	Tr.	52	10	.8	1,100	.02	.06	1.4	7
Pears:												
Raw, 1 pear (3 by 2½ in. diam.)	83	100	1	1	25	13	.5	30	.04	.07	.2	7
Canned in syrup, 2 medium size halves and 2 tablespoons syrup	80	90	Tr.	Tr.	23	6	.2	Tr.	.01	.02	.2	2
Pineapple:												
Raw, diced, 1 cup	85	75	1	Tr.	19	24	.7	100	.12	.04	.3	24
Canned in syrup, 2 small or 1 large slice and 2 tablespoons juice	80	90	Tr.	Tr.	24	13	.4	50	.09	.03	.2	8
Pineapple juice, canned, 1 cup	86	135	1	Tr.	34	37	.7	120	.12	.04	.5	22
Plums, raw, 1 plum, (2 in. diam.)	87	25	Tr.	Tr.	7	7	.3	140	.02	.02	.3	3
Prunes, cooked, unsweetened, 1 cup (16–18 prunes and ⅓ cup liquid)	66	295	2	1	78	60	4.5	1,860	.08	.18	1.7	2
Prune juice, canned, 1 cup	80	200	1	Tr.	49	36	10.5	—	.02	.03	1.1	4
Raisins, dried, 1 cup	18	460	4	Tr.	124	99	5.6	30	.18	.13	.9	2
Raspberries, red, raw, 1 cup	84	70	1	1	17	27	1.1	160	.04	.11	1.1	31
Rhubarb, cooked with sugar, 1 cup	63	385	1	Tr.	98	212	1.6	220	.06	.15	.7	17

Strawberries:												
Raw, 1 cup	90	55	1	1	13	31	1.5	90	.04	.10	1.0	88
Frozen, 10-ounce carton	71	310	1	1	79	40	2.0	90	.06	.17	1.5	150
Tangerines, 1 medium (2½ in. diam., about 4 per lb.)	87	40	1	Tr.	10	34	.3	350	.05	.02	.1	26
Watermelons, 1 wedge (4 × 8 in.)	93	115	2	1	27	30	2.1	2,510	.13	.13	.7	30
CEREAL—BREAD:												
Biscuits, enriched flour, 1 biscuit (2½ in. diam.)	27	140	3	6	17	46	.6	Tr.	.08	.08	.7	Tr.
Bran flakes, 1 ounce	3	85	3	1	23	20	1.2	0	.11	.05	1.7	0
Breads, 1 slice:												
Boston brown, unenriched	45	100	3	1	22	43	.9	0	.05	.03	.6	0
Rye (⅓ rye, ⅔ wheat)	36	55	2	Tr.	12	17	.4	0	.04	.02	.3	0
White, unenriched, 4 percent non-fat milk solids	36	45	1	1	9	14	.1	Tr.	.01	.01	.2	Tr.
White, enriched, 4 percent nonfat milk solids	36	45	1	1	9	14	.4	Tr.	.04	.04	.4	Tr.
Whole wheat	36	55	2	1	11	23	.5	Tr.	.06	.03	.7	Tr.
Cakes:												
Angel food, 2-inch sector	32	110	3	Tr.	24	4	.1	0	Tr.	.06	.1	0
Doughnuts, cake-type, 1 doughnut	24	125	1	6	16	13	.4	30	.05	.05	.4	Tr.
Gingerbread, 1 piece (2 by 2 by 2 in.)	31	175	2	6	29	37	1.3	50	.06	.06	.5	0
Plain cake and cupcakes, 1 cupcake (2¾ in. diam.)	24	145	2	6	22	26	.2	70	.01	.03	.1	Tr.
Sponge, 2-inch sector (1/12 of cake, 8 in. diam.)	32	120	3	2	22	12	.5	180	.02	.06	.1	Tr.
Cookies, plain and assorted, 1 3-inch	3	120	1	5	18	9	.2	20	.01	.01	.1	Tr.
Corn bread or muffins made with enriched, degermed corn meal, 1 muffin (2¾ in. diam.)	33	150	3	5	23	50	.8	80	.09	.11	.8	Tr.
Corn flakes, 1 ounce	4	110	2	Tr.	24	5	.4	0	.12	.02	.6	0
Crackers:												
Graham, 4 small or 2 medium	6	55	1	1	10	6	.2	0	.01	.03	.2	0
Soda, plain, 2 crackers (2½ in. diam.)	4	50	1	1	8	2	.2	0	Tr.	Tr.	.1	0
Farina, enriched, cooked, 1 cup	90	100	3	Tr.	21	10	.7	0	.11	.07	1.0	0

CEREAL—BREAD—Continued

FOOD AND APPROXIMATE MEASURE OR COMMON WEIGHT	WATER	FOOD ENERGY	PROTEIN	FAT	TOTAL CARBOHYDRATE	CALCIUM	IRON	VITAMIN A VALUE	THIAMINE	RIBOFLAVIN	NIACIN VALUE	ASCORBIC ACID
	Pct.	Cal.	Gm.	Gm.	Gm.	Mg.	Mg.	I.U.	Mg.	Mg.	Mg.	Mg.
Macaroni, cooked, 1 cup:												
Unenriched	64	190	6	1	39	14	.6	0	.02	.02	.5	0
Enriched	64	190	6	1	39	14	1.4	0	.23	.14	1.9	0
Muffins, made with enriched flour, 1 muffin (2¾ in. diam.)	38	140	4	5	20	50	.8	50	.08	.11	.7	Tr.
Oatmeal or rolled oats:												
Cooked, 1 cup	86	130	5	2	23	21	1.4	0	.19	.05	.3	0
Pancakes, baked, wheat, with enriched flour, 1 cake (4 in. diam.)	50	60	2	2	9	27	.4	30	.05	.06	.3	Tr.
Pies, 4-inch sector (9 in. diam.):												
Apple	48	345	3	15	51	11	.4	40	.03	.02	.5	1
Custard	58	280	8	14	30	125	.8	300	.07	.21	.4	0
Lemon meringue	47	305	4	12	45	17	.6	200	.04	.10	.2	4
Mince	43	365	3	16	56	38	1.4	Tr.	.09	.05	.5	1
Pumpkin	59	275	5	15	32	66	.6	3,210	.04	.13	.6	Tr.
Pretzels, 5 small sticks	8	20	Tr.	Tr.	4	1	0	Tr.	Tr.	Tr.	Tr.	0
Rice, enriched cooked, 1 cup:												
Converted, long-grain, parboiled	73	185	4	Tr.	41	33	1.4	0	.19	.02	2.0	0
White or milled	73	185	3	Tr.	41	17	1.5	0	.19	.01	1.6	0
Rice, puffed, 1 cup	4	55	1	Tr.	13	3	.3	0	.06	.01	.6	0
Rolls, plain, enriched, 1 roll (12 per pound)	31	115	3	2	20	28	.7	Tr.	.11	.07	.8	Tr.
Spaghetti, unenriched, cooked, 1 cup	72	155	5	1	32	11	.6	0	.02	.02	.4	0
Waffles, baked, with enriched flour, 1 waffle (4½ by 5⅝ by ½ in.)	41	210	7	7	28	85	1.3	250	.13	.19	1.0	Tr.
Wheat flours:												
Whole, 1 cup stirred	12	400	16	2	85	49	4.0	0	.66	.14	5.2	0
All purpose or family flour:												
Unenriched, 1 cup sifted	12	400	12	1	84	18	.9	0	.07	.05	1.0	0
Enriched, 1 cup sifted	12	400	12	1	84	18	3.2	0	.48	.29	3.8	0
Wheat germ, 1 cup stirred	11	245	18	7	32	49	6.4	0	1.36	0.46	2.9	0
Wheat, shredded, 1 large biscuit, 1 ounce	7	100	3	1	23	12	1.0	0	.06	.03	1.2	0

VEGETABLES:

Asparagus:											
Cooked, 1 cup cut spears	94	35	4	Tr.	6	37	1.0	1,580	.27	.32	2.4	46
Beans, lima, immature, cooked, 1 cup, fresh	71	180	12	1	32	75	4.0	450	.29	.16	2.0	28
Beans, snap, green, cooked, 1 cup	92	30	2	Tr.	7	62	.8	680	.08	.11	.6	16
Beets, cooked, diced, 1 cup	91	50	2	Tr.	12	23	.8	40	.04	.07	.5	11
Broccoli, cooked, flower stalks, 1 cup	91	40	5	Tr.	7	132	1.2	3,750	.14	.29	1.2	135
Brussels sprouts, cooked, 1 cup	88	45	5	1	8	42	1.4	680	.10	.18	1.1	113
Cabbage, 1 cup:											
Raw, shredded	92	25	1	Tr.	5	49	.4	130	.05	.05	.3	47
Cooked	94	35	2	Tr.	7	75	.5	220	.07	.07	.5	56
Carrots:											
Raw, grated, 1 cup	88	45	1	Tr.	11	41	.8	12,100	.06	.06	.7	9
Cooked, diced, 1 cup	91	45	1	Tr.	10	48	.9	15,220	.08	.07	.7	9
Cauliflower, cooked, flower buds, 1 cup	93	25	3	Tr.	5	25	.8	70	.11	.10	.7	66
Celery, raw, diced 1 cup:	94	15	1	Tr.	4	39	.3	240	.03	.03	.3	9
Collards, cooked, 1 cup	91	55	5	1	9	289	1.1	10,260	.27	.37	2.4	87
Corn, sweet:											
Cooked, 1 ear (5 in. long)	74	70	3	1	16	2	.5	310	.09	.08	1.0	7
Canned, solids and liquid, 1 cup	81	170	5	2	40	10	1.0	690	.07	.12	2.3	13
Cucumbers, 10 ounce, raw, pared (7½ × 2 in.)	96	30	1	Tr.	7	35	.6	Tr.	.07	.09	.4	23
Endive, raw, 2 ounces	93	10	1	Tr.	2	46	1.0	1,870	.04	.08	.3	6
Kale, cooked, 1 cup	91	30	4	1	4	147	1.3	8,140	—	—	—	68
Lettuce, Boston, 1 head, raw (4 in. diam.)	95	30	3	Tr.	6	77	4.4	2,130	.14	.13	.6	18
Mushrooms, canned, solids and liquid, 1 cup	93	40	5	Tr.	6	15	1.2	Tr.	.04	.60	4.8	4
Mustard greens, cooked, 1 cup	93	35	3	1	6	193	2.5	8,120	.11	.19	.9	68
Okra, cooked, 8 pods	91	25	2	Tr.	5	78	.4	420	.11	.15	.8	17
Onions, raw:											
Mature, 1 onion (2½ in. diam.)	89	40	2	Tr.	10	30	.6	40	.04	.04	.2	11
Young green, 6 small onions without tops	88	20	1	Tr.	5	20	.3	Tr.	.02	.02	.2	12

VEGETABLES—Continued

FOOD AND APPROXIMATE MEASURE OR COMMON WEIGHT	WATER	FOOD ENERGY	PROTEIN	FAT	TOTAL CARBOHYDRATE	CALCIUM	IRON	VITAMIN A VALUE	THIAMINE	RIBOFLAVIN	NIACIN VALUE	ASCORBIC ACID
	Pct.	Cal.	Gm.	Gm.	Gm.	Mg.	Mg.	I.U.	Mg.	Mg.	Mg.	Mg.
Parsnips, cooked, 1 cup	82	100	2	1	23	70	.9	50	.11	.13	.2	16
Peas, green:												
Cooked, 1 cup	82	115	9	1	19	37	2.9	860	.44	.17	3.7	33
Peppers, green, raw, 1 medium	93	15	1	Tr.	3	6	.4	260	.05	.05	.3	79
Potatoes:												
Baked, 1 medium (2½ in. diam.)	75	90	3	Tr.	21	9	.7	Tr.	.10	.04	1.7	20
Boiled in skin, 1 medium (2½ in. diam.)	80	105	3	Tr.	23	10	.8	Tr.	.13	.05	2.0	22
Boiled after peeling, 1 medium (2½ in. diam.)	83	80	2	Tr.	18	7	.6	Tr.	.11	.04	1.4	20
French-fried, 10 pieces (2 by ½ by ½ in.)	45	155	2	7	20	9	.7	Tr.	.07	.04	1.8	12
Potato chips, 10 medium (2 in. diam.)	2	115	1	8	10	8	.4	Tr.	.04	.01	1.0	3
Pumpkin, canned, 1 cup	90	75	2	1	18	57	.9	14,590	.07	.12	1.3	12
Radishes, raw, 4 small	94	5	Tr.	Tr.	1	12	.4	Tr.	.01	.01	.1	10
Sauerkraut, canned, drained solids, 1 cup	93	45	2	Tr.	9	85	1.2	120	.07	.09	.4	33
Soybean sprouts, raw, 1 cup	89	40	6	2	4	46	.7	90	.17	.16	.8	4
Spinach:												
Cooked, 1 cup	92	40	5	1	6	167	4.0	14,580	.13	.25	1.0	50
Squash:												
Summer, cooked, diced, 1 cup	96	30	2	Tr.	7	52	.8	820	.10	.16	1.6	21
Winter, baked, mashed, 1 cup	81	130	4	1	32	57	1.6	8,610	.10	.27	1.4	27
Sweet potatoes, peeled, 1 sweet potato:												
Baked (5 by 2 in.)	64	155	2	1	36	44	1.0	8,910	.10	.07	.7	24
Boiled (5 by 2½ in.)	71	170	2	1	39	47	1.0	11,610	.13	.09	.9	25
Tomatoes:												
Raw, 1 medium (2 by 2½ in.)	94	35	2	Tr.	7	20	0.8	1,350	0.10	0.06	1.0	34
Canned or cooked, 1 cup	94	50	2	Tr.	10	15	1.2	2,180	.13	.07	1.7	40
Tomato juice, canned, 1 cup	94	45	2	Tr.	10	17	2.2	1,940	.13	.07	1.8	39

Food												
Turnips, cooked, diced, 1 cup	94	35	1	Tr.	8	54	.6	Tr.	.06	.08	.5	33
Turnip greens, cooked, 1 cup	93	30	3	Tr.	5	267	1.6	9,140	.21	.36	.8	100
MATURE BEANS AND PEAS; NUTS:												
Almonds, shelled, unblanched, 1 cup	5	850	26	77	28	332	6.7	0	.34	1.31	5.0	Tr.
Beans, canned or cooked, 1 cup:												
Kidney, red	76	230	15	1	42	74	4.6	Tr.	.13	.10	1.5	—
Lima, dried, cooked	64	260	16	1	48	56	5.6	Tr.	.26	.12	1.3	Tr.
Navy or other varieties with:												
Tomato sauce and pork	71	320	16	7	50	141	4.7	340	.20	.08	1.5	5
Tomato sauce, no pork	68	310	16	1	60	177	5.2	160	.18	.09	1.5	5
Coconut; dried, shredded (sweetened), 1 cup	3	340	2	24	33	10	1.2	0	.02	.02	.2	0
Peanuts, roasted, shelled, 1 cup	2	840	37	72	27	107	3.0	—	.46	.19	24.7	0
Peanut butter, 1 tablespoon	2	95	4	8	3	9	.3	—	.02	.02	2.4	0
Peas, split, dry, 1 cup, cooked	70	290	20	1	52	28	4.2	100	.37	.22	2.2	—
Pecans, 1 cup halves	3	740	10	77	16	79	2.6	140	.93	.14	1.0	2
Walnuts, English, 1 cup halves	4	650	15	64	16	99	3.1	30	.33	.13	.9	3
MEAT, POULTRY, FISH:												
Beef, 3 ounces, without bone, cooked:												
Chuck, lean and fat, braised	53	245	23	16	0	10	2.9	30	.04	.18	3.5	—
Hamburger, regular, broiled	54	245	21	17	0	9	2.7	30	.07	.18	4.6	—
Sirloin, relatively fat, broiled	44	330	20	27	0	9	2.5	50	.05	.16	4.0	—
Beef, dried, 2 ounces	48	115	19	4	0	11	2.9	—	.04	.18	2.2	—
Chicken, 3 ounces:												
Canned, boned	65	170	18	10	0	18	1.3	200	.03	.11	3.7	3
Flesh only, broiled	71	115	20	3	0	8	1.4	80	.05	.16	7.4	—
Clams, raw, meat only, 3 ounces	82	65	11	1	2	59	5.2	90	.08	.15	1.1	8
Crab meat, canned or cooked, 3 ounces	77	85	15	2	1	38	.7	—	.07	.07	1.6	—
Haddock, fried, 1 fillet (4 by 3 by ½ in.), 3 ounces	66	140	17	5	5	34	1.0	—	.03	.06	2.7	2

MEAT, POULTRY, FISH—Continued

FOOD AND APPROXIMATE MEASURE OR COMMON WEIGHT	WATER	FOOD ENERGY	PRO- TEIN	FAT	TOTAL CARBO- HYDRATE	CAL- CIUM	IRON	VITAMIN A VALUE	THIA- MINE	RIBO- FLAVIN	NIA- CIN VALUE	ASCOR- BIC ACID
	Pct.	Cal.	Gm.	Gm.	Gm.	Mg.	Mg.	I.U.	Mg.	Mg.	Mg.	Mg.
Heart, beef, braised, 3 ounces	61	160	27	5	1	5	5.0	20	.21	1.04	6.5	1
Lamb, leg roast, cooked, 3 ounces	54	235	22	16	0	9	1.4	—	.13	.23	4.7	—
Liver, beef, fried, 2 ounces	57	130	15	6	3	6	5.0	30,280	.15	2.37	9.4	15
Oysters, meat only, raw, 1 cup (13–19 medium size oysters, selects)	85	160	20	4	8	226	13.2	740	.33	.43	6.0	—
Pork loin or chops, cooked, 3 ounces without bone	46	310	21	24	0	9	2.7	0	.78	.22	4.7	—
Pork, cured ham, cooked, 3 ounces without bone	54	245	18	19	0	8	2.2	0	.40	.16	3.1	—
Pork luncheon meat, canned, spiced, 2 ounces	55	165	8	14	1	5	1.2	0	.18	.12	1.6	—
Salmon, canned, pink, 3 ounces	71	120	17	5	0	167	.7	60	.03	.16	6.8	—
Sardines, canned in oil, drained solids, 3 ounces	62	175	20	9	0	372	2.5	190	.02	.17	4.6	—
Shrimp, canned, 3 ounces	70	100	21	1	1	98	2.6	50	.01	.03	1.5	—
Tuna, canned in oil, drained, 3 ounces	61	170	24	7	0	7	1.6	70	.04	.10	10.1	—

FATS, OILS, RELATED PRODUCTS:

FOOD AND APPROXIMATE MEASURE OR COMMON WEIGHT	WATER	FOOD ENERGY	PRO- TEIN	FAT	TOTAL CARBO- HYDRATE	CAL- CIUM	IRON	VITAMIN A VALUE	THIA- MINE	RIBO- FLAVIN	NIA- CIN VALUE	ASCOR- BIC ACID
Bacon, medium fat, broiled or fried, 2 slices	8	100	5	8	1	2	.5	0	.08	.05	.8	—
Butter, 1 tablespoon	16	100	Tr.	11	Tr.	3	0	460	—	—	—	0
Fats, cooking (vegetable fats):												
1 cup	0	1,770	0	200	0	0	0	—	0	0	0	0
1 tablespoon	0	110	0	12	0	0	0	—	0	0	0	0
Lard, 1 tablespoon	0	125	0	14	0	0	0	0	0	0	0	0
Margarine, 1 tablespoon	16	100	Tr.	11	Tr.	3	0	460	—	—	—	0
Oils, salad or cooking, 1 tablespoon	0	125	0	14	0	0	0	—	0	0	0	0
Salad dressings, 1 tablespoon:												
French	39	60	Tr.	6	3	2	.1	—	—	—	—	—
Home-cooked	68	30	1	2	3	15	.1	80	.01	.03	Tr.	Tr.
Mayonnaise	15	110	Tr.	12	Tr.	3	.1	40	Tr.	.01	Tr.	0

SUGARS, SWEETS:

Candy, 1 ounce:												
Caramels	8	115	1	3	22	42	.4	Tr.	.01	.05	Tr.	Tr.
Chocolate, sweetened milk,	1	150	2	9	16	65	.3	80	.02	.09	.1	Tr.
Fudge, plain	8	115	1	3	21	22	.3	Tr.	.01	.03	.1	Tr.
Hard	1	110	0	Tr.	28	6	.5	0	0	0	0	0
Marshmallows	17	90	1	Tr.	23	5	.5	0	0	Tr.	Tr.	0
Chocolate syrup, 1 tablespoon	32	50	Tr.	Tr.	13	3	.3	—	Tr.	.01	.1	0
Honey, strained or extracted, 1 tablespoon	17	65	Tr.	0	17	1	.1	0	Tr.	.01	.1	Tr.
Jams, marmalades, preserves, 1 tablespoon	29	55	Tr.	Tr.	14	4	.2	Tr.	Tr.	.01	Tr.	Tr.
Molasses, cane, 1 tablespoon:												
Light	24	50	—	—	13	33	.9	—	.01	.01	Tr.	—
Blackstrap	24	45	—	—	11	137	3.2	—	.02	.04	.4	—
Sugar, 1 tablespoon:												
Granulated, cane or beet	Tr.	45	0	0	12	0	Tr.	0	0	0	0	0
Brown	2	50	0	0	13	12	.5	0	Tr.	Tr.	Tr.	0

MISCELLANEOUS:

Beverages, carbonated, cola type, 1 cup	90	95	0	0	24	—	—	0	0	0	0	0
Bouillon cubes, 1 cube	4	5	1	Tr.	Tr.	—	—	—	—	—	—	—
Chocolate, unsweetened, 1 ounce	2	145	3	15	8	22	1.9	20	.01	.07	.4	0
Gelatin dessert, plain, ready-to-serve, 1 cup	84	140	4	0	34	—	—	—	—	—	—	0
Sherbet, 1 cup	67	260	2	2	59	31	Tr.	110	.02	.06	Tr.	4
Yeast:												
Compressed, baker's, 1 ounce	71	25	3	Tr.	3	4	1.4	Tr.	.20	.47	3.2	Tr.
Dried brewer's, 1 tablespoon	5	25	3	Tr.	3	17	1.4	Tr.	1.25	.34	3.0	Tr.

Index

(References to illustrations and tables are italicized; those to recipes are in bold type.)